RENT-A-GIRLFRIEND

VOLUME 6

REIJI MIYAJIMA

CONTENTS

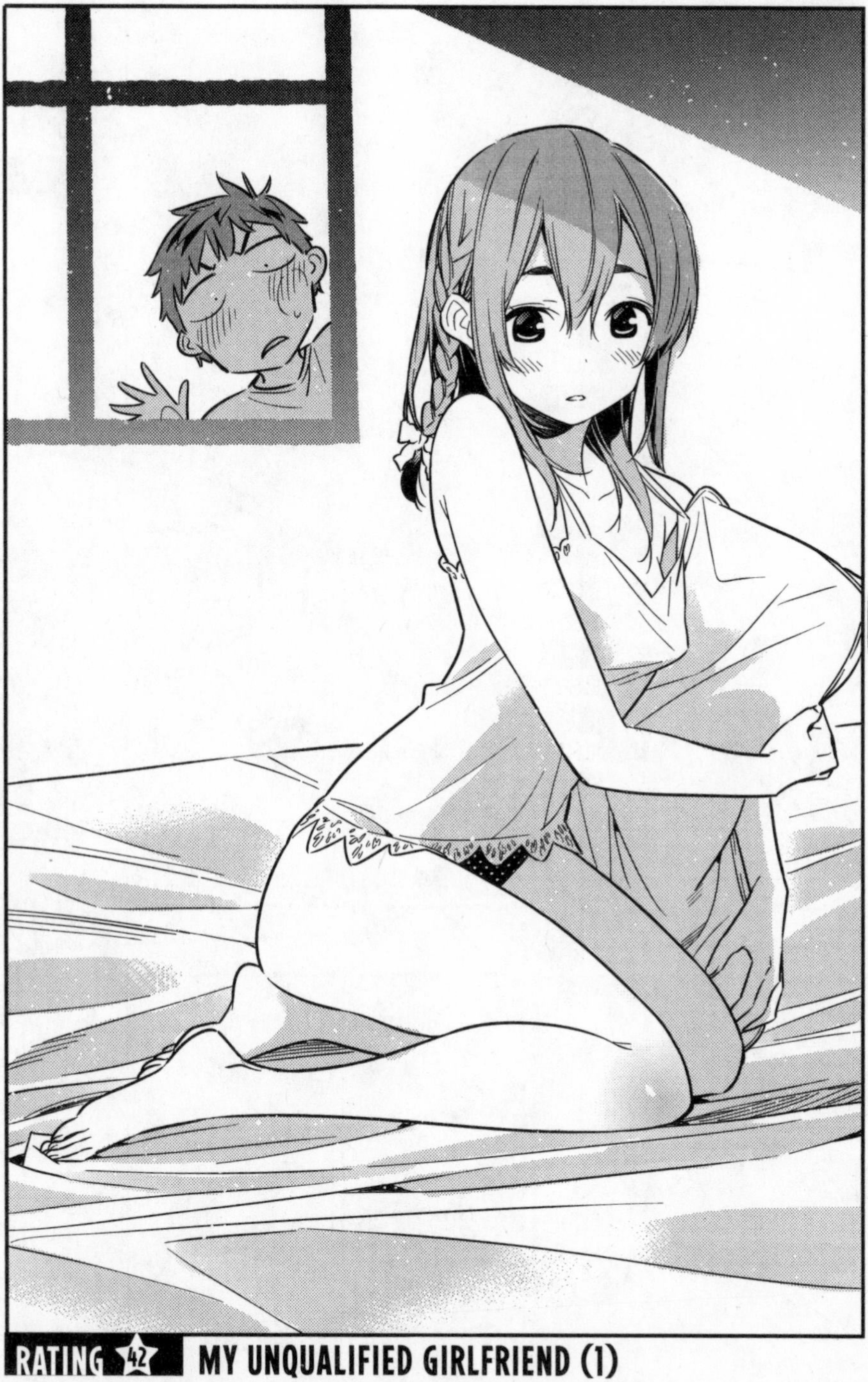

RATING 42 MY UNQUALIFIED GIRLFRIEND (1)

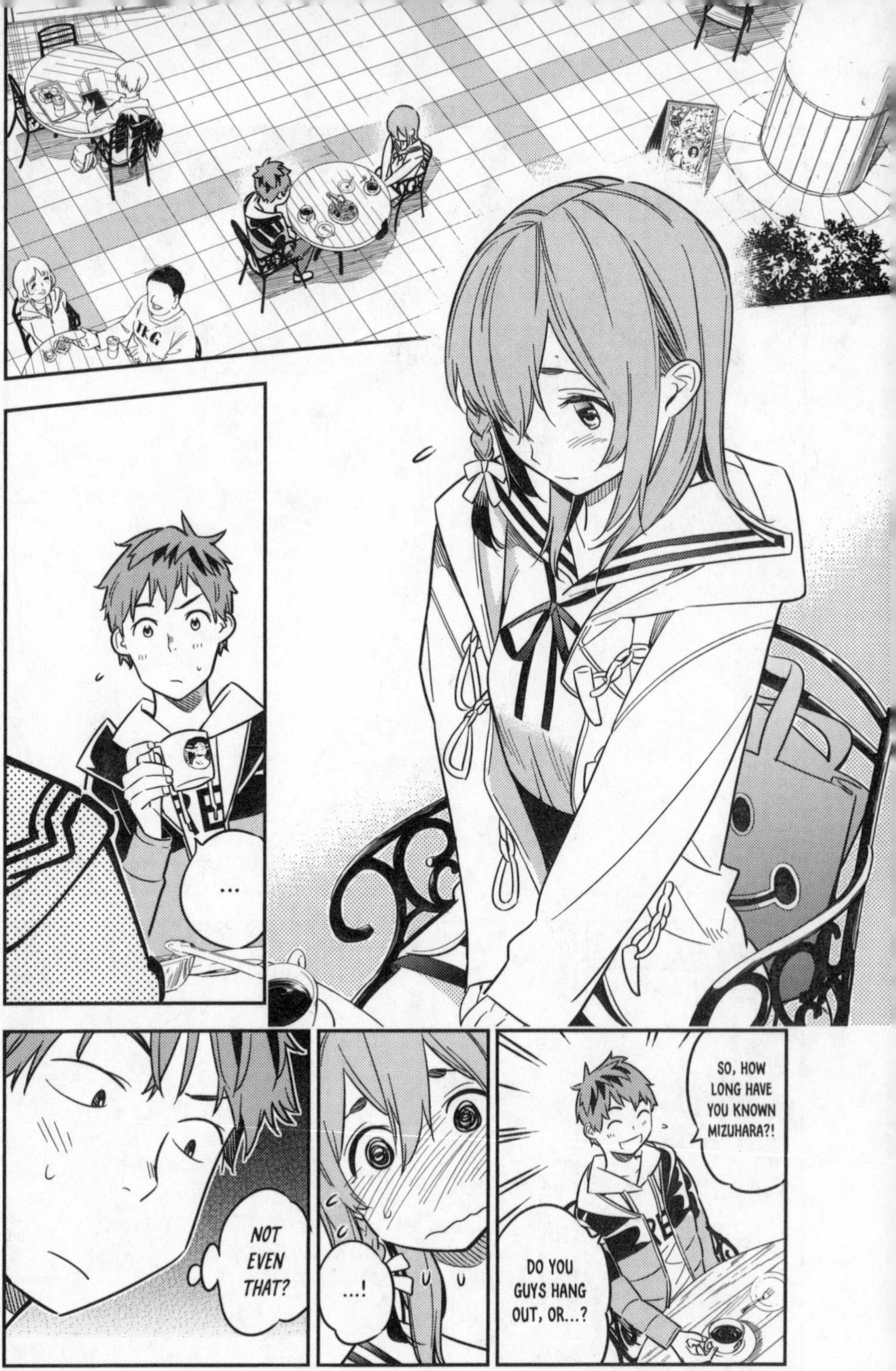
...
SO, HOW LONG HAVE YOU KNOWN MIZUHARA?!
DO YOU GUYS HANG OUT, OR...?
...!
NOT EVEN THAT?

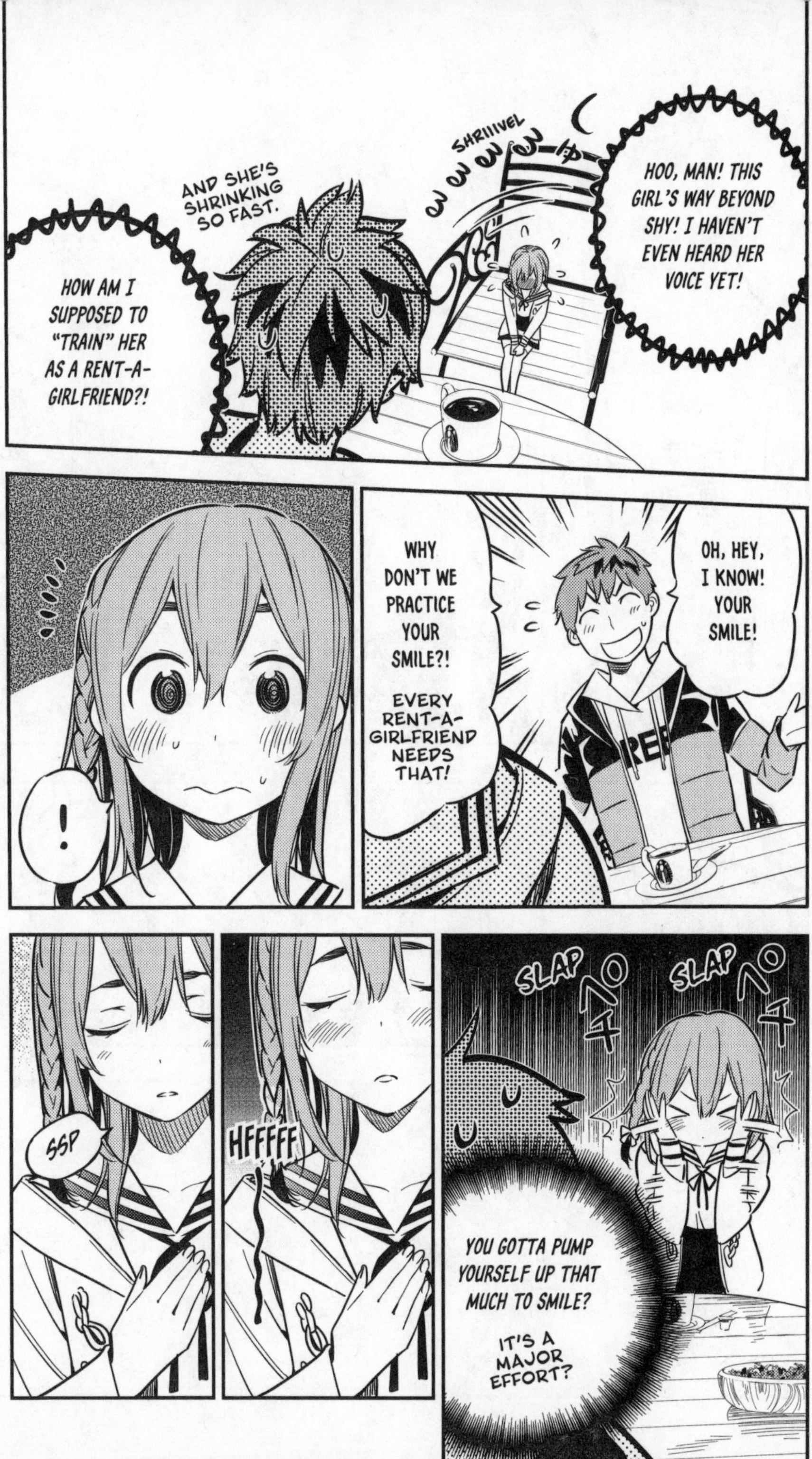
HOO, MAN! THIS GIRL'S WAY BEYOND SHY! I HAVEN'T EVEN HEARD HER VOICE YET!
SHRIIIVEL
AND SHE'S SHRINKING SO FAST.
HOW AM I SUPPOSED TO "TRAIN" HER AS A RENT-A-GIRLFRIEND?!
OH, HEY, I KNOW! YOUR SMILE!
WHY DON'T WE PRACTICE YOUR SMILE?!
EVERY RENT-A-GIRLFRIEND NEEDS THAT!
!
SLAP
SLAP
YOU GOTTA PUMP YOURSELF UP THAT MUCH TO SMILE?
IT'S A MAJOR EFFORT?
HFFFFF
SSP

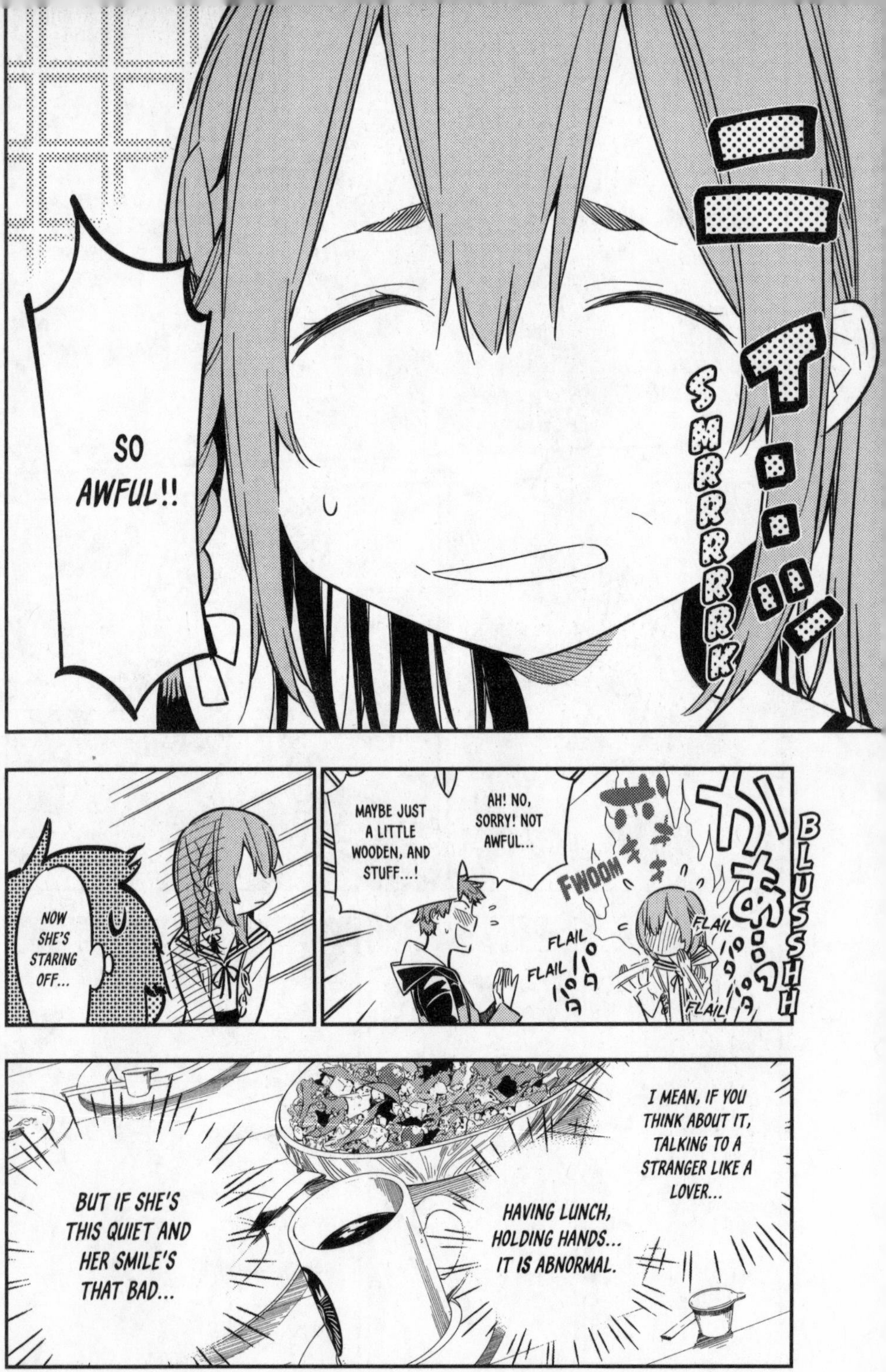
SMRRRRK
SO AWFUL!!
BLUSSHH
FWOOM
FLAIL
FLAIL
AH! NO, SORRY! NOT AWFUL...
MAYBE JUST A LITTLE WOODEN, AND STUFF...!
FLAIL
FLAIL
NOW SHE'S STARING OFF...
I MEAN, IF YOU THINK ABOUT IT, TALKING TO A STRANGER LIKE A LOVER...
HAVING LUNCH, HOLDING HANDS... IT IS ABNORMAL.
BUT IF SHE'S THIS QUIET AND HER SMILE'S THAT BAD...

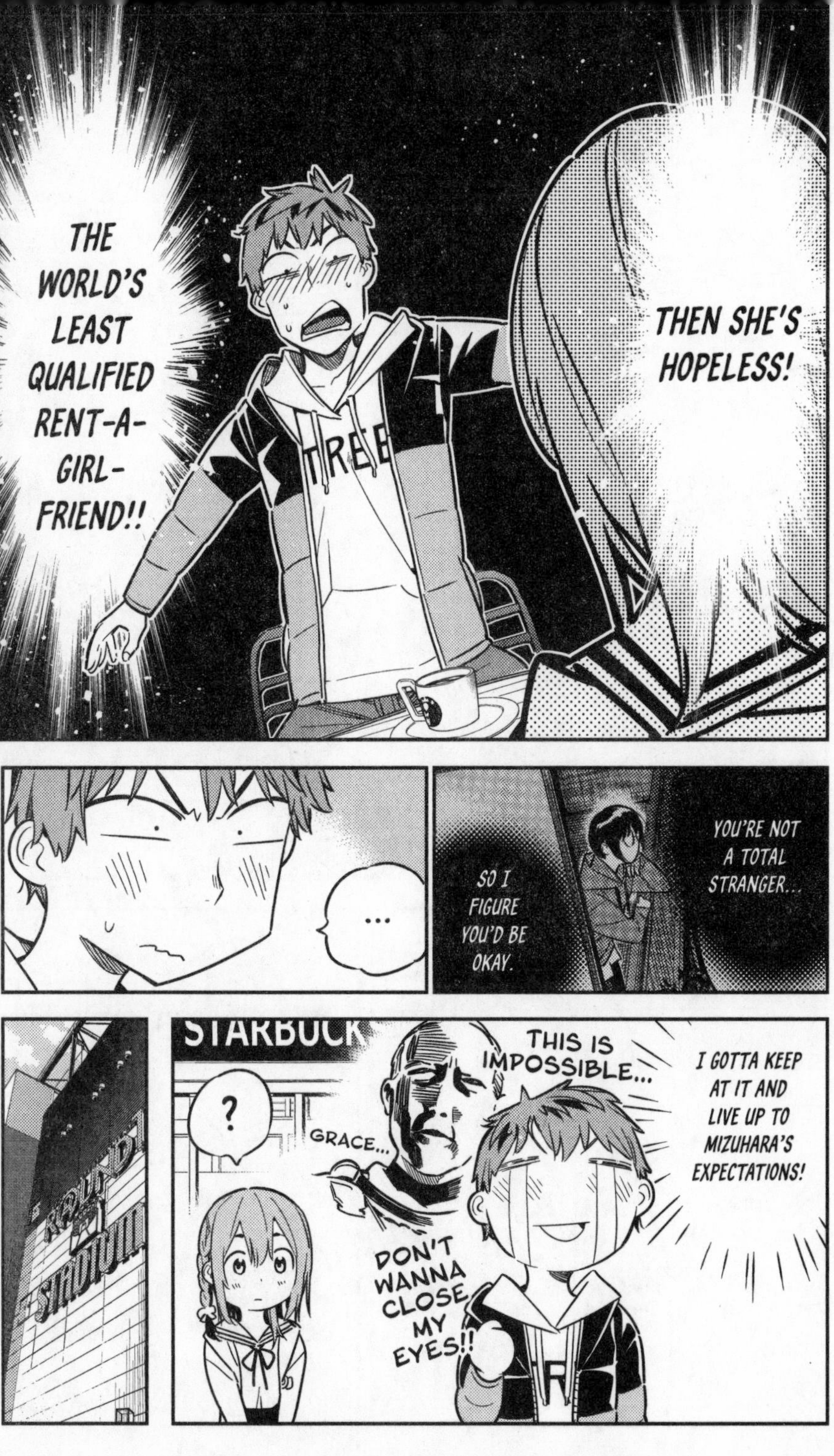
THEN SHE'S HOPELESS!
THE WORLD'S LEAST QUALIFIED RENT-A-GIRL-FRIEND!!
YOU'RE NOT A TOTAL STRANGER...
SO I FIGURE YOU'D BE OKAY.
...
I GOTTA KEEP AT IT AND LIVE UP TO MIZUHARA'S EXPECTATIONS!
THIS IS IMPOSSIBLE...
STARBUCK
?
GRACE...
DON'T WANNA CLOSE MY EYES!!

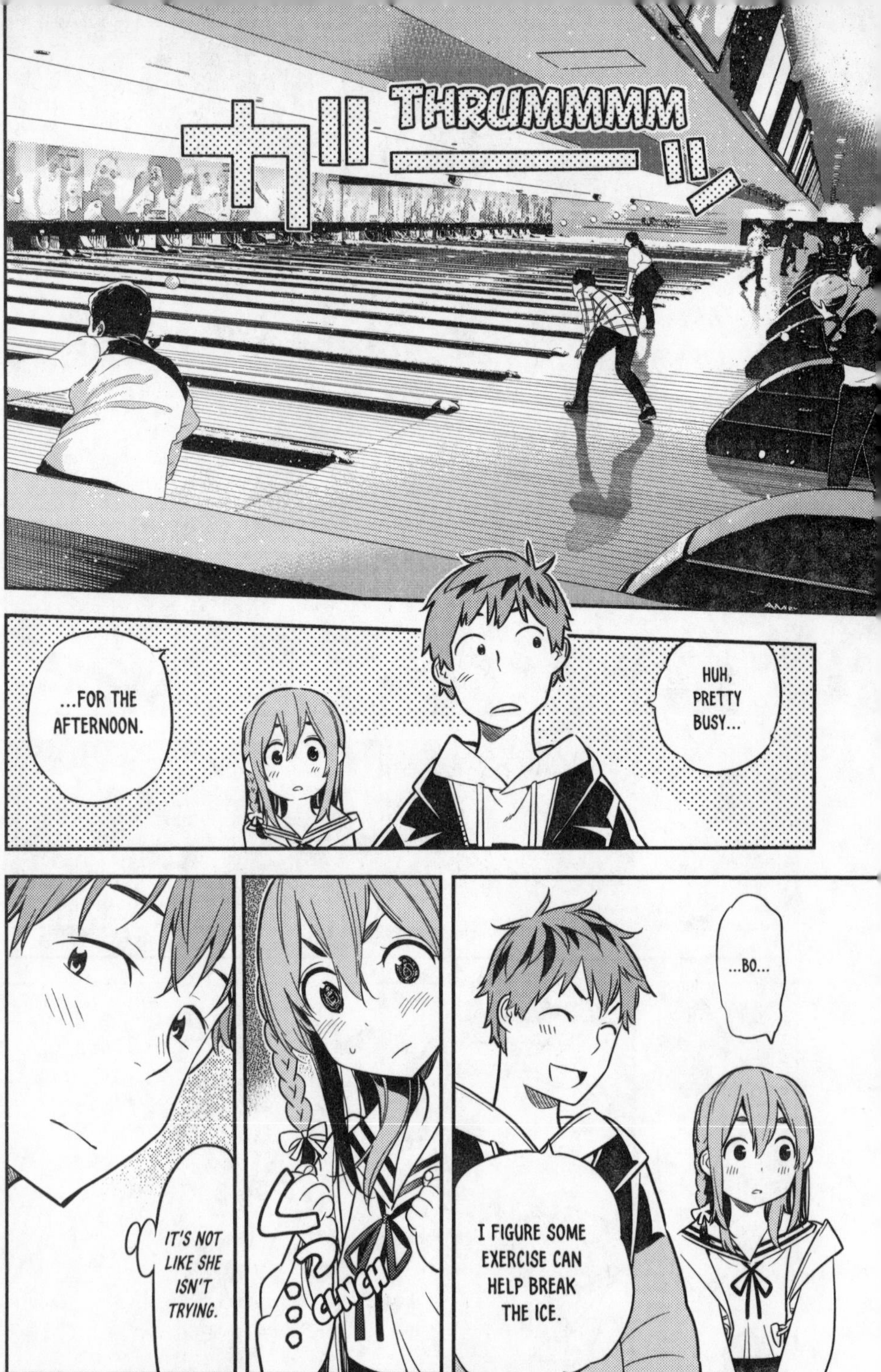
THRUMMMMM
HUH, PRETTY BUSY...
...FOR THE AFTERNOON.
...BO...
I FIGURE SOME EXERCISE CAN HELP BREAK THE ICE.
CLNCH
IT'S NOT LIKE SHE ISN'T TRYING.

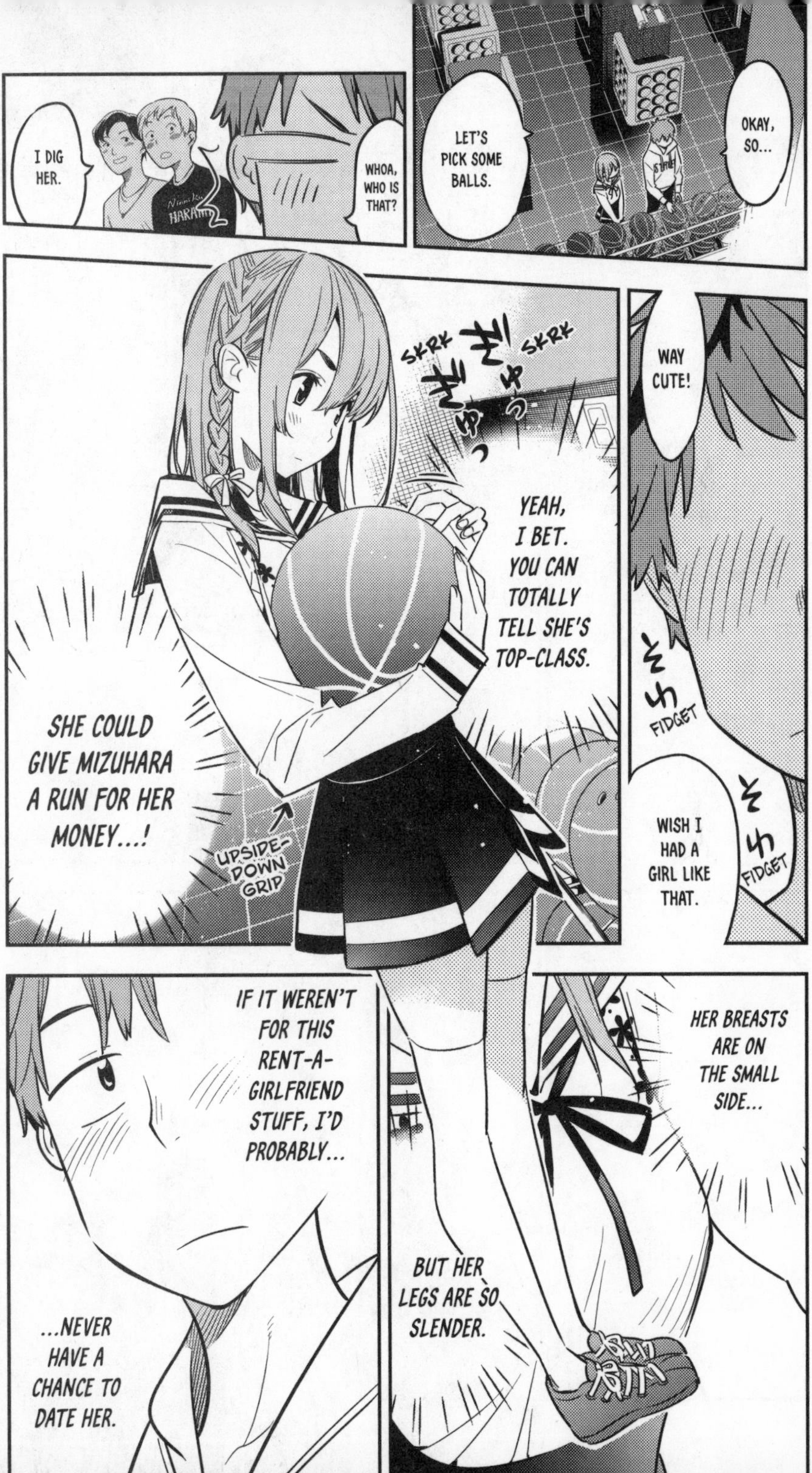
OKAY, SO...
LET'S PICK SOME BALLS.
WHOA, WHO IS THAT?
I DIG HER.
WAY CUTE!
FIDGET
WISH I HAD A GIRL LIKE THAT.
FIDGET
SKRK SKRK
YEAH, I BET. YOU CAN TOTALLY TELL SHE'S TOP-CLASS.
SHE COULD GIVE MIZUHARA A RUN FOR HER MONEY...!
UPSIDE-DOWN GRIP
HER BREASTS ARE ON THE SMALL SIDE...
BUT HER LEGS ARE SO SLENDER.
IF IT WEREN'T FOR THIS RENT-A-GIRLFRIEND STUFF, I'D PROBABLY...
...NEVER HAVE A CHANCE TO DATE HER.

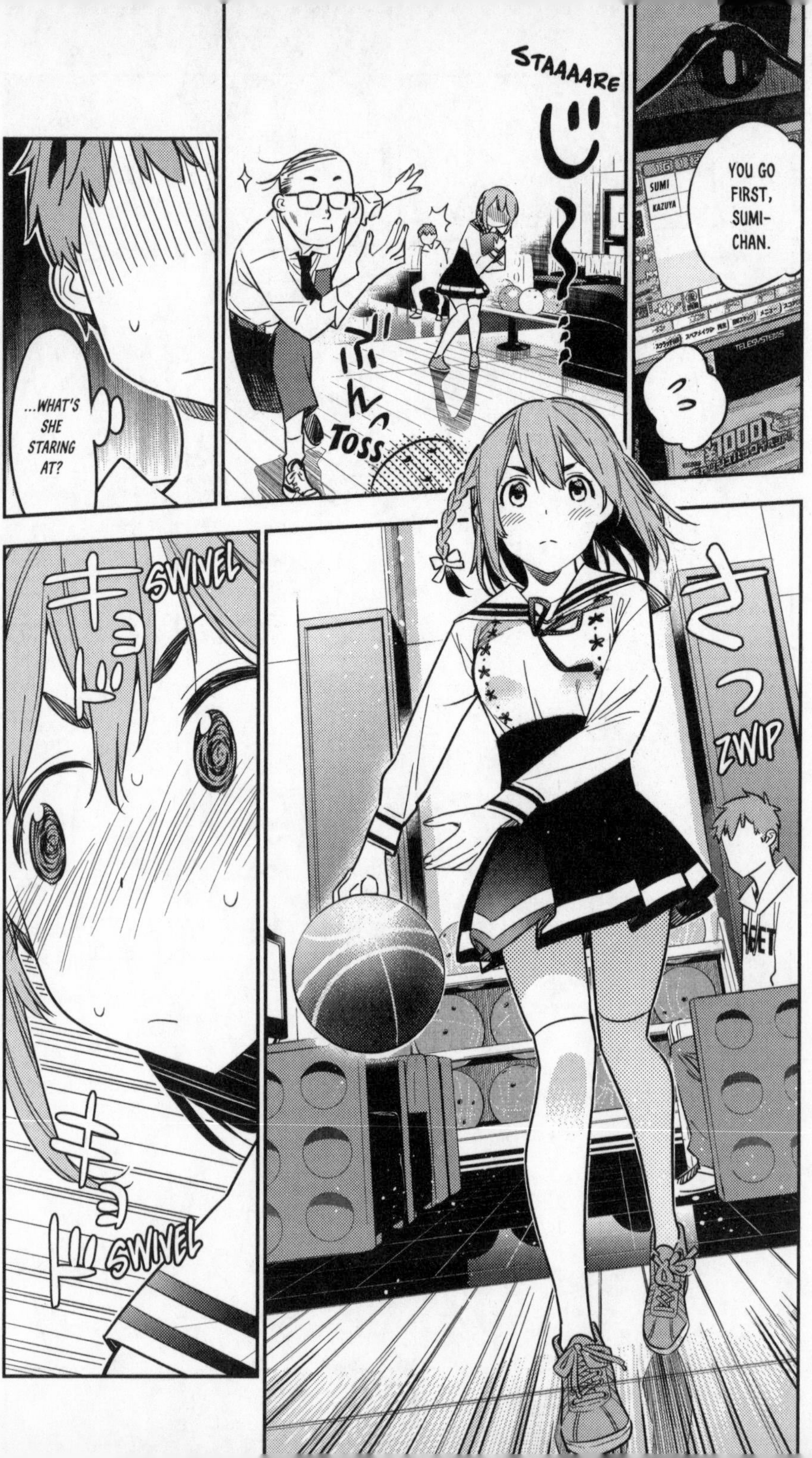
YOU GO FIRST, SUMI-CHAN.
SUMI
KAZUYA
STAAAARE
TOSS
...WHAT'S SHE STARING AT?
ZWIP
SWIVEL
SWIVEL

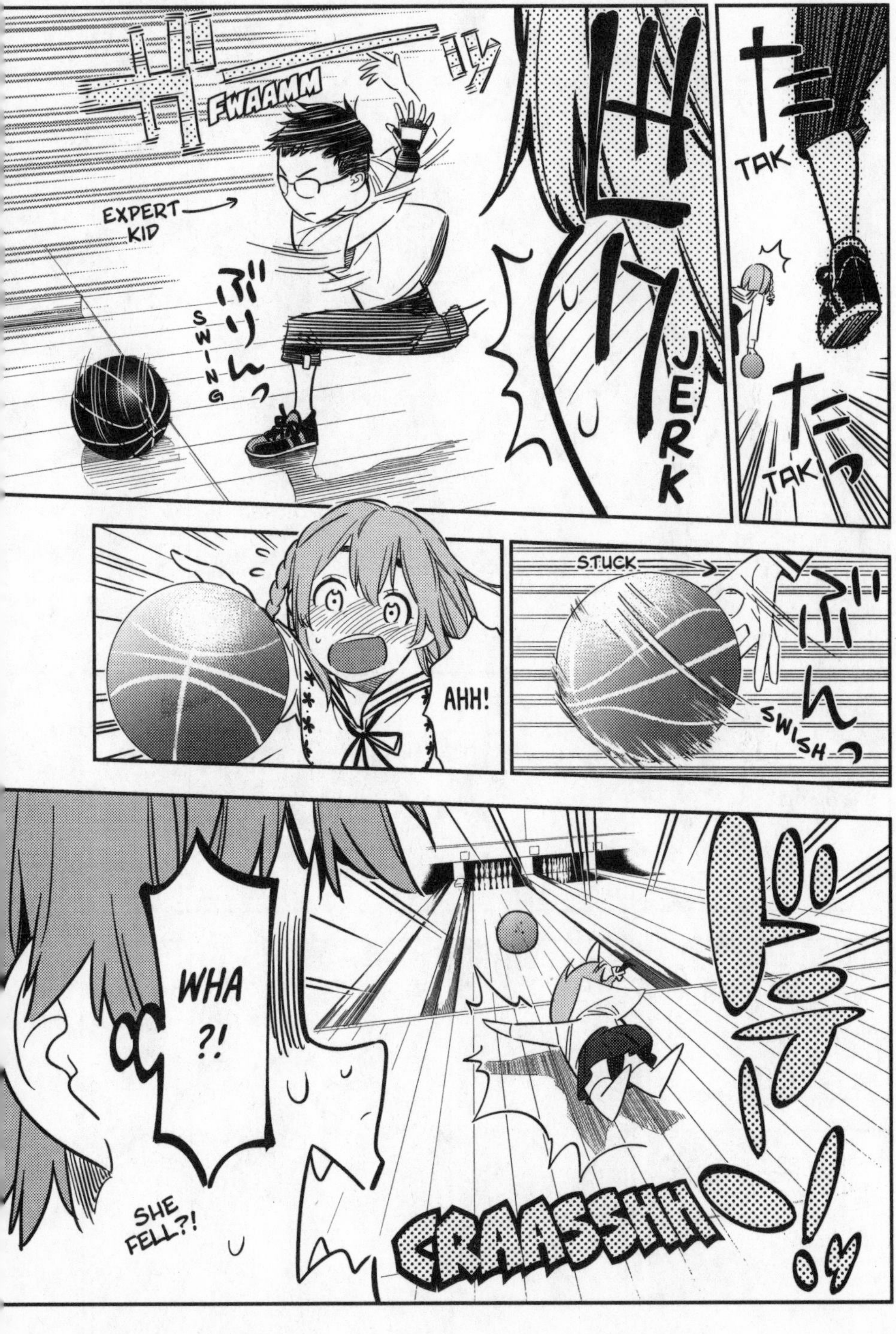
TAK
TAK
JERK
FWAAMM
EXPERT KID
SWING
STUCK
SWISH
AHH!
CRAASHH
WHA ?!
SHE FELL?!

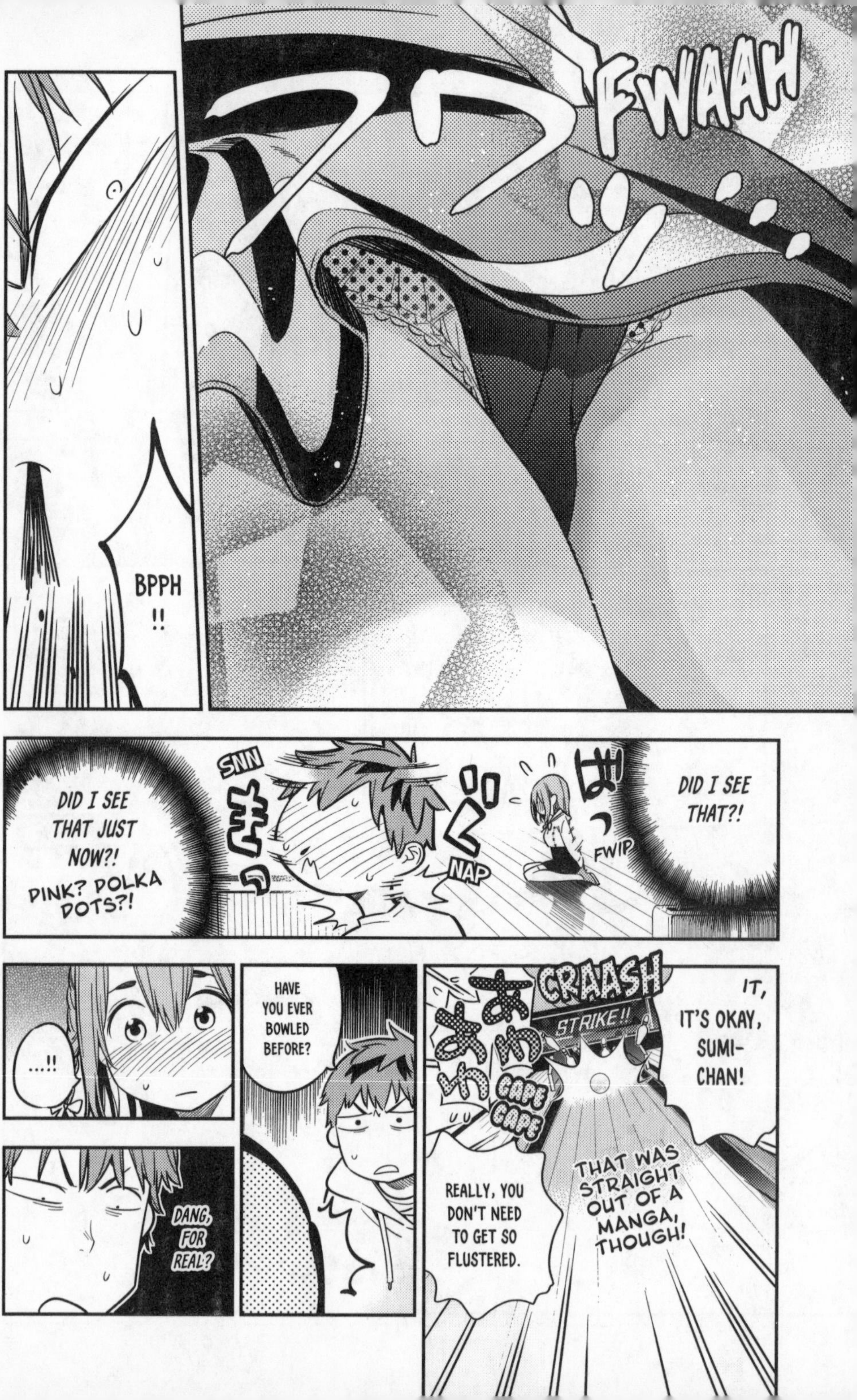
FWAAH
BPPH !!
DID I SEE THAT?!
FWIP
SNN
NAP
DID I SEE THAT JUST NOW?! PINK? POLKA DOTS?!
CRAASH
STRIKE!!
IT, IT'S OKAY, SUMI-CHAN!
CAPE CAPE
THAT WAS STRAIGHT OUT OF A MANGA, THOUGH!
REALLY, YOU DON'T NEED TO GET SO FLUSTERED.
HAVE YOU EVER BOWLED BEFORE?
...!!
DANG, FOR REAL?

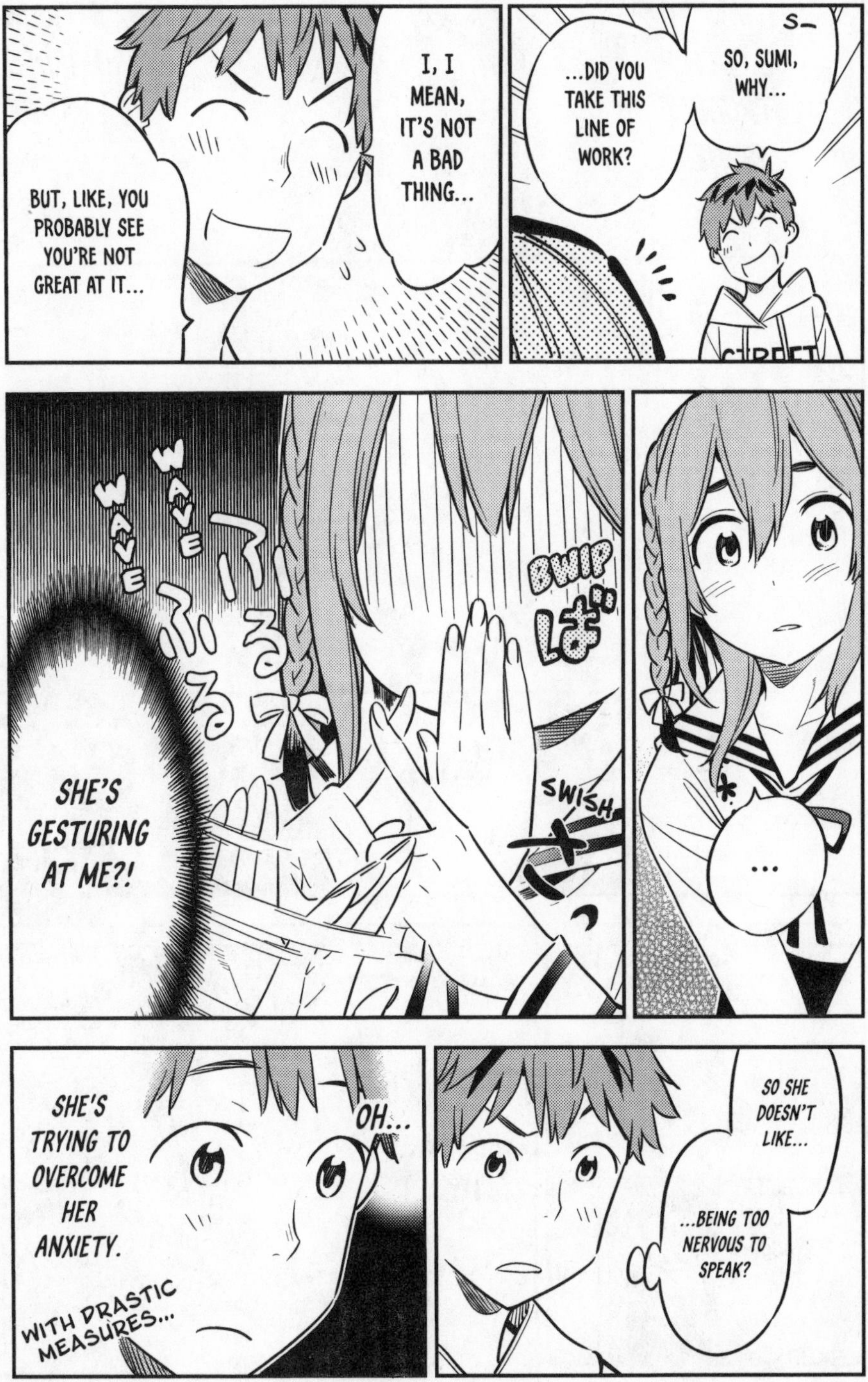

S–
SO, SUMI, WHY...
...DID YOU TAKE THIS LINE OF WORK?
I, I MEAN, IT'S NOT A BAD THING...
BUT, LIKE, YOU PROBABLY SEE YOU'RE NOT GREAT AT IT...
...
BWIP ば
SWISH さっ
WAVE WAVE ふるふる
SHE'S GESTURING AT ME?!
SO SHE DOESN'T LIKE...
...BEING TOO NERVOUS TO SPEAK?
OH...
SHE'S TRYING TO OVERCOME HER ANXIETY.
WITH DRASTIC MEASURES...

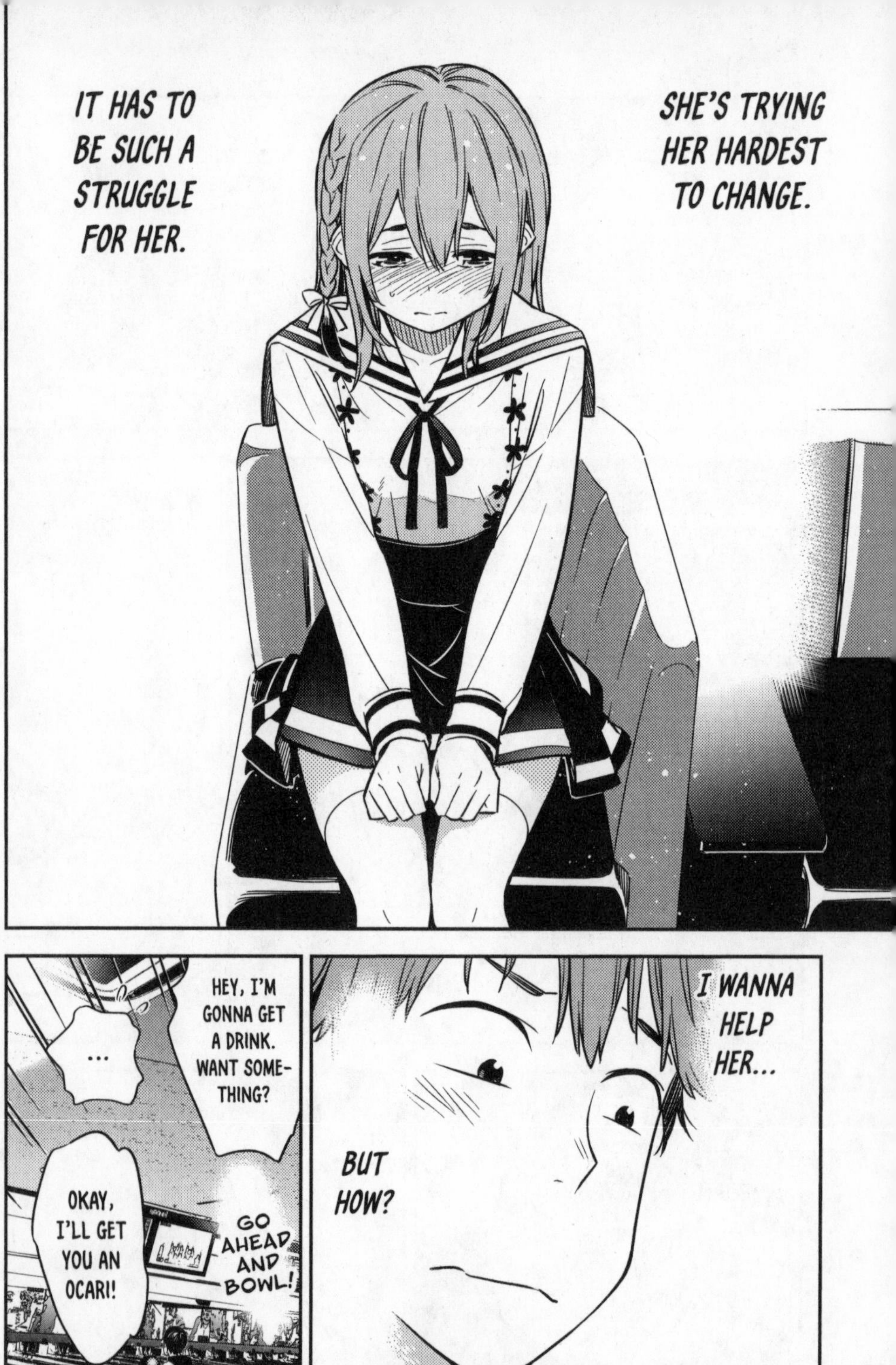
SHE'S TRYING HER HARDEST TO CHANGE.
IT HAS TO BE SUCH A STRUGGLE FOR HER.
I WANNA HELP HER...
BUT HOW?
HEY, I'M GONNA GET A DRINK. WANT SOME-THING?
...
OKAY, I'LL GET YOU AN OCARI!
GO AHEAD AND BOWL!

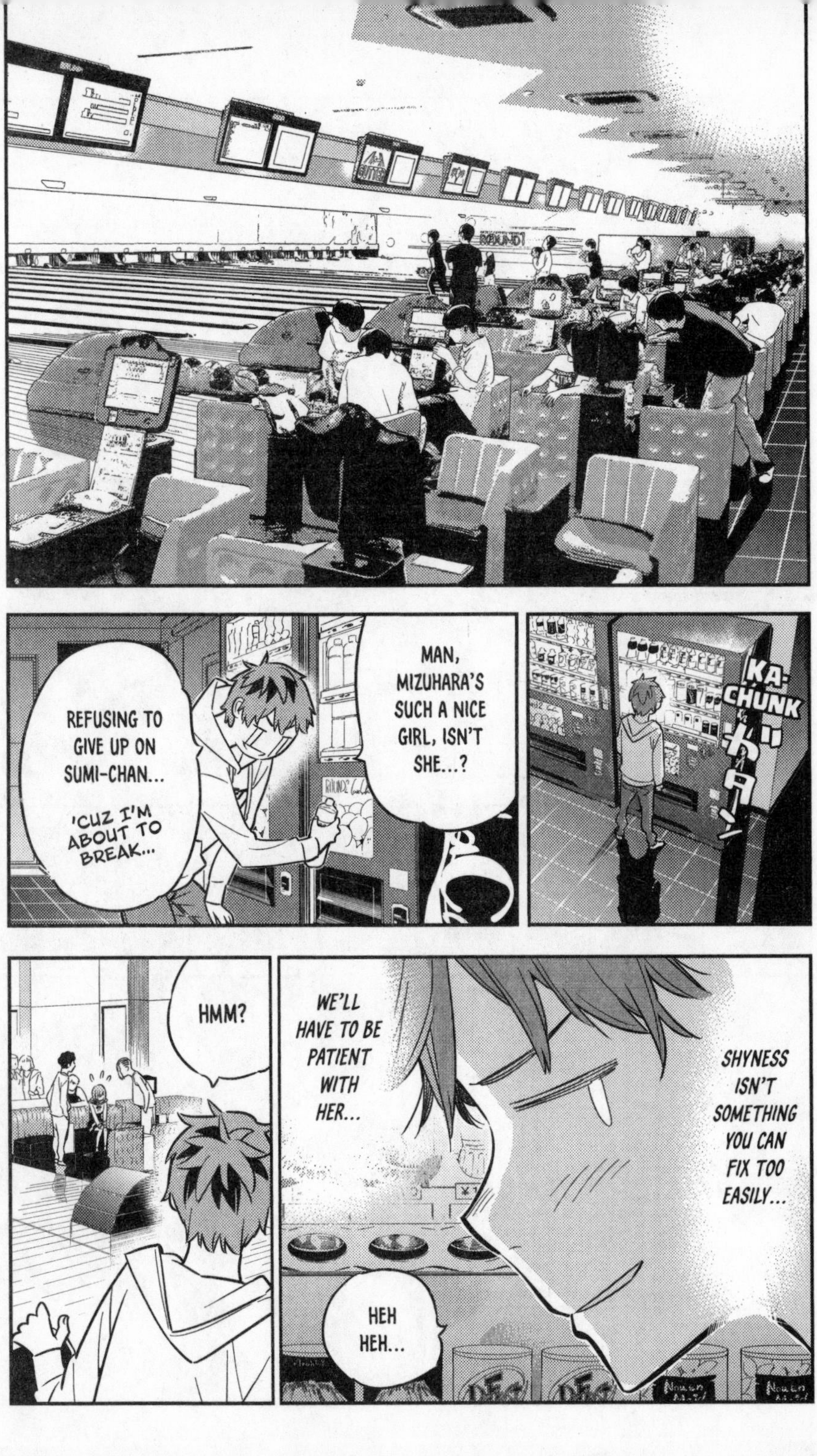
KA-CHUNK
MAN, MIZUHARA'S SUCH A NICE GIRL, ISN'T SHE...?
REFUSING TO GIVE UP ON SUMI-CHAN...
'CUZ I'M ABOUT TO BREAK...
SHYNESS ISN'T SOMETHING YOU CAN FIX TOO EASILY...
WE'LL HAVE TO BE PATIENT WITH HER...
HEH HEH...
HMM?

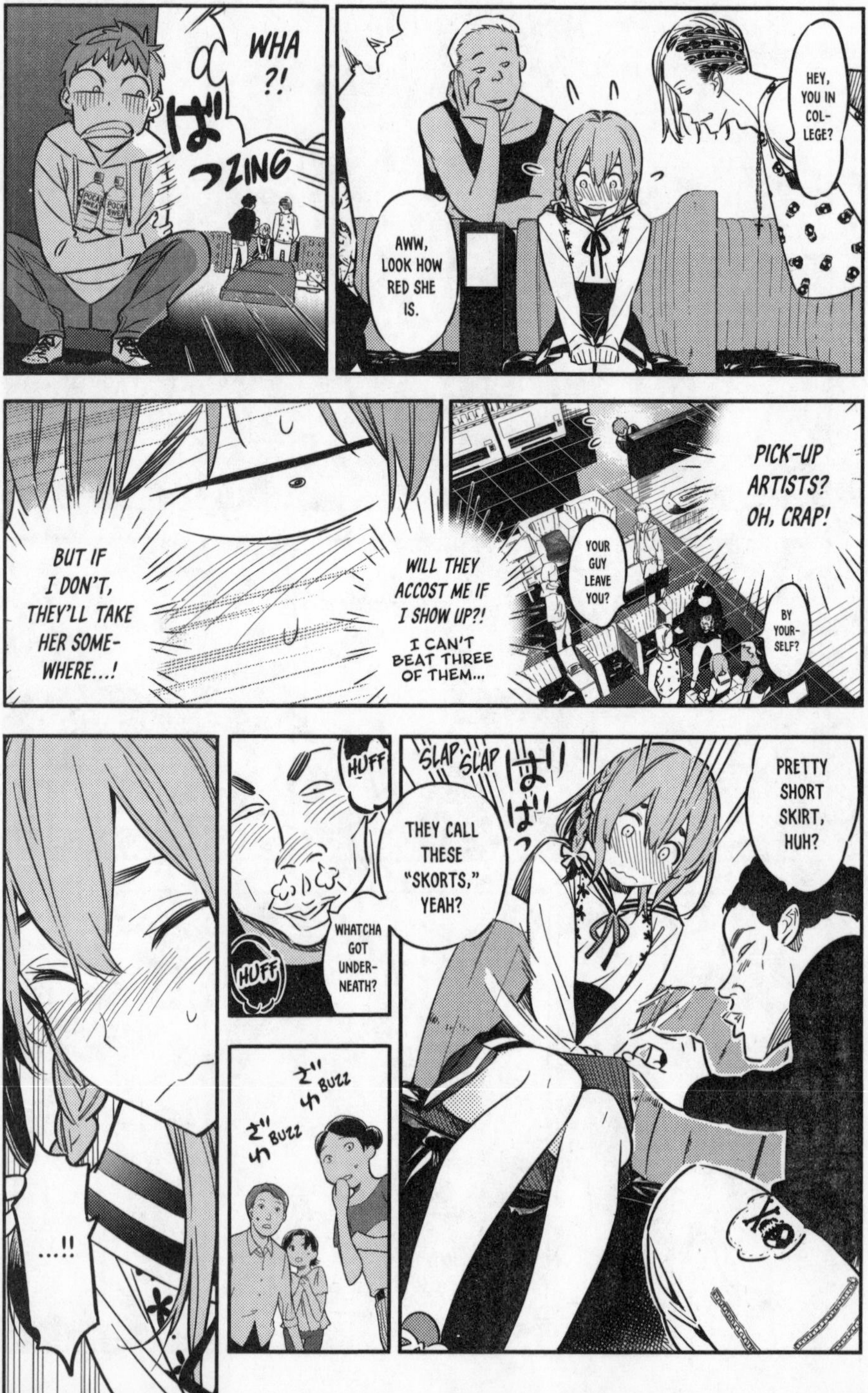
HEY, YOU IN COL-LEGE?
AWW, LOOK HOW RED SHE IS.
WHA ?!
ばっ
ZING
PICK-UP ARTISTS? OH, CRAP!
BY YOUR-SELF?
YOUR GUY LEAVE YOU?
WILL THEY ACCOST ME IF I SHOW UP?!
I CAN'T BEAT THREE OF THEM...
BUT IF I DON'T, THEY'LL TAKE HER SOME-WHERE...!
PRETTY SHORT SKIRT, HUH?
SLAP, SLAP
HUFF
THEY CALL THESE "SKORTS," YEAH?
WHATCHA GOT UNDER-NEATH?
HUFF
ざわ BUZZ
ざわ BUZZ
...!!

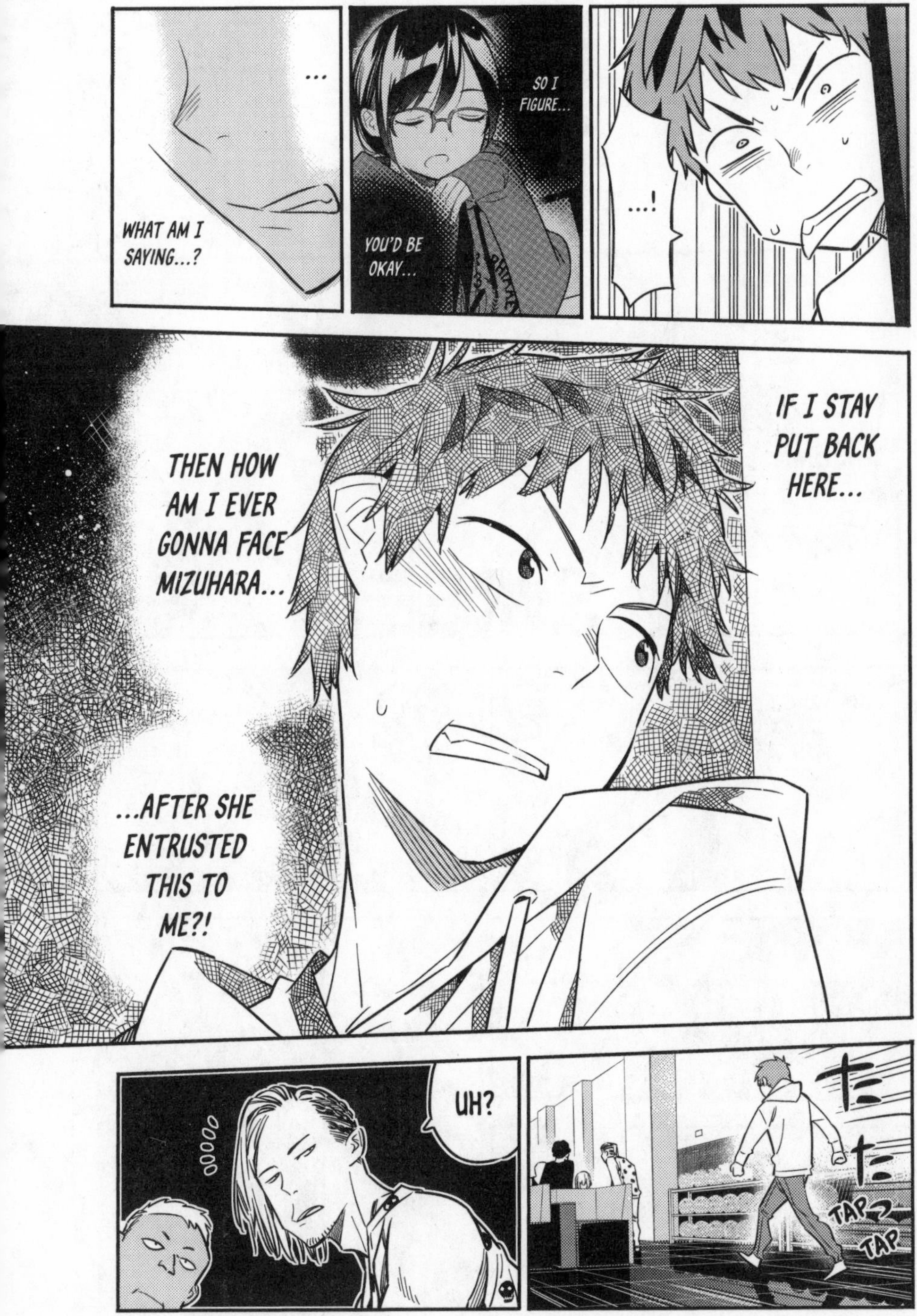
...!
SO I FIGURE...
YOU'D BE OKAY...
...
WHAT AM I SAYING...?
IF I STAY PUT BACK HERE...
THEN HOW AM I EVER GONNA FACE MIZUHARA...
...AFTER SHE ENTRUSTED THIS TO ME?!
TAP TAP
UH?

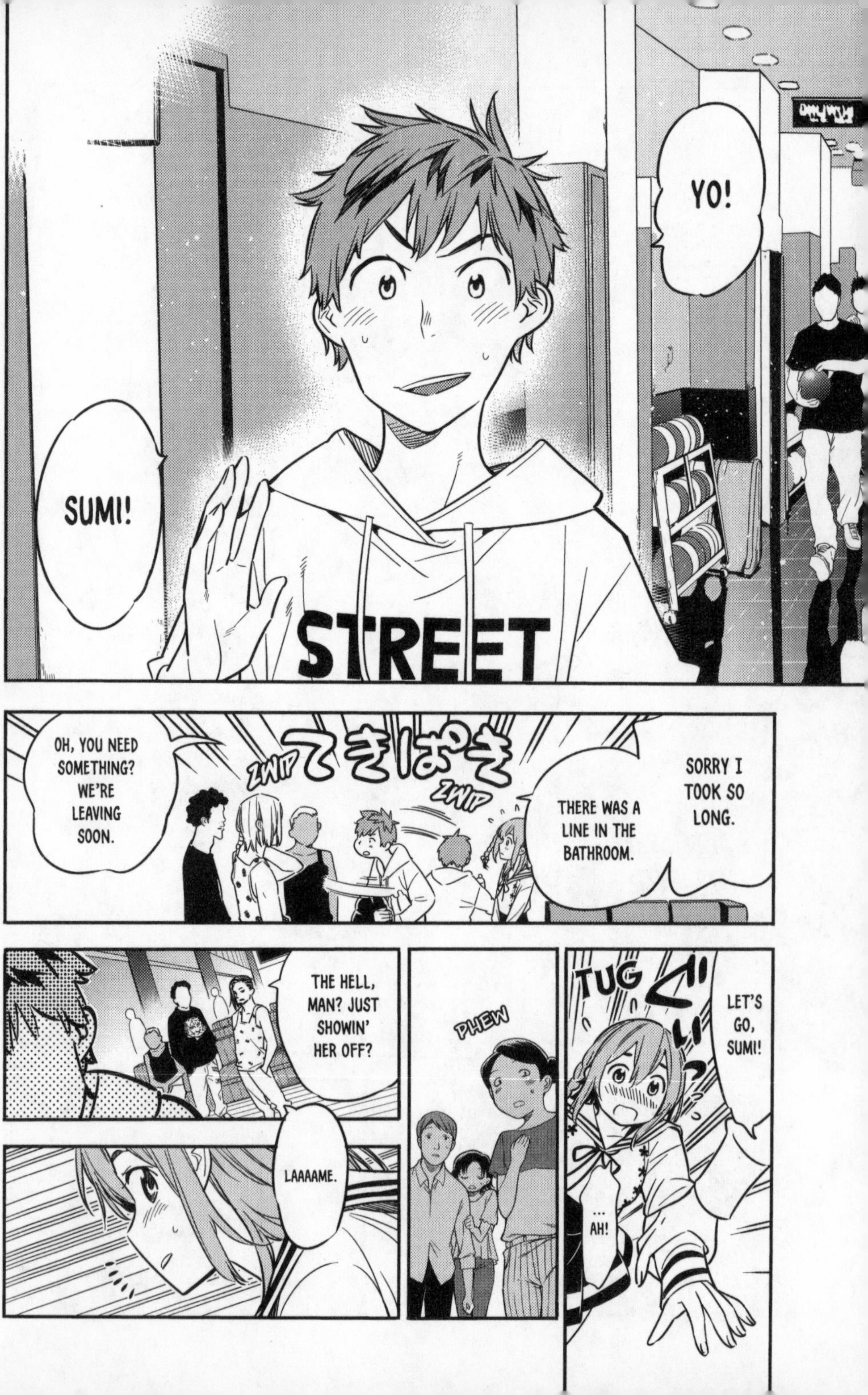
YO!
SUMI!
SORRY I TOOK SO LONG.
THERE WAS A LINE IN THE BATHROOM.
ZWIP てきぱき ZWIP
OH, YOU NEED SOMETHING? WE'RE LEAVING SOON.
TUG ぐいっ
LET'S GO, SUMI!
...AH!
PHEW
THE HELL, MAN? JUST SHOWIN' HER OFF?
LAAAAME.

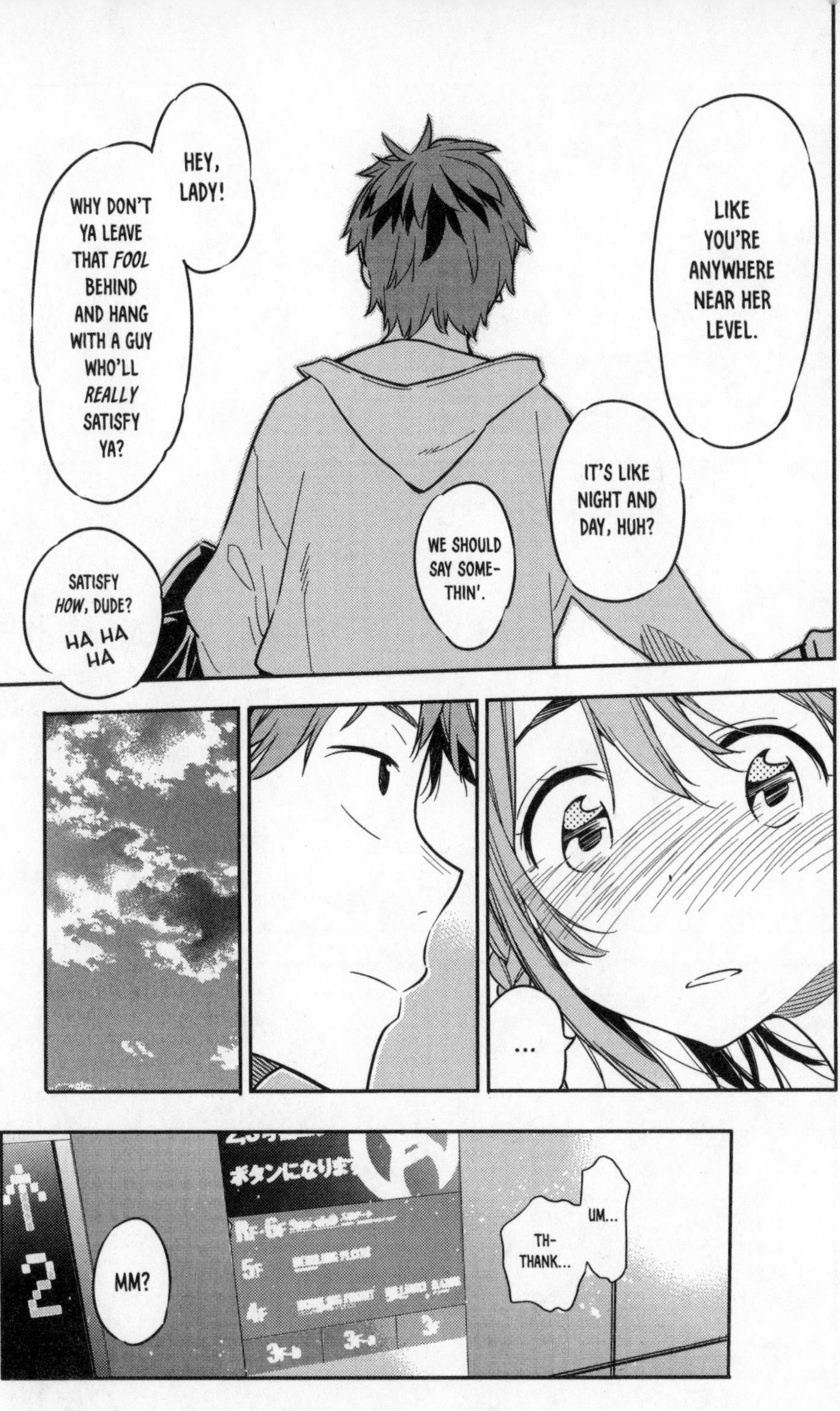
LIKE YOU'RE ANYWHERE NEAR HER LEVEL.
HEY, LADY!
WHY DON'T YA LEAVE THAT *FOOL* BEHIND AND HANG WITH A GUY WHO'LL *REALLY* SATISFY YA?
IT'S LIKE NIGHT AND DAY, HUH?
WE SHOULD SAY SOME-THIN'.
SATISFY *HOW*, DUDE?
HA HA HA
...
UM...
TH-THANK...
MM?

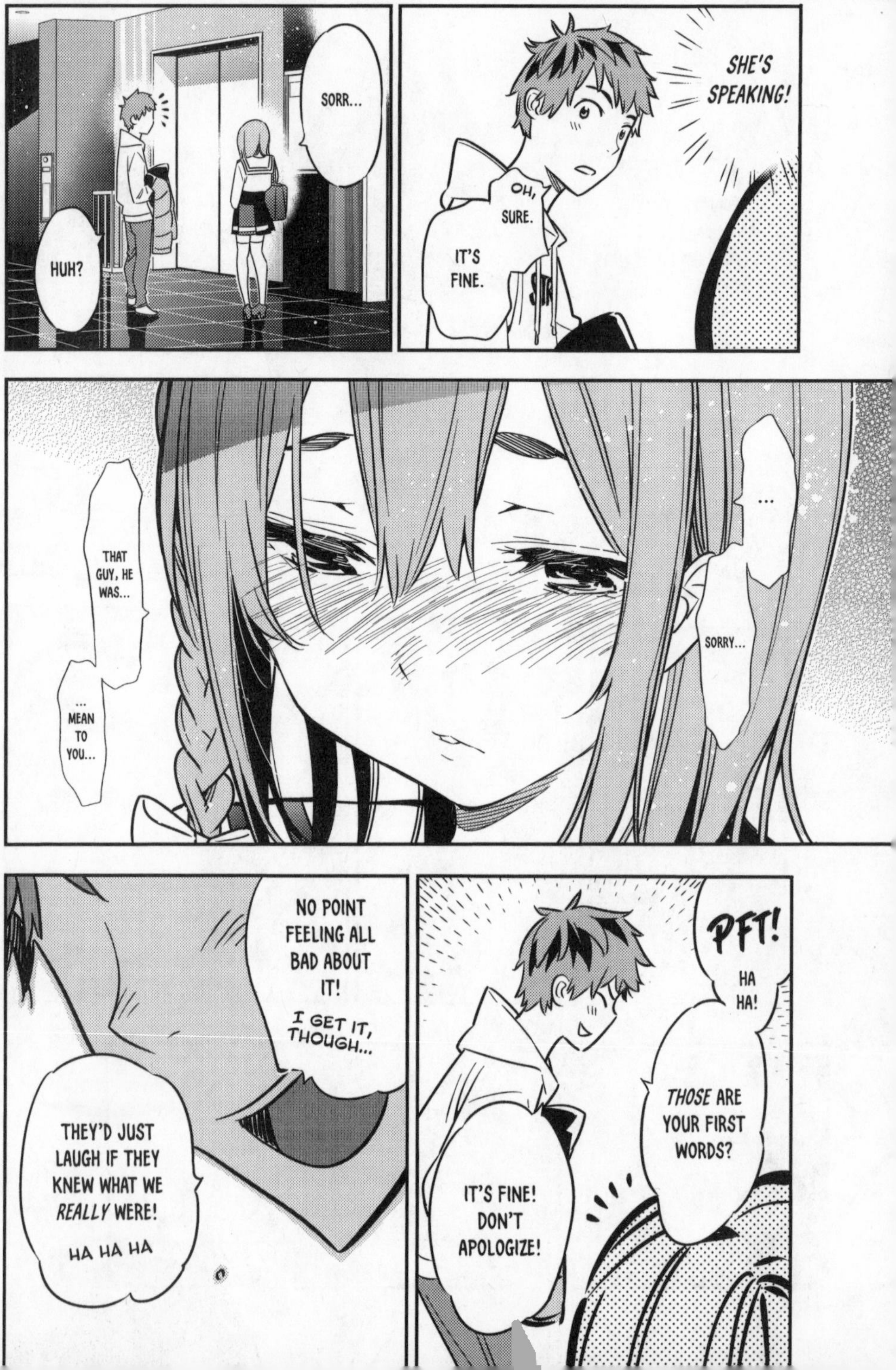
SHE'S SPEAKING!
OH, SURE.
IT'S FINE.
SORR...
HUH?
...
SORRY...
THAT GUY, HE WAS...
... MEAN TO YOU...
PFT!
HA HA!
THOSE ARE YOUR FIRST WORDS?
IT'S FINE! DON'T APOLOGIZE!
NO POINT FEELING ALL BAD ABOUT IT!
I GET IT, THOUGH...
THEY'D JUST LAUGH IF THEY KNEW WHAT WE REALLY WERE!
HA HA HA

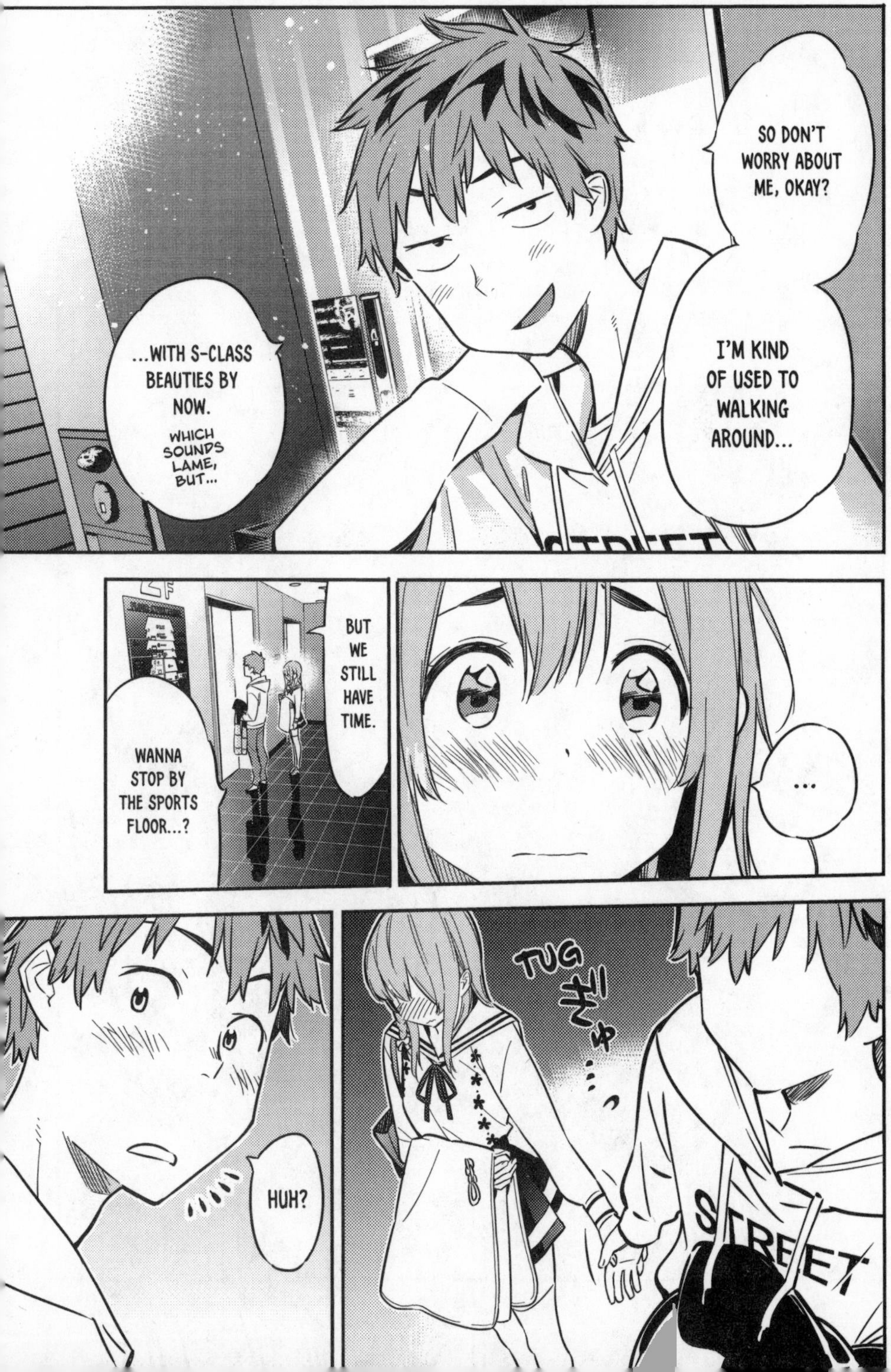
SO DON'T WORRY ABOUT ME, OKAY?
I'M KIND OF USED TO WALKING AROUND...
...WITH S-CLASS BEAUTIES BY NOW.
WHICH SOUNDS LAME, BUT...
...
BUT WE STILL HAVE TIME.
WANNA STOP BY THE SPORTS FLOOR...?
TUG
ぎゅ...っ
STREET
HUH?

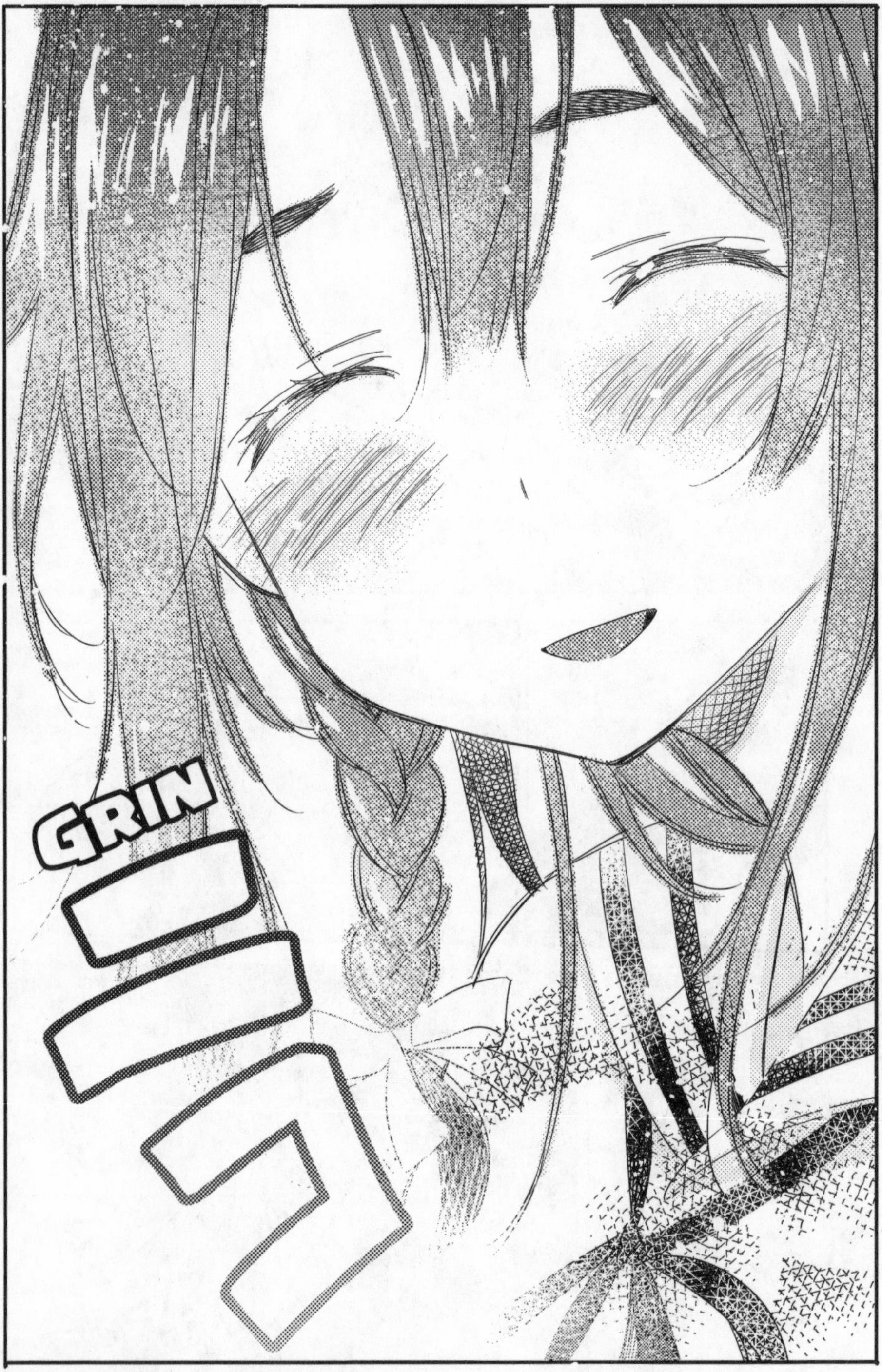
GRIN

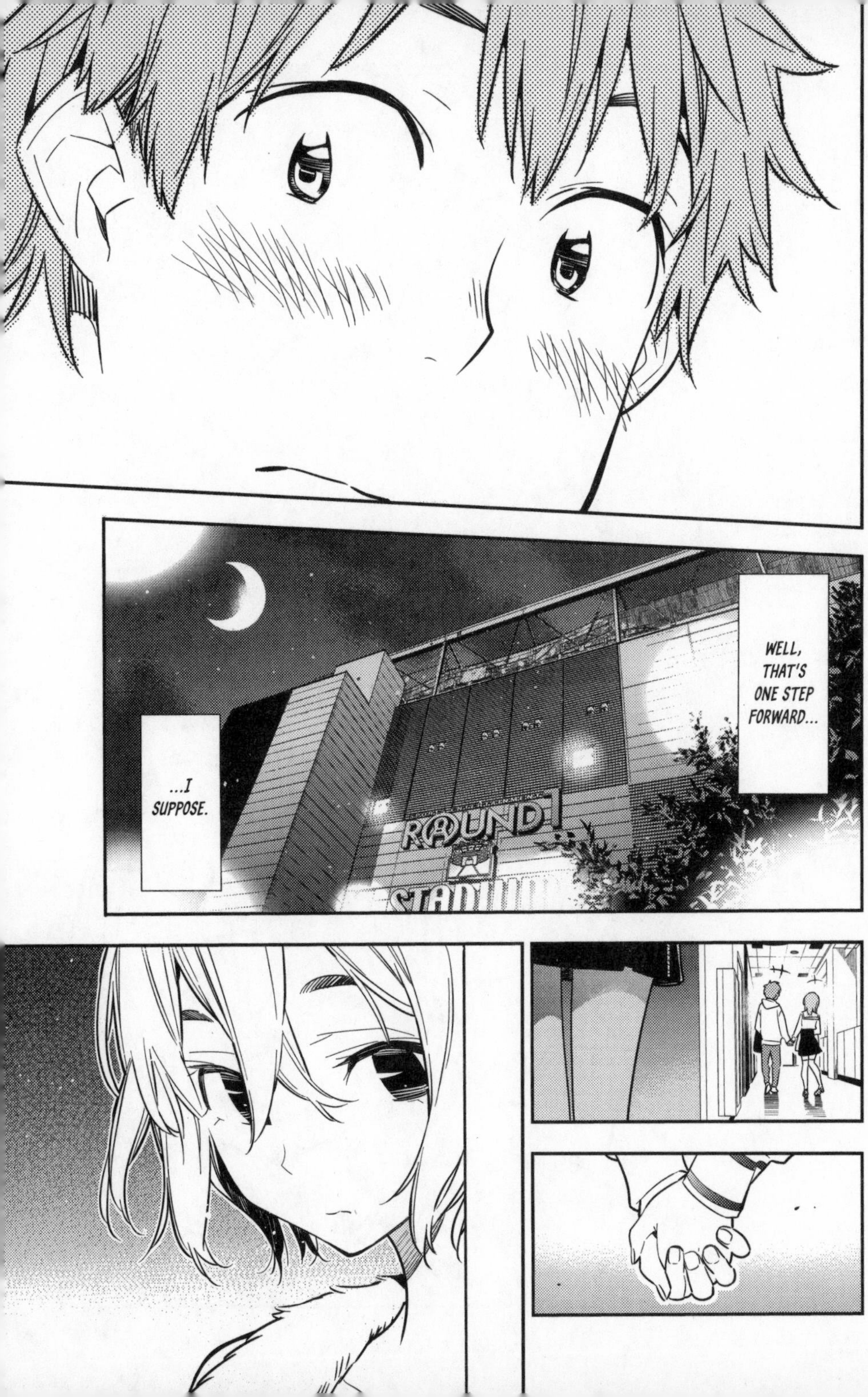
WELL, THAT'S ONE STEP FORWARD...
ROUND1
...I SUPPOSE.

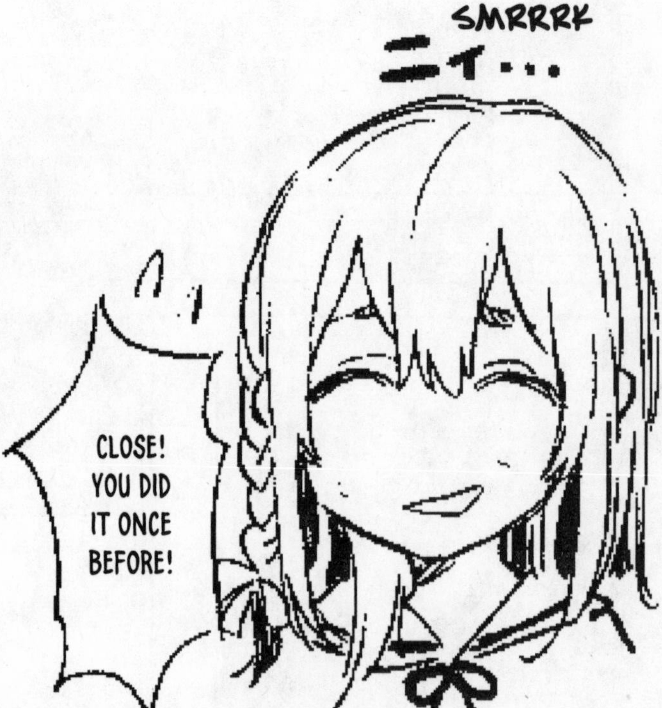
SMRRRK
ニィ…
CLOSE! YOU DID IT ONCE BEFORE!

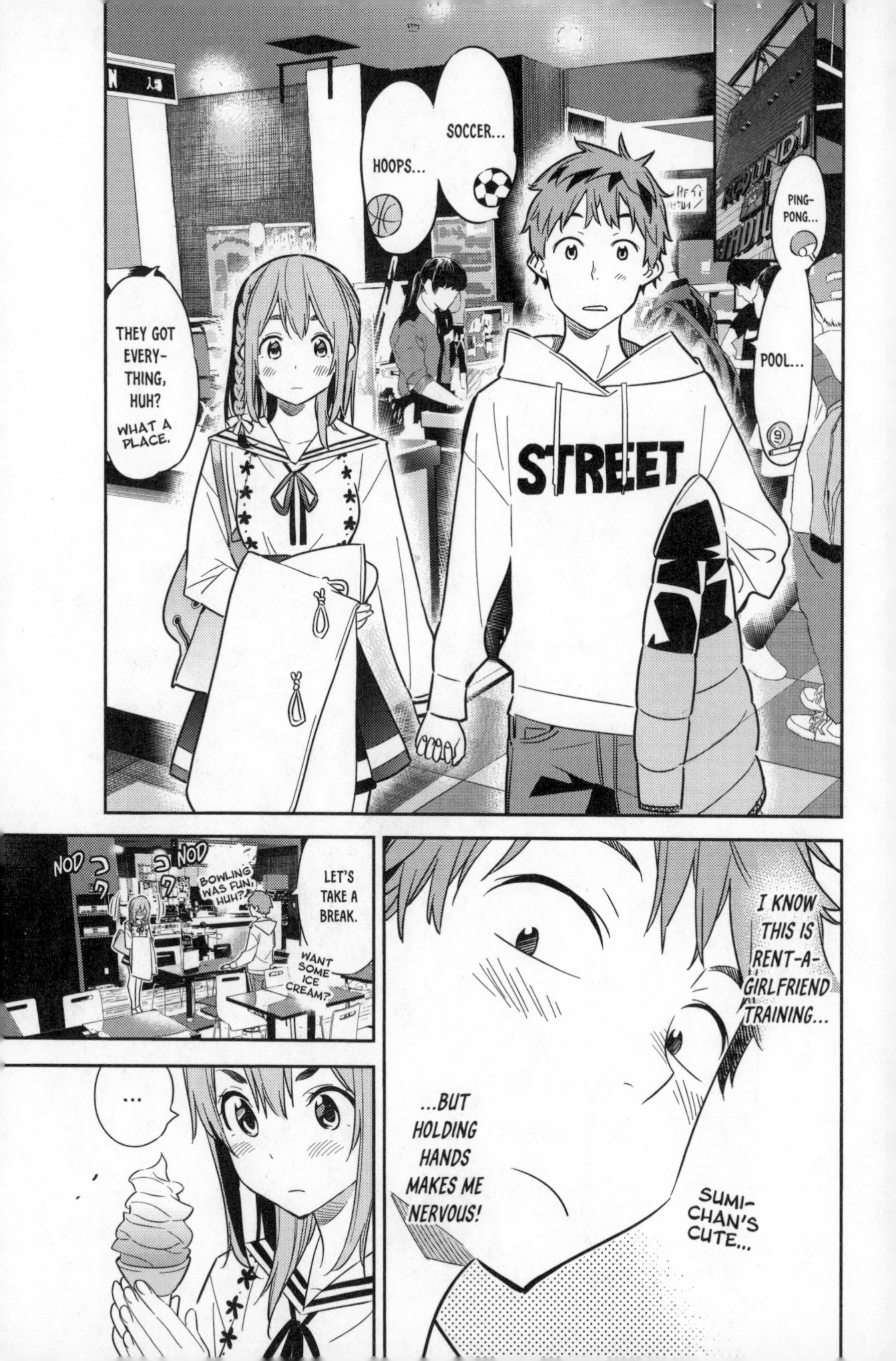
PING-PONG...
POOL...
SOCCER...
HOOPS...
THEY GOT EVERYTHING, HUH? WHAT A PLACE.
I KNOW THIS IS RENT-A-GIRLFRIEND TRAINING...
...BUT HOLDING HANDS MAKES ME NERVOUS!
SUMI-CHAN'S CUTE...
LET'S TAKE A BREAK.
BOWLING WAS FUN, HUH?
WANT SOME ICE CREAM?
NOD NOD
...

RATING 43 MY UNQUALIFIED GIRLFRIEND (2)

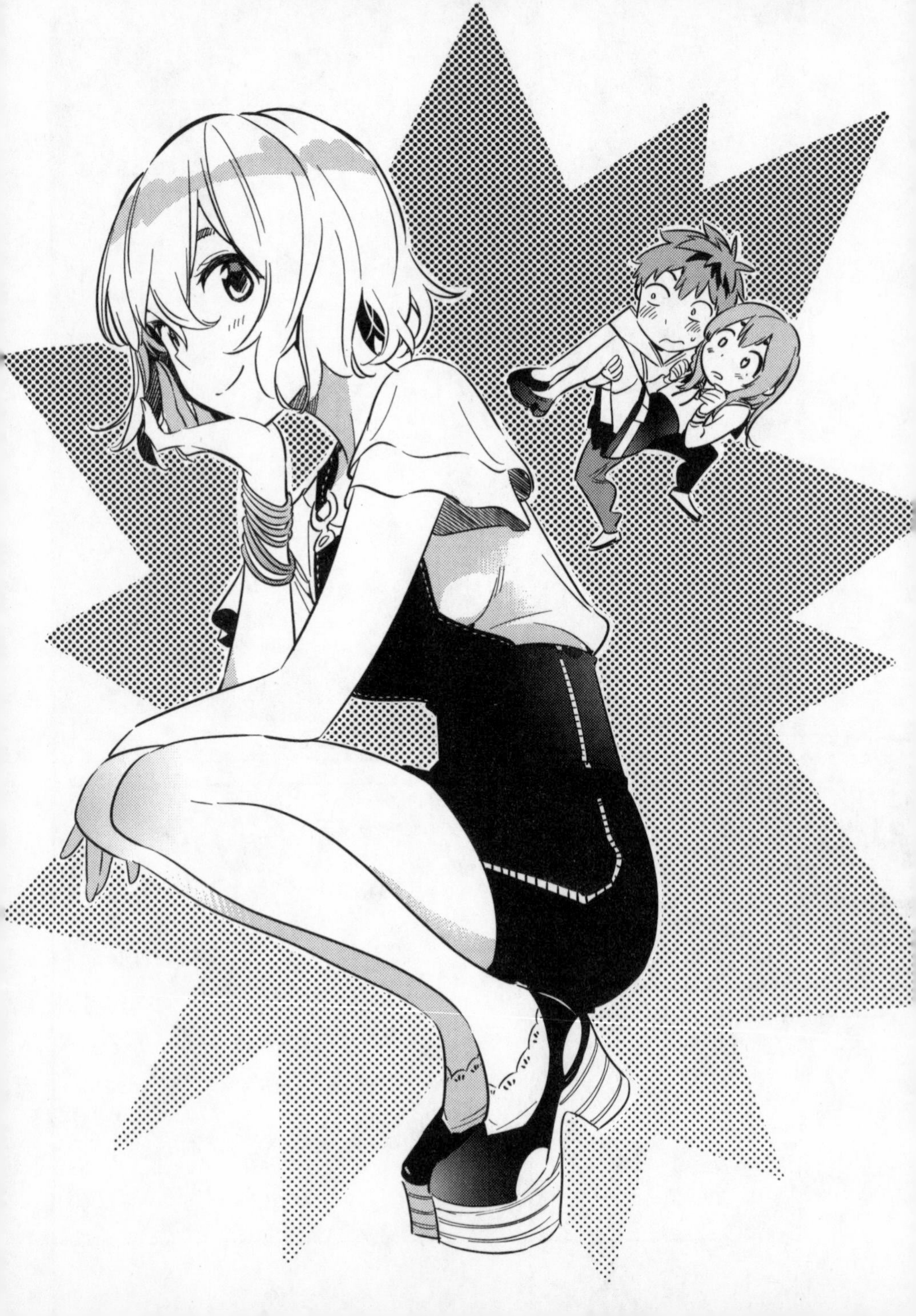

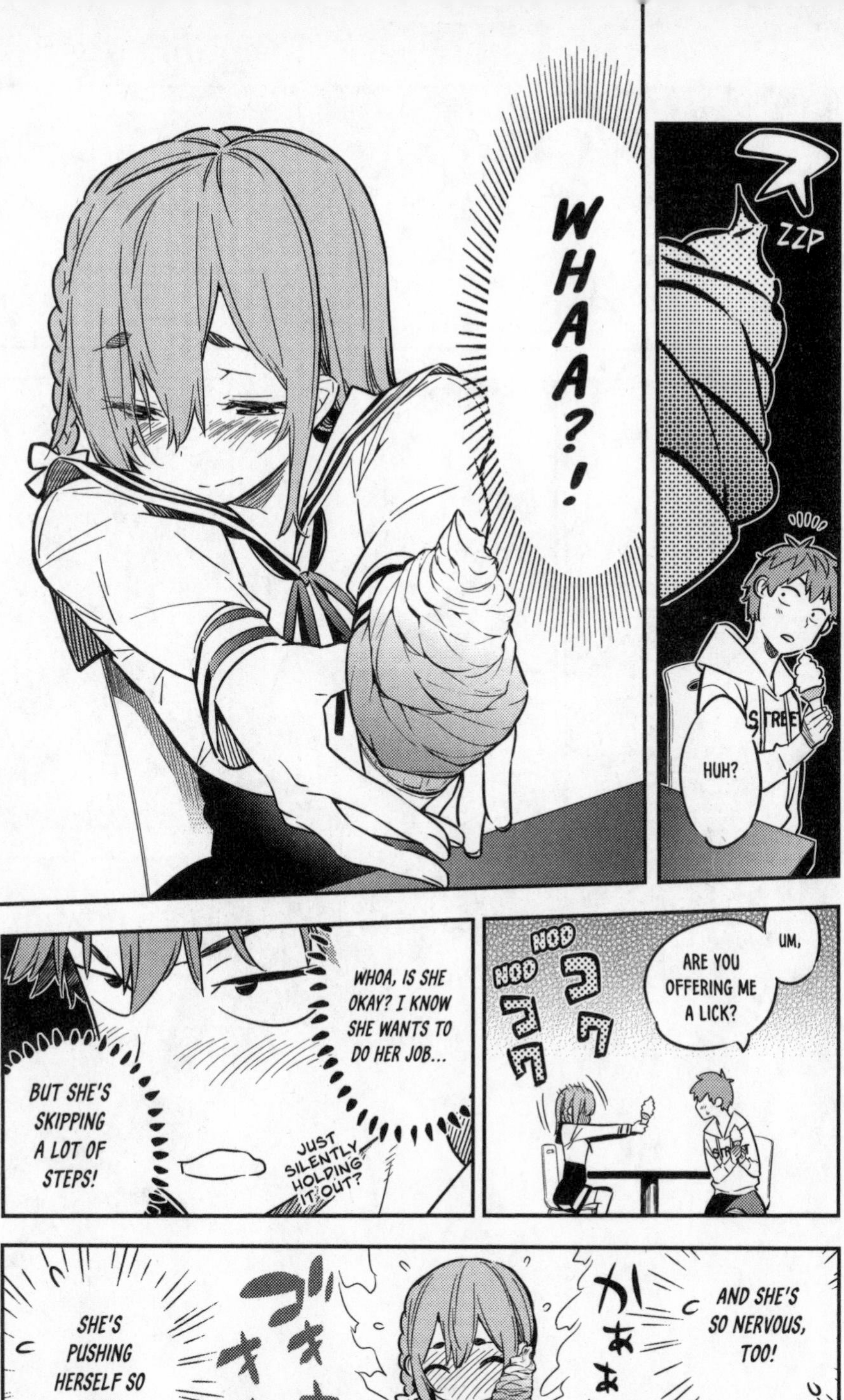

ZZP
HUH?
WHAAA?!
NOO NOO NOO
UM,
ARE YOU OFFERING ME A LICK?
WHOA, IS SHE OKAY? I KNOW SHE WANTS TO DO HER JOB...
BUT SHE'S SKIPPING A LOT OF STEPS!
JUST SILENTLY HOLDING IT OUT?
AND SHE'S SO NERVOUS, TOO!
BLUSHHHH
ROAARRR
SHE'S PUSHING HERSELF SO HARD!

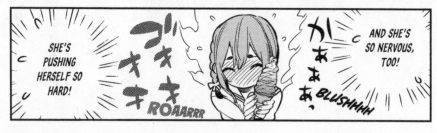

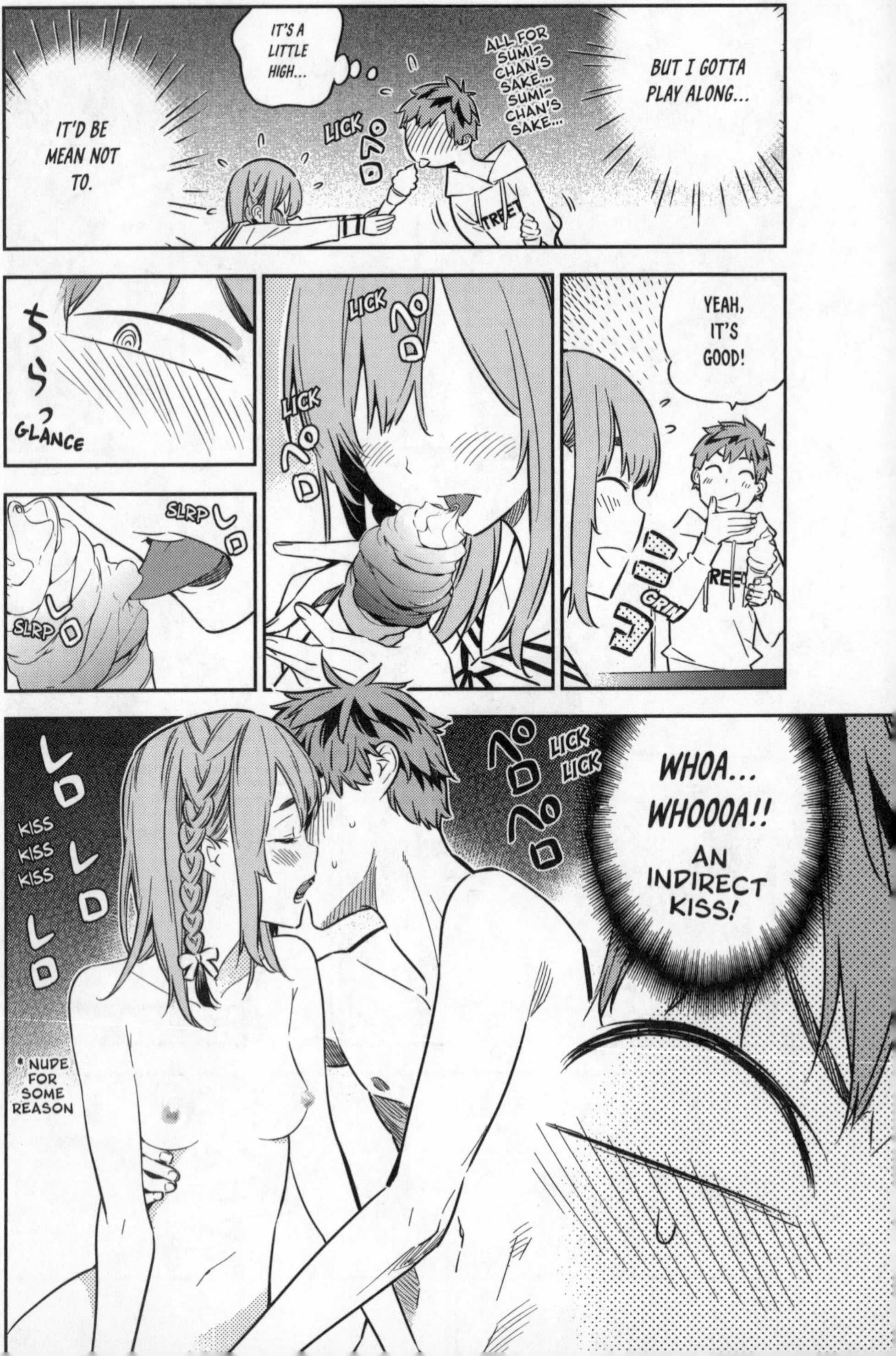
BUT I GOTTA PLAY ALONG...
ALL FOR SUMI-CHAN'S SAKE... SUMI-CHAN'S SAKE...
IT'S A LITTLE HIGH...
LICK
IT'D BE MEAN NOT TO.
YEAH, IT'S GOOD!
GRIN
LICK
LICK
GLANCE
SLRP
SLRP
WHOA... WHOOOA!!
AN INDIRECT KISS!
LICK LICK
KISS KISS KISS
* NUDE FOR SOME REASON

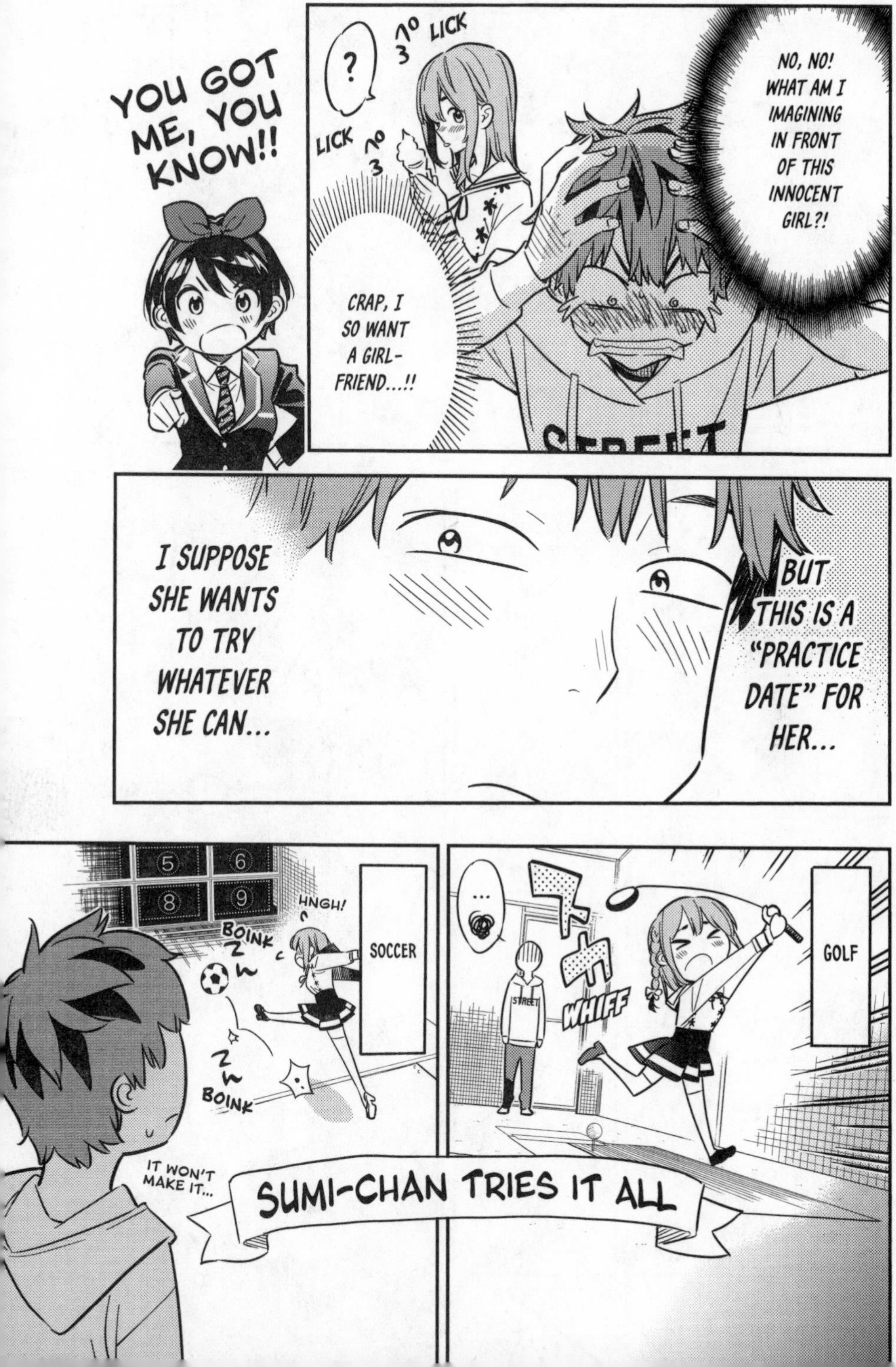
NO, NO! WHAT AM I IMAGINING IN FRONT OF THIS INNOCENT GIRL?!
LICK
?
LICK
CRAP, I SO WANT A GIRL-FRIEND...!!
YOU GOT ME, YOU KNOW!!
BUT THIS IS A "PRACTICE DATE" FOR HER...
I SUPPOSE SHE WANTS TO TRY WHATEVER SHE CAN...
GOLF
...
WHIFF
SOCCER
HNGH!
BOINK
BOINK
IT WON'T MAKE IT...
SUMI-CHAN TRIES IT ALL

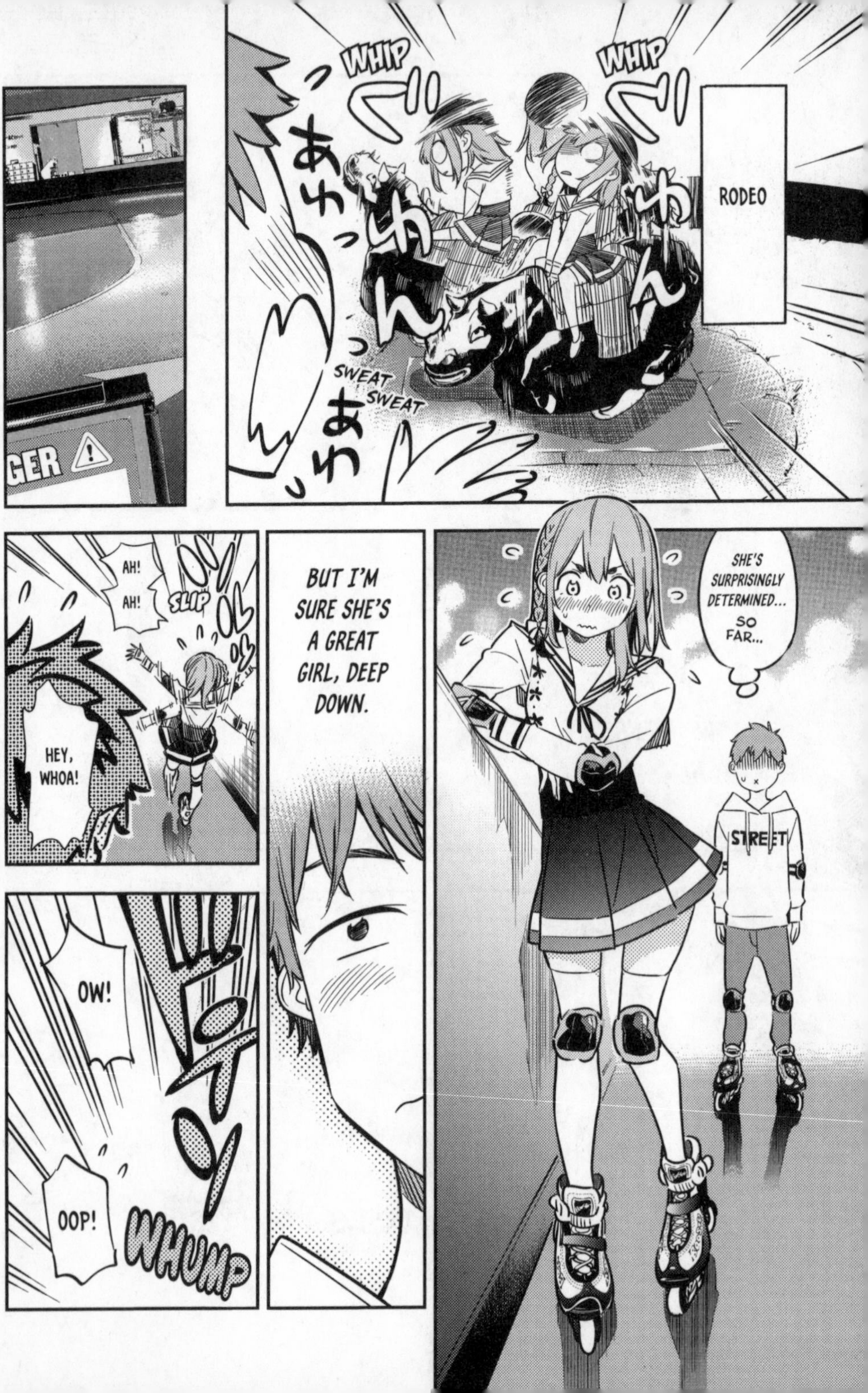
RODEO
WHIP
WHIP
SWEAT
SWEAT
GER
SHE'S SURPRISINGLY DETERMINED... SO FAR...
STREET
BUT I'M SURE SHE'S A GREAT GIRL, DEEP DOWN.
AH! AH!
SLIP
HEY, WHOA!
OW!
OOP!
WHUMP

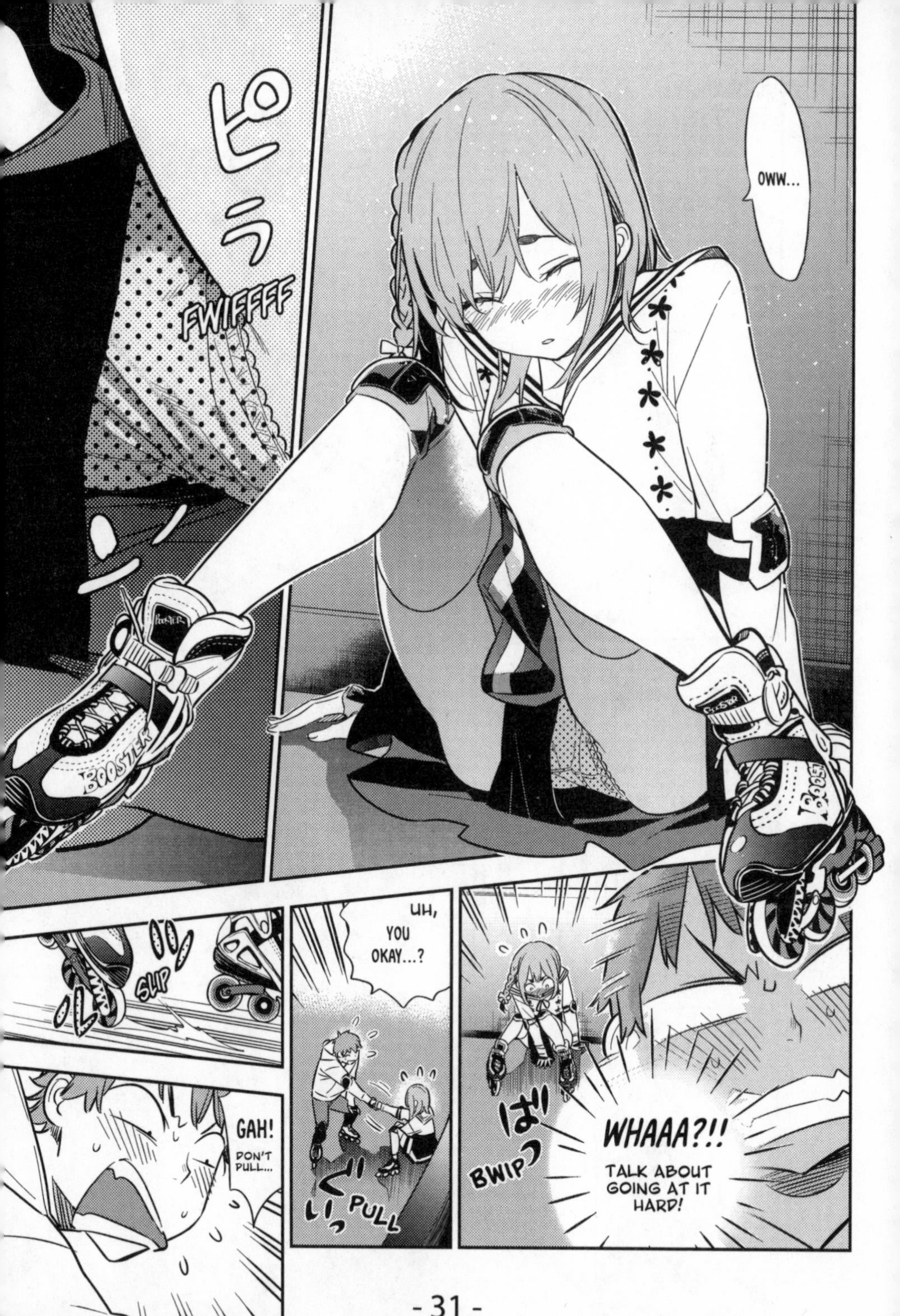
OWW...
ピラ
FWIFFFF
ぱっ
BWIP
WHAAA?!!
TALK ABOUT GOING AT IT HARD!
UH, YOU OKAY...?
ぐいっ
PULL
SLIP
GAH!
DON'T PULL...

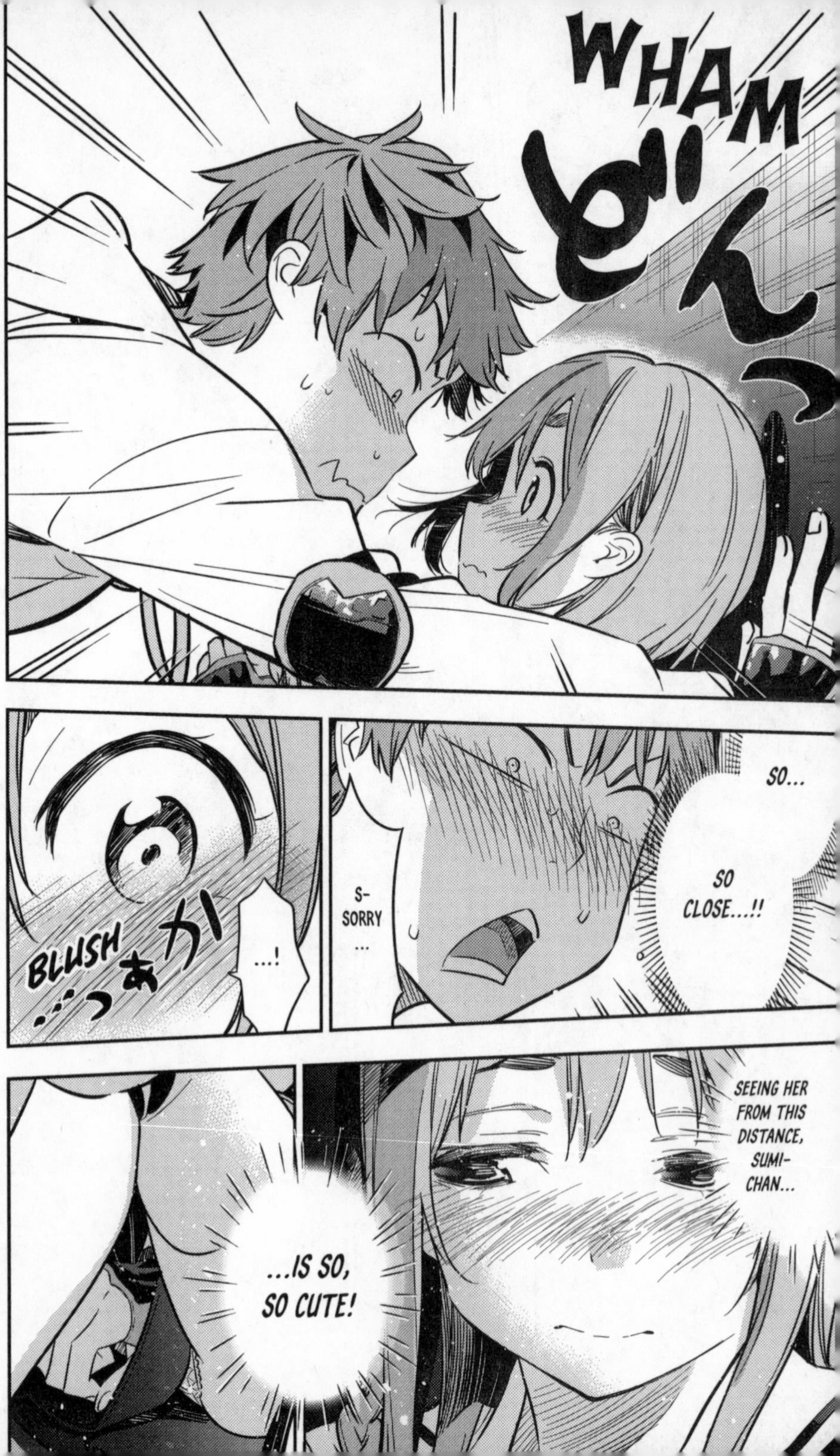
WHAM
どんっ
SO...
SO CLOSE...!!
S-SORRY...
...!
BLUSH
かあっ
SEEING HER FROM THIS DISTANCE, SUMI-CHAN...
...IS SO, SO CUTE!

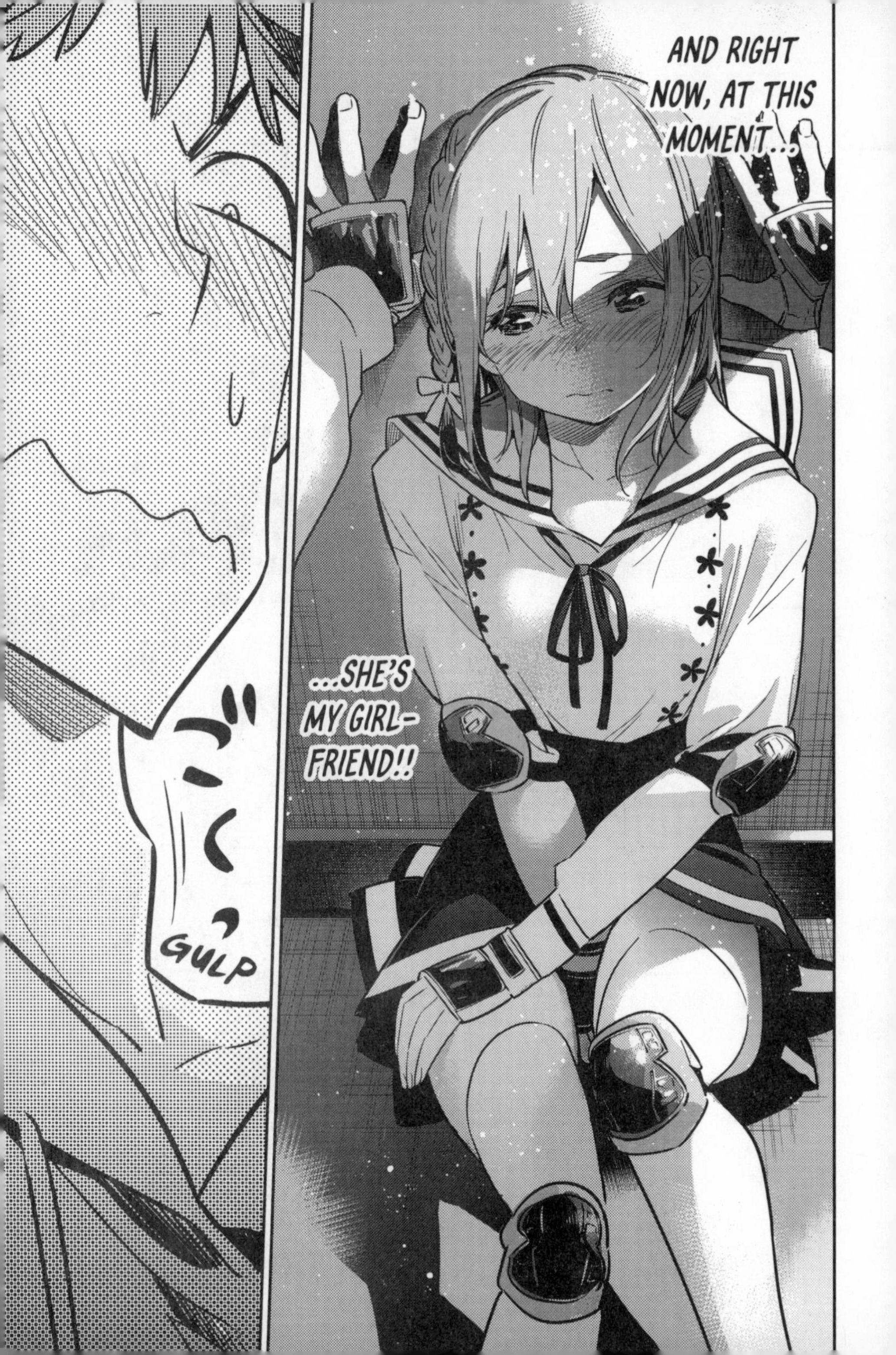
AND RIGHT NOW, AT THIS MOMENT...
...SHE'S MY GIRL-FRIEND!!
GULP

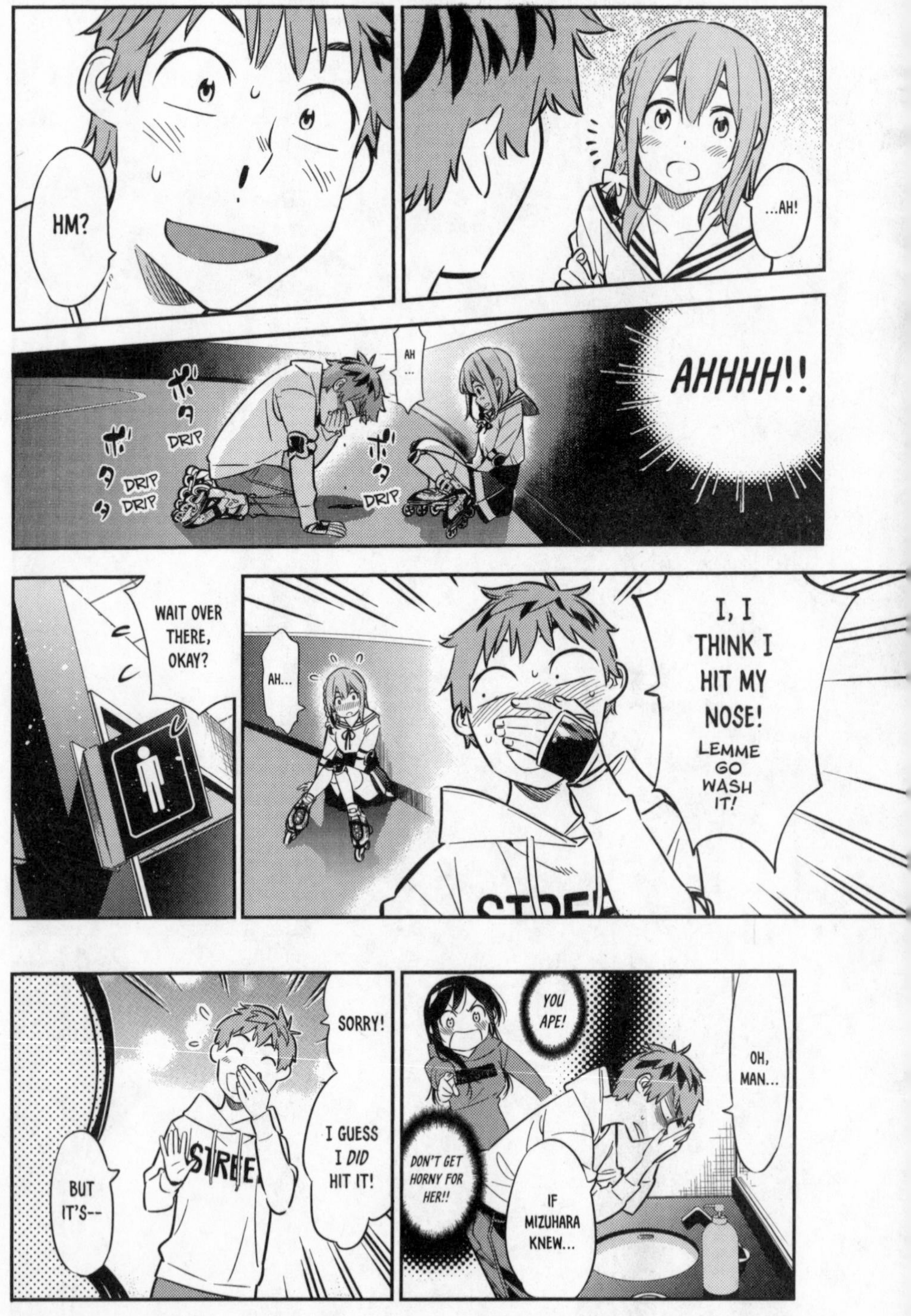
...AH!
HM?
AHHHH!!
AH ...
ポタ
DRIP
ポタ
DRIP
ポタ
DRIP
ポタ
DRIP
I, I THINK I HIT MY NOSE! LEMME GO WASH IT!
AH...
WAIT OVER THERE, OKAY?
OH, MAN...
YOU APE!
DON'T GET HORNY FOR HER!!
IF MIZUHARA KNEW...
SORRY!
I GUESS I *DID* HIT IT!
BUT IT'S--

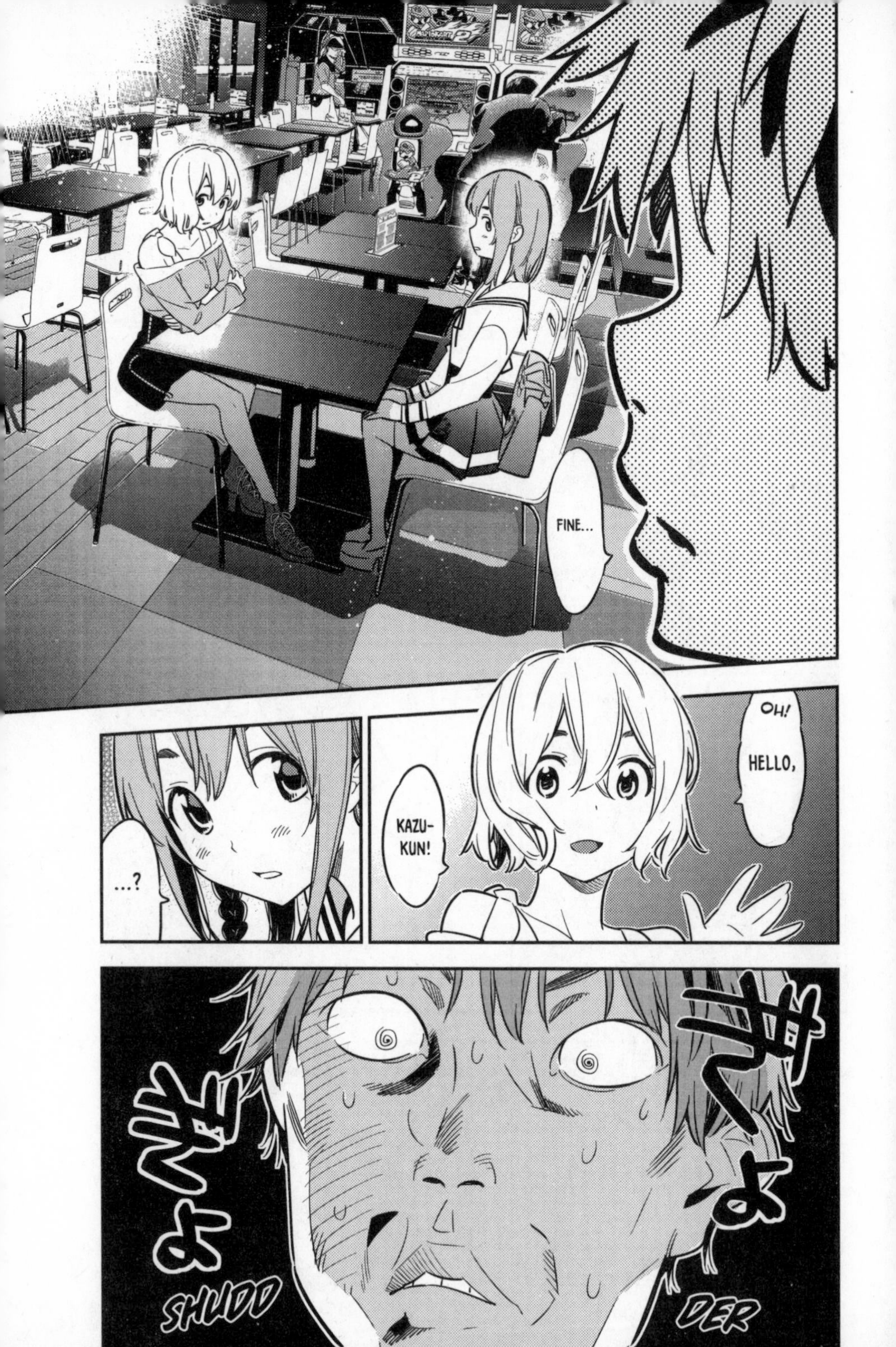
FINE...
OH!
HELLO,
KAZU-KUN!
...?
SHUDD
DER

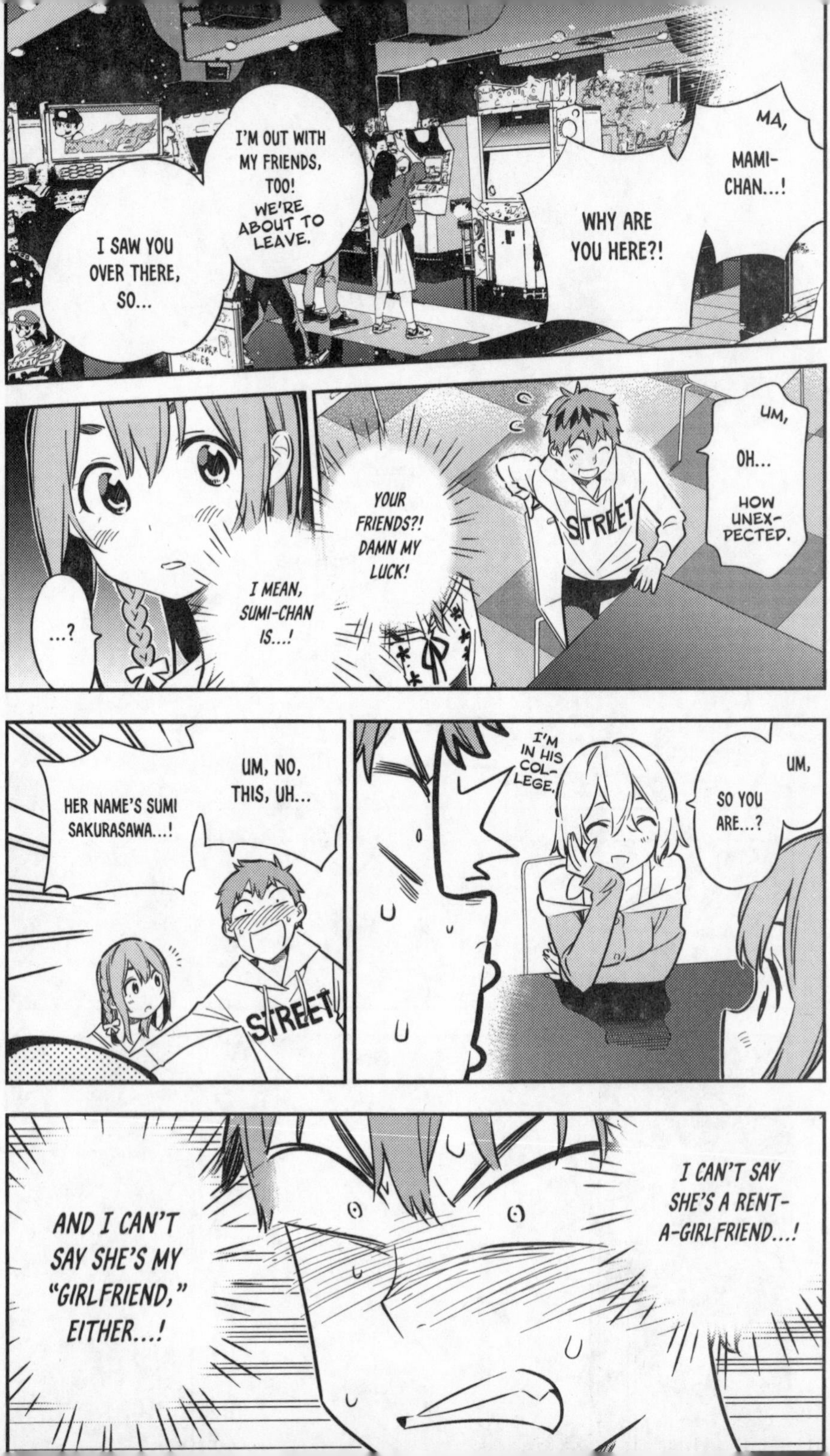
MA, MAMI-CHAN...!
WHY ARE YOU HERE?!
I'M OUT WITH MY FRIENDS, TOO! WE'RE ABOUT TO LEAVE.
I SAW YOU OVER THERE, SO...
UM, OH... HOW UNEXPECTED.
YOUR FRIENDS?! DAMN MY LUCK!
I MEAN, SUMI-CHAN IS...!
...?
UM, SO YOU ARE...?
I'M IN HIS COLLEGE.
UM, NO, THIS, UH...
HER NAME'S SUMI SAKURASAWA...!
I CAN'T SAY SHE'S A RENT-A-GIRLFRIEND...!
AND I CAN'T SAY SHE'S MY "GIRLFRIEND," EITHER...!

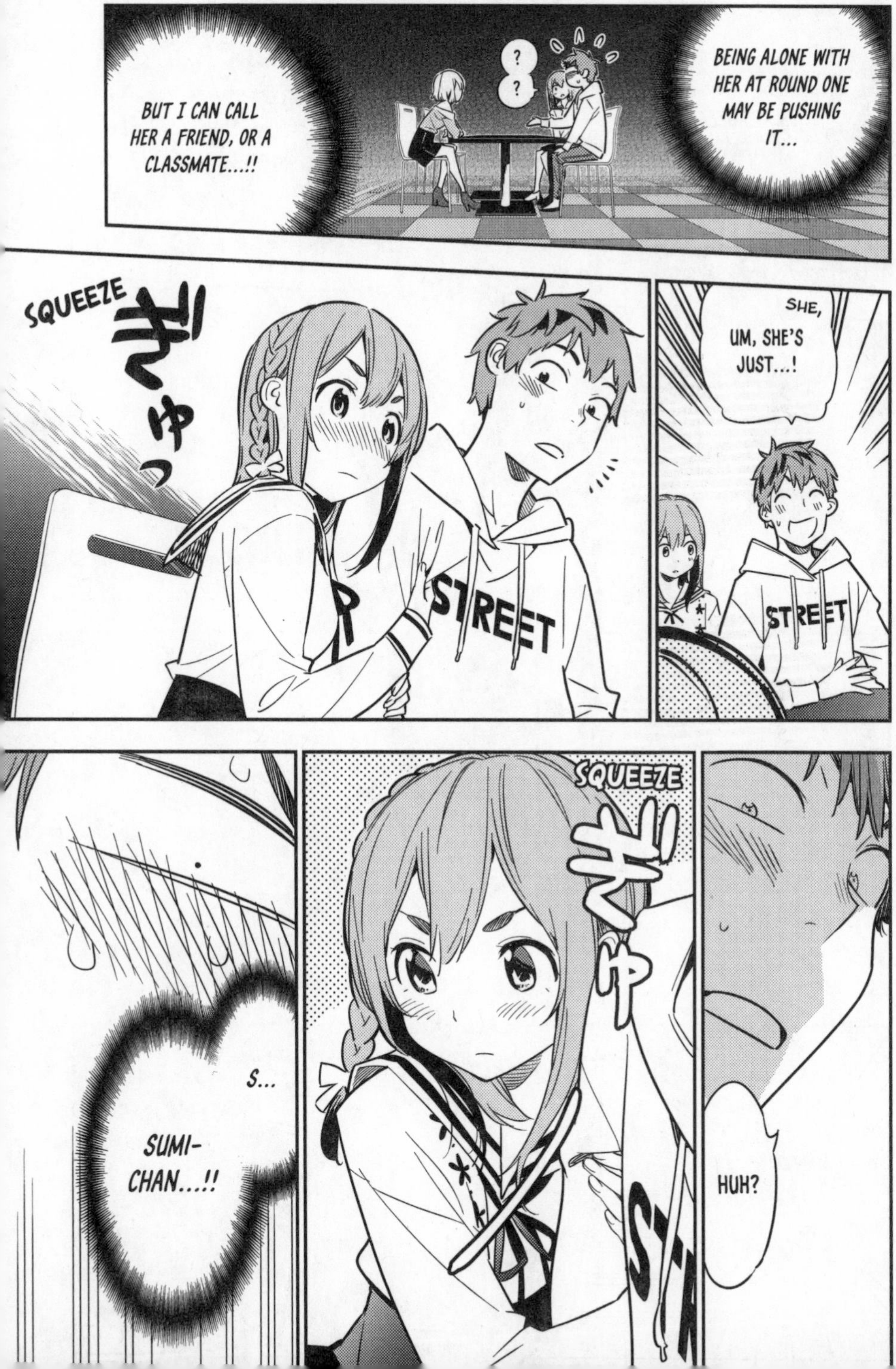
BEING ALONE WITH HER AT ROUND ONE MAY BE PUSHING IT...
?
?
BUT I CAN CALL HER A FRIEND, OR A CLASSMATE...!!
SHE, UM, SHE'S JUST...!
SQUEEZE
ぎゅっ
STREET
STREET
HUH?
SQUEEZE
ぎゅ
S...
SUMI-CHAN...!!

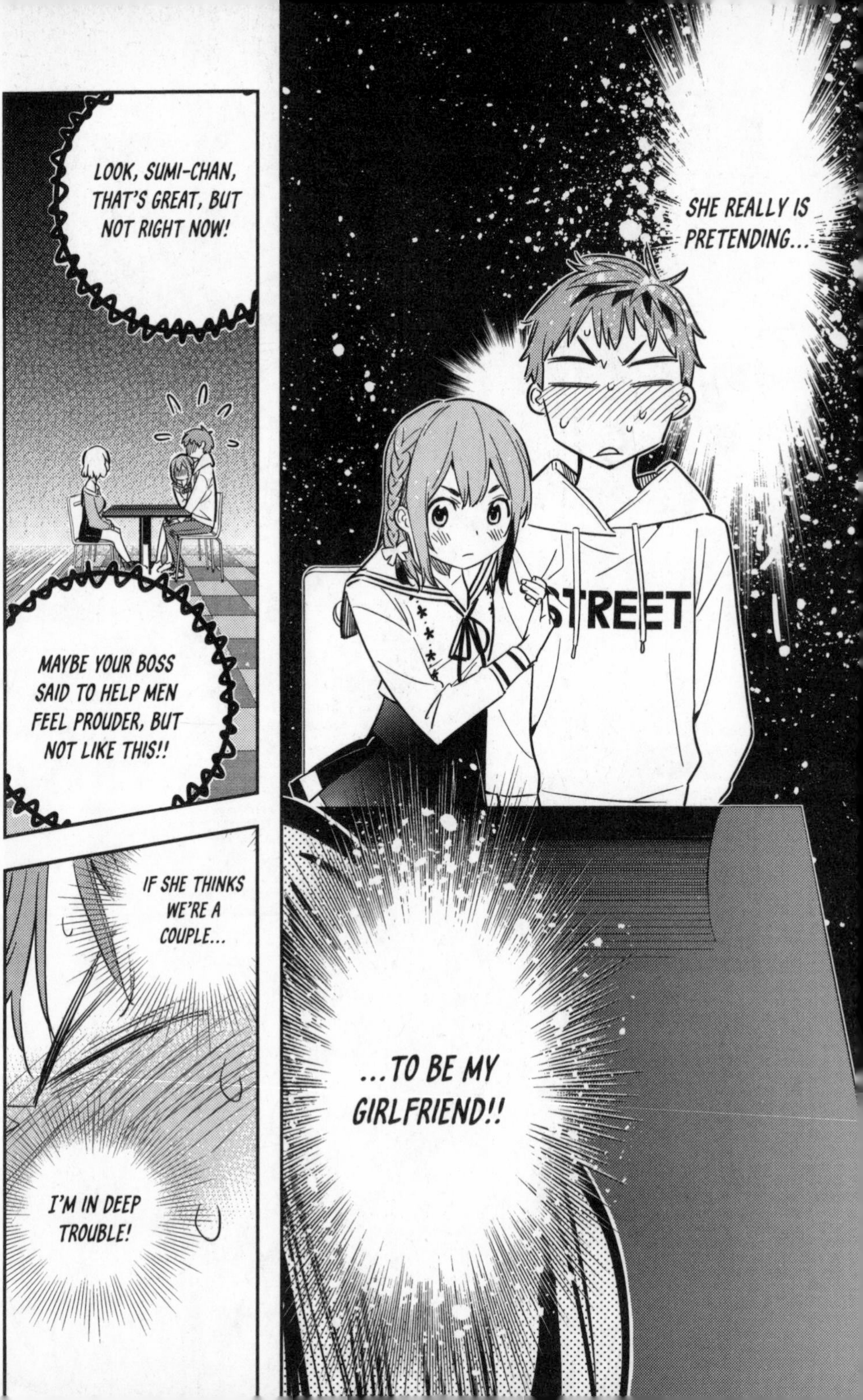
SHE REALLY IS PRETENDING...
STREET
...TO BE MY GIRLFRIEND!!
LOOK, SUMI-CHAN, THAT'S GREAT, BUT NOT RIGHT NOW!
MAYBE YOUR BOSS SAID TO HELP MEN FEEL PROUDER, BUT NOT LIKE THIS!!
IF SHE THINKS WE'RE A COUPLE...
I'M IN DEEP TROUBLE!

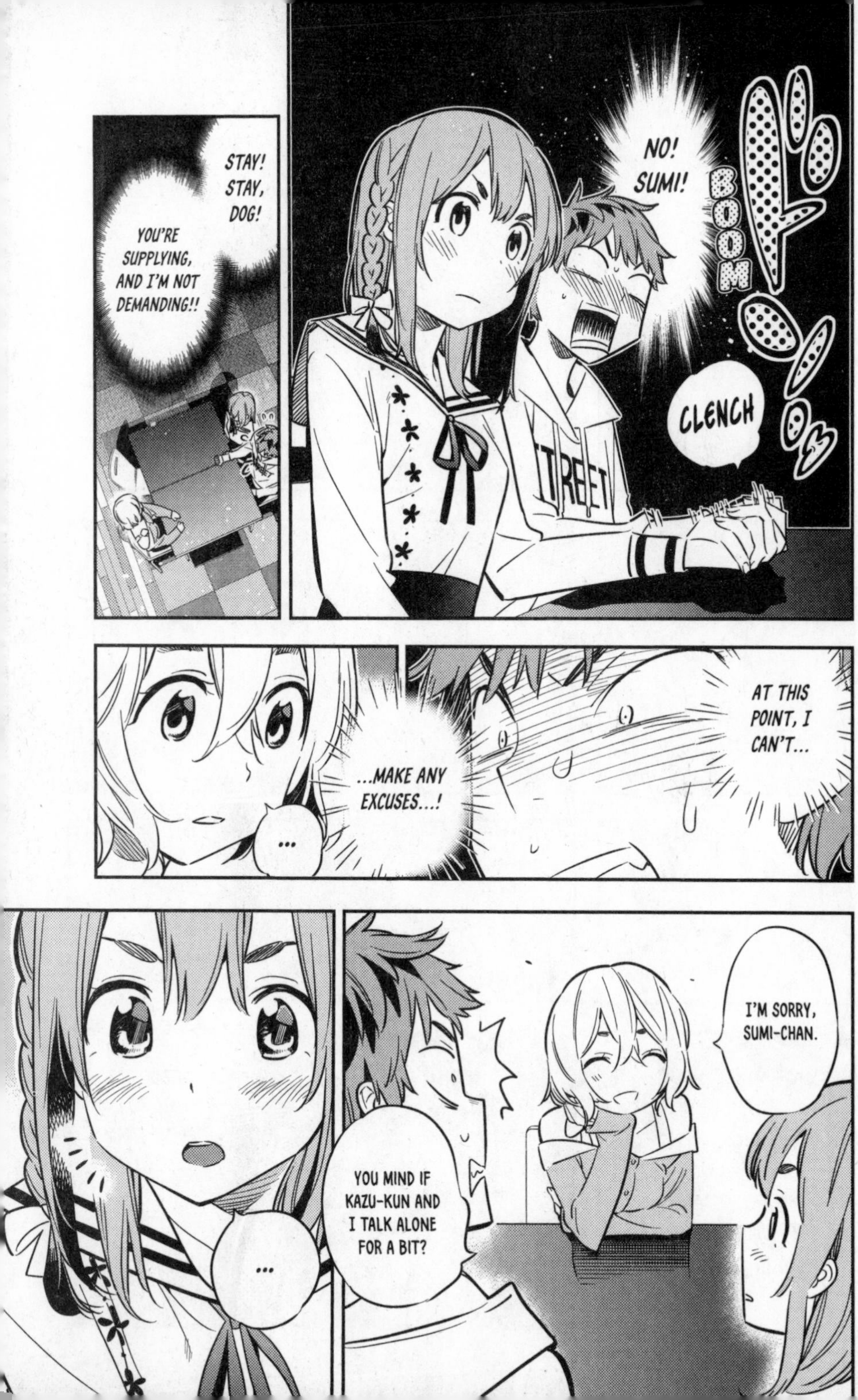
NO! SUMI!
BOOM
CLENCH
STAY! STAY, DOG!
YOU'RE SUPPLYING, AND I'M NOT DEMANDING!!
AT THIS POINT, I CAN'T...
...MAKE ANY EXCUSES...!
...
I'M SORRY, SUMI-CHAN.
YOU MIND IF KAZU-KUN AND I TALK ALONE FOR A BIT?
...

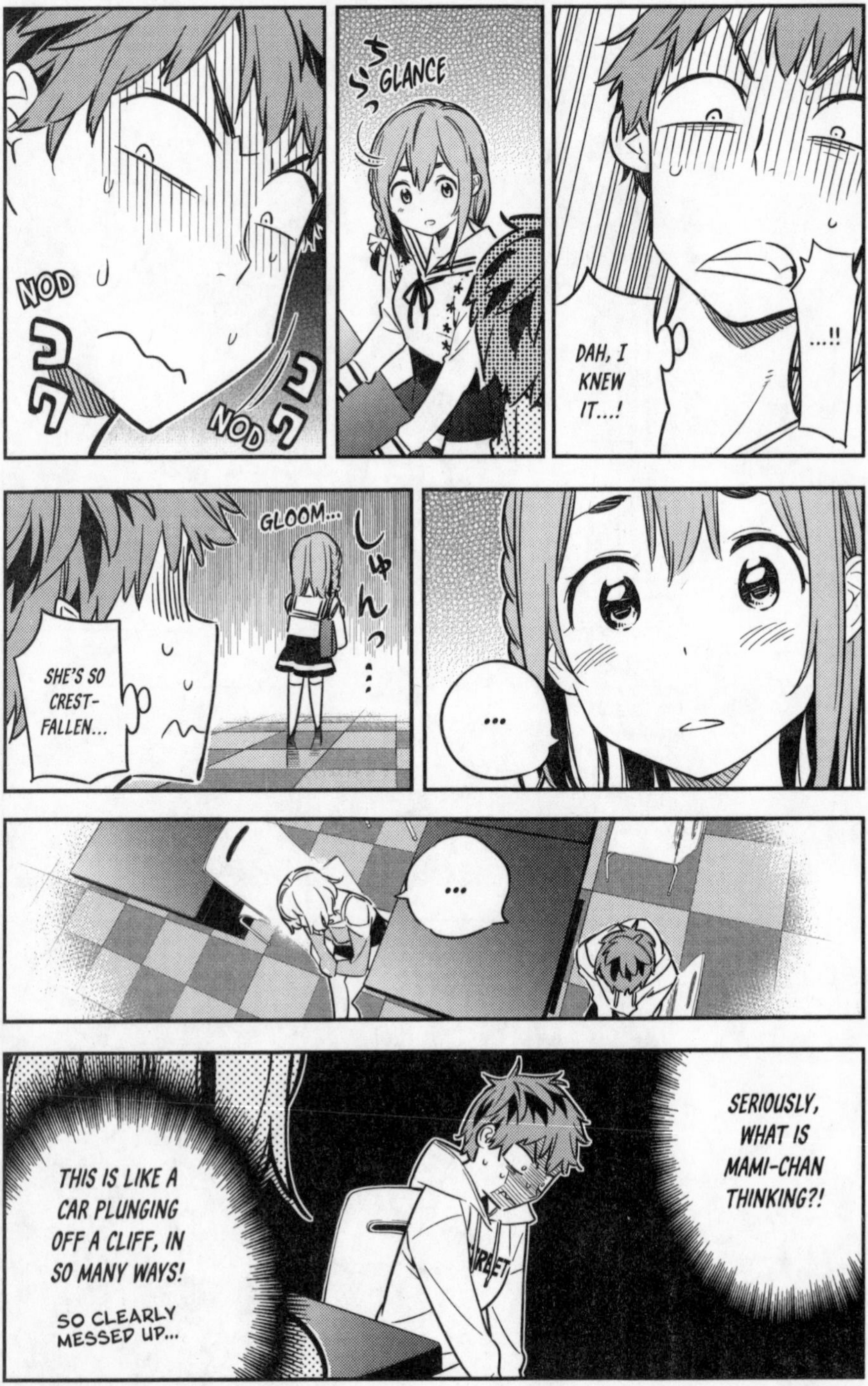
...!!
DAH, I KNEW IT...!
ちらっ
GLANCE
NOD
コク
NOD
コク
...
GLOOM...
しゅんっ...
SHE'S SO CREST-FALLEN...
...
SERIOUSLY, WHAT IS MAMI-CHAN THINKING?!
THIS IS LIKE A CAR PLUNGING OFF A CLIFF, IN SO MANY WAYS!
SO CLEARLY MESSED UP...

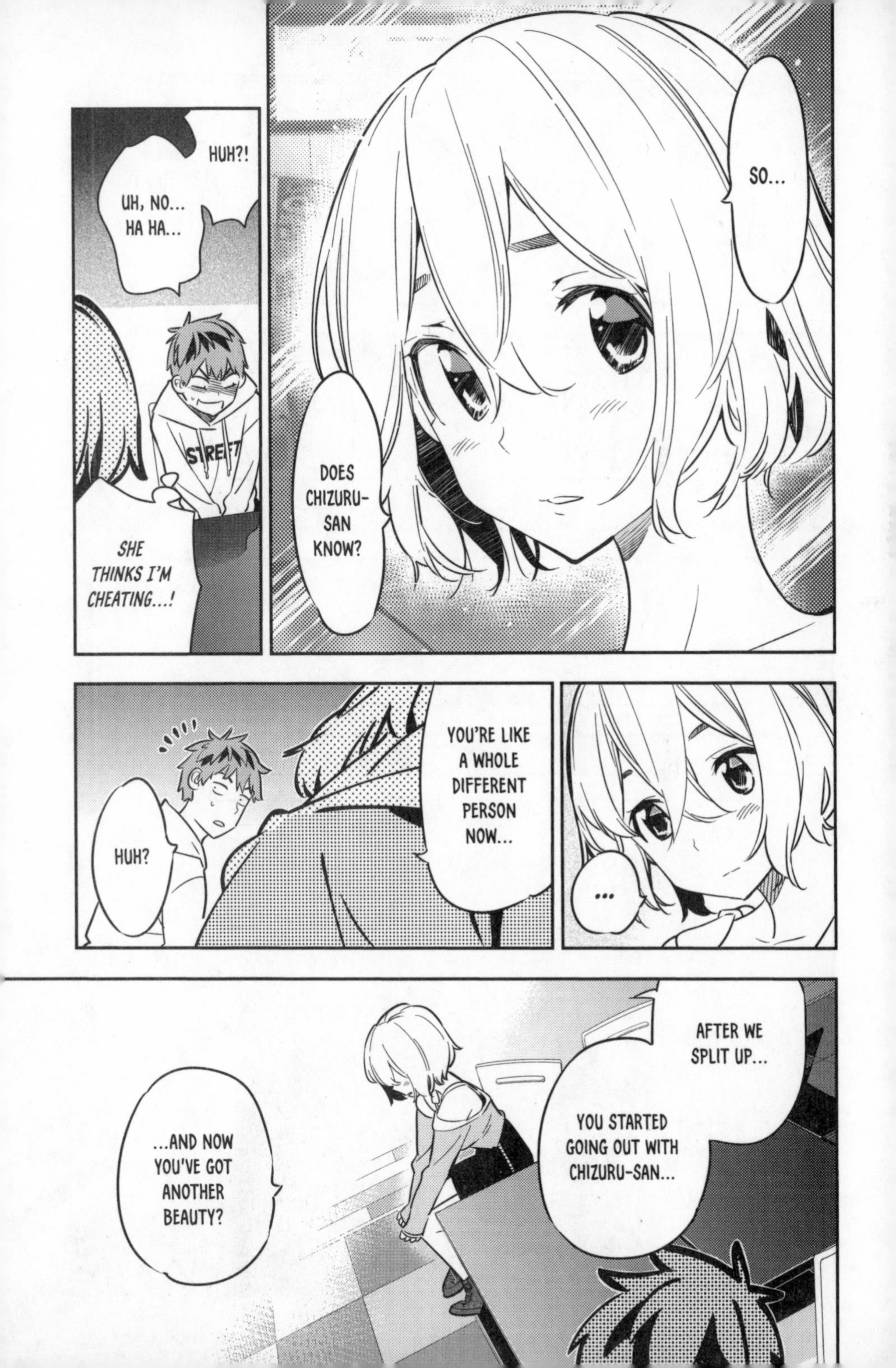
SO...
DOES CHIZURU-SAN KNOW?
HUH?!
UH, NO... HA HA...
SHE THINKS I'M CHEATING...!
...
YOU'RE LIKE A WHOLE DIFFERENT PERSON NOW...
HUH?
AFTER WE SPLIT UP...
YOU STARTED GOING OUT WITH CHIZURU-SAN...
...AND NOW YOU'VE GOT ANOTHER BEAUTY?

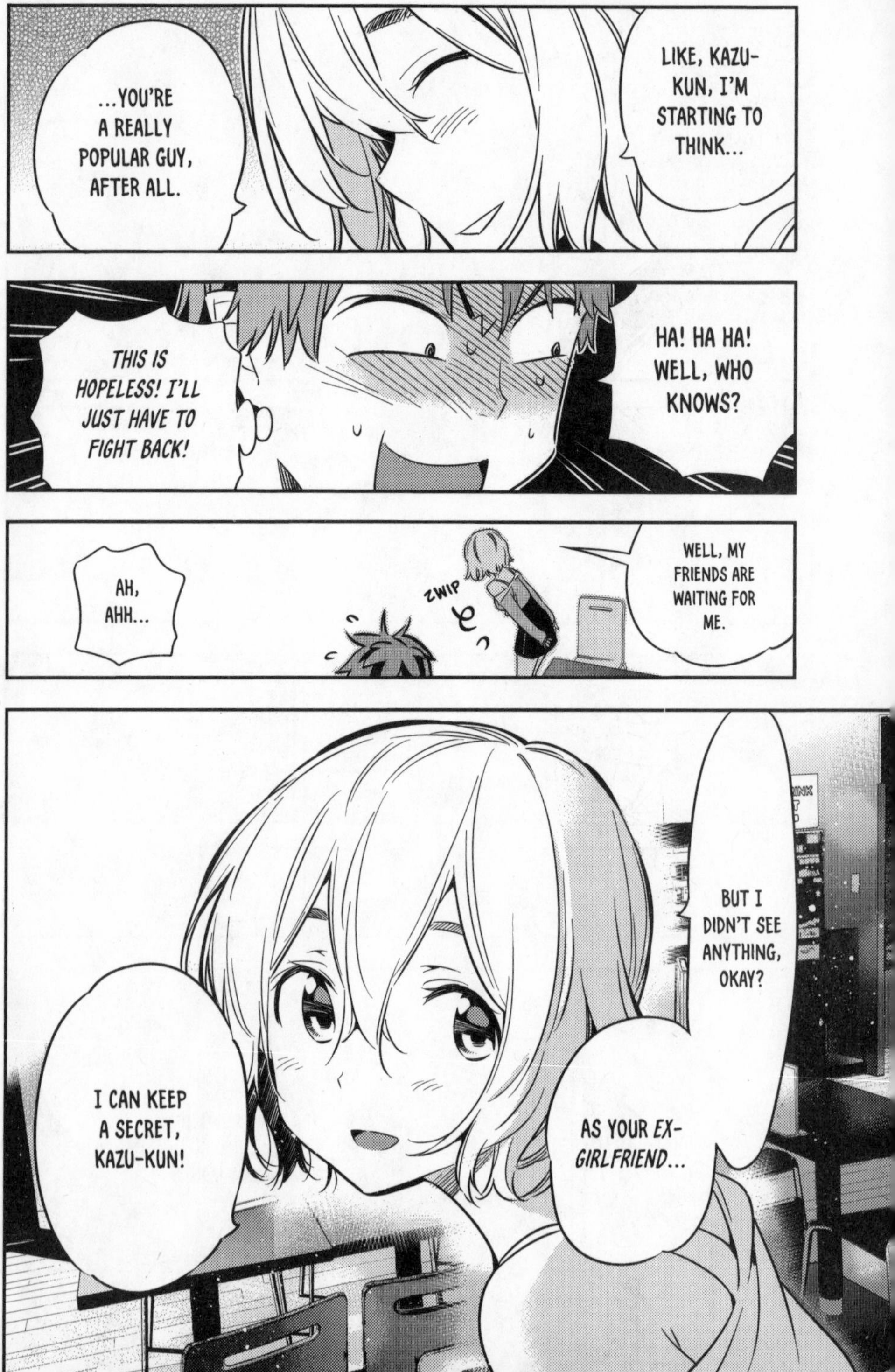
LIKE, KAZU-KUN, I'M STARTING TO THINK...
...YOU'RE A REALLY POPULAR GUY, AFTER ALL.
HA! HA HA! WELL, WHO KNOWS?
THIS IS HOPELESS! I'LL JUST HAVE TO FIGHT BACK!
WELL, MY FRIENDS ARE WAITING FOR ME.
ZWIP
AH, AHH...
BUT I DIDN'T SEE ANYTHING, OKAY?
AS YOUR *EX-GIRLFRIEND*...
I CAN KEEP A SECRET, KAZU-KUN!

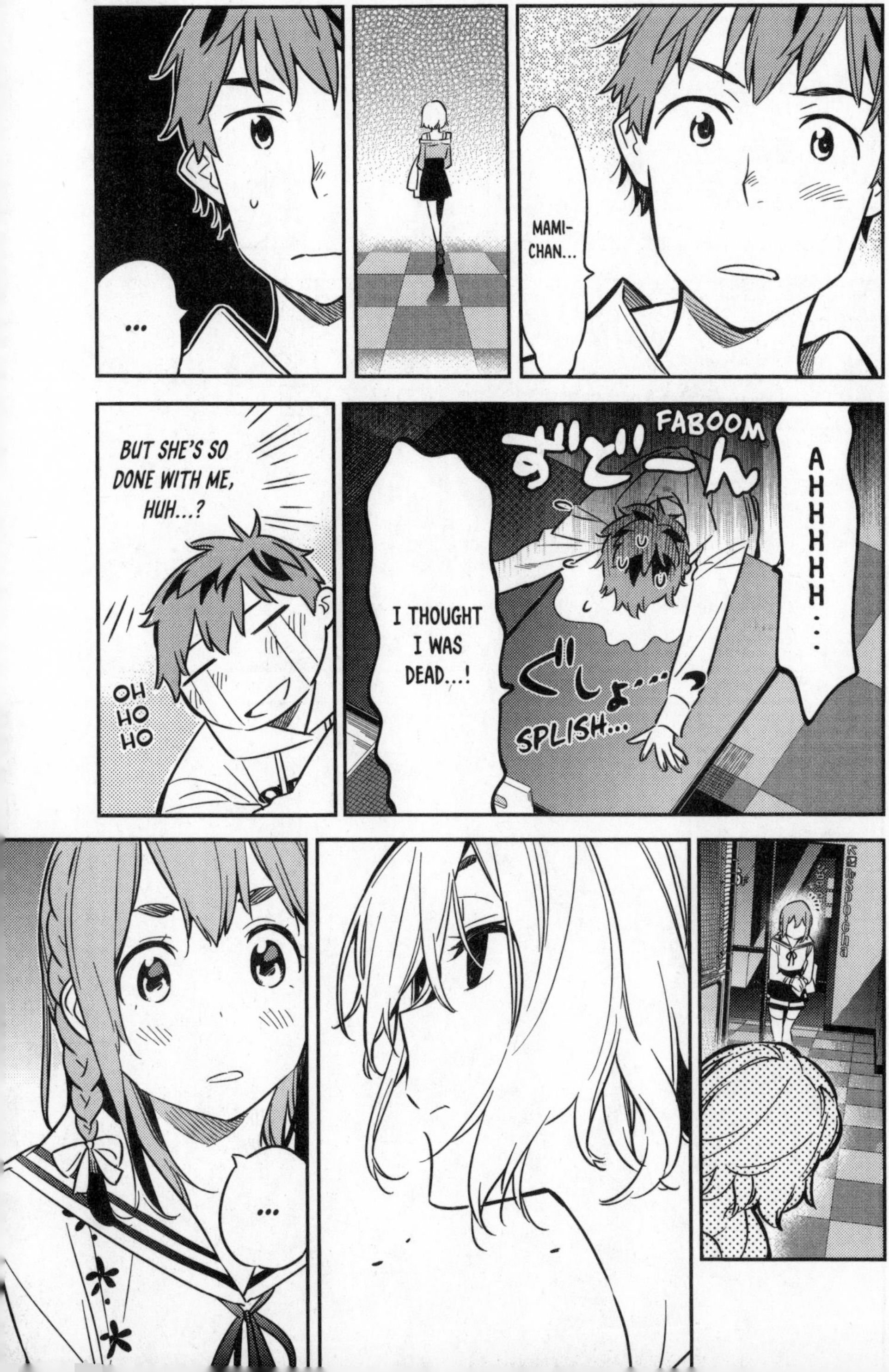
MAMI-CHAN...
...
AHHHHHH...
FABOOM
ずどーん
I THOUGHT I WAS DEAD...!
ぐしょ...
SPLISH...
BUT SHE'S SO DONE WITH ME, HUH...?
OH HO HO
...

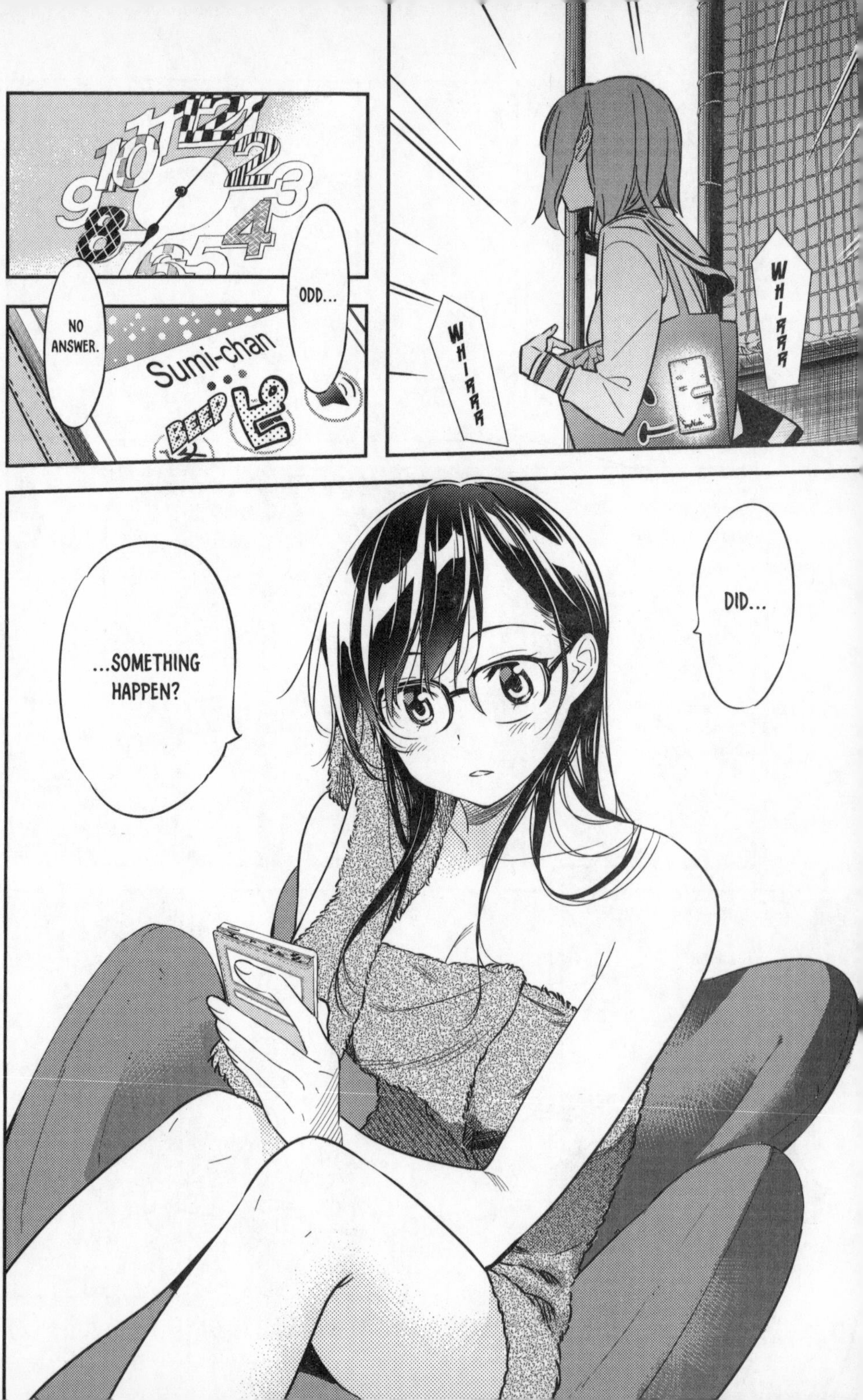
WHIRRR
WHIRRR
ODD...
NO ANSWER.
Sumi-chan
BEEP
DID...
...SOMETHING HAPPEN?

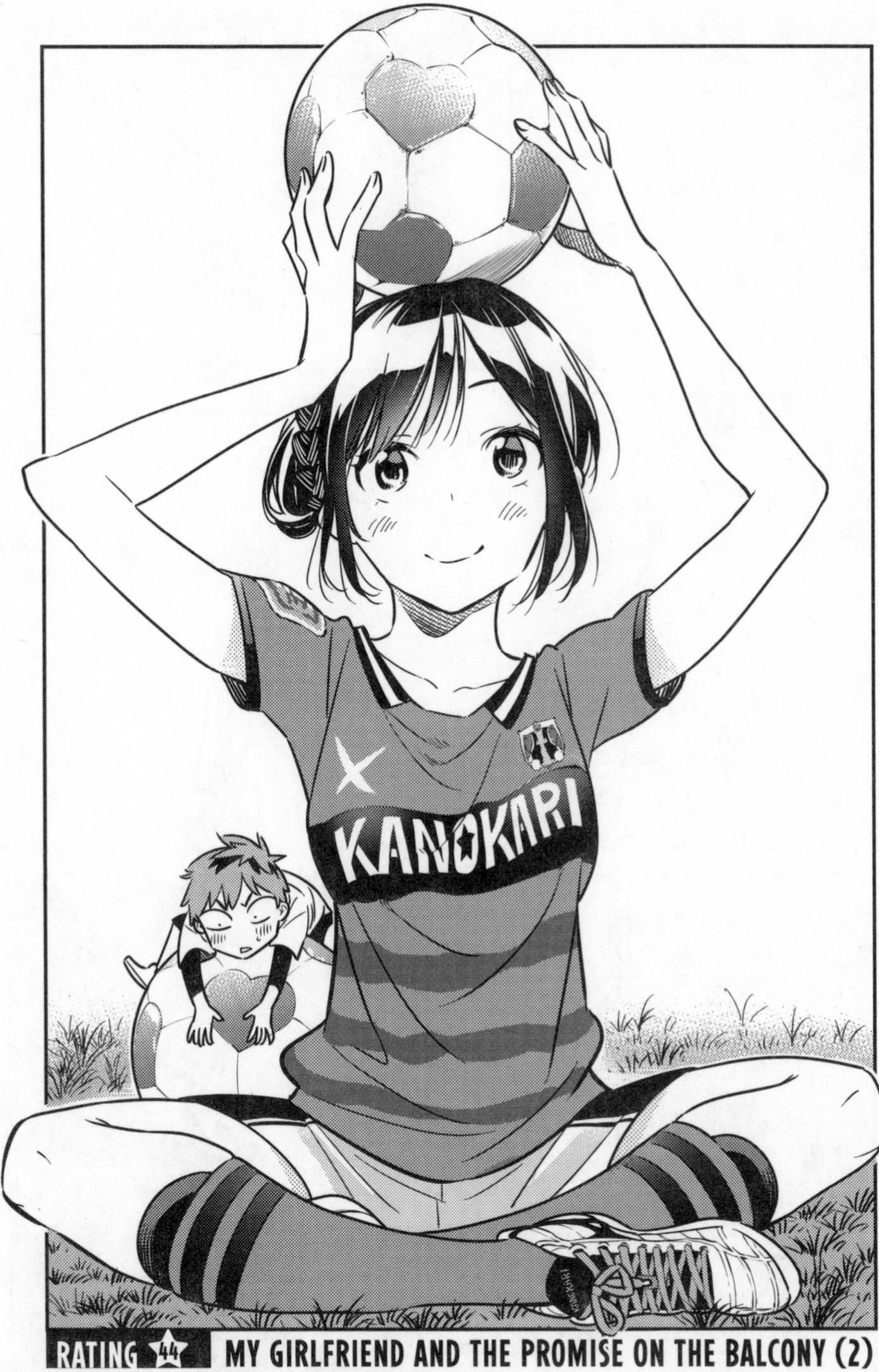
KANOKARI

RATING 44 MY GIRLFRIEND AND THE PROMISE ON THE BALCONY (2)

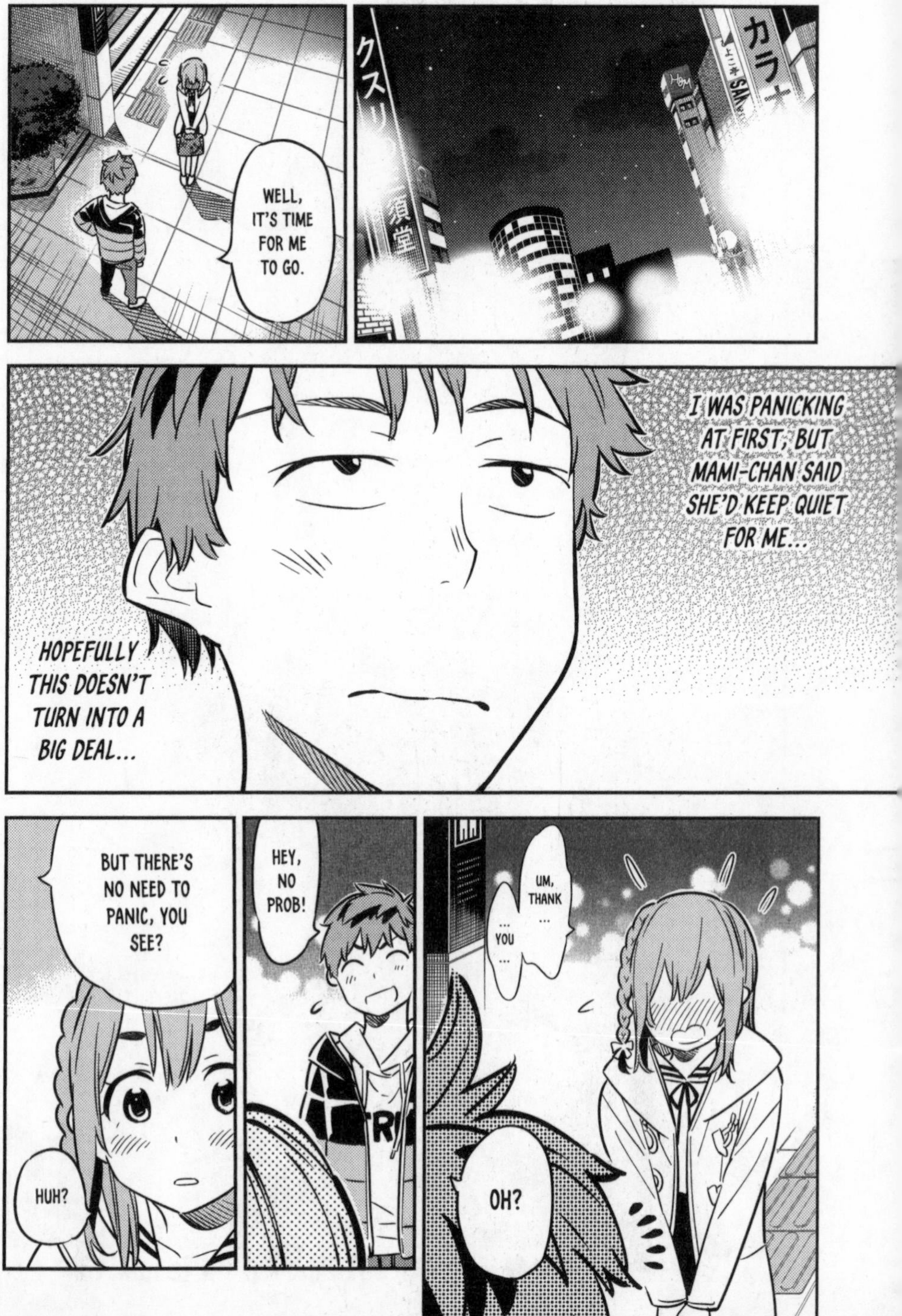
WELL, IT'S TIME FOR ME TO GO.
I WAS PANICKING AT FIRST, BUT MAMI-CHAN SAID SHE'D KEEP QUIET FOR ME...
HOPEFULLY THIS DOESN'T TURN INTO A BIG DEAL...
UM, THANK ...
... YOU ...
OH?
HEY, NO PROB!
BUT THERE'S NO NEED TO PANIC, YOU SEE?
HUH?

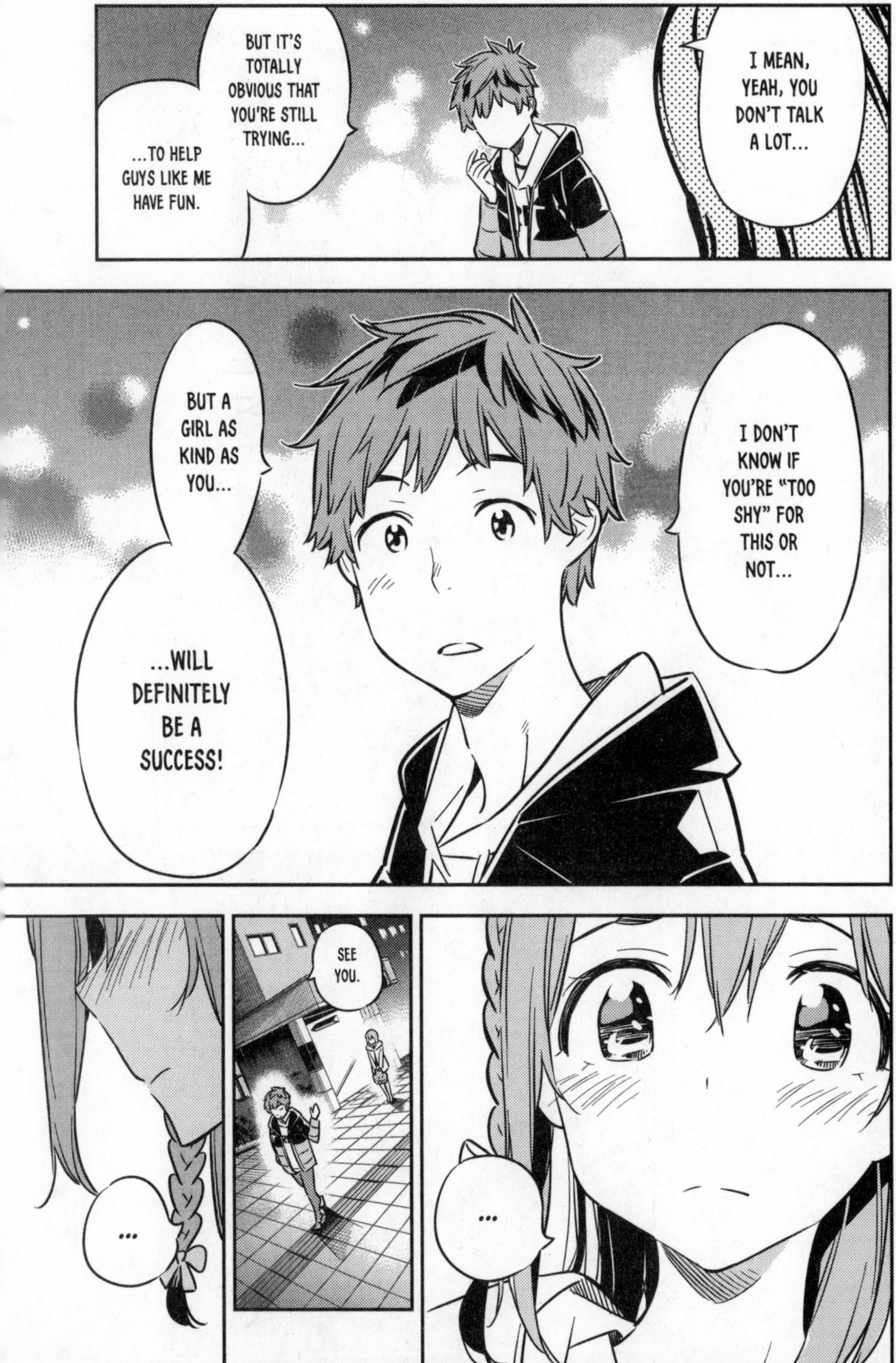
I MEAN, YEAH, YOU DON'T TALK A LOT...
BUT IT'S TOTALLY OBVIOUS THAT YOU'RE STILL TRYING...
...TO HELP GUYS LIKE ME HAVE FUN.
I DON'T KNOW IF YOU'RE "TOO SHY" FOR THIS OR NOT...
BUT A GIRL AS KIND AS YOU...
...WILL DEFINITELY BE A SUCCESS!
...
SEE YOU.
...

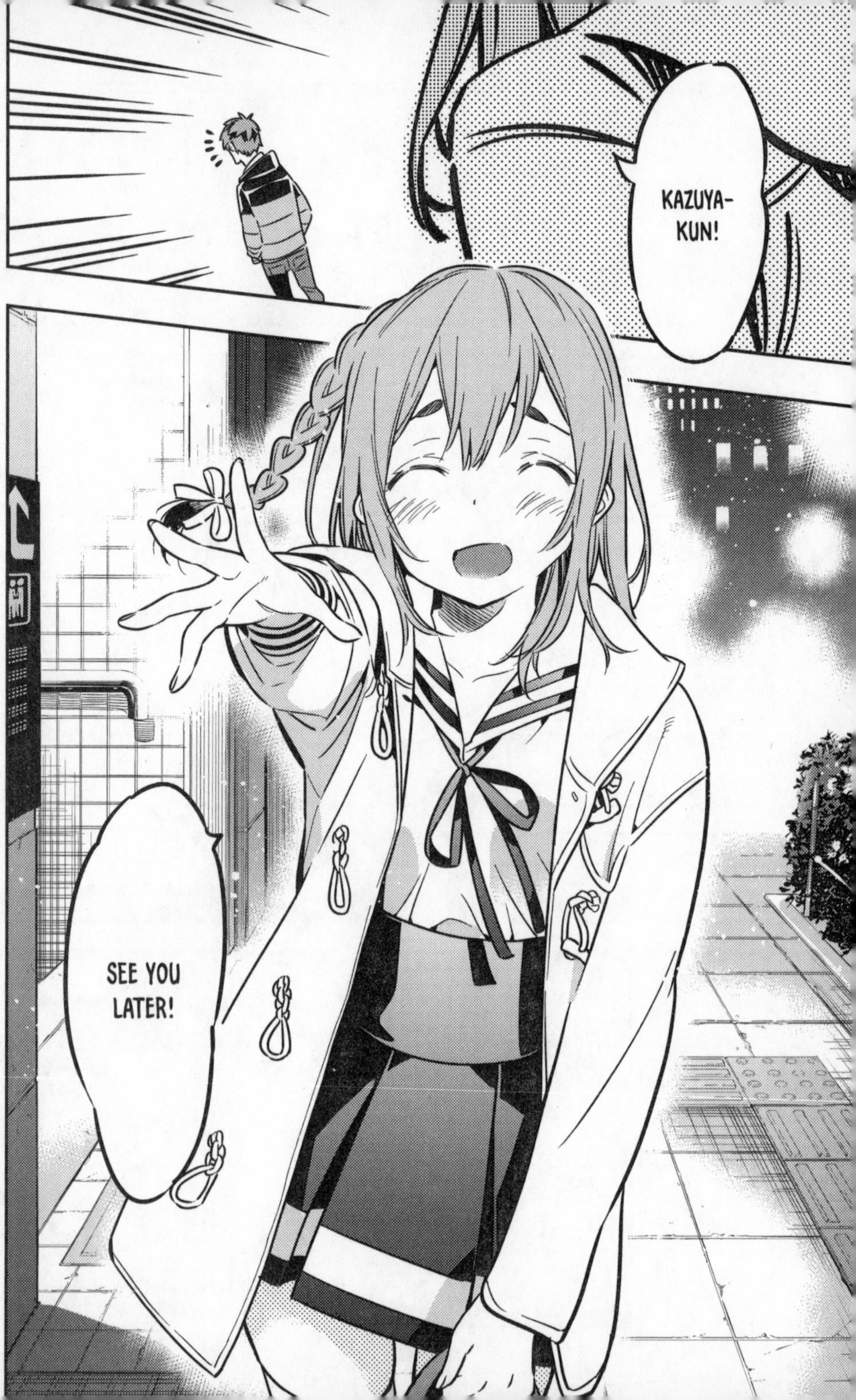
KAZUYA-KUN!
SEE YOU LATER!

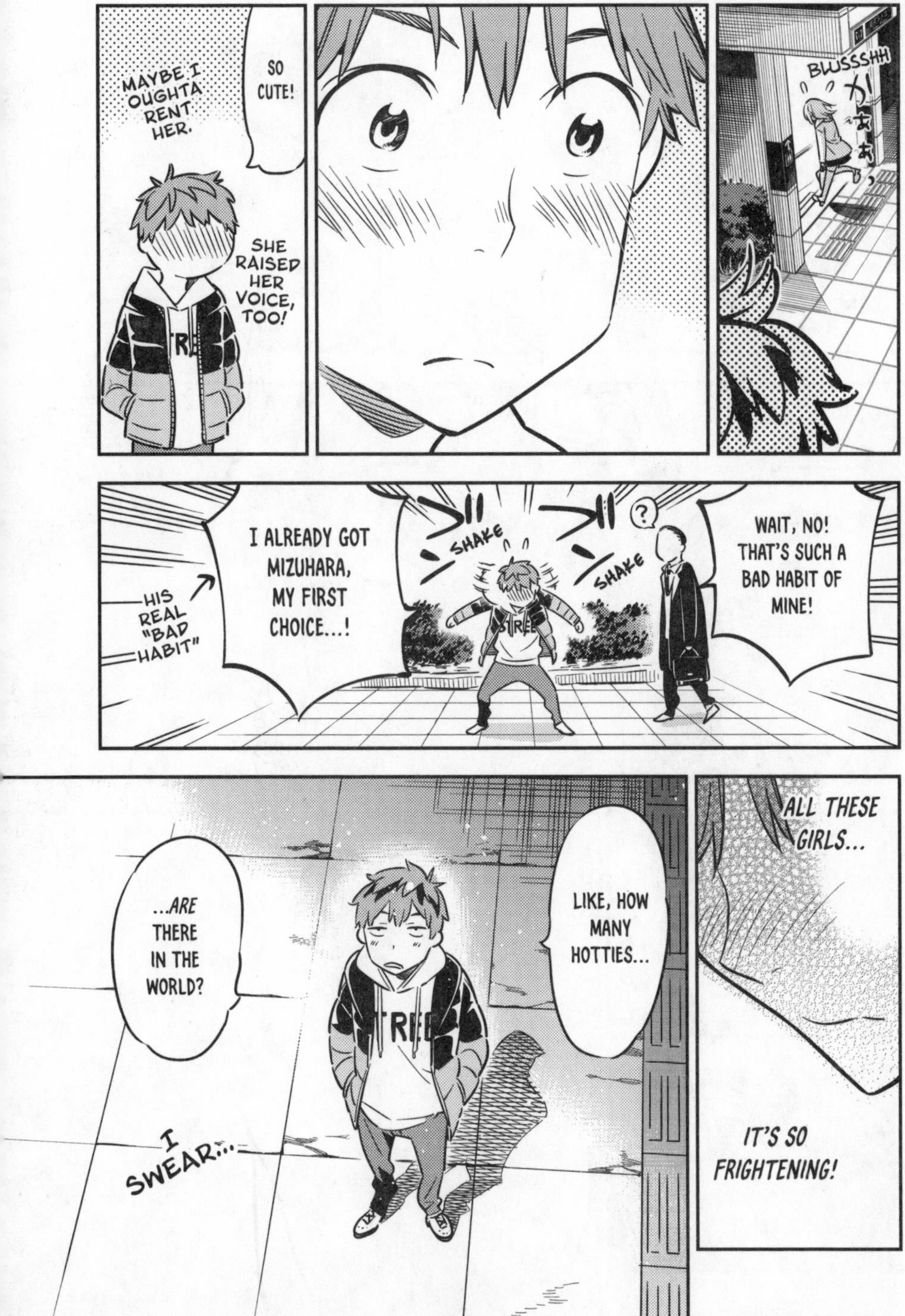
BLUSSSHH
SO CUTE!
MAYBE I OUGHTA RENT HER.
SHE RAISED HER VOICE, TOO!
WAIT, NO! THAT'S SUCH A BAD HABIT OF MINE!
?
SHAKE
SHAKE
I ALREADY GOT MIZUHARA, MY FIRST CHOICE...!
HIS REAL "BAD HABIT"
ALL THESE GIRLS...
IT'S SO FRIGHTENING!
LIKE, HOW MANY HOTTIES...
...ARE THERE IN THE WORLD?
I SWEAR...

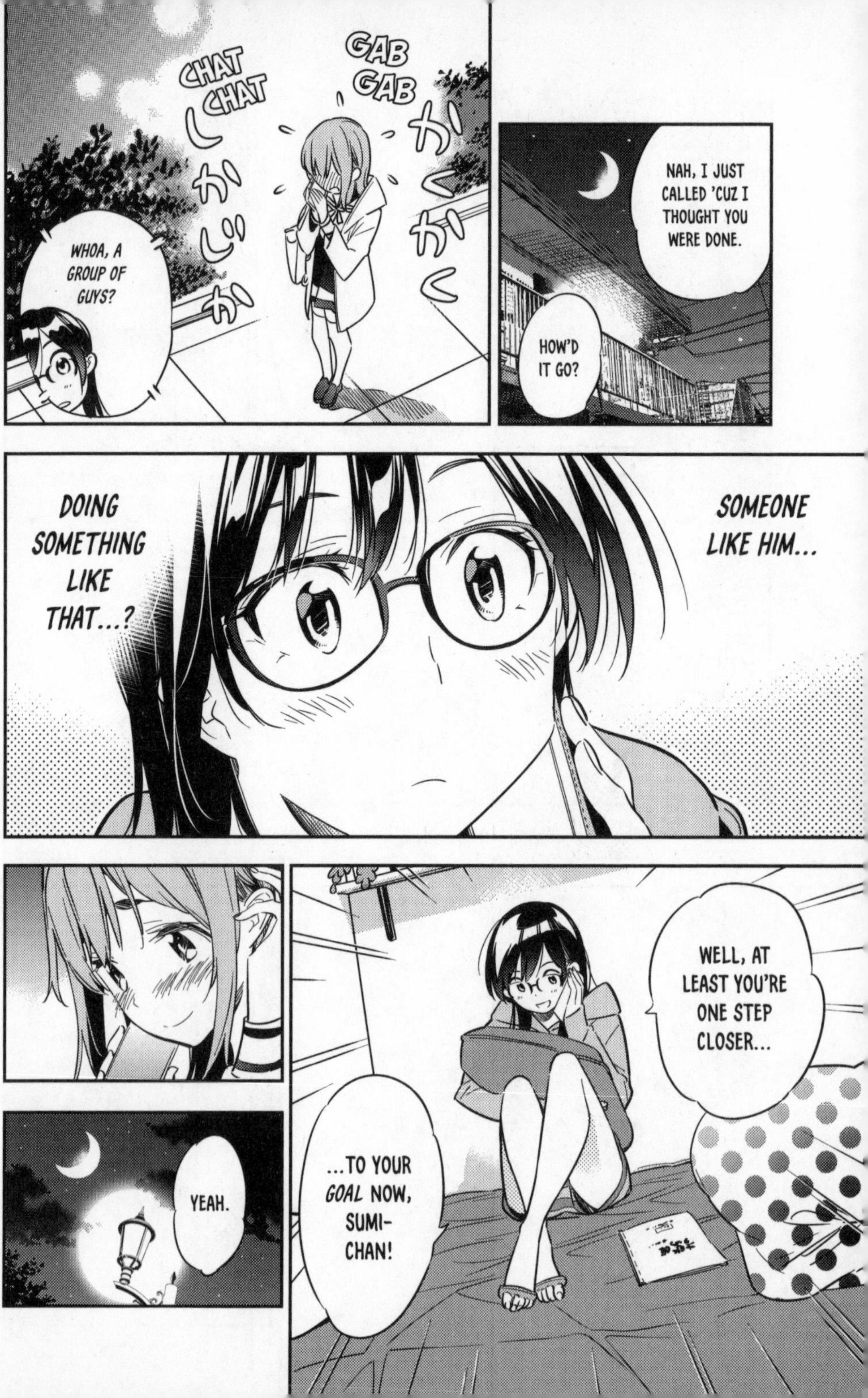
NAH, I JUST CALLED 'CUZ I THOUGHT YOU WERE DONE.
HOW'D IT GO?
GAB GAB
かくかく
CHAT CHAT
しかじか
WHOA, A GROUP OF GUYS?
SOMEONE LIKE HIM...
DOING SOMETHING LIKE THAT...?
WELL, AT LEAST YOU'RE ONE STEP CLOSER...
...TO YOUR *GOAL* NOW, SUMI-CHAN!
YEAH.

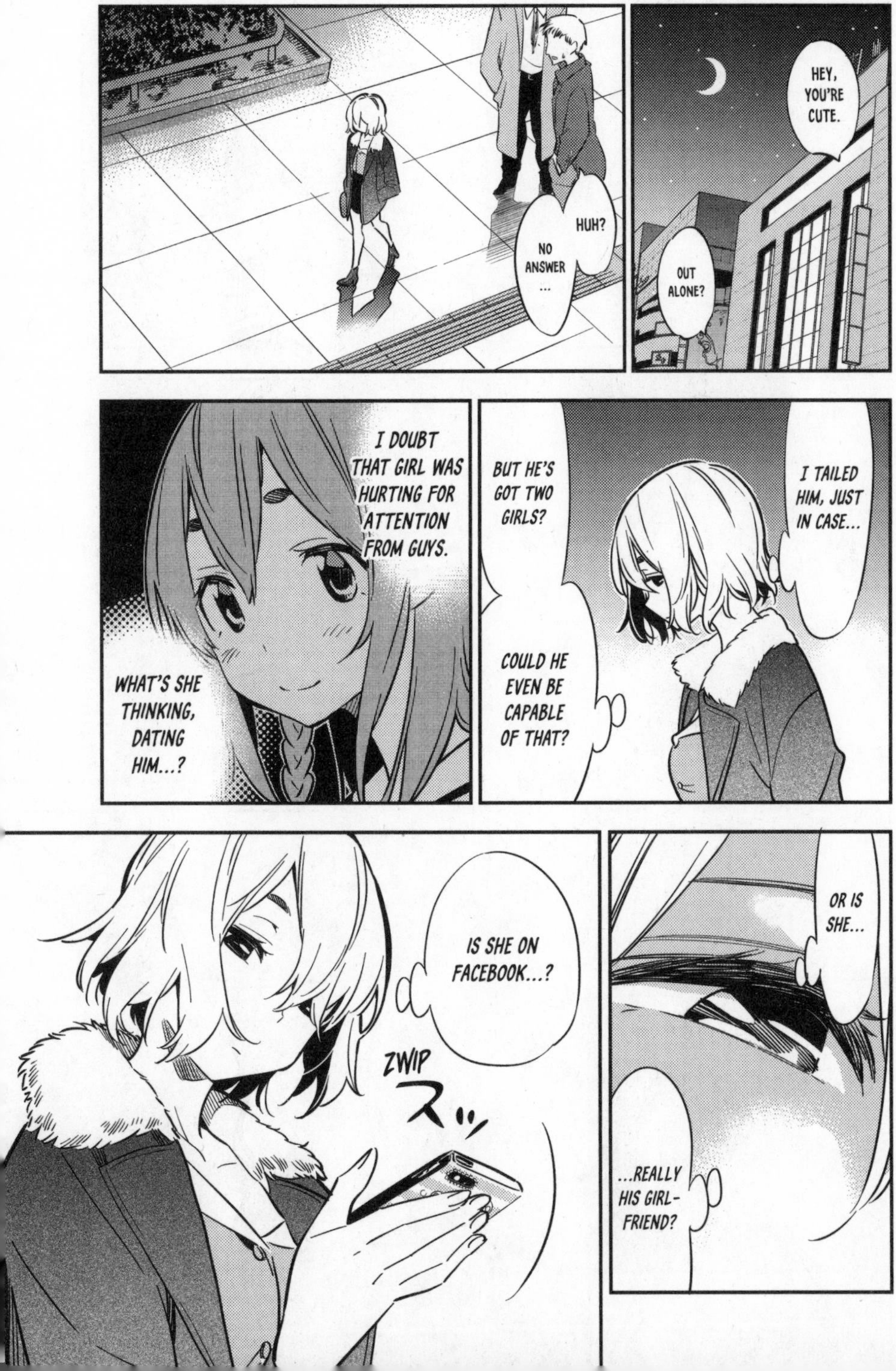
HEY, YOU'RE CUTE.
OUT ALONE?
HUH?
NO ANSWER ...
I TAILED HIM, JUST IN CASE...
BUT HE'S GOT TWO GIRLS?
COULD HE EVEN BE CAPABLE OF THAT?
I DOUBT THAT GIRL WAS HURTING FOR ATTENTION FROM GUYS.
WHAT'S SHE THINKING, DATING HIM...?
OR IS SHE...
...REALLY HIS GIRL-FRIEND?
IS SHE ON FACEBOOK...?
ZWIP
スッ

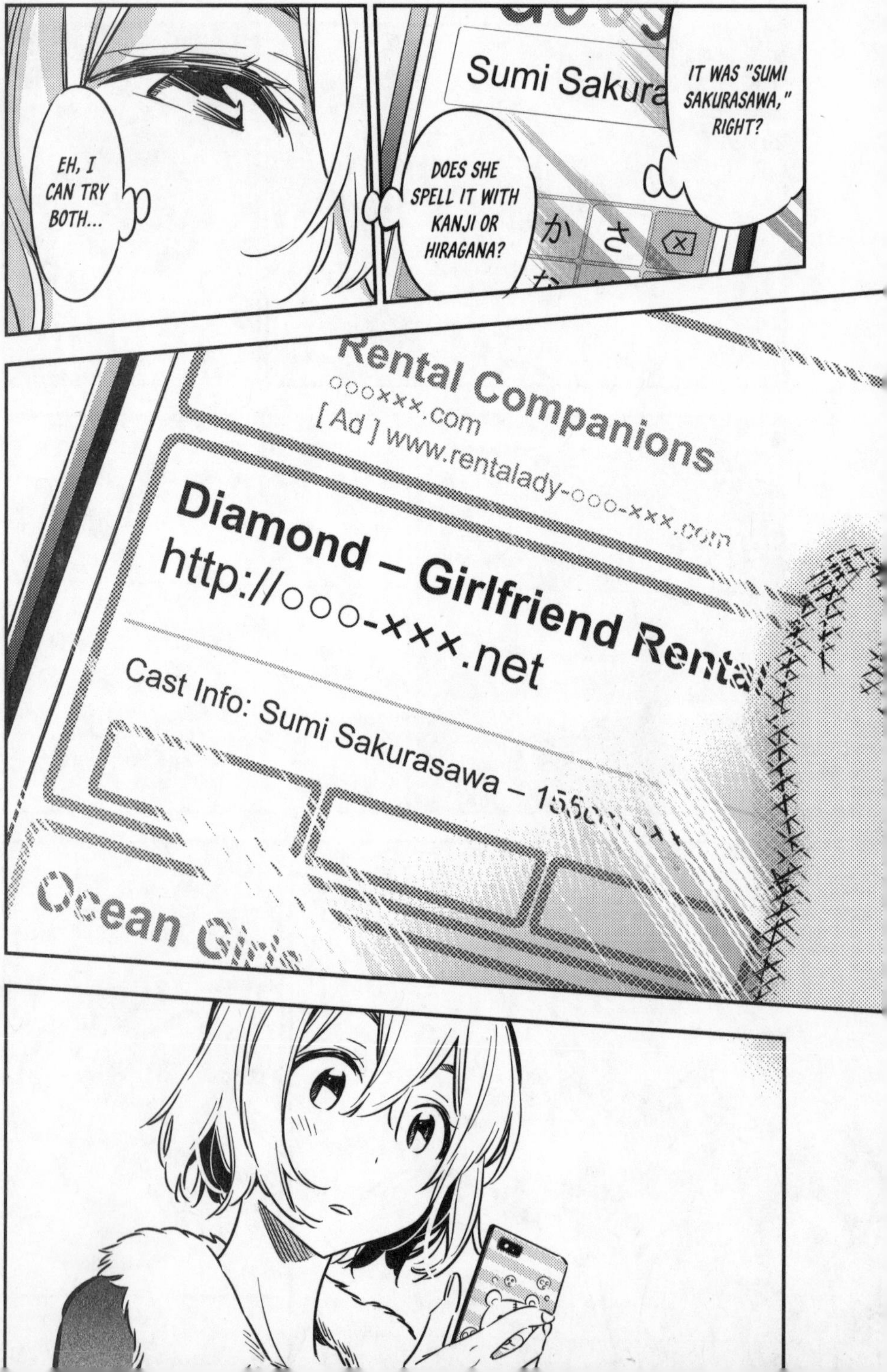
Sumi Sakura
IT WAS "SUMI SAKURASAWA," RIGHT?
DOES SHE SPELL IT WITH KANJI OR HIRAGANA?
か さ
EH, I CAN TRY BOTH...
Rental Companions
○○○×××.com
[Ad] www.rentalady-○○○-×××.com
Diamond – Girlfriend Rental
http://○○○-×××.net
Cast Info: Sumi Sakurasawa – 155cm
Ocean Girls

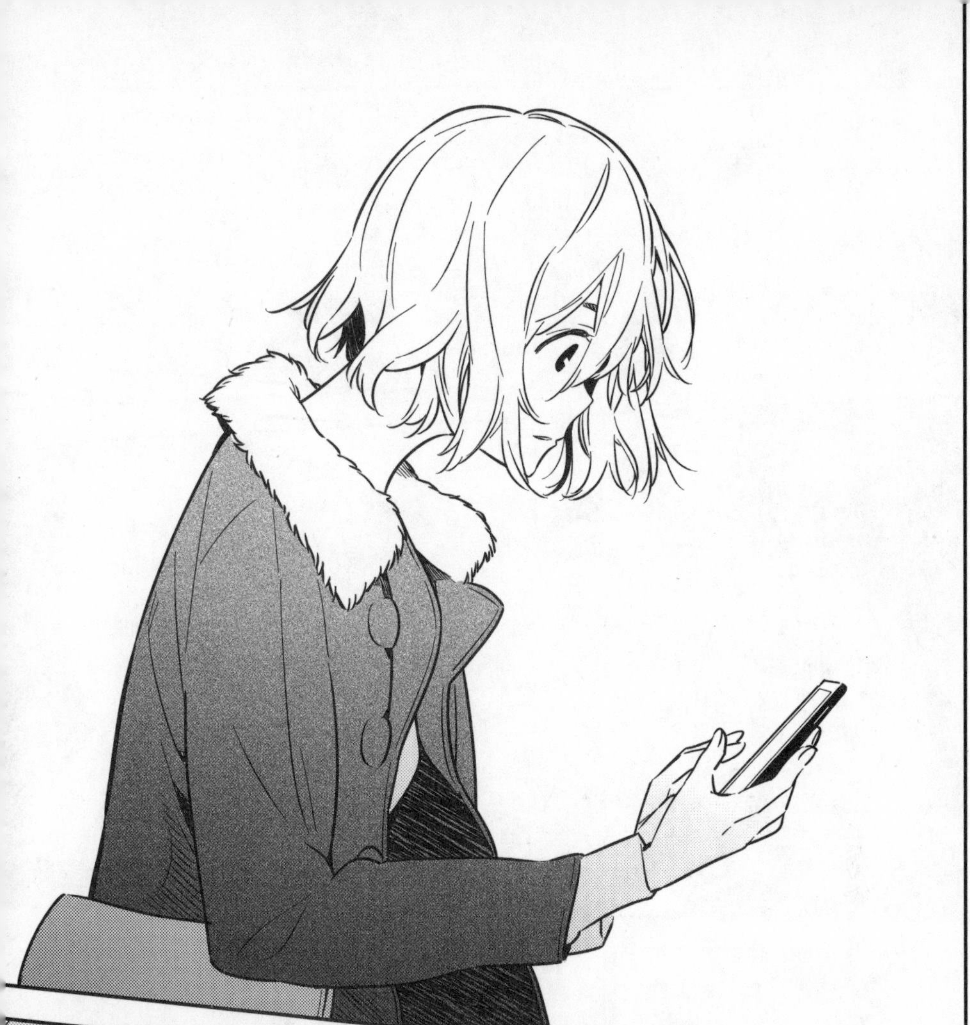
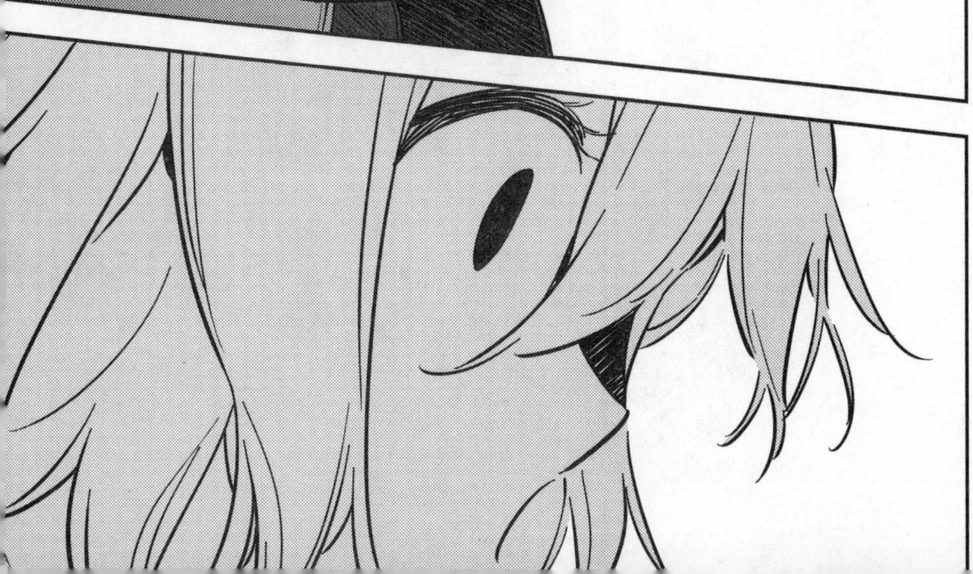

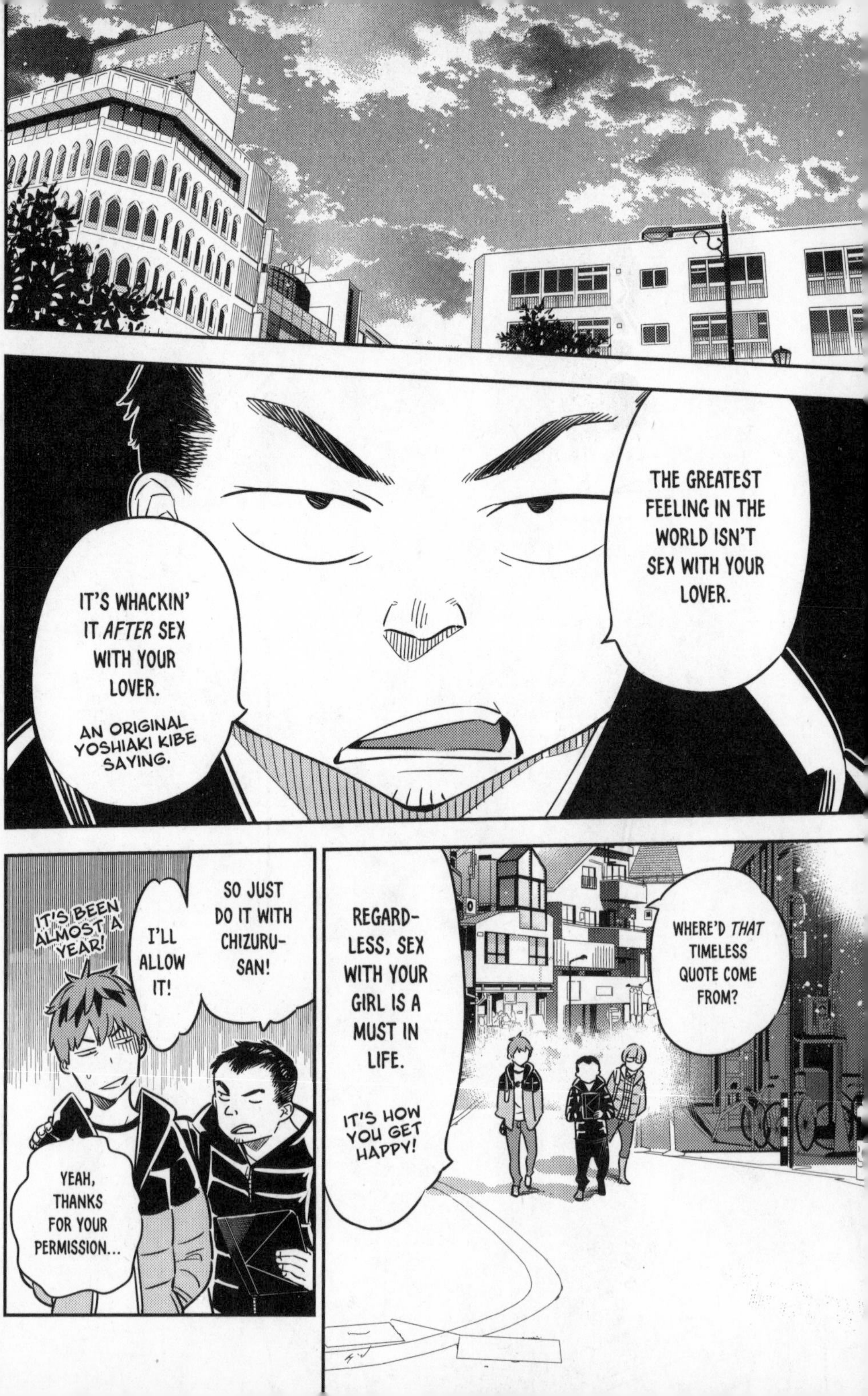
THE GREATEST FEELING IN THE WORLD ISN'T SEX WITH YOUR LOVER.
IT'S WHACKIN' IT *AFTER* SEX WITH YOUR LOVER.
AN ORIGINAL YOSHIAKI KIBE SAYING.
WHERE'D *THAT* TIMELESS QUOTE COME FROM?
REGARD-LESS, SEX WITH YOUR GIRL IS A MUST IN LIFE.
IT'S HOW YOU GET HAPPY!
SO JUST DO IT WITH CHIZURU-SAN!
I'LL ALLOW IT!
IT'S BEEN ALMOST A YEAR!
YEAH, THANKS FOR YOUR PERMISSION...

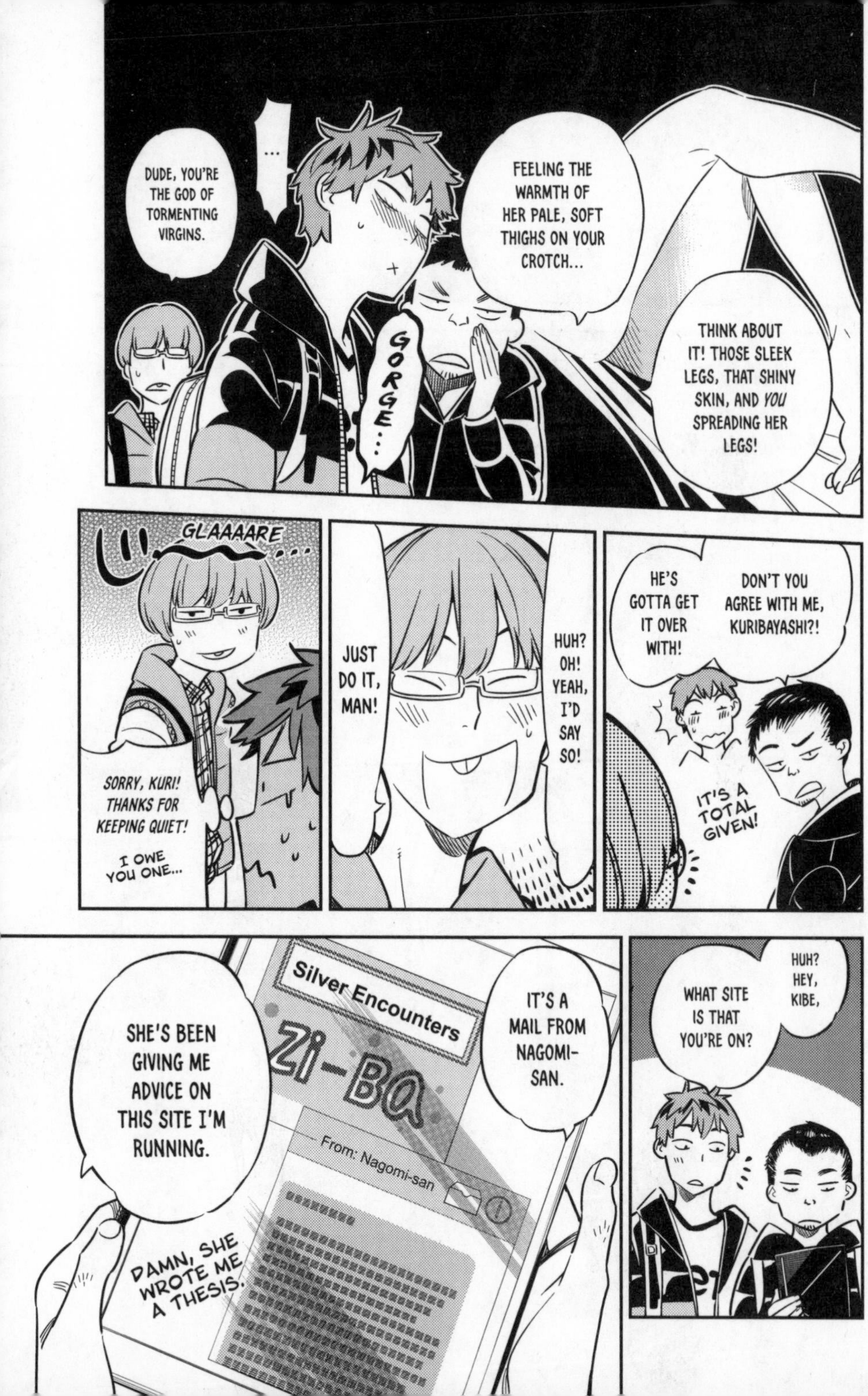
FEELING THE WARMTH OF HER PALE, SOFT THIGHS ON YOUR CROTCH...
THINK ABOUT IT! THOSE SLEEK LEGS, THAT SHINY SKIN, AND *YOU* SPREADING HER LEGS!
...
DUDE, YOU'RE THE GOD OF TORMENTING VIRGINS.
GORGE...
DON'T YOU AGREE WITH ME, KURIBAYASHI?!
HE'S GOTTA GET IT OVER WITH!
IT'S A TOTAL GIVEN!
HUH? OH! YEAH, I'D SAY SO!
JUST DO IT, MAN!
GLAAAARE...
SORRY, KURI! THANKS FOR KEEPING QUIET!
I OWE YOU ONE...
HUH? HEY, KIBE,
WHAT SITE IS THAT YOU'RE ON?
IT'S A MAIL FROM NAGOMI-SAN.
SHE'S BEEN GIVING ME ADVICE ON THIS SITE I'M RUNNING.
Silver Encounters
Zi-BA
From: Nagomi-san
DAMN, SHE WROTE ME A THESIS.

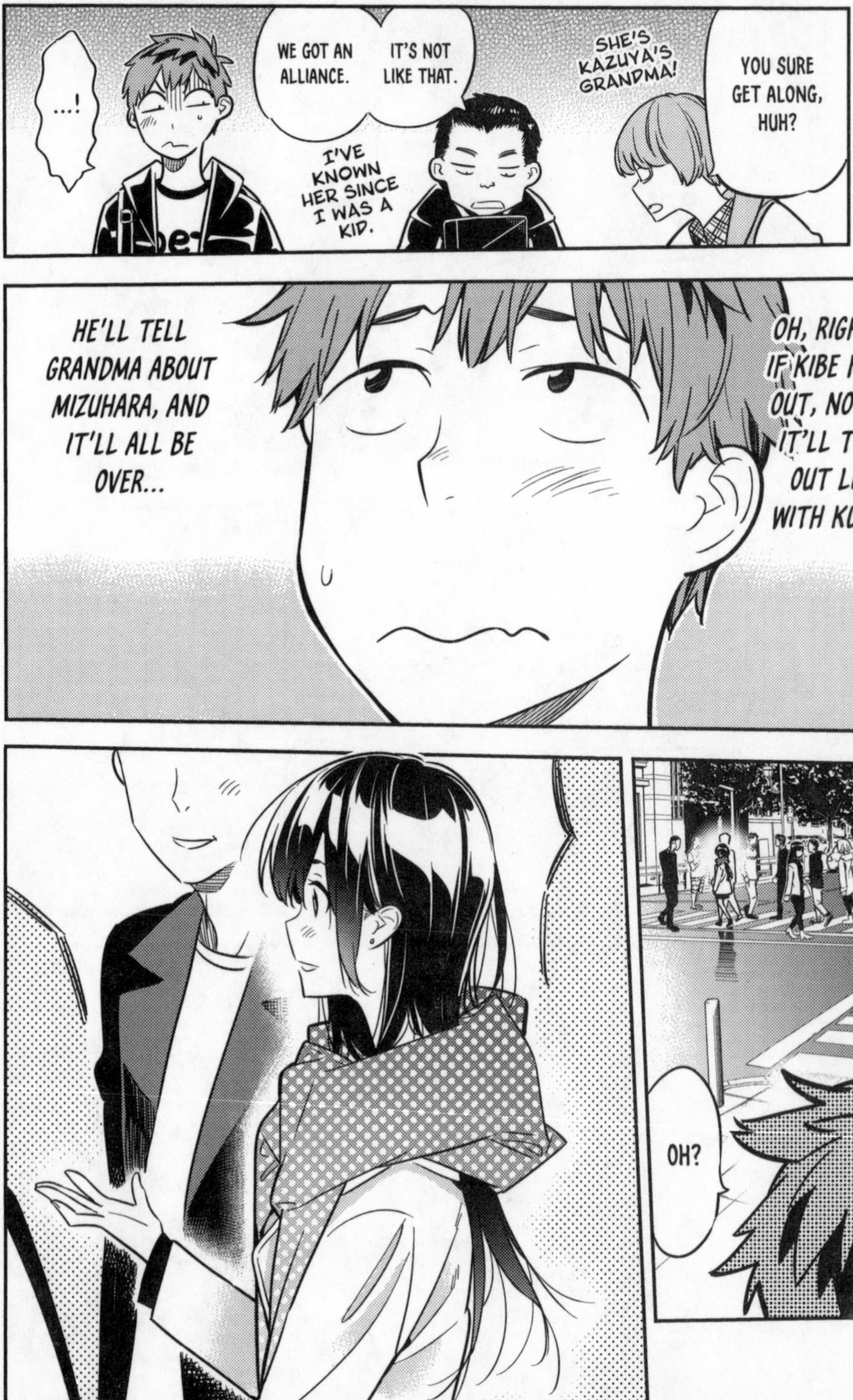
YOU SURE GET ALONG, HUH?
SHE'S KAZUYA'S GRANDMA!
IT'S NOT LIKE THAT.
WE GOT AN ALLIANCE.
I'VE KNOWN HER SINCE I WAS A KID.
...!
OH, RIGHT... IF KIBE FINDS OUT, NO WAY IT'LL TURN OUT LIKE WITH KURI...
HE'LL TELL GRANDMA ABOUT MIZUHARA, AND IT'LL ALL BE OVER...
OH?

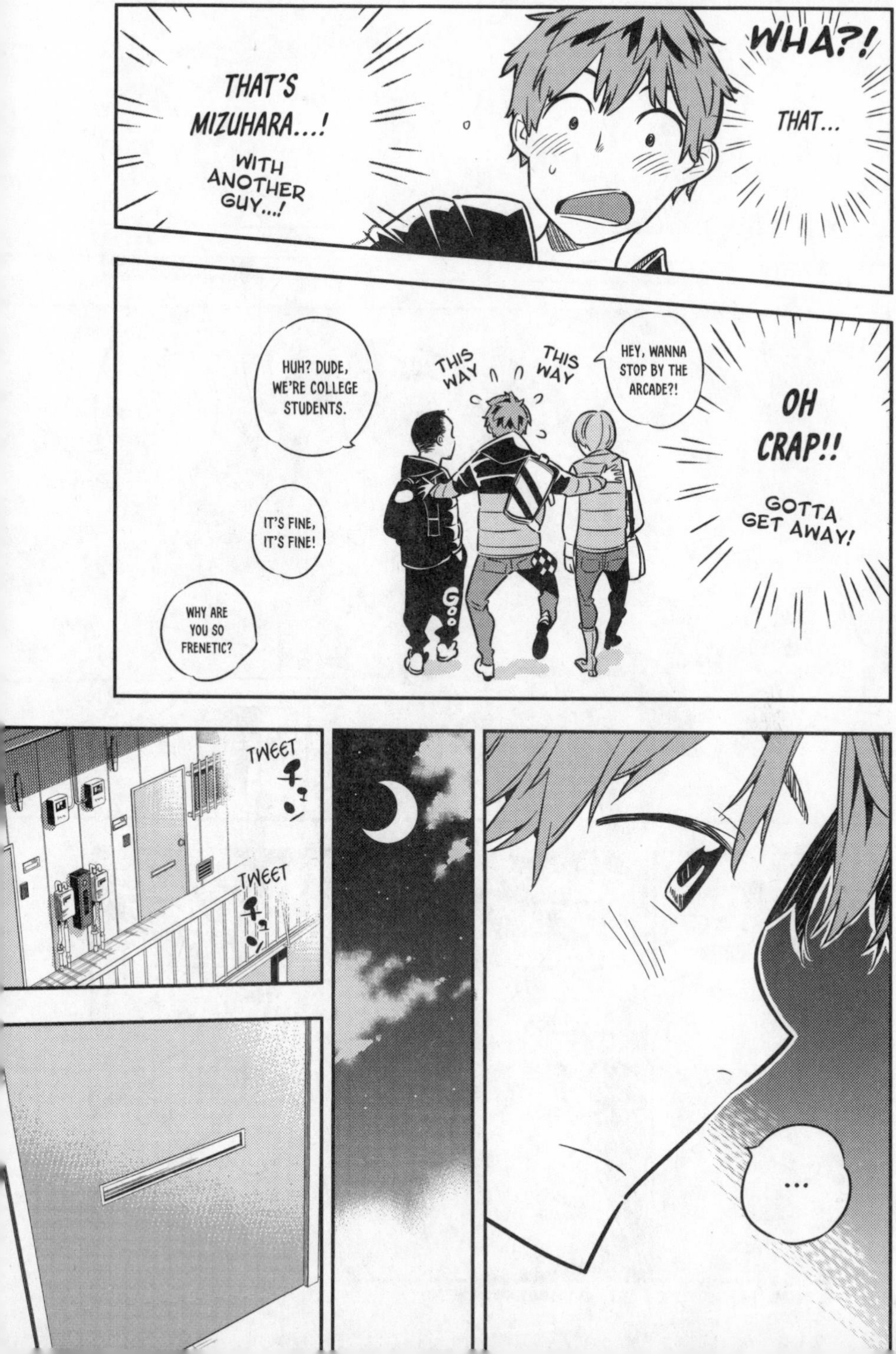
WHA?!
THAT...
THAT'S MIZUHARA...!
WITH ANOTHER GUY...!
OH CRAP!!
GOTTA GET AWAY!
HEY, WANNA STOP BY THE ARCADE?!
THIS WAY
THIS WAY
HUH? DUDE, WE'RE COLLEGE STUDENTS.
IT'S FINE, IT'S FINE!
WHY ARE YOU SO FRENETIC?
...
TWEET
TWEET

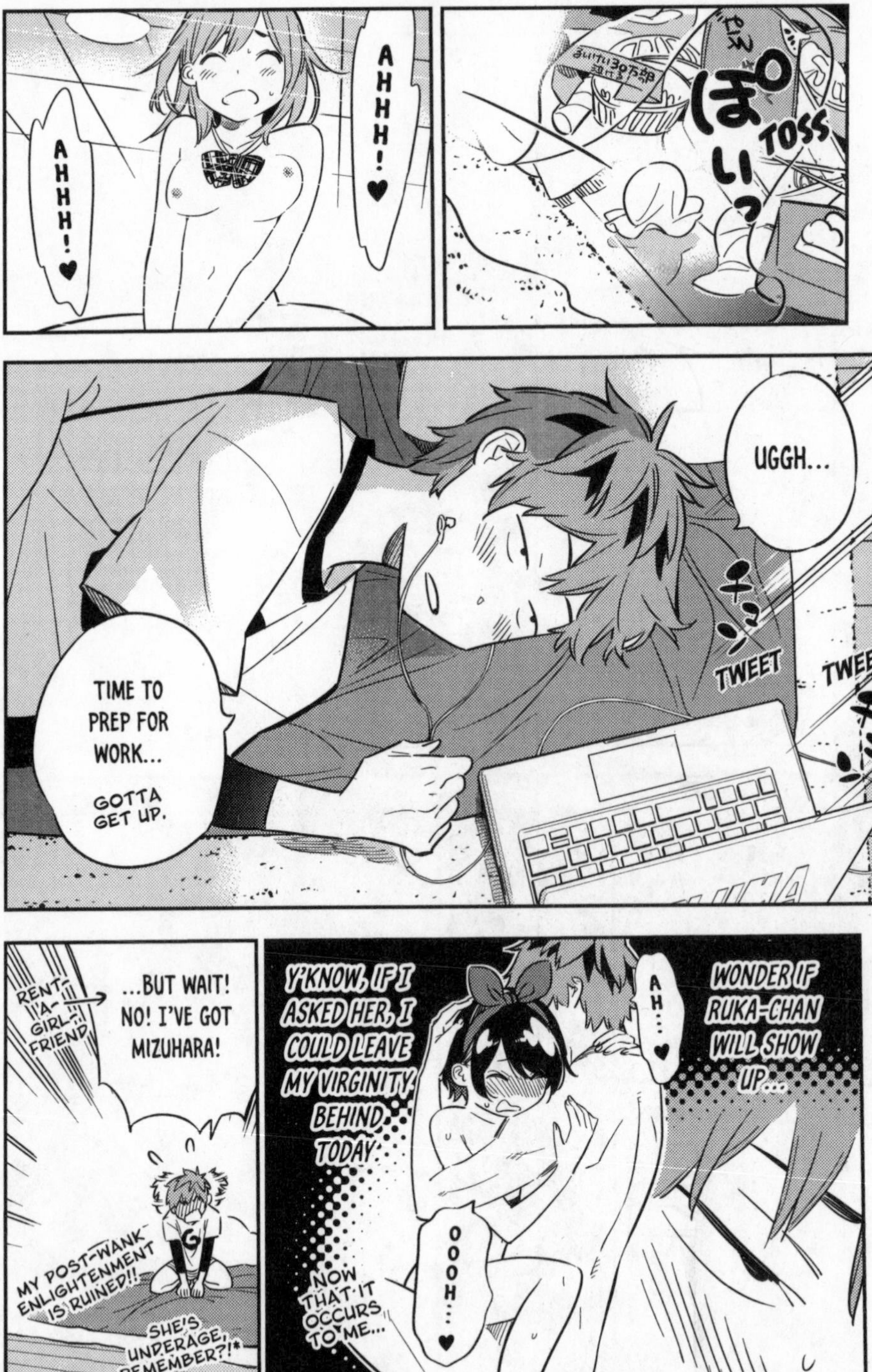
ぽいっ
TOSS
AHHHH!♥
AHHH!♥
UGGH...
チュン
TWEET
TWEET
チュン
TIME TO PREP FOR WORK...
GOTTA GET UP.
WONDER IF RUKA-CHAN WILL SHOW UP...
AH...♥
Y'KNOW, IF I ASKED HER, I COULD LEAVE MY VIRGINITY BEHIND TODAY
OOOH...♥
NOW THAT IT OCCURS TO ME...
...BUT WAIT! NO! I'VE GOT MIZUHARA!
RENT-A-GIRLFRIEND
MY POST-WANK ENLIGHTENMENT IS RUINED!!
SHE'S UNDERAGE, REMEMBER?!*

* IN JAPAN, THE AGE OF MAJORITY IS 20 (WITH PLANS TO LOWER IT TO 18 IN 2021).

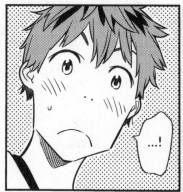

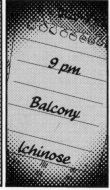

CLACK
!
9 pm
Balcony
Ichinose
...!
SIGH...
Water Issues?
Apartments
65,000
NOT A THING... JUST ADS.
WAITING FOR THESE NOTES...
IT'S SO STUPID.
MIZUHARA HASN'T SPOKEN TO ME SINCE THEN...
ISN'T SHE IN CONTACT WITH SUMI-CHAN?
SO SHE CALLED ME OUT JUST FOR HER CO-WORKER'S SAKE?
NO SPECIAL MEANING TO IT?
...OH.
I'M OUT OF SOCKS.
THE BALCONY...

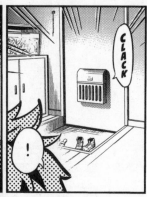

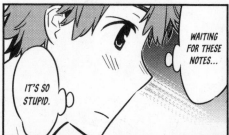

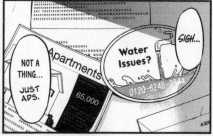

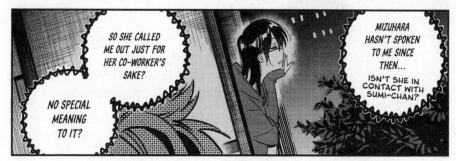

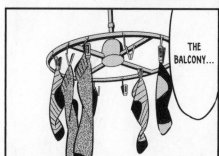

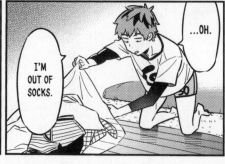

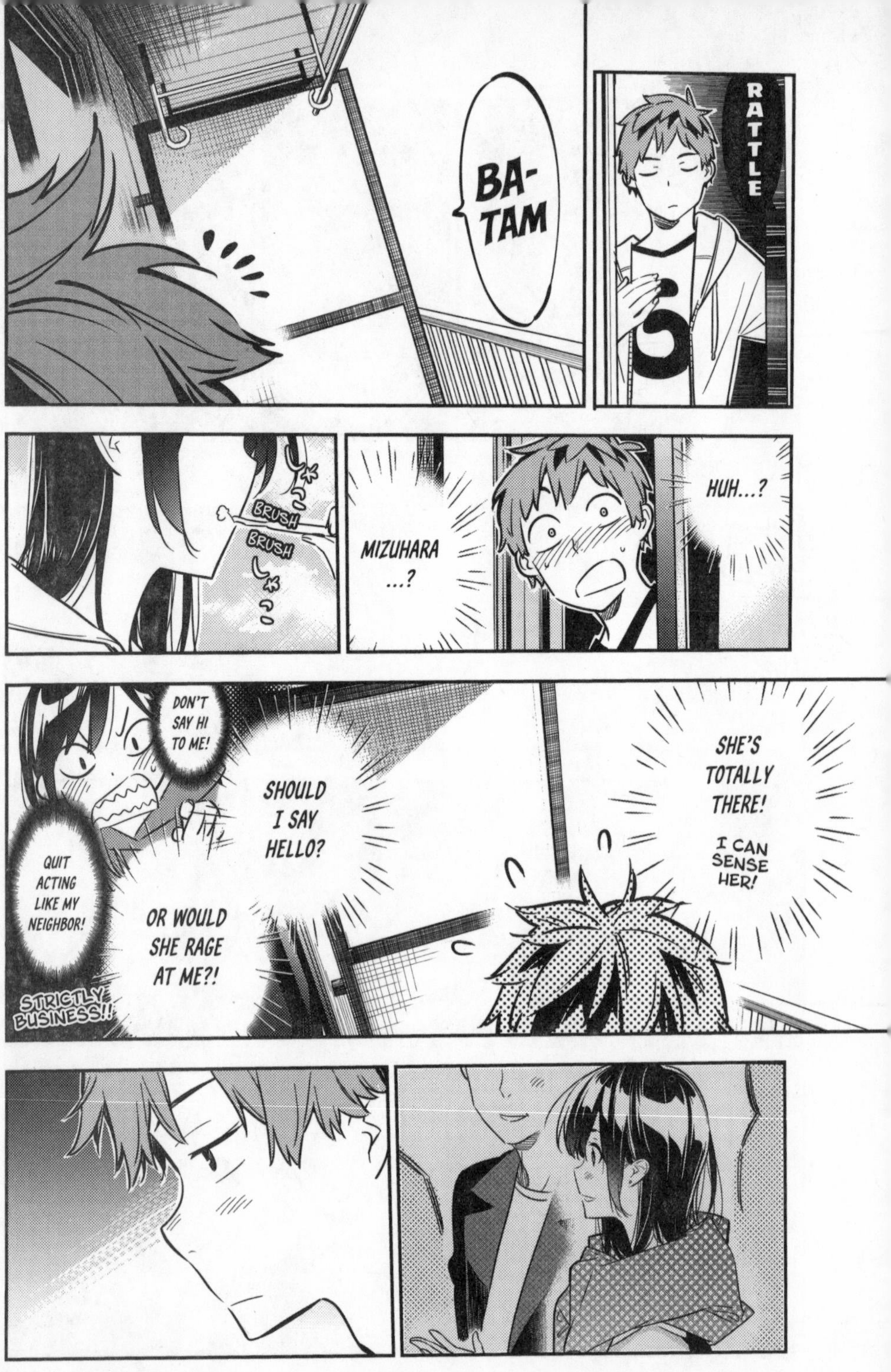
RATTLE
BA-TAM
HUH...?
MIZUHARA ...?
BRUSH
BRUSH
SHE'S TOTALLY THERE!
I CAN SENSE HER!
SHOULD I SAY HELLO?
OR WOULD SHE RAGE AT ME?!
DON'T SAY HI TO ME!
QUIT ACTING LIKE MY NEIGHBOR!
STRICTLY BUSINESS!!

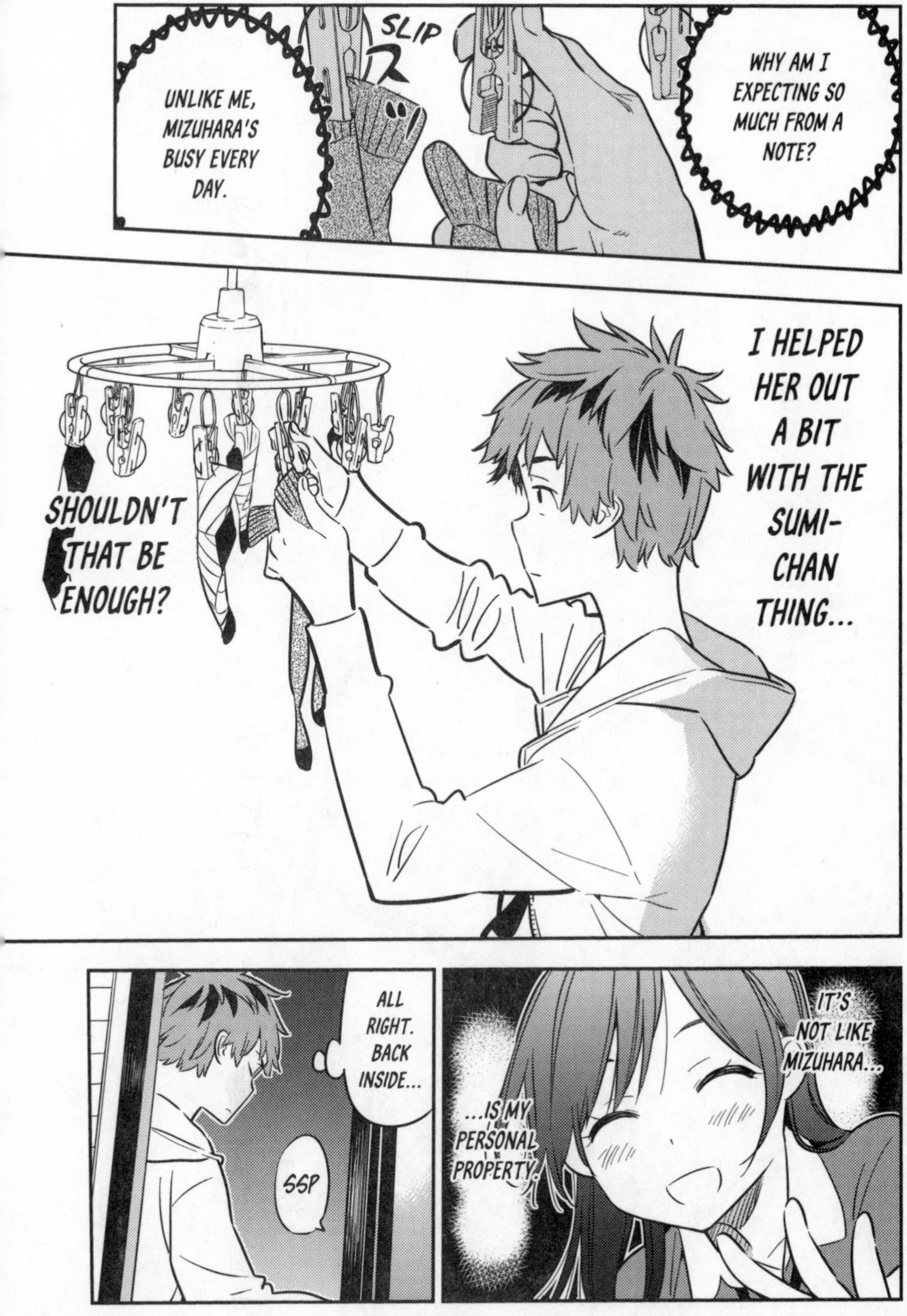
WHY AM I EXPECTING SO MUCH FROM A NOTE?
SLIP
UNLIKE ME, MIZUHARA'S BUSY EVERY DAY.
I HELPED HER OUT A BIT WITH THE SUMI-CHAN THING...
SHOULDN'T THAT BE ENOUGH?
IT'S NOT LIKE MIZUHARA...
...IS MY PERSONAL PROPERTY.
ALL RIGHT. BACK INSIDE...
SSP

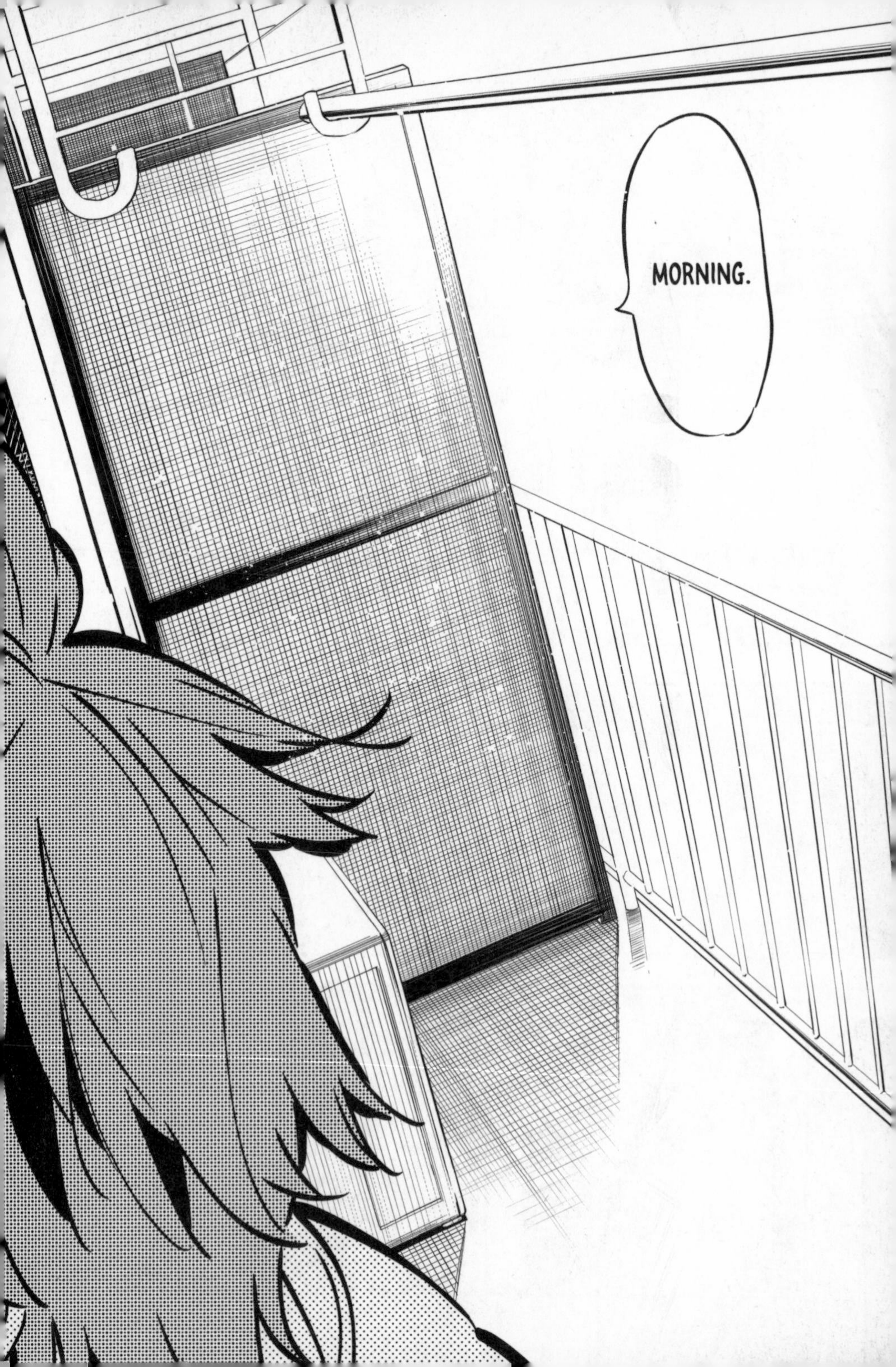
MORNING.

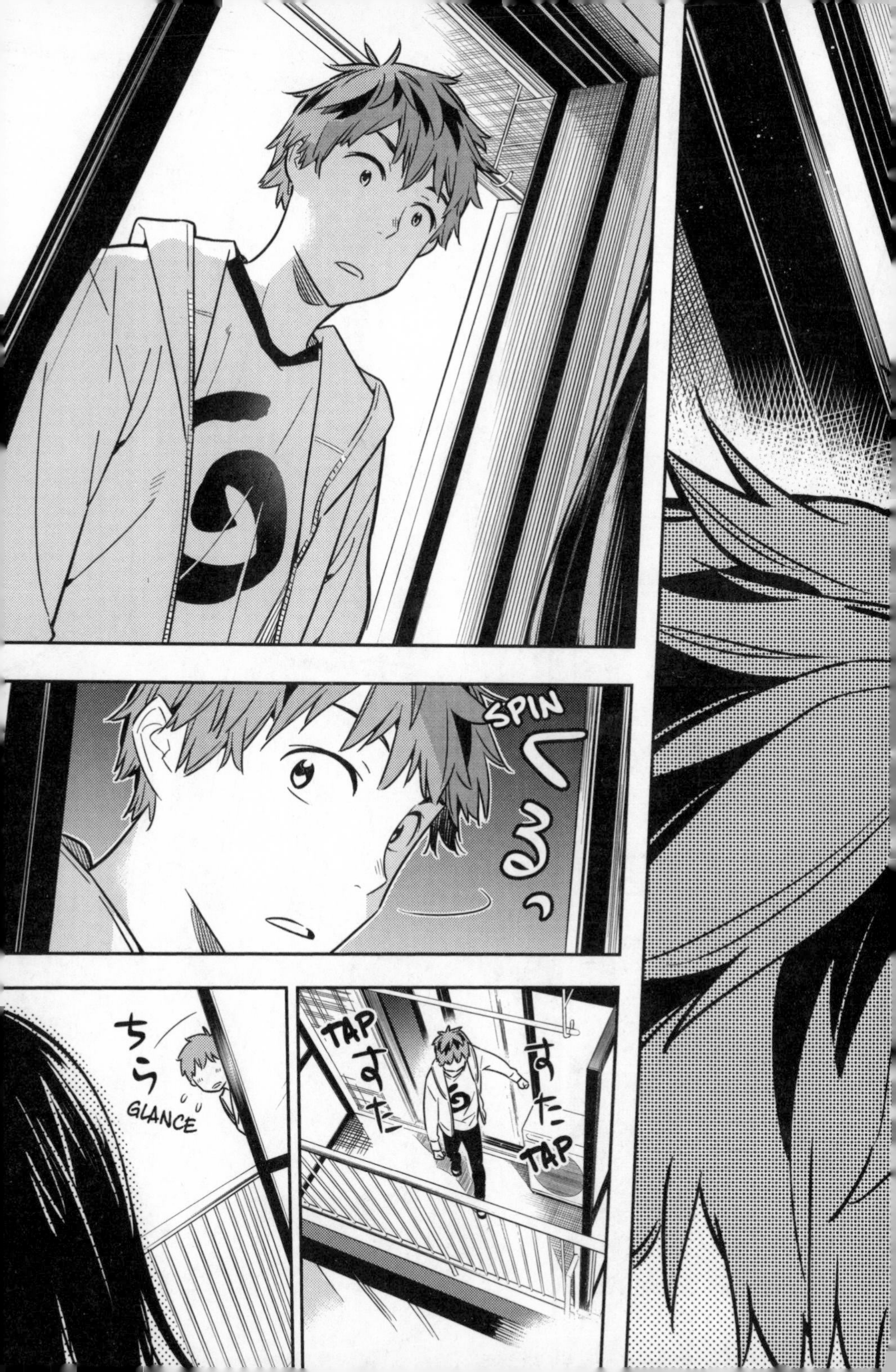
SPIN
くるっ
すた
TAP
TAP
すた
ちら
GLANCE

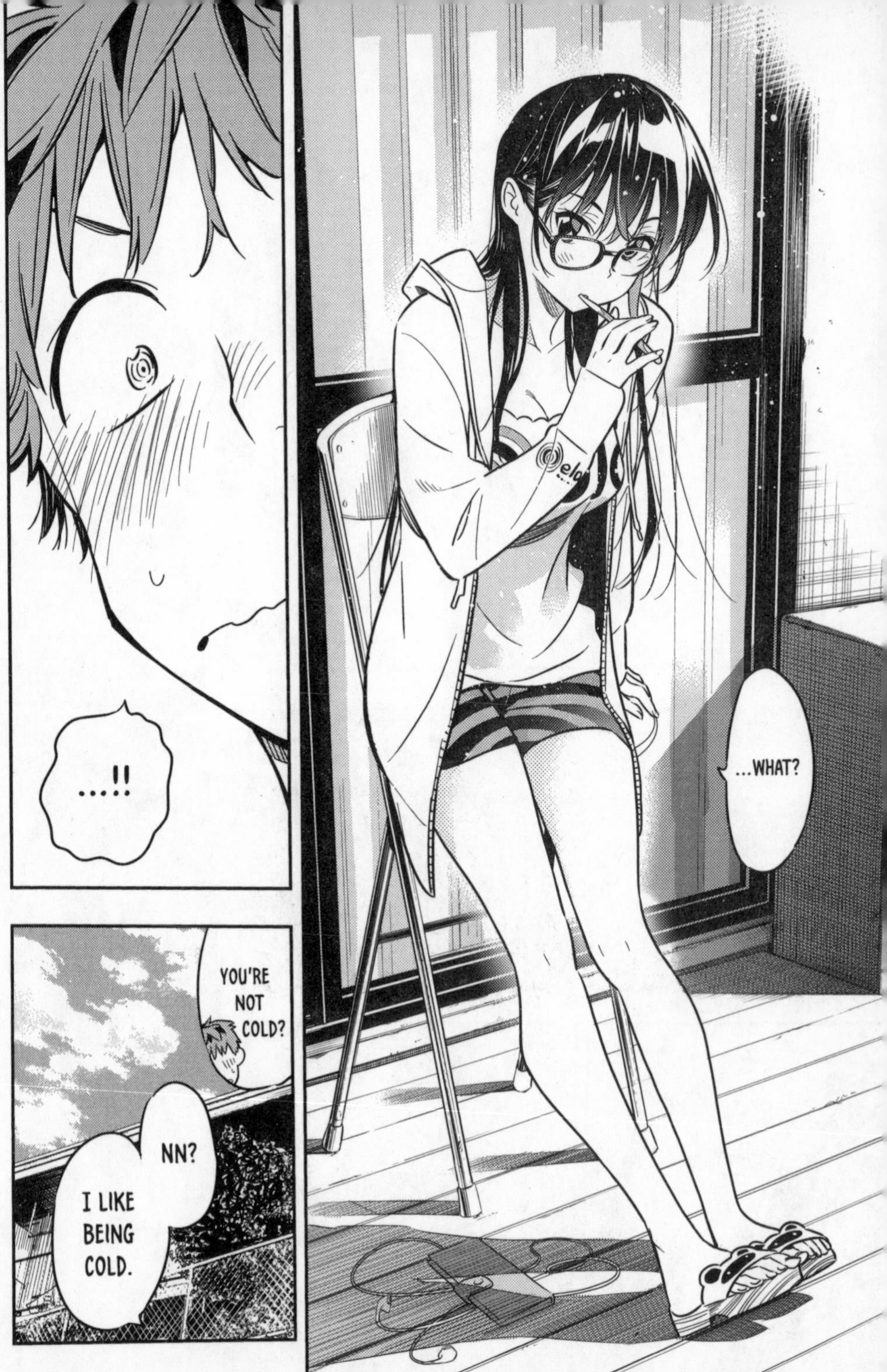
...WHAT?
...!!
YOU'RE NOT COLD?
NN?
I LIKE BEING COLD.

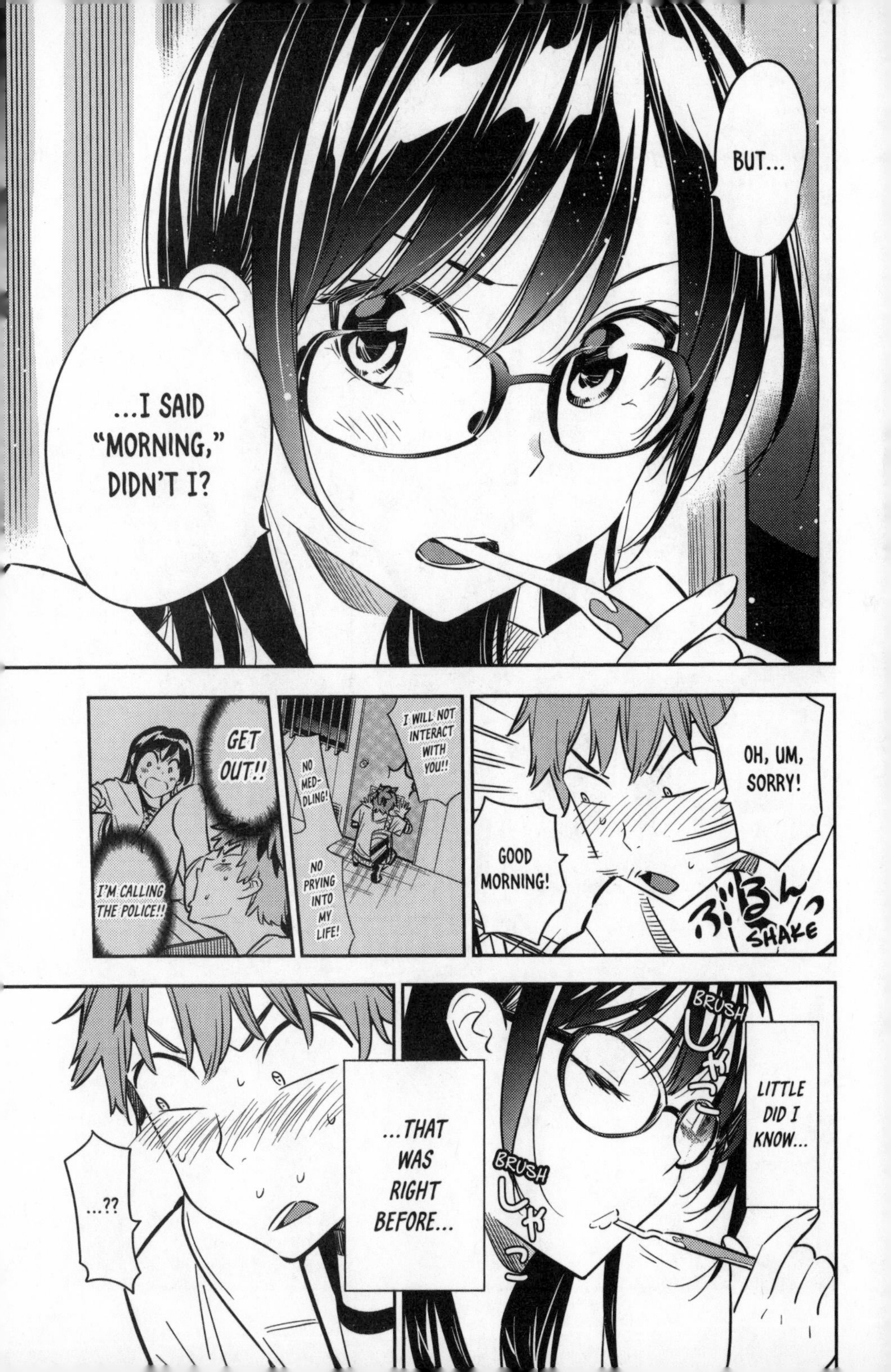
BUT...
...I SAID "MORNING," DIDN'T I?
OH, UM, SORRY!
GOOD MORNING!
SHAKE
I WILL NOT INTERACT WITH YOU!!
NO MED-DLING!
NO PRYING INTO MY LIFE!
GET OUT!!
I'M CALLING THE POLICE!!
BRUSH
LITTLE DID I KNOW...
BRUSH
...THAT WAS RIGHT BEFORE...
...??

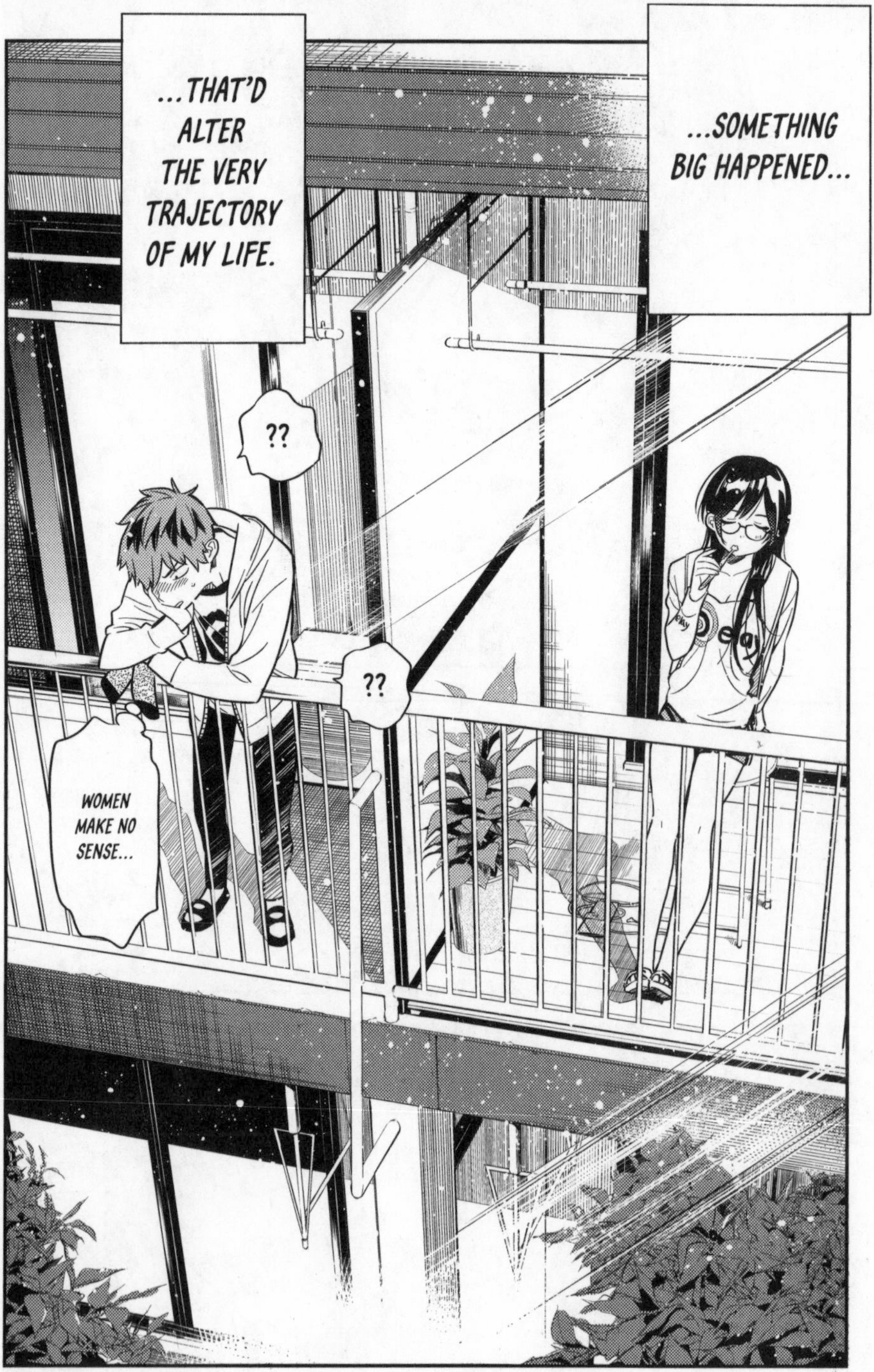
...SOMETHING BIG HAPPENED...
...THAT'D ALTER THE VERY TRAJECTORY OF MY LIFE.
??
??
WOMEN MAKE NO SENSE...

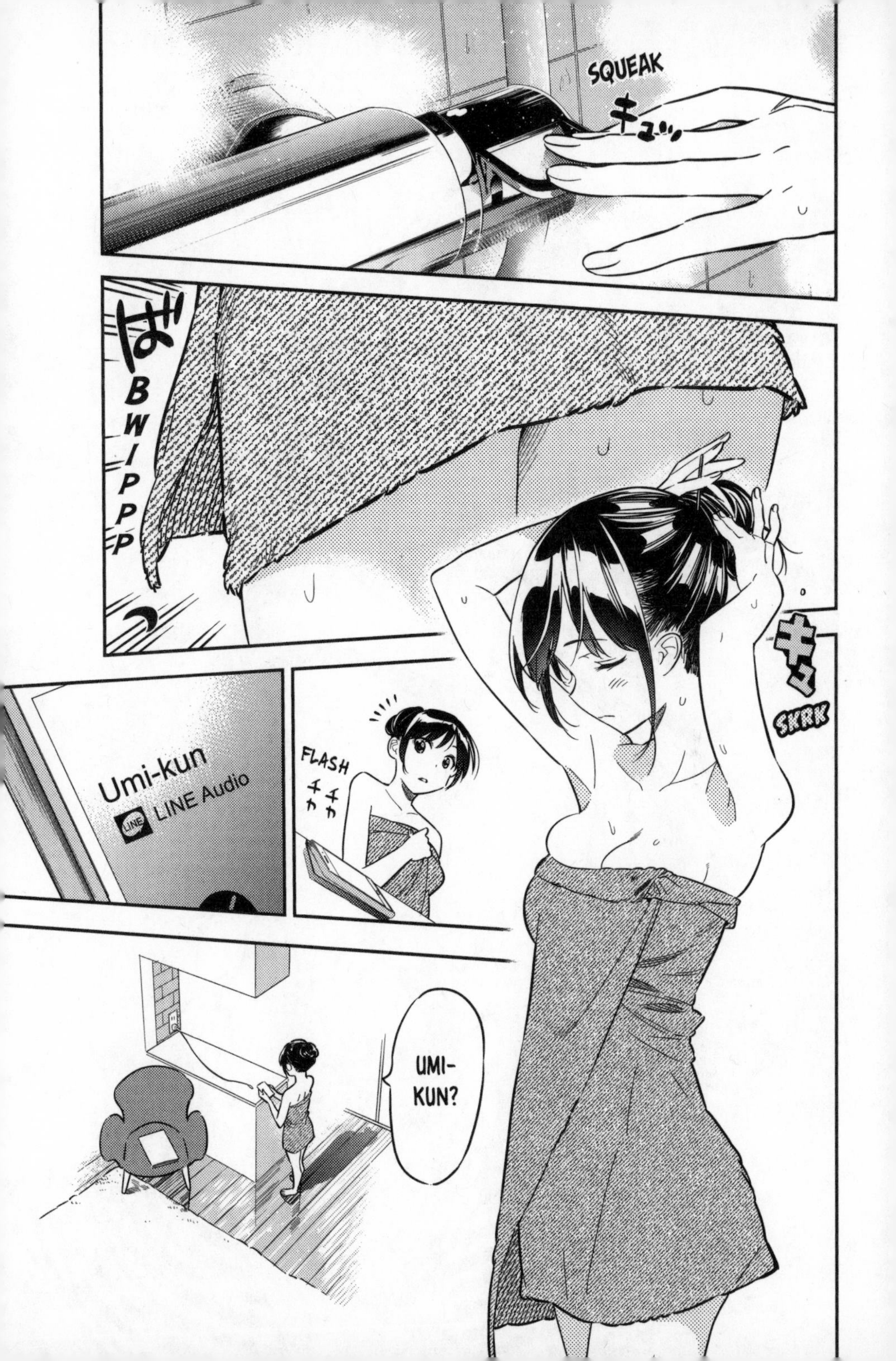
SQUEAK
キュッ
ばっ
BWIPPP
キュ
SKRK
FLASH
チカチカ
Umi-kun
LINE Audio
UMI-KUN?

RATING 45 MY GIRLFRIEND AND THE BREAK-OFF POINT (1)

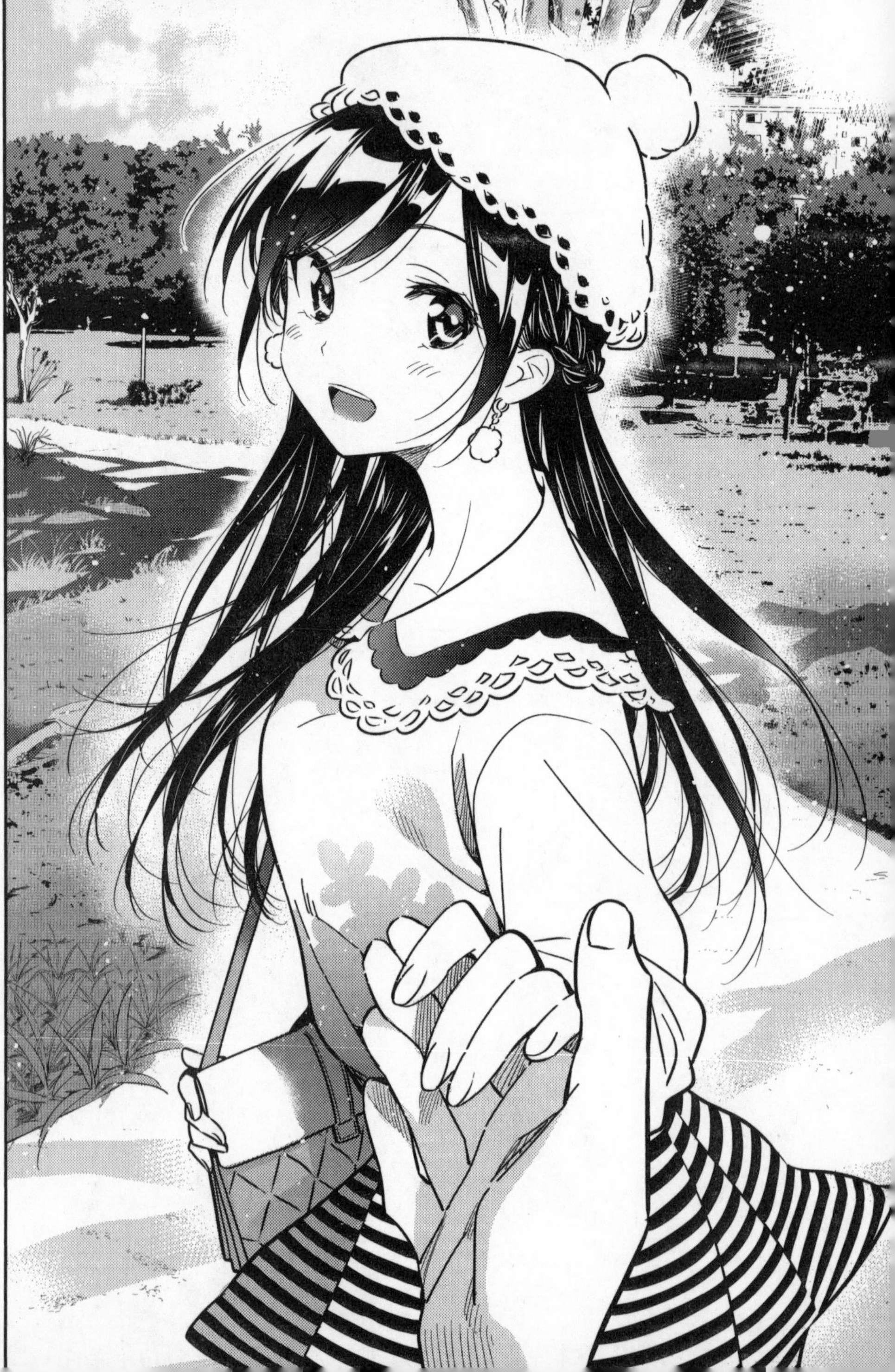

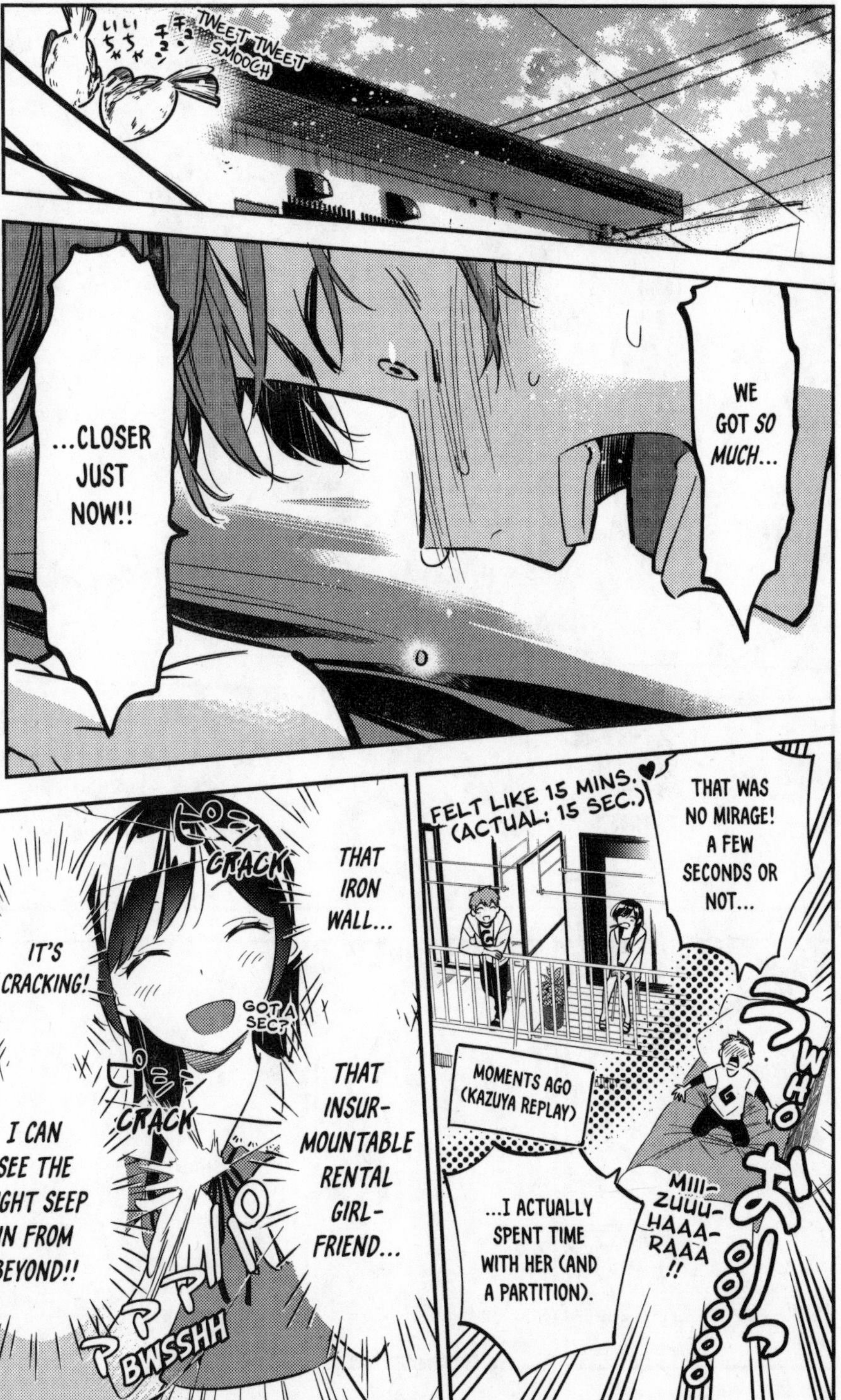

チュンチュン
いちゃいちゃ
TWEET TWEET
SMOOCH
WE GOT SO MUCH...
...CLOSER JUST NOW!!
THAT WAS NO MIRAGE! A FEW SECONDS OR NOT...
FELT LIKE 15 MINS. (ACTUAL: 15 SEC.)
WHOOOOOOO
MIIIZUUU-HAAAA-RAAAA!!
MOMENTS AGO (KAZUYA REPLAY)
...I ACTUALLY SPENT TIME WITH HER (AND A PARTITION).
THAT IRON WALL...
CRACK
THAT INSUR-MOUNTABLE RENTAL GIRL-FRIEND...
IT'S CRACKING!
GOT A SEC?
CRACK
I CAN SEE THE LIGHT SEEP IN FROM BEYOND!!
BWSSHH

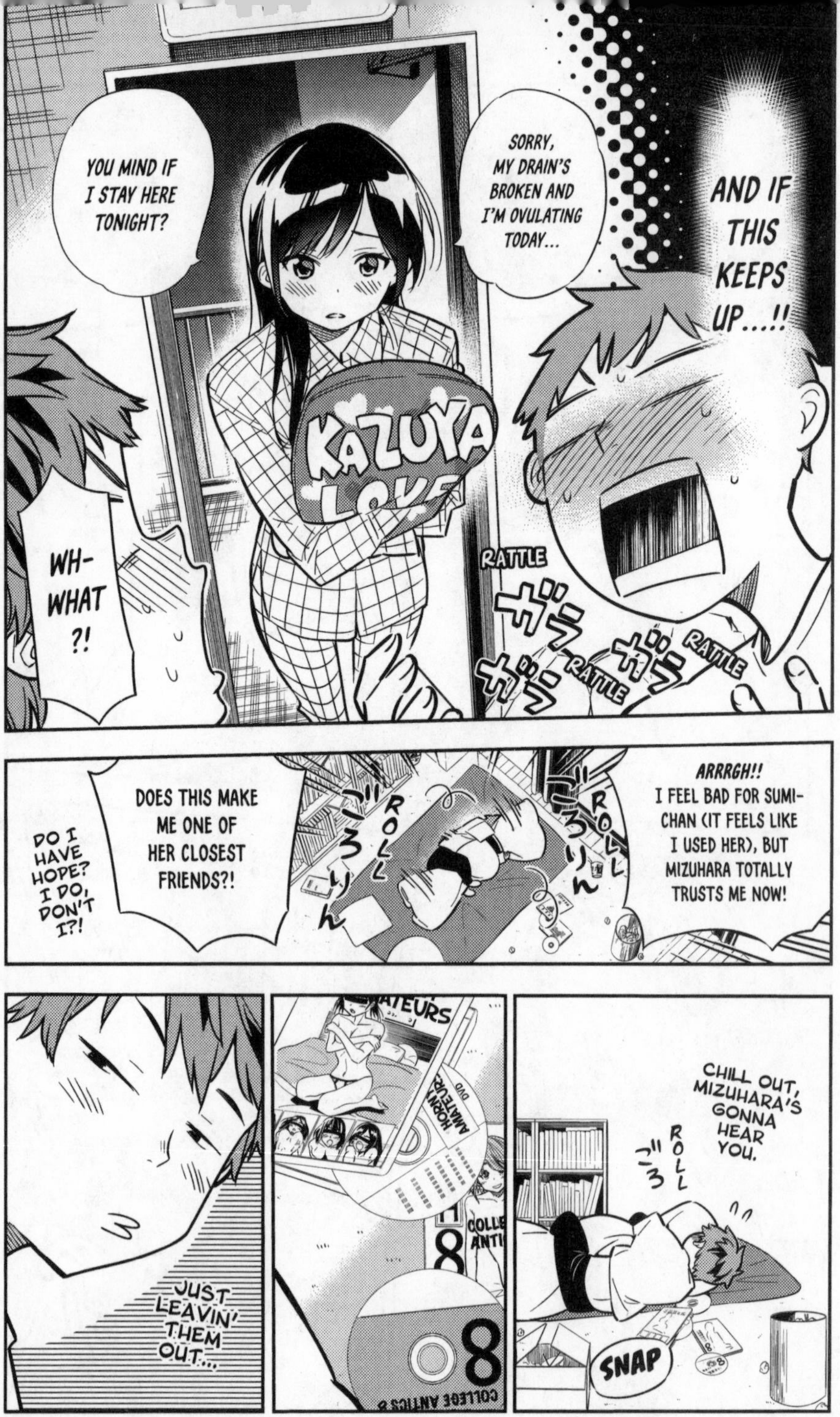
AND IF THIS KEEPS UP....!!
SORRY, MY DRAIN'S BROKEN AND I'M OVULATING TODAY...
YOU MIND IF I STAY HERE TONIGHT?
KAZUYA LOVE
WH-WHAT?!
RATTLE
ガラ
RATTLE
ガラ
RATTLE
ガラ
RATTLE
ガラ
ARRRGH!! I FEEL BAD FOR SUMI-CHAN (IT FEELS LIKE I USED HER), BUT MIZUHARA TOTALLY TRUSTS ME NOW!
ROLL
ごろりん
ROLL
ごろりん
DOES THIS MAKE ME ONE OF HER CLOSEST FRIENDS?!
DO I HAVE HOPE? I DO, DON'T I?!
CHILL OUT, MIZUHARA'S GONNA HEAR YOU.
ROLL
ごろ
SNAP
HORNY AMATEURS
DVD
COLLEGE ANTICS 8
JUST LEAVIN' THEM OUT...

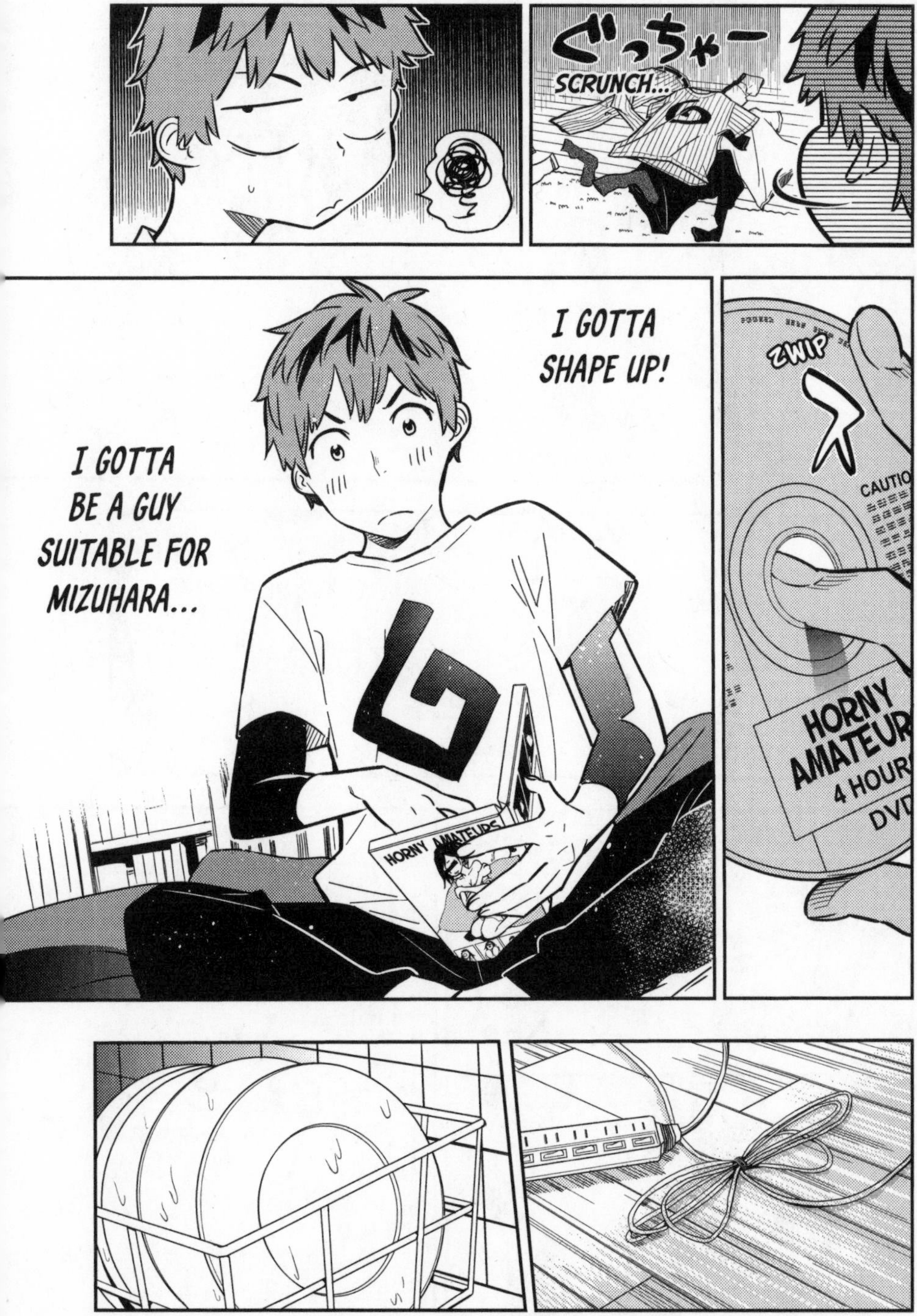
ぐっちゃー
SCRUNCH...
ZWIP
ス
I GOTTA SHAPE UP!
I GOTTA BE A GUY SUITABLE FOR MIZUHARA...
HORNY AMATEURS

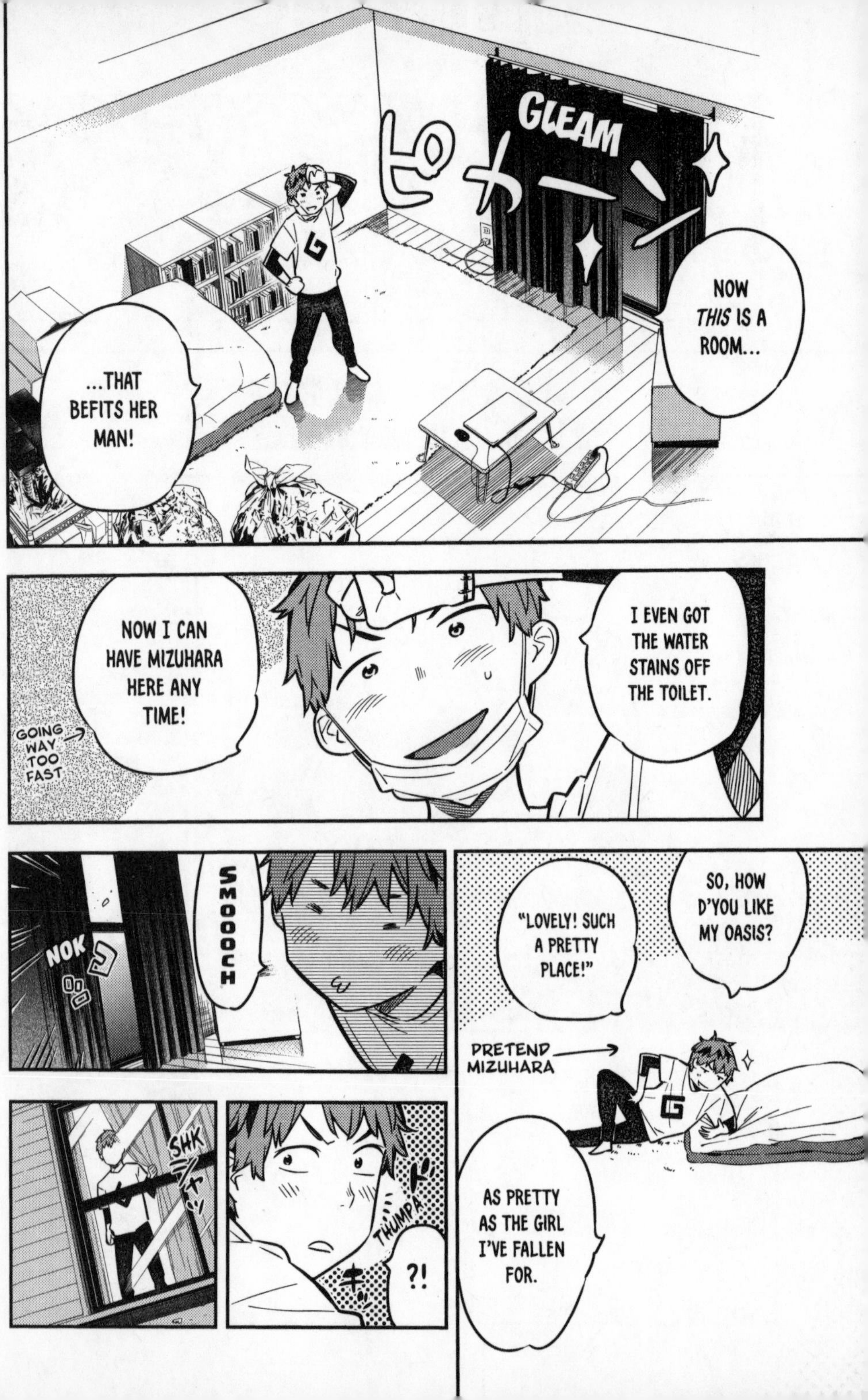
GLEAM
NOW THIS IS A ROOM...
...THAT BEFITS HER MAN!
I EVEN GOT THE WATER STAINS OFF THE TOILET.
NOW I CAN HAVE MIZUHARA HERE ANY TIME!
GOING WAY TOO FAST
SO, HOW D'YOU LIKE MY OASIS?
"LOVELY! SUCH A PRETTY PLACE!"
PRETEND MIZUHARA
AS PRETTY AS THE GIRL I'VE FALLEN FOR.
SMOOOCH
NOK
THUMPA
?!
SHK

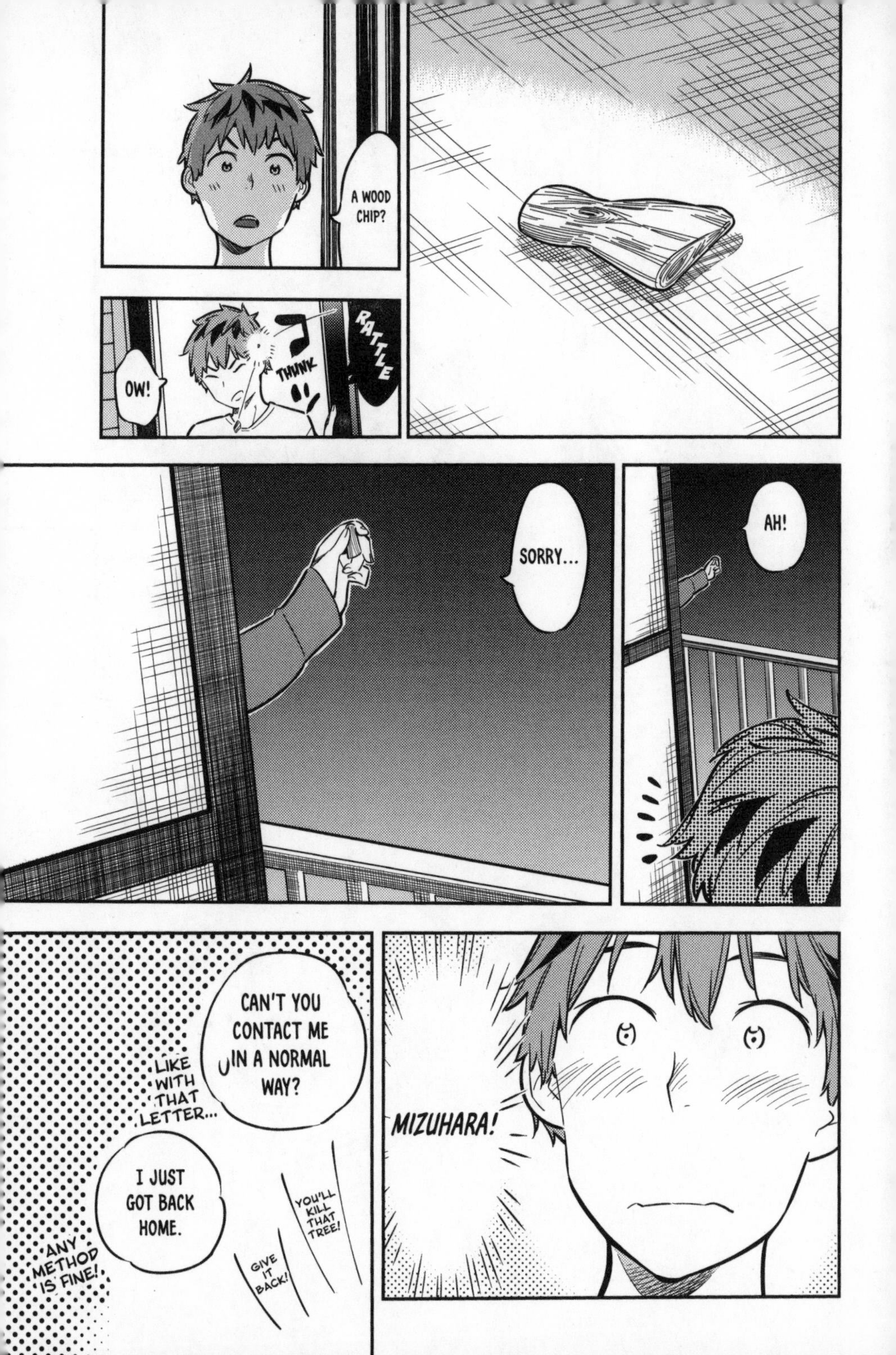
A WOOD CHIP?
RATTLE
THUNK
OW!
AH!
SORRY...
MIZUHARA!
CAN'T YOU CONTACT ME IN A NORMAL WAY?
LIKE WITH THAT LETTER...
YOU'LL KILL THAT TREE!
GIVE IT BACK!
I JUST GOT BACK HOME.
ANY METHOD IS FINE!

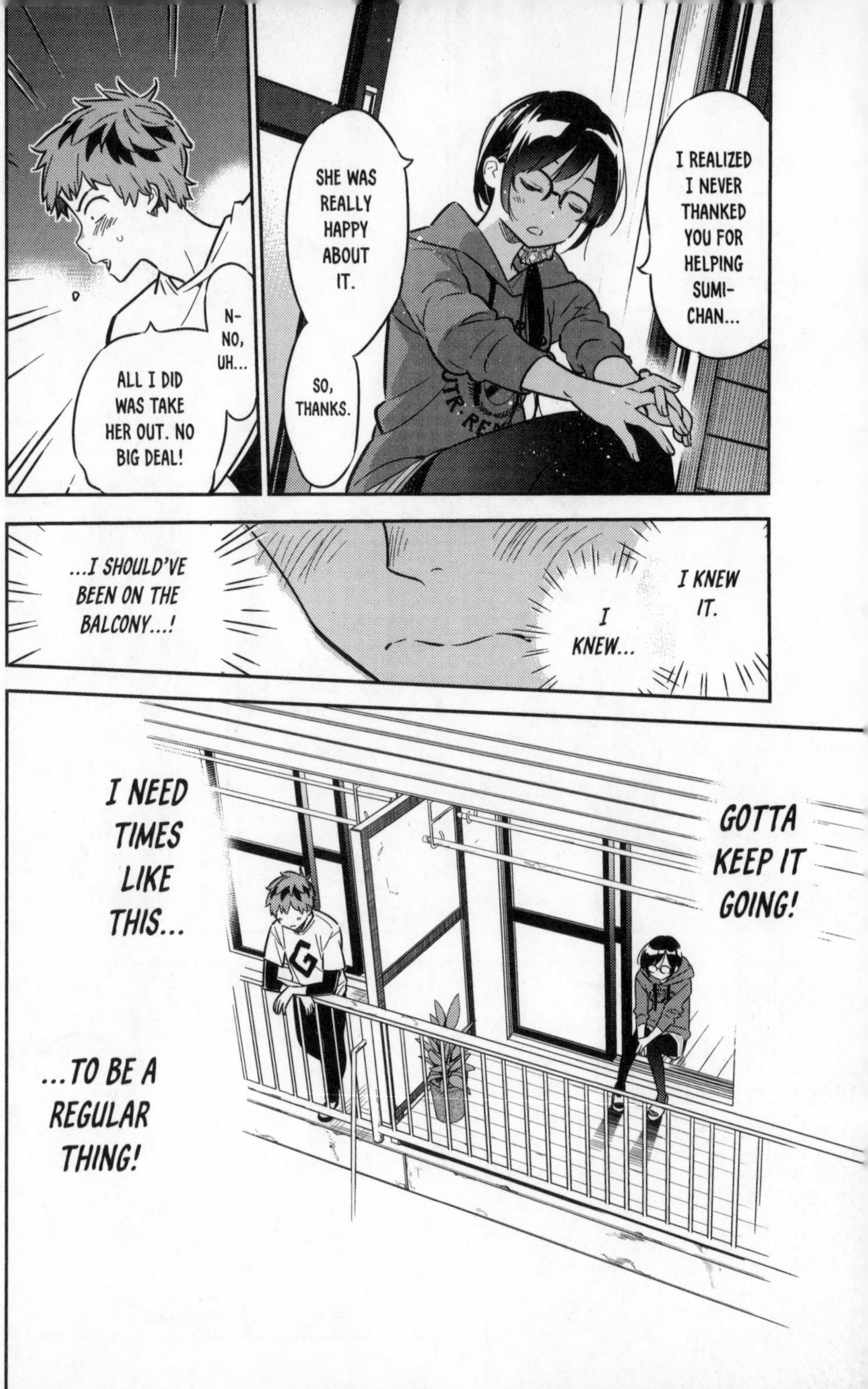
I REALIZED I NEVER THANKED YOU FOR HELPING SUMI-CHAN...
SHE WAS REALLY HAPPY ABOUT IT.
SO, THANKS.
N-NO, UH...
ALL I DID WAS TAKE HER OUT. NO BIG DEAL!
I KNEW IT.
I KNEW...
...I SHOULD'VE BEEN ON THE BALCONY...!
I NEED TIMES LIKE THIS...
...TO BE A REGULAR THING!
GOTTA KEEP IT GOING!

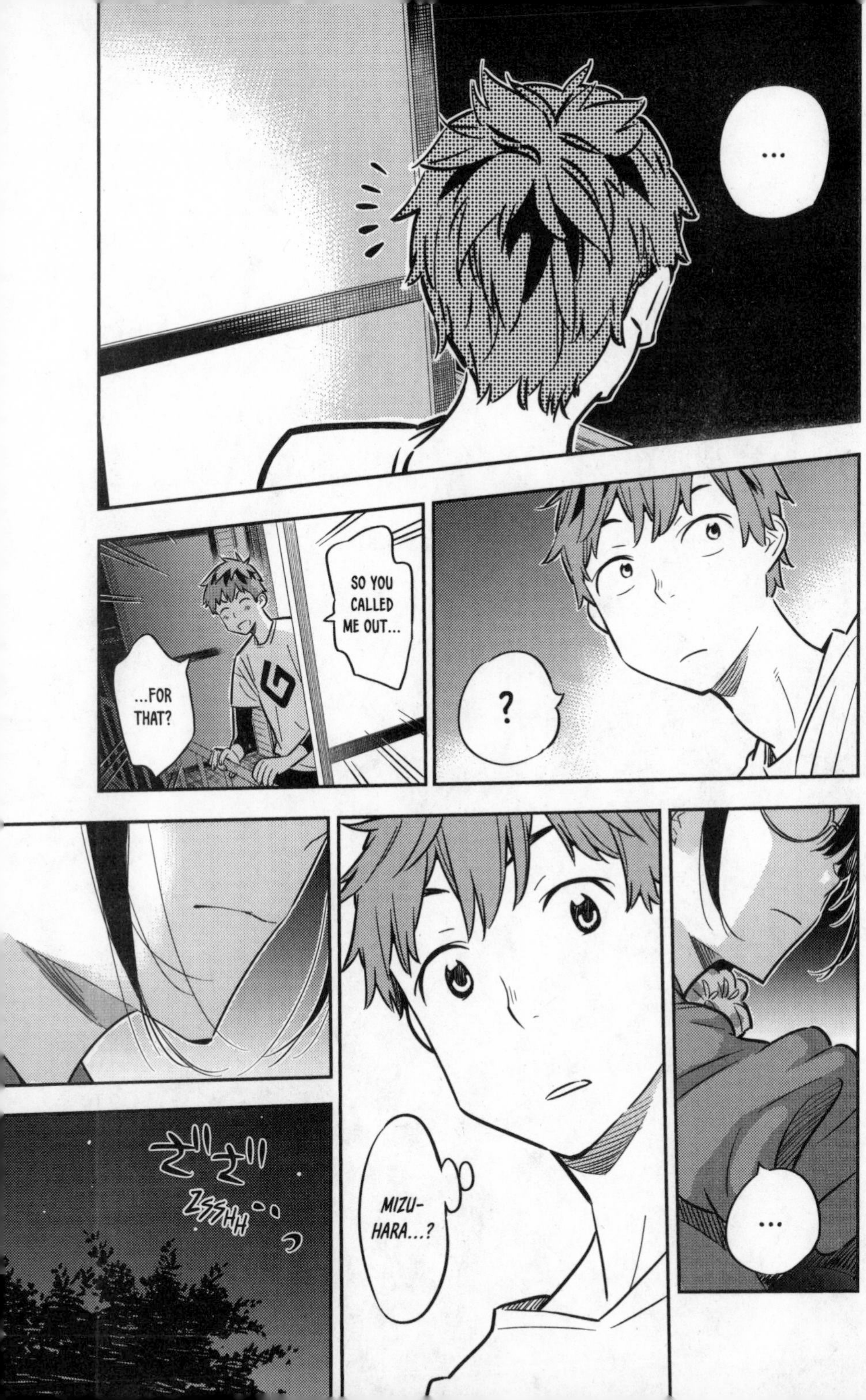
...
?
SO YOU CALLED ME OUT...
...FOR THAT?
...
MIZU-HARA...?
ZSSHH

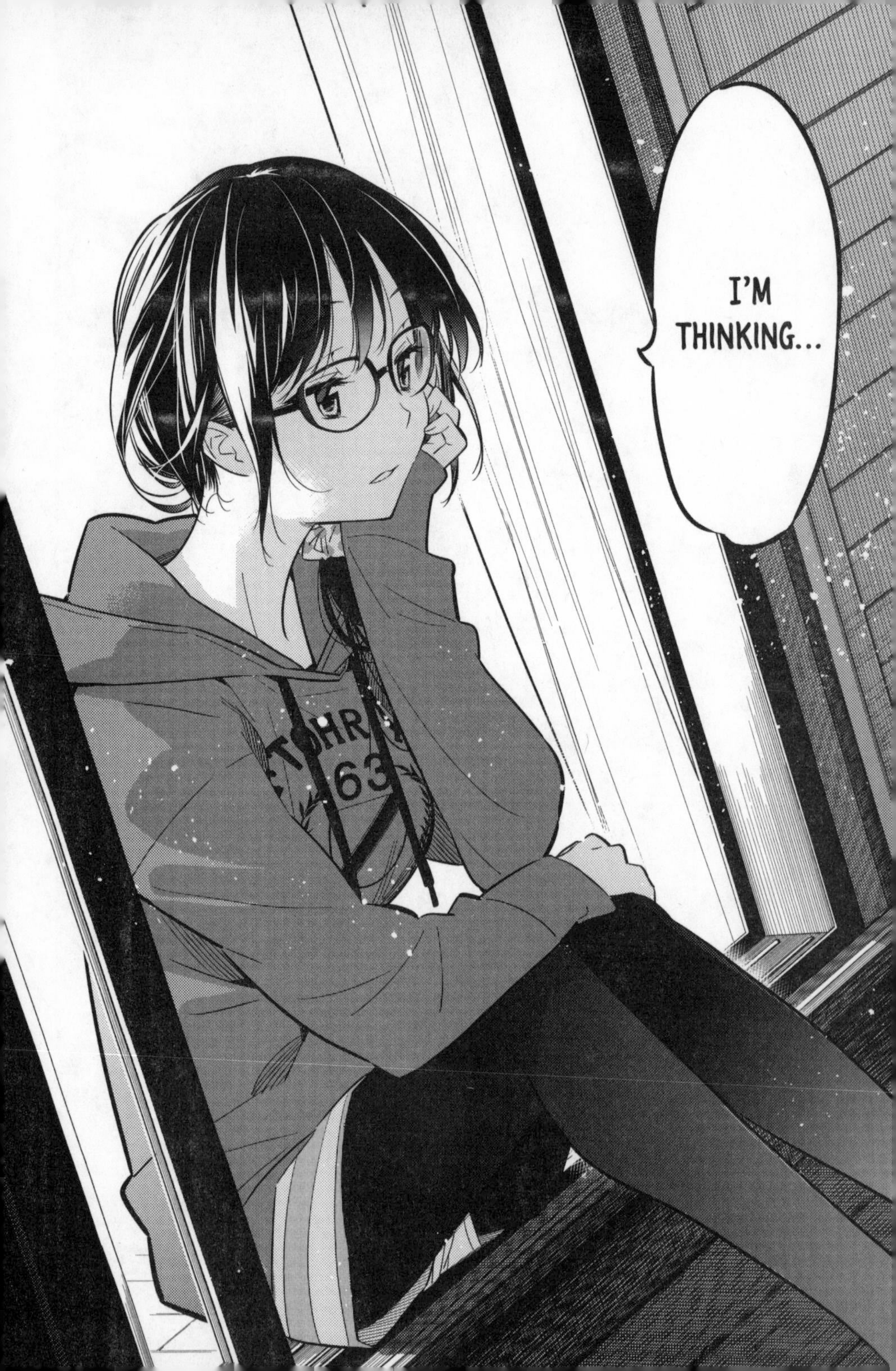
I'M THINKING...

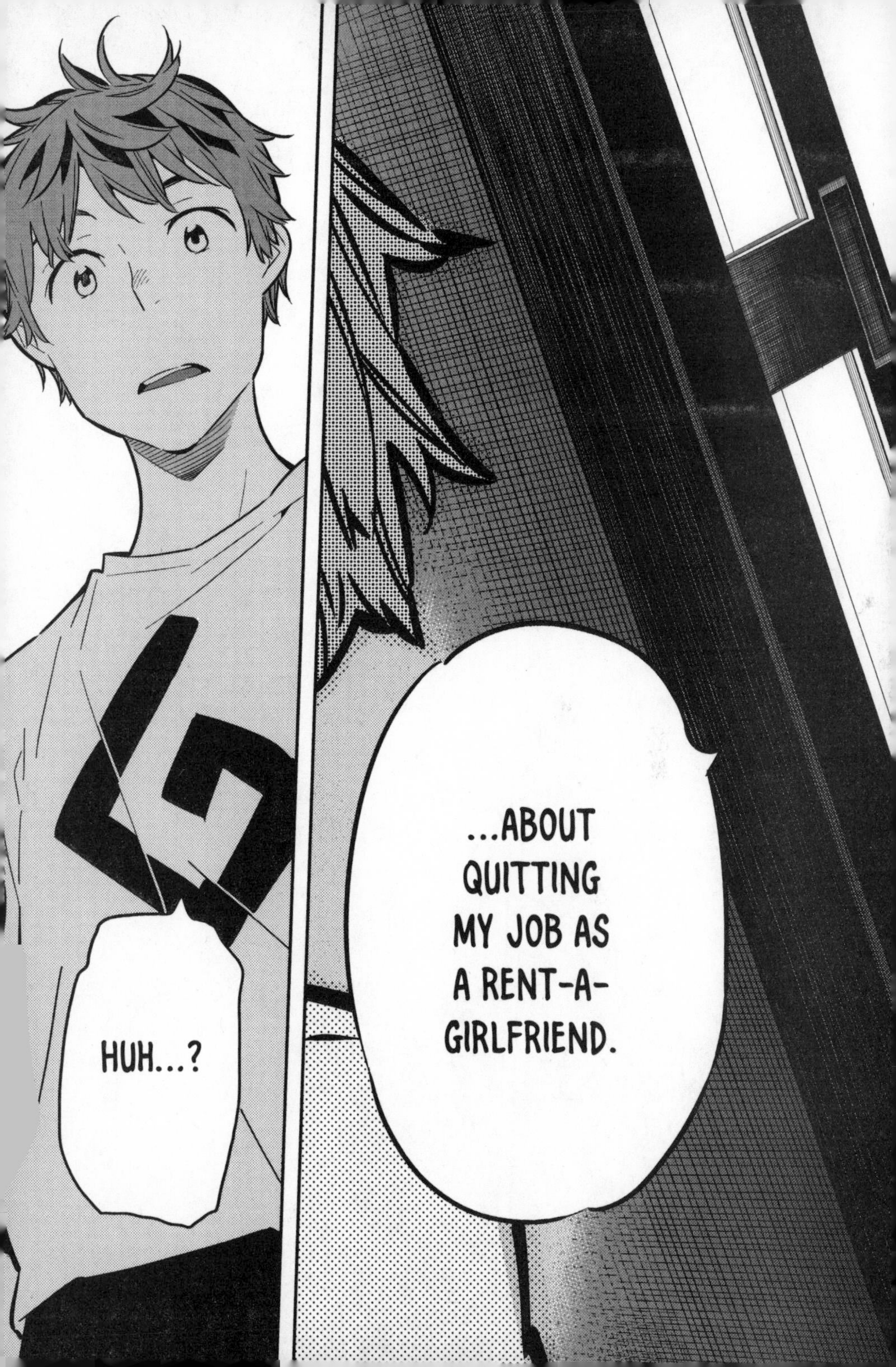
...ABOUT QUITTING MY JOB AS A RENT-A-GIRLFRIEND.
HUH...?

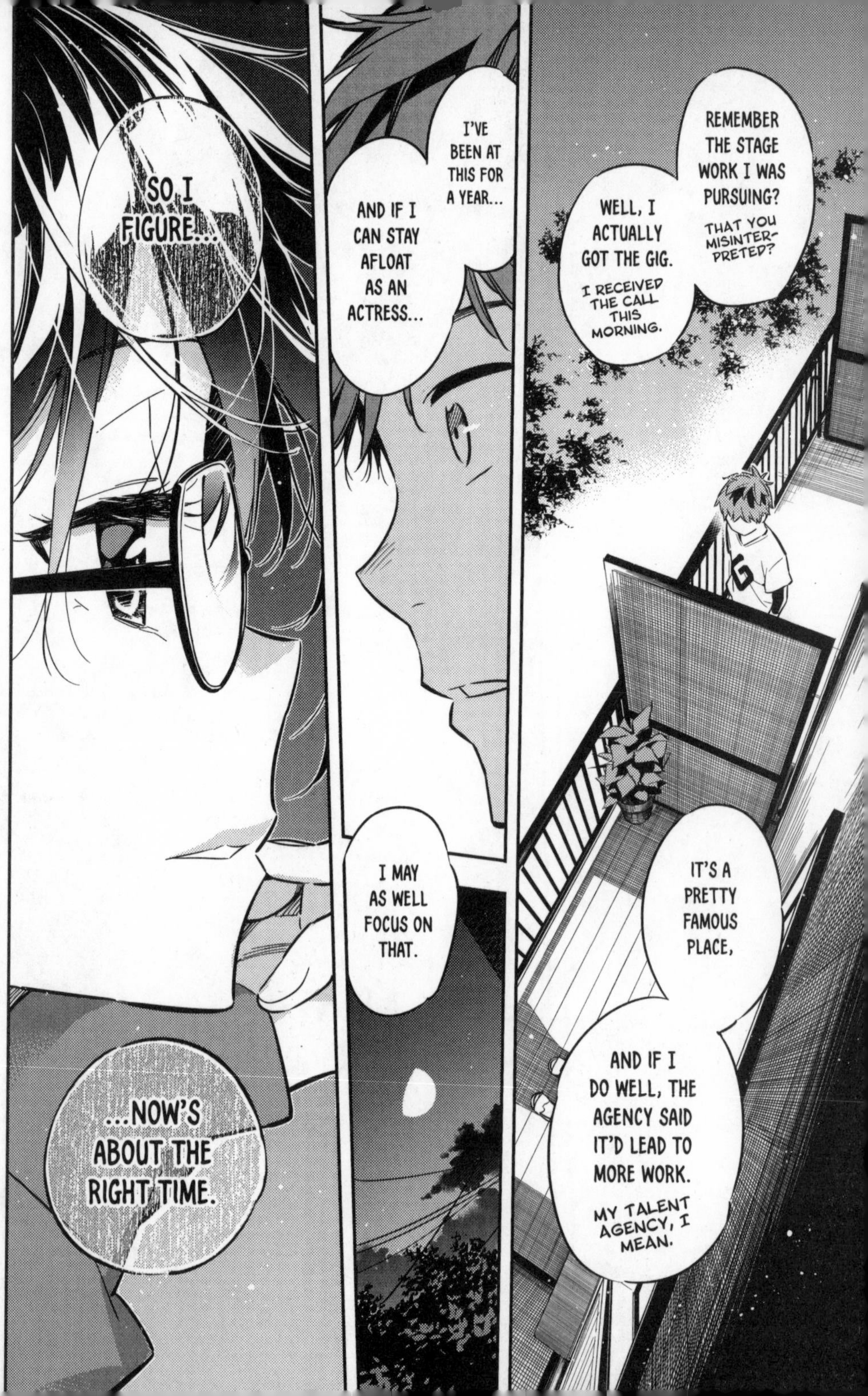
REMEMBER THE STAGE WORK I WAS PURSUING?
THAT YOU MISINTERPRETED?
WELL, I ACTUALLY GOT THE GIG.
I RECEIVED THE CALL THIS MORNING.
IT'S A PRETTY FAMOUS PLACE,
AND IF I DO WELL, THE AGENCY SAID IT'D LEAD TO MORE WORK.
MY TALENT AGENCY, I MEAN.
I'VE BEEN AT THIS FOR A YEAR...
AND IF I CAN STAY AFLOAT AS AN ACTRESS...
I MAY AS WELL FOCUS ON THAT.
SO I FIGURE...
...NOW'S ABOUT THE RIGHT TIME.

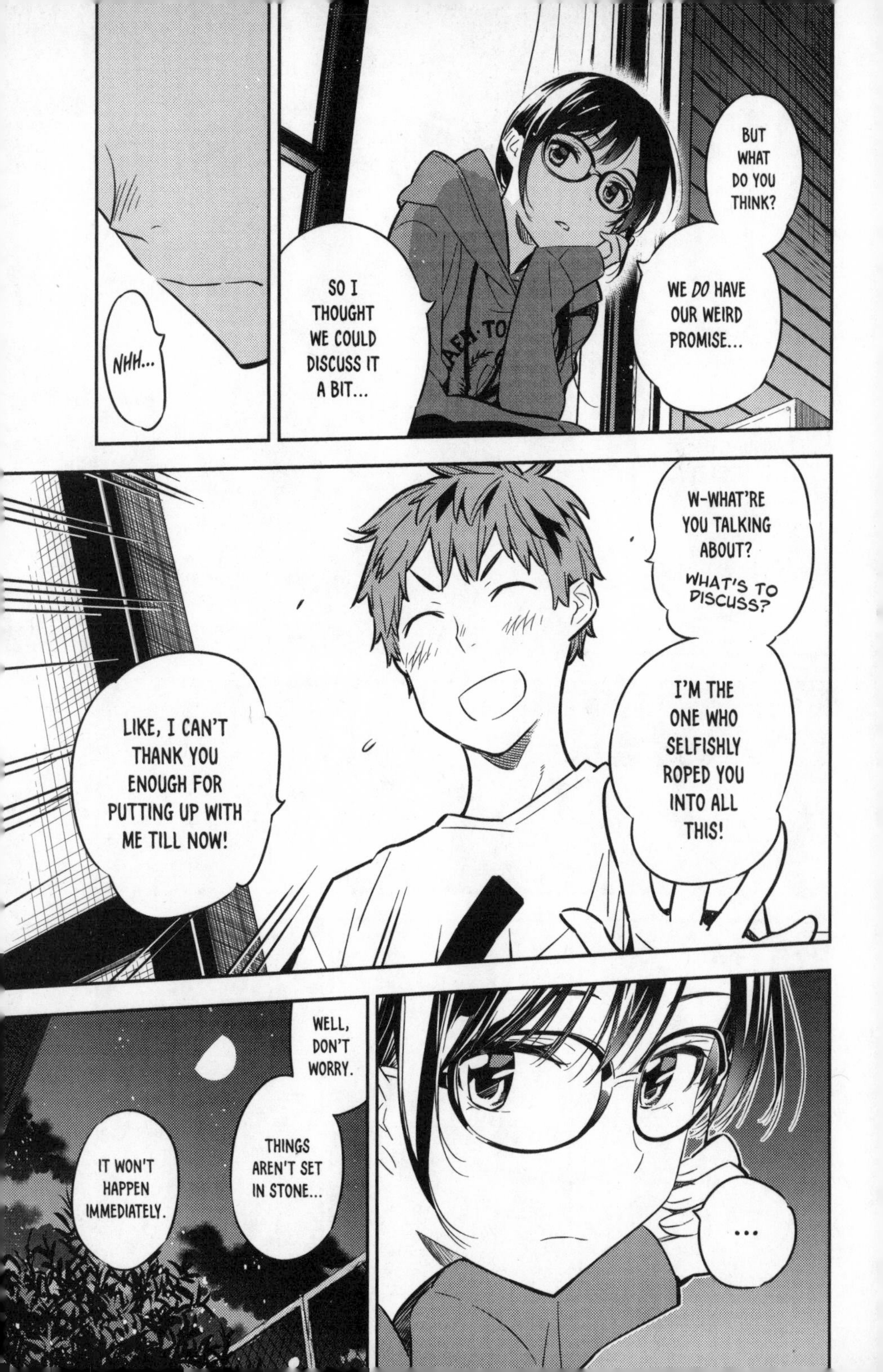
BUT WHAT DO YOU THINK?
WE *DO* HAVE OUR WEIRD PROMISE...
SO I THOUGHT WE COULD DISCUSS IT A BIT...
NHH...
W-WHAT'RE YOU TALKING ABOUT?
WHAT'S TO DISCUSS?
I'M THE ONE WHO SELFISHLY ROPED YOU INTO ALL THIS!
LIKE, I CAN'T THANK YOU ENOUGH FOR PUTTING UP WITH ME TILL NOW!
...
WELL, DON'T WORRY.
THINGS AREN'T SET IN STONE...
IT WON'T HAPPEN IMMEDIATELY.

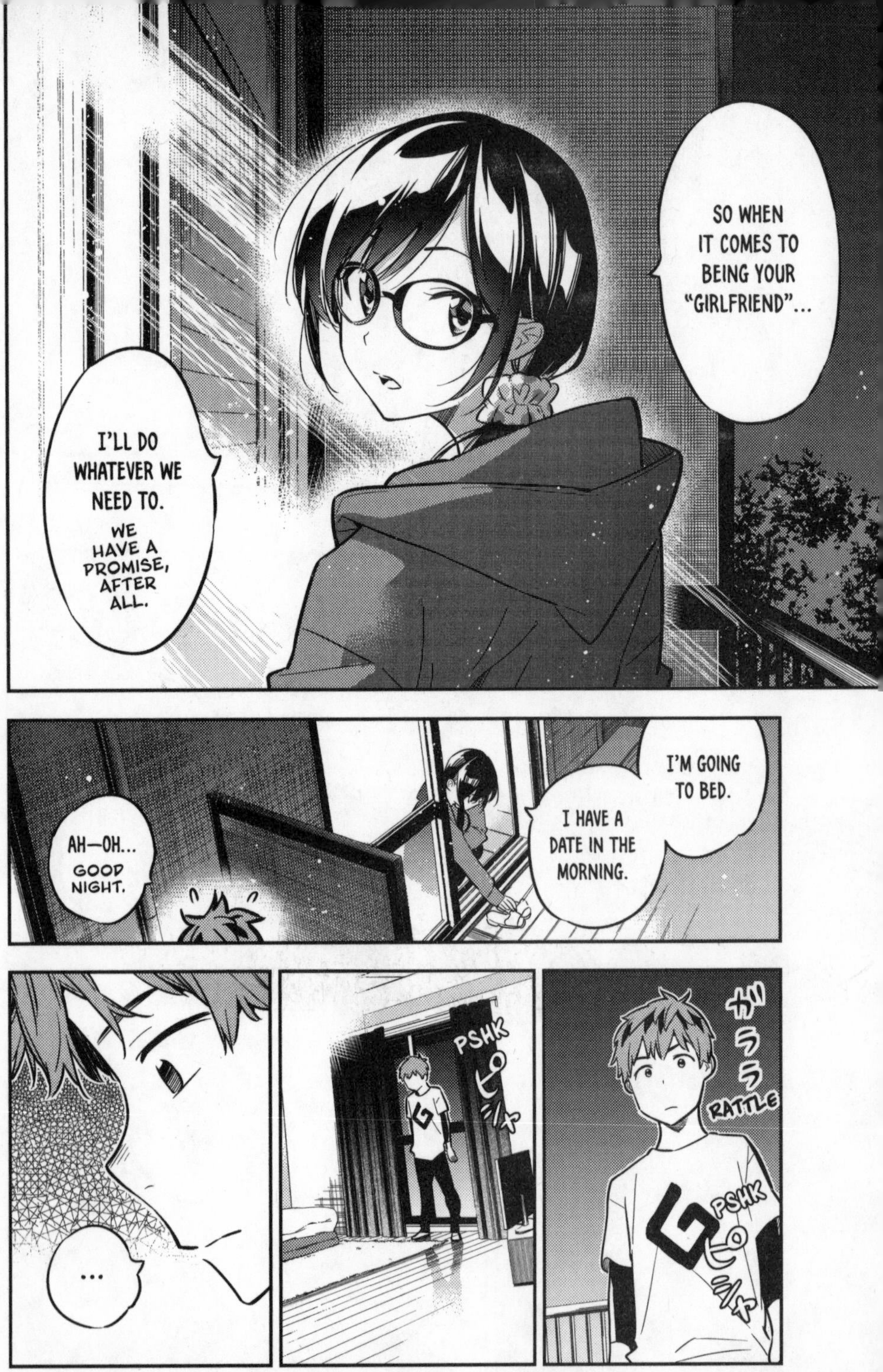
SO WHEN IT COMES TO BEING YOUR "GIRLFRIEND"...
I'LL DO WHATEVER WE NEED TO.
WE HAVE A PROMISE, AFTER ALL.
I'M GOING TO BED.
I HAVE A DATE IN THE MORNING.
AH—OH...
GOOD NIGHT.
がララ
RATTLE
PSHK
ピシャ
PSHK
ピシャ
...

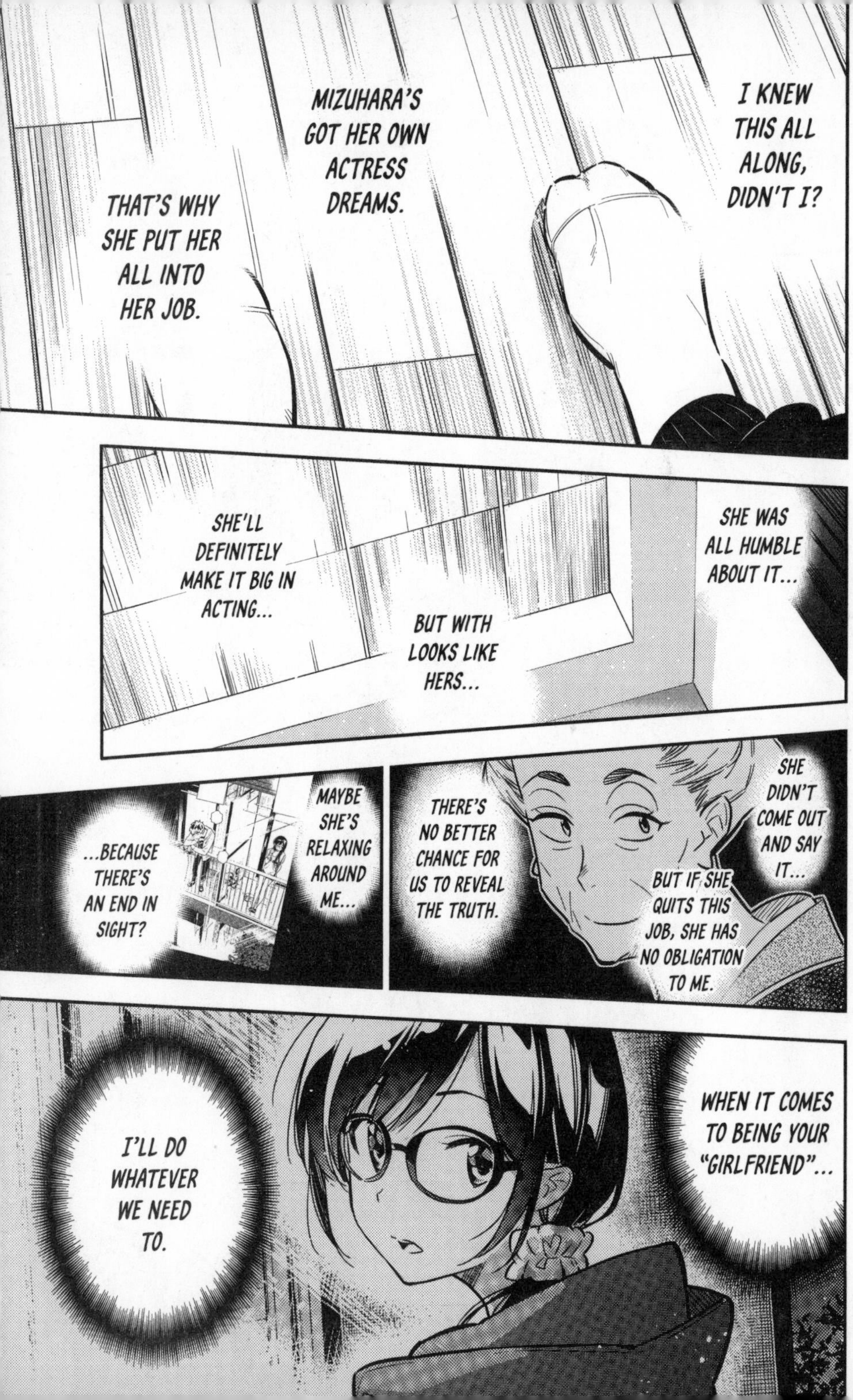
I KNEW THIS ALL ALONG, DIDN'T I?
MIZUHARA'S GOT HER OWN ACTRESS DREAMS.
THAT'S WHY SHE PUT HER ALL INTO HER JOB.
SHE WAS ALL HUMBLE ABOUT IT...
BUT WITH LOOKS LIKE HERS...
SHE'LL DEFINITELY MAKE IT BIG IN ACTING...
SHE DIDN'T COME OUT AND SAY IT...
BUT IF SHE QUITS THIS JOB, SHE HAS NO OBLIGATION TO ME.
THERE'S NO BETTER CHANCE FOR US TO REVEAL THE TRUTH.
MAYBE SHE'S RELAXING AROUND ME...
...BECAUSE THERE'S AN END IN SIGHT?
WHEN IT COMES TO BEING YOUR "GIRLFRIEND"...
I'LL DO WHATEVER WE NEED TO.

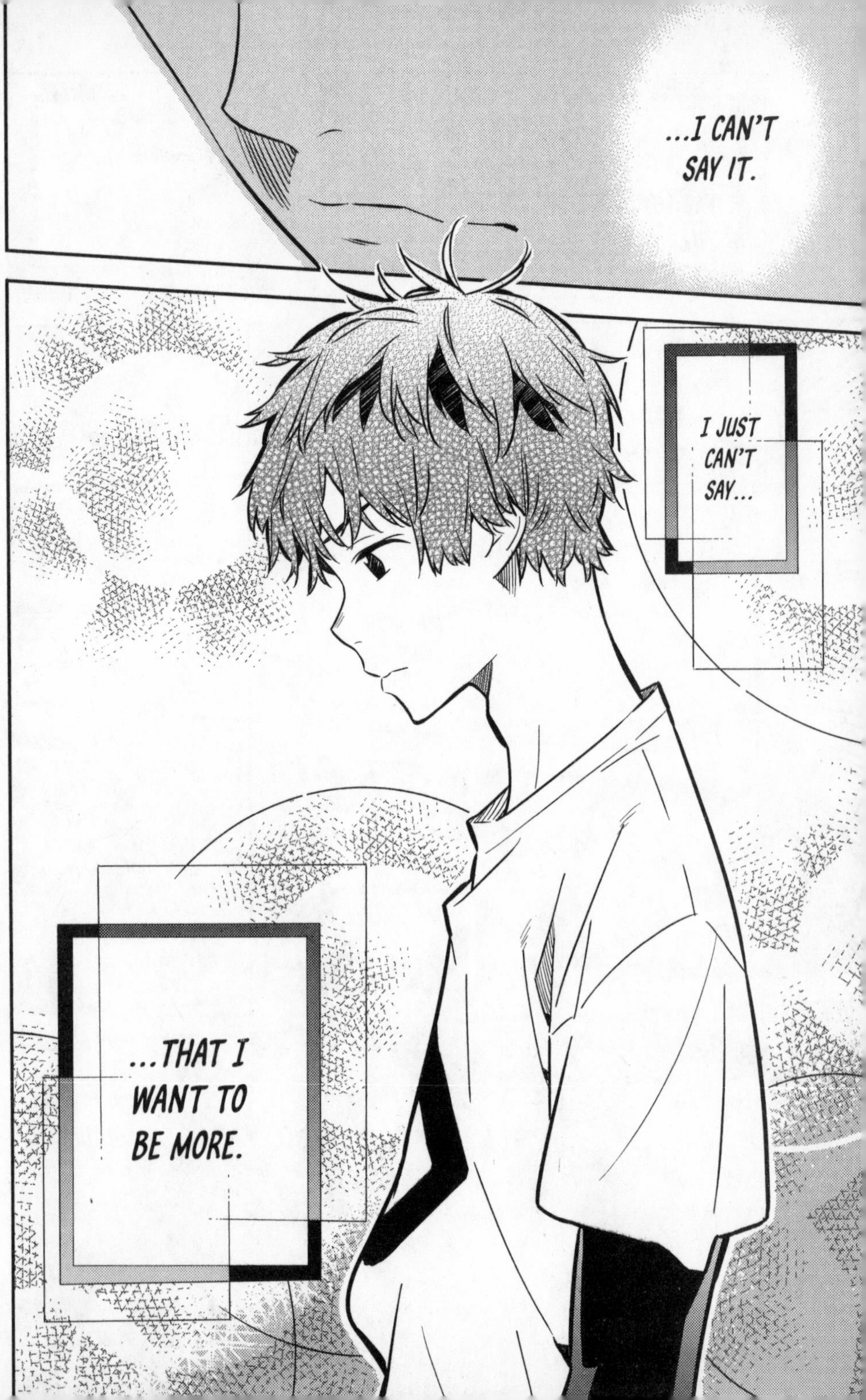
...I CAN'T SAY IT.
I JUST CAN'T SAY...
...THAT I WANT TO BE MORE.

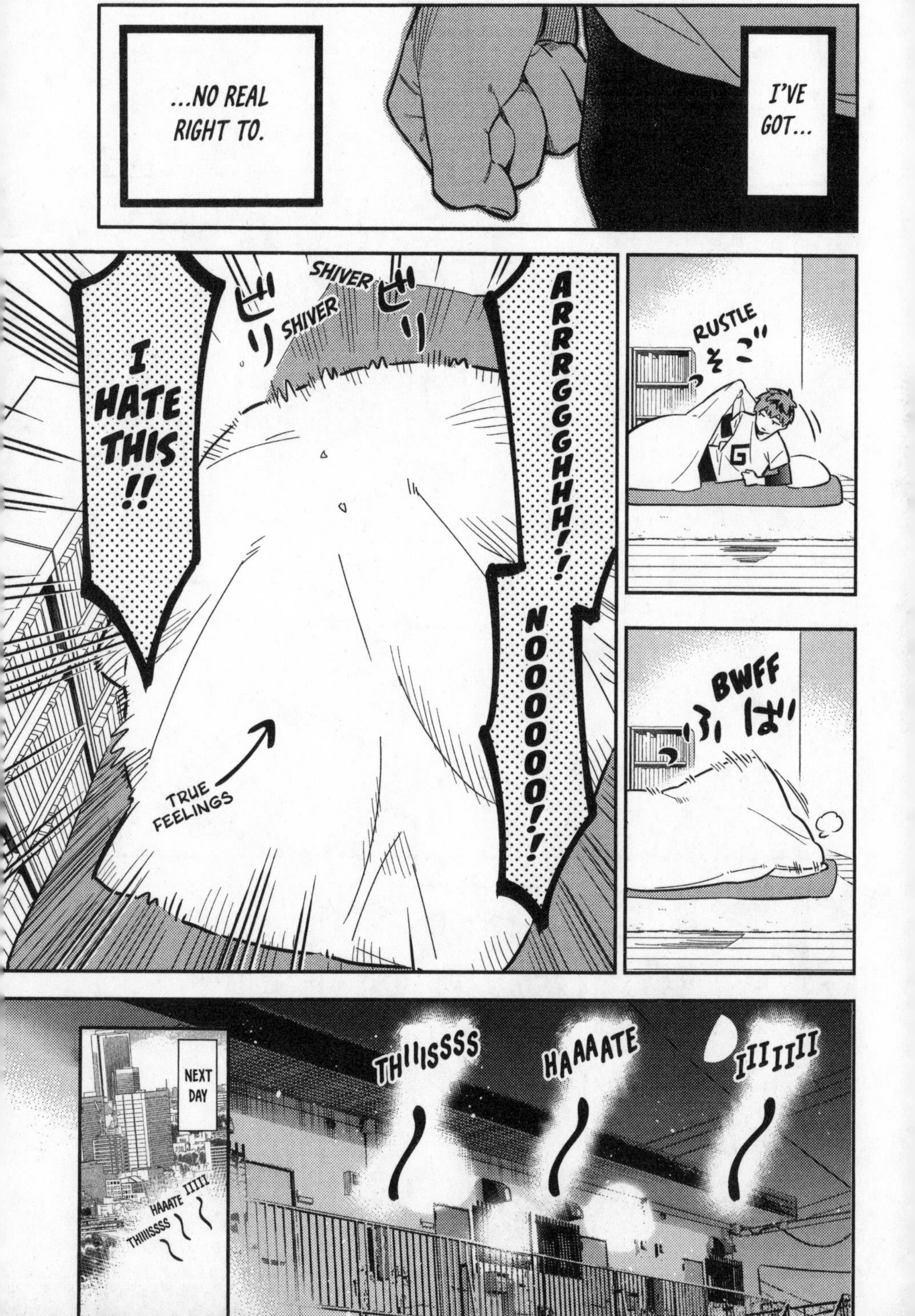
I'VE GOT...
...NO REAL RIGHT TO.
RUSTLE
BWFF
ARRRGGGHHH!!
NOOOOOOO!!
SHIVER
SHIVER
I HATE THIS!!
TRUE FEELINGS
IIIIII
HAAAATE
THIIISSSS
NEXT DAY
IIIII
HAAATE
THIIISSSS

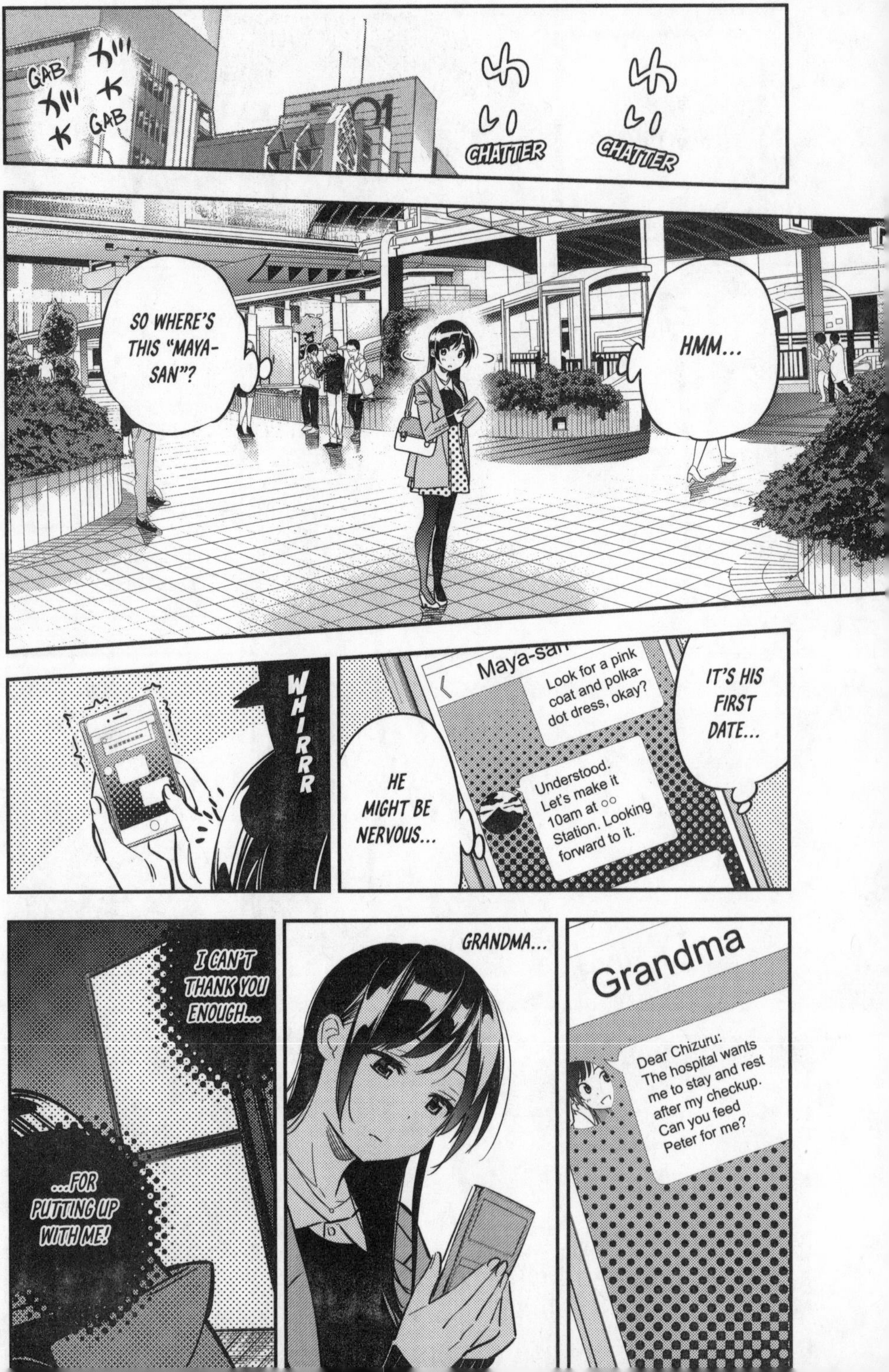
CHATTER
CHATTER
GAB
GAB
HMM...
SO WHERE'S THIS "MAYA-SAN"?
IT'S HIS FIRST DATE...
Maya-san
Look for a pink coat and polka-dot dress, okay?
Understood. Let's make it 10am at ○○ Station. Looking forward to it.
HE MIGHT BE NERVOUS...
WHIRRR
Grandma
Dear Chizuru: The hospital wants me to stay and rest after my checkup. Can you feed Peter for me?
GRANDMA...
I CAN'T THANK YOU ENOUGH...
...FOR PUTTING UP WITH ME!

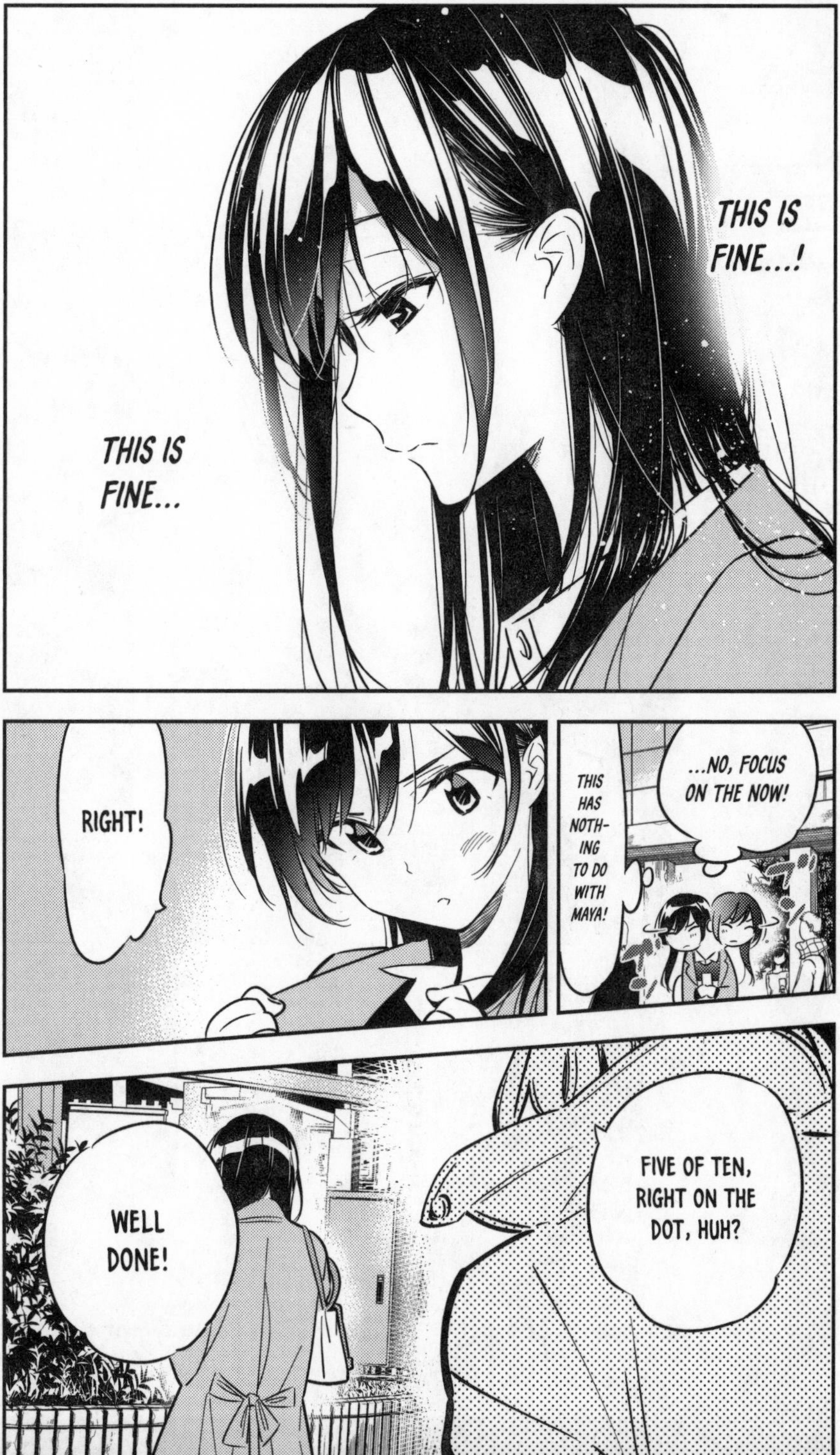
THIS IS FINE...!
THIS IS FINE...
...NO, FOCUS ON THE NOW!
THIS HAS NOTHING TO DO WITH MAYA!
RIGHT!
FIVE OF TEN, RIGHT ON THE DOT, HUH?
WELL DONE!

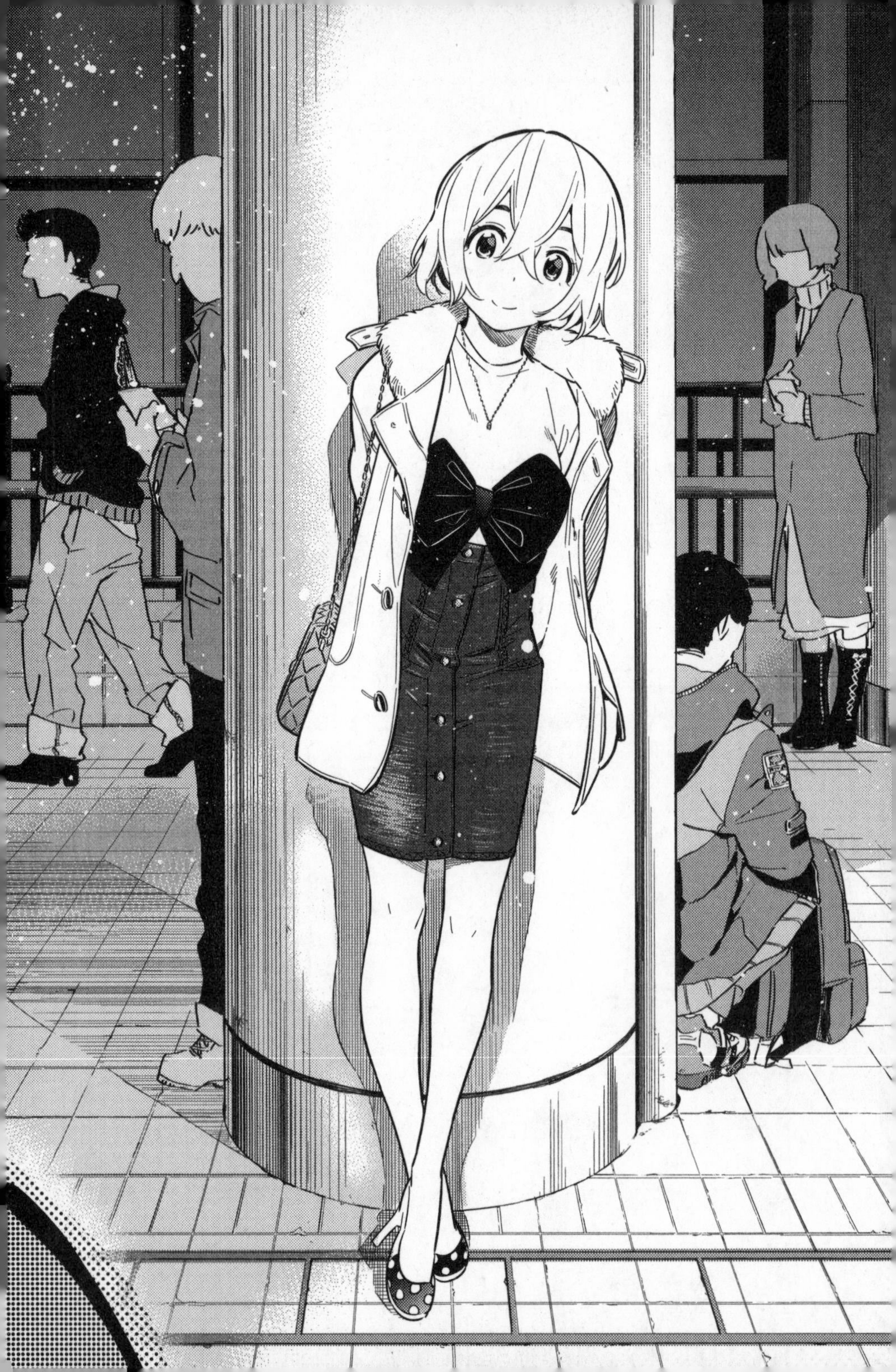

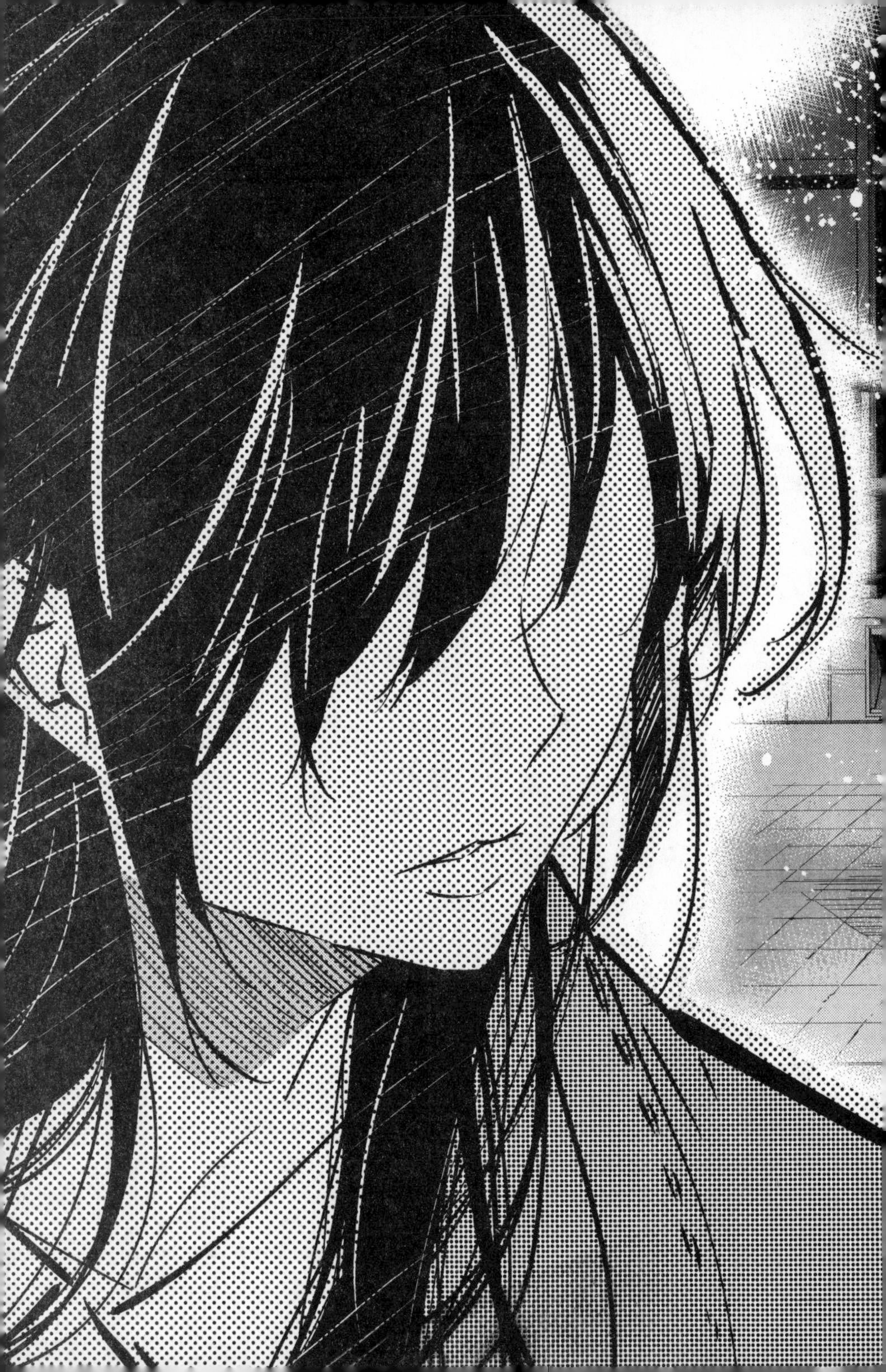

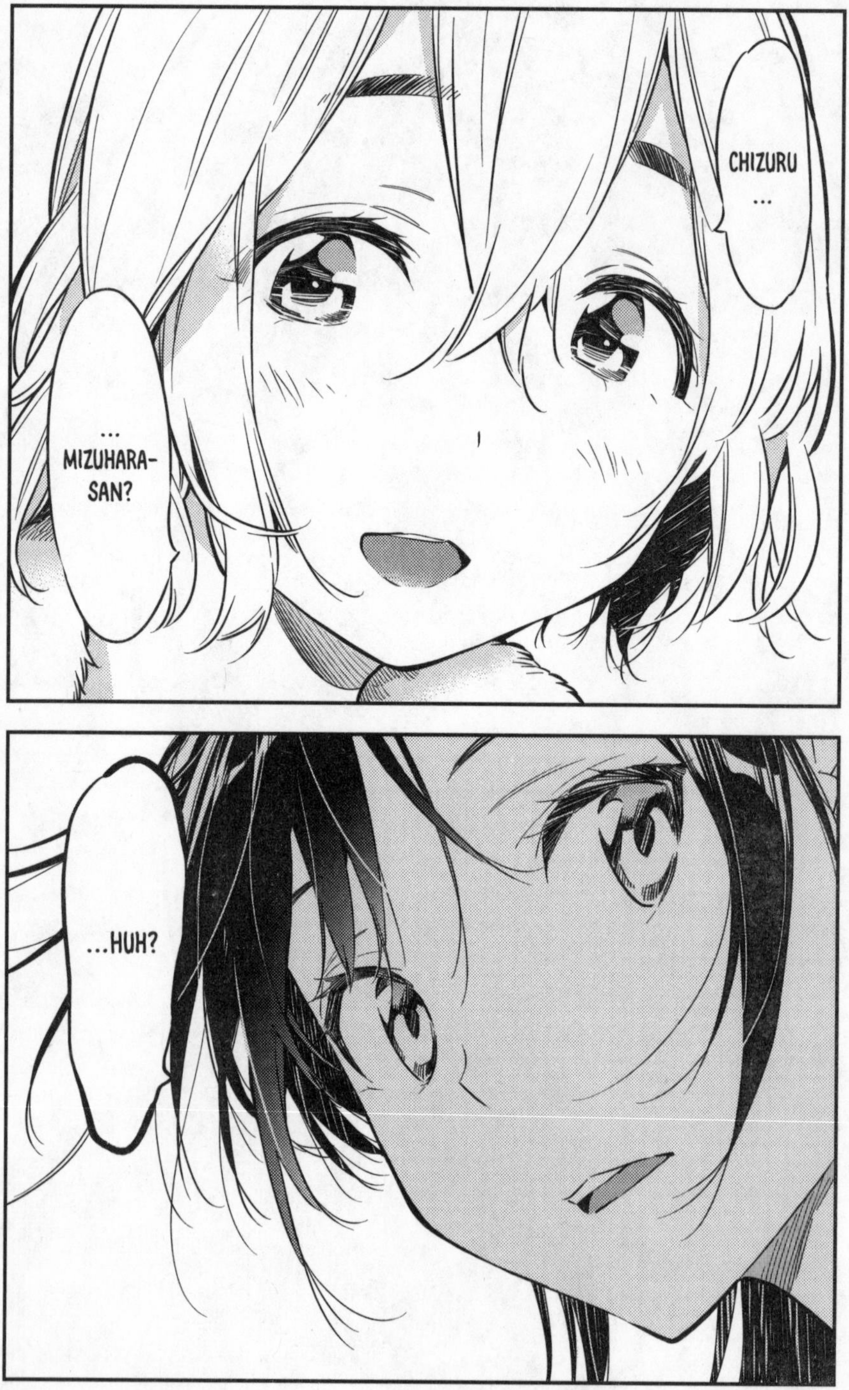
CHIZURU ...
... MIZUHARA-SAN?
...HUH?

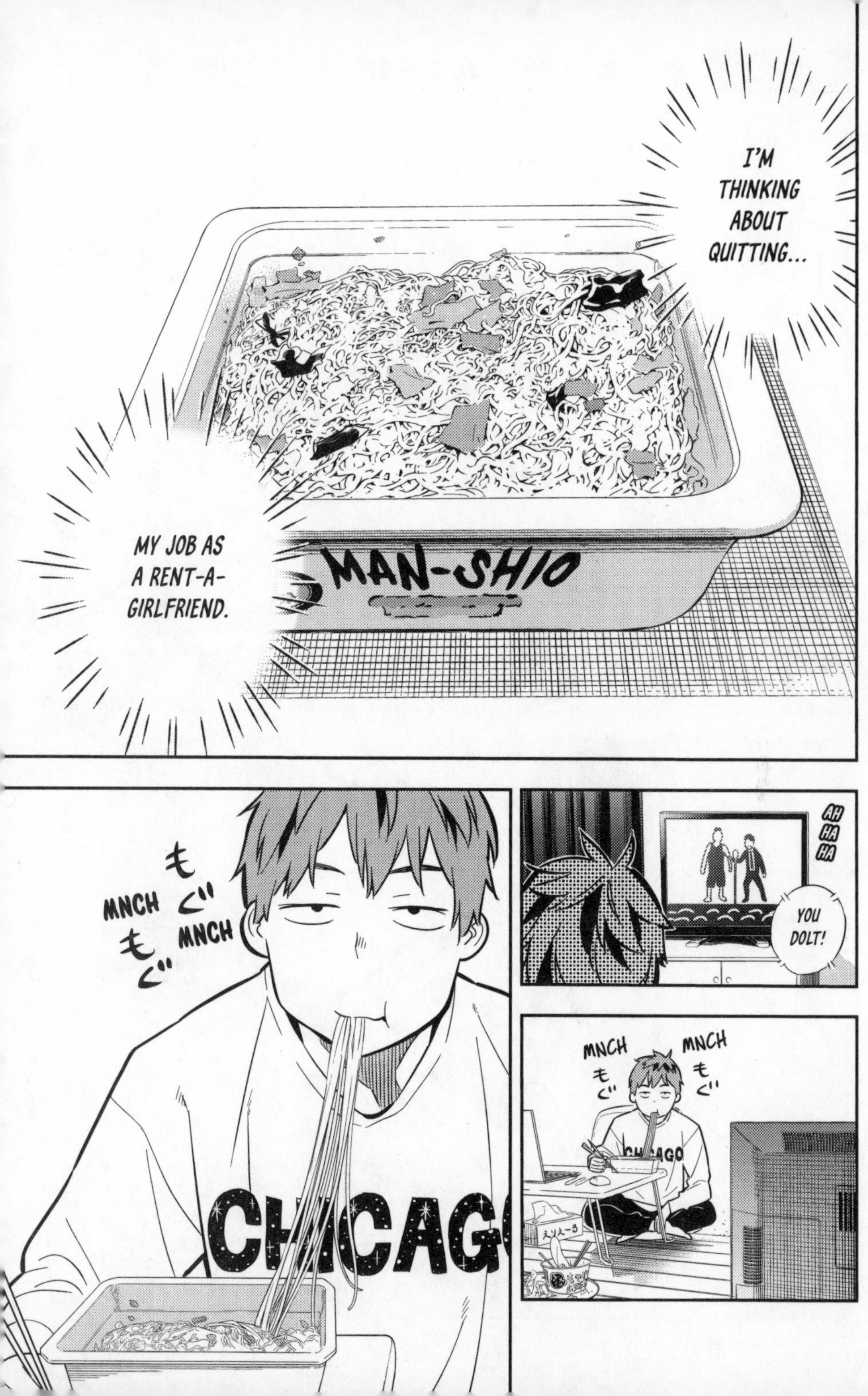
I'M THINKING ABOUT QUITTING...
MY JOB AS A RENT-A-GIRLFRIEND.
MAN-SHIO
AH HA HA
YOU DOLT!
MNCH もぐ
MNCH もぐ
MNCH もぐ
MNCH もぐ

RATING 46 MY GIRLFRIEND AND THE BREAK-OFF POINT (2)

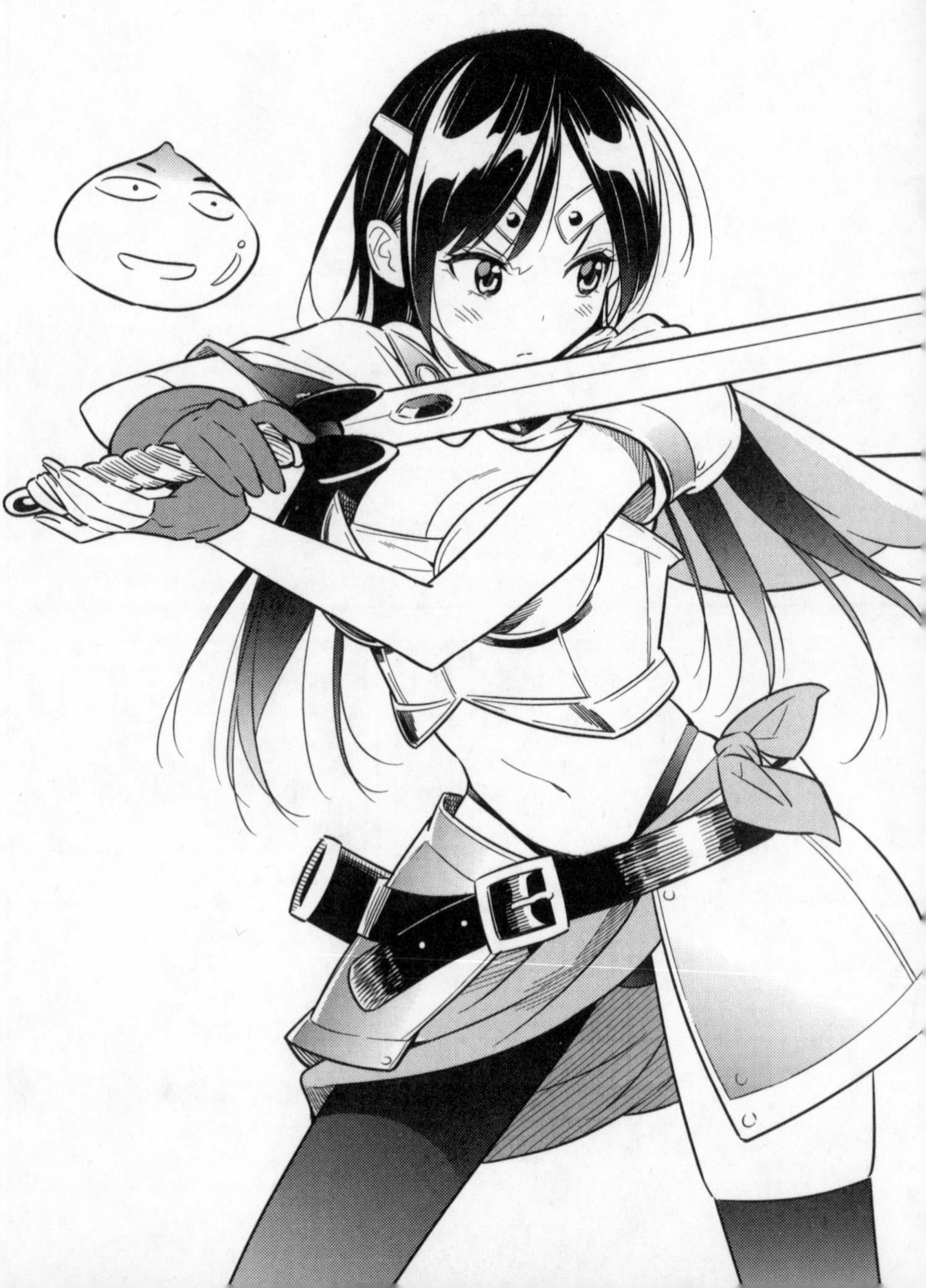

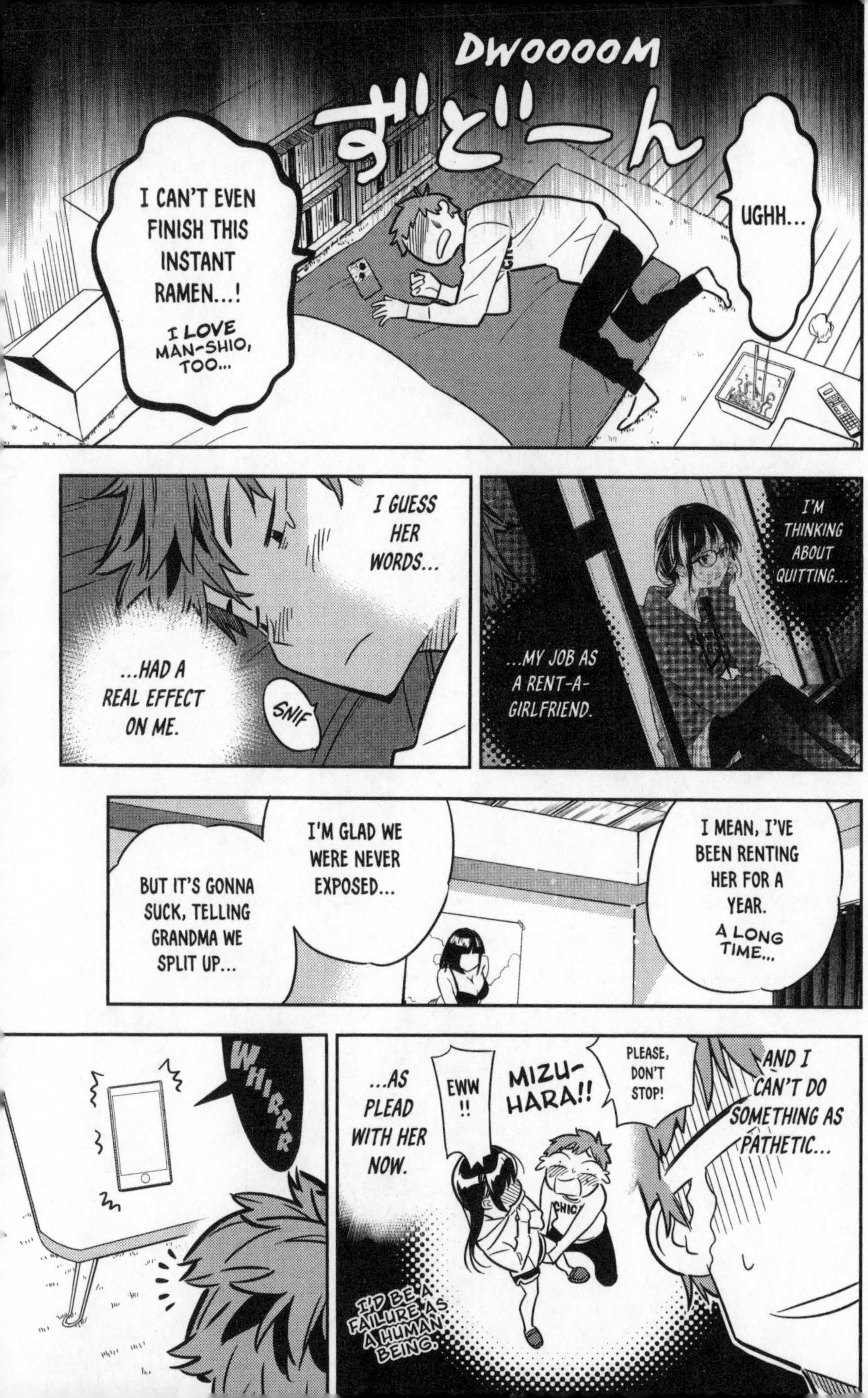
DWOOOOM
ずどーん
UGHH...
I CAN'T EVEN FINISH THIS INSTANT RAMEN...!
I LOVE MAN-SHIO, TOO...
I'M THINKING ABOUT QUITTING...
...MY JOB AS A RENT-A-GIRLFRIEND.
I GUESS HER WORDS...
...HAD A REAL EFFECT ON ME.
SNIF
I MEAN, I'VE BEEN RENTING HER FOR A YEAR.
A LONG TIME...
I'M GLAD WE WERE NEVER EXPOSED...
BUT IT'S GONNA SUCK, TELLING GRANDMA WE SPLIT UP...
AND I CAN'T DO SOMETHING AS PATHETIC...
PLEASE, DON'T STOP!
MIZU-HARA!!
EWW!!
...AS PLEAD WITH HER NOW.
I'D BE A FAILURE AS A HUMAN BEING.
WHIRRR

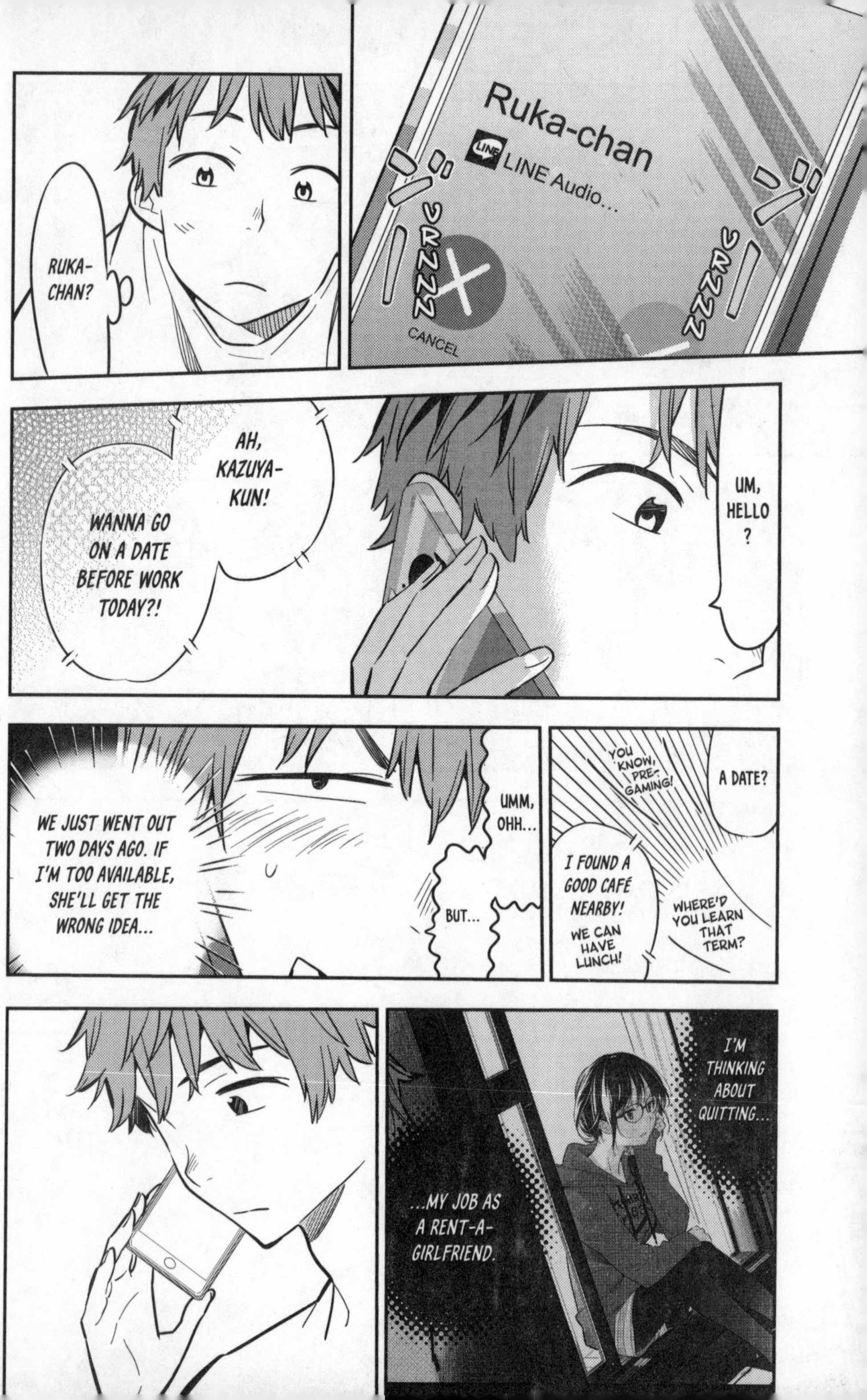

Ruka-chan
LINE Audio...
VRZZZZZ
VRZZZZ
CANCEL
RUKA-CHAN?
UM, HELLO?
AH, KAZUYA-KUN!
WANNA GO ON A DATE BEFORE WORK TODAY?!
A DATE?
YOU KNOW, PRE-GAMING!
WHERE'D YOU LEARN THAT TERM?
I FOUND A GOOD CAFÉ NEARBY!
WE CAN HAVE LUNCH!
UMM, OHH...
BUT...
WE JUST WENT OUT TWO DAYS AGO. IF I'M TOO AVAILABLE, SHE'LL GET THE WRONG IDEA...
I'M THINKING ABOUT QUITTING...
...MY JOB AS A RENT-A-GIRLFRIEND.

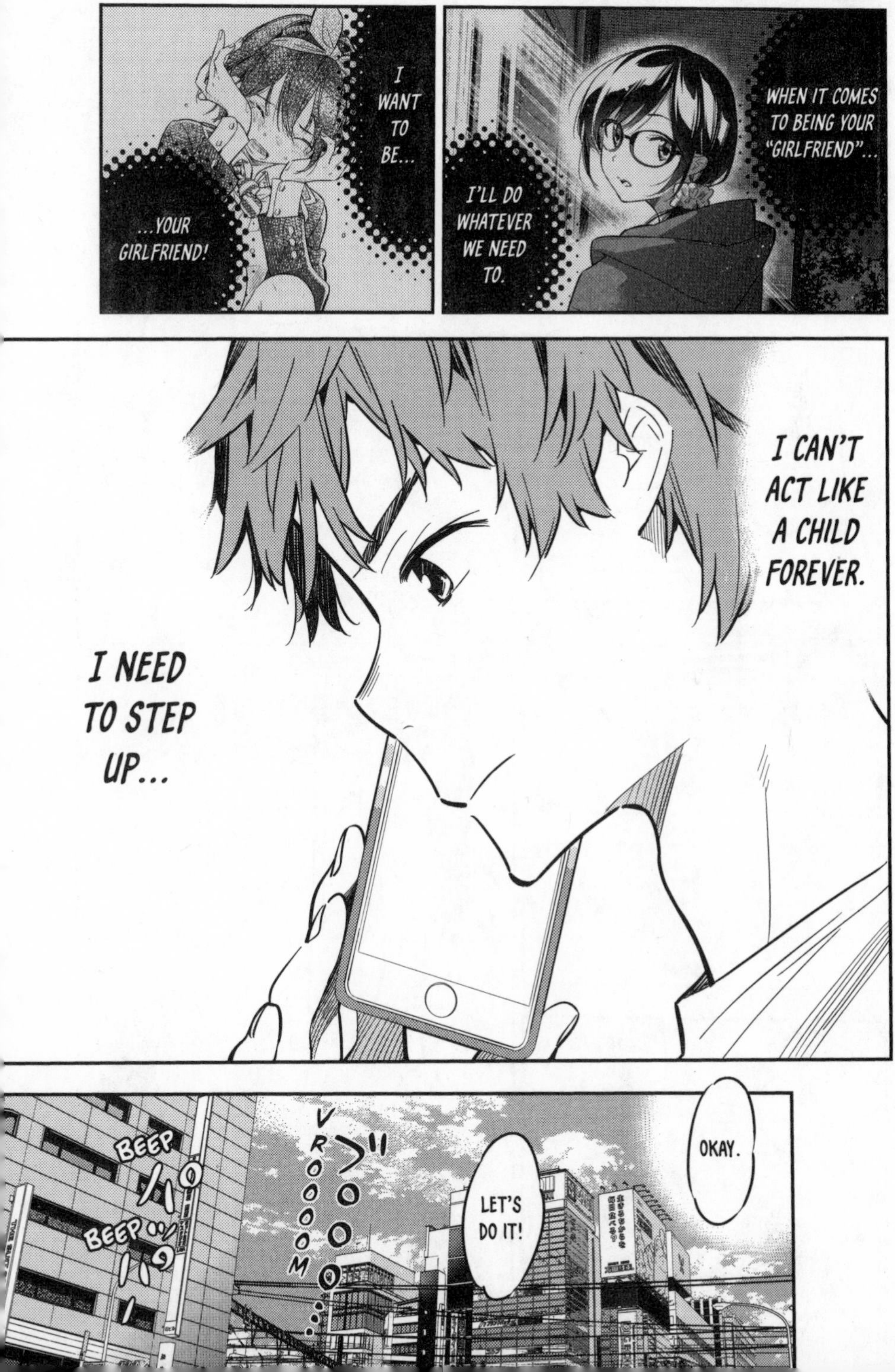
WHEN IT COMES TO BEING YOUR "GIRLFRIEND"...
I'LL DO WHATEVER WE NEED TO.
I WANT TO BE...
...YOUR GIRLFRIEND!
I CAN'T ACT LIKE A CHILD FOREVER.
I NEED TO STEP UP...
OKAY.
LET'S DO IT!
VROOOOOOM
BEEP
BEEP

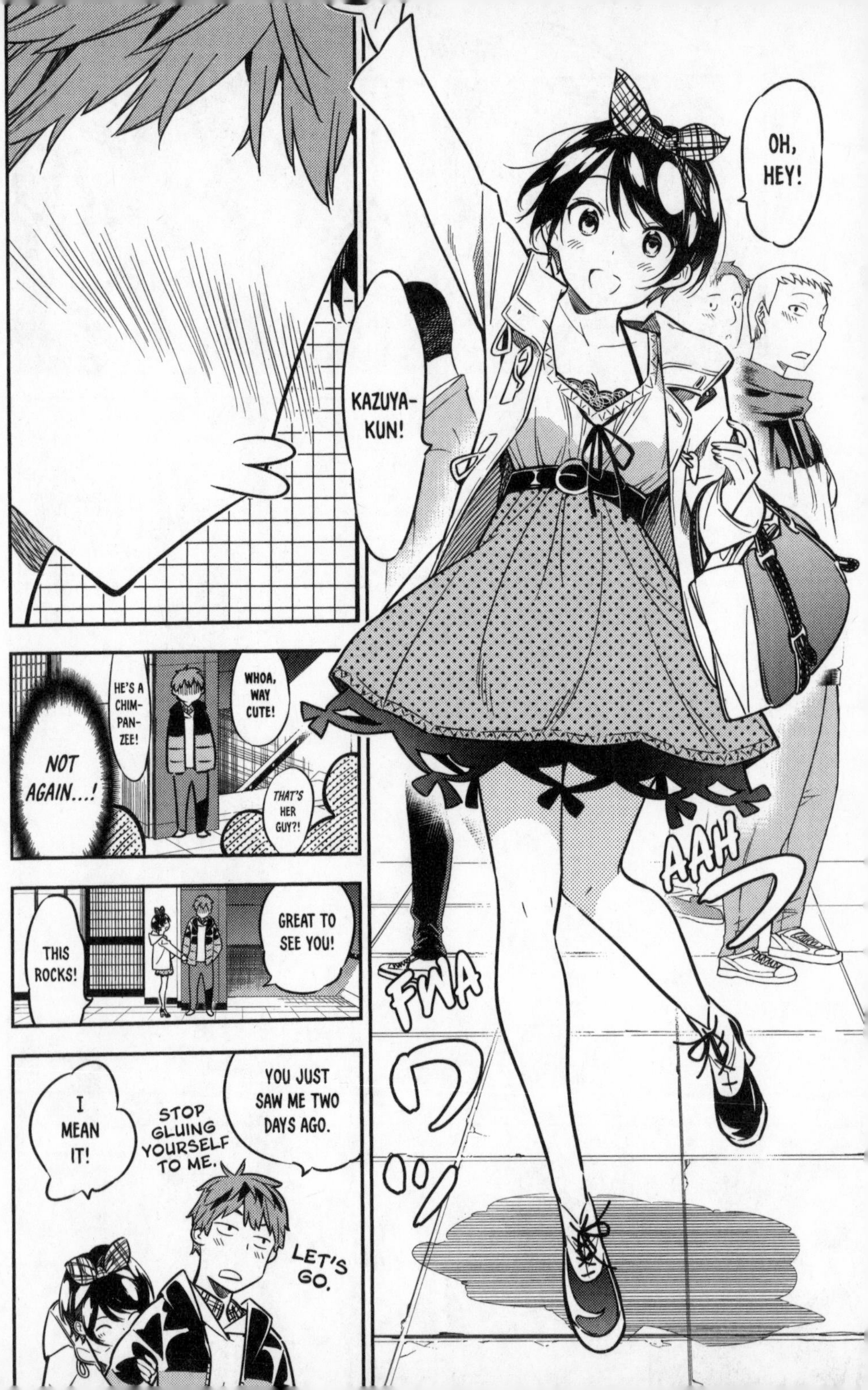
OH, HEY!
KAZUYA-KUN!
AAH
FWA
WHOA, WAY CUTE!
HE'S A CHIMPANZEE!
THAT'S HER GUY?!
NOT AGAIN...!
GREAT TO SEE YOU!
THIS ROCKS!
YOU JUST SAW ME TWO DAYS AGO.
STOP GLUING YOURSELF TO ME.
I MEAN IT!
LET'S GO.

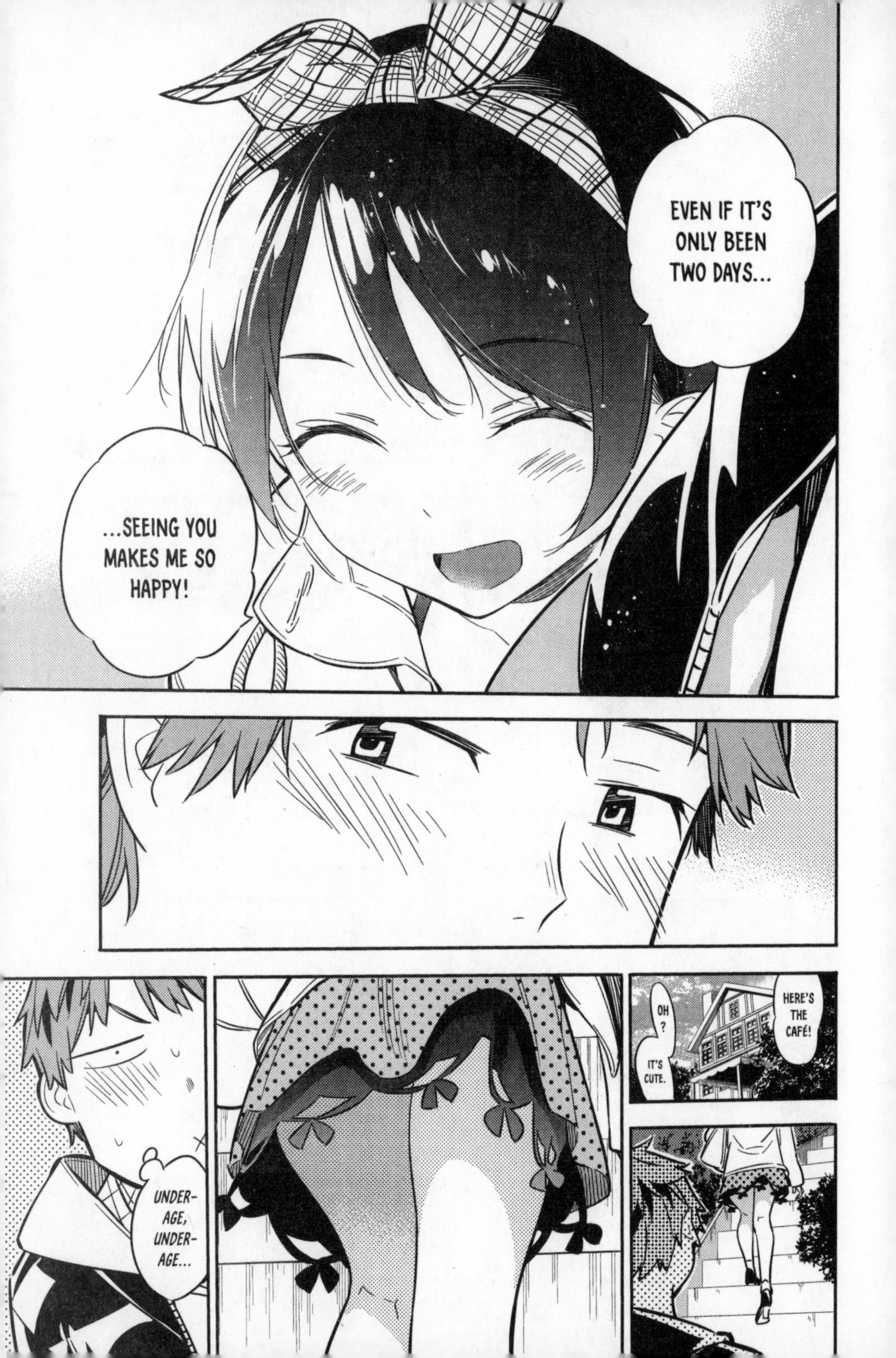
EVEN IF IT'S ONLY BEEN TWO DAYS...
...SEEING YOU MAKES ME SO HAPPY!
HERE'S THE CAFÉ!
OH? IT'S CUTE.
UNDER-AGE, UNDER-AGE...

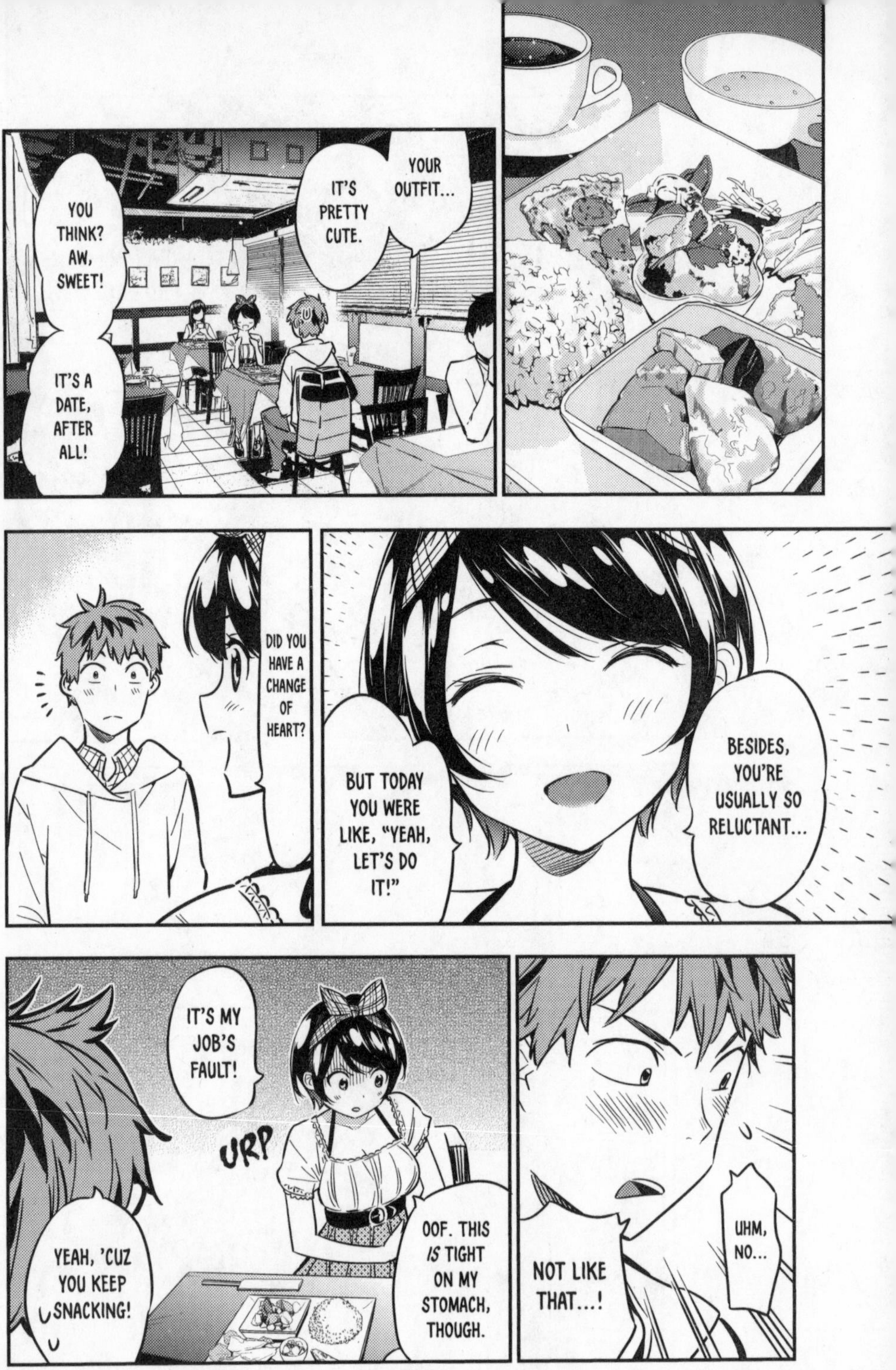
YOUR OUTFIT...
IT'S PRETTY CUTE.
YOU THINK? AW, SWEET!
IT'S A DATE, AFTER ALL!
BESIDES, YOU'RE USUALLY SO RELUCTANT...
BUT TODAY YOU WERE LIKE, "YEAH, LET'S DO IT!"
DID YOU HAVE A CHANGE OF HEART?
UHM, NO...
NOT LIKE THAT...!
IT'S MY JOB'S FAULT!
URP
OOF. THIS *IS* TIGHT ON MY STOMACH, THOUGH.
YEAH, 'CUZ YOU KEEP SNACKING!

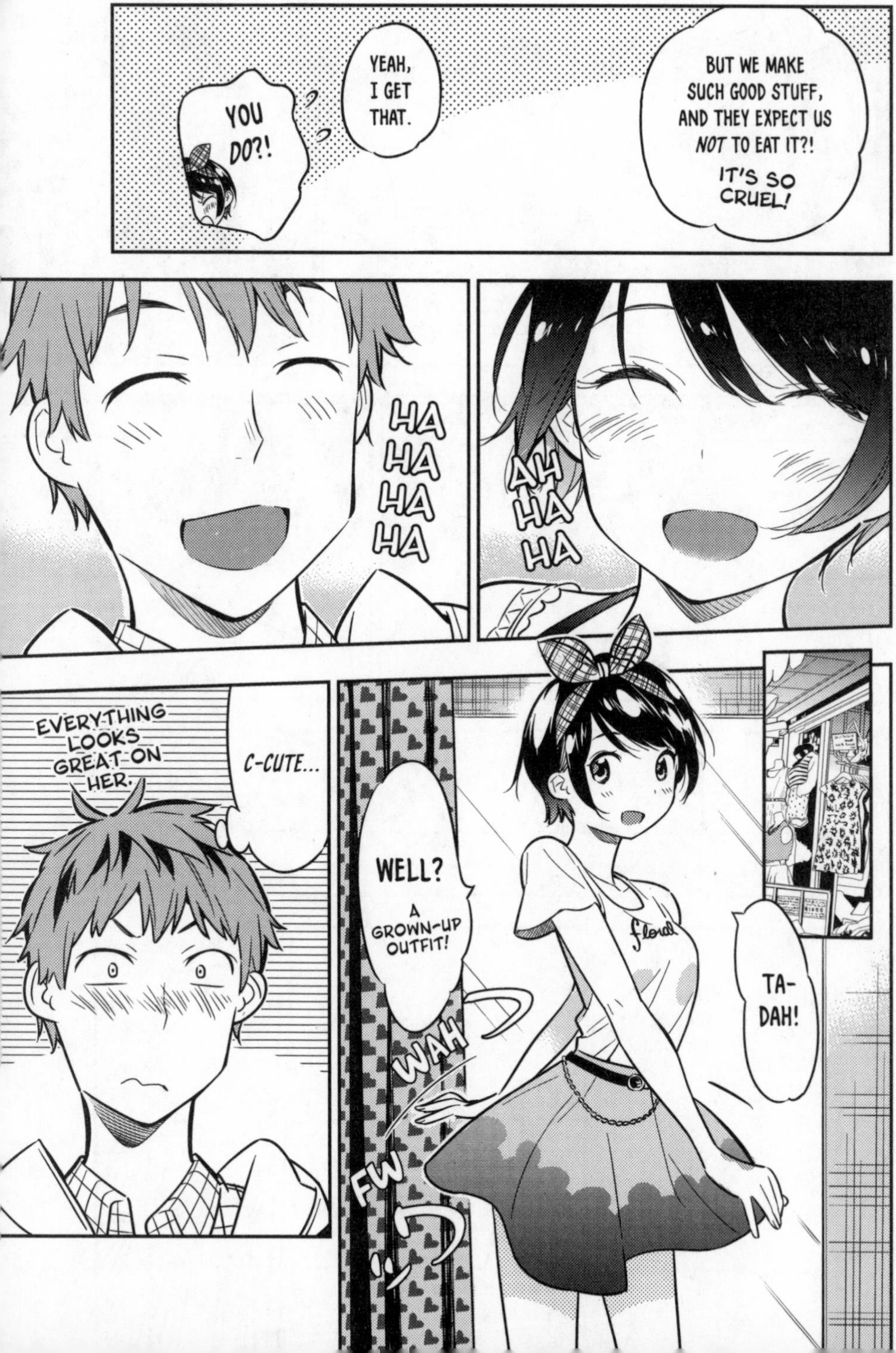
BUT WE MAKE SUCH GOOD STUFF, AND THEY EXPECT US *NOT* TO EAT IT?!
IT'S SO CRUEL!
YEAH, I GET THAT.
YOU DO?!
AH HA HA HA
HA HA HA HA
TA-DAH!
WELL?
A GROWN-UP OUTFIT!
floral
WAH
FW
C-CUTE...
EVERYTHING LOOKS GREAT ON HER.

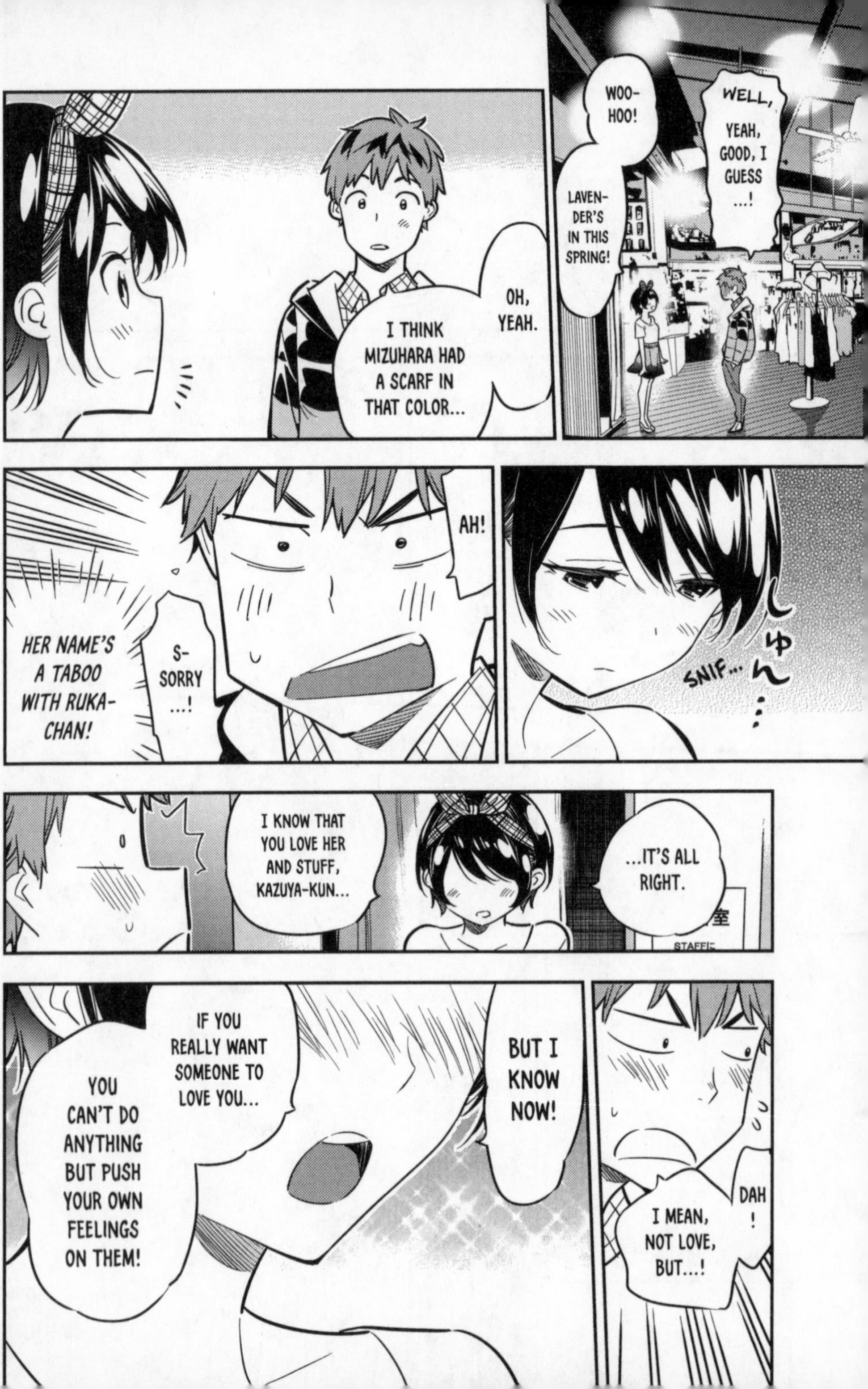
WELL, YEAH, GOOD, I GUESS ...!
WOO-HOO!
LAVENDER'S IN THIS SPRING!
OH, YEAH.
I THINK MIZUHARA HAD A SCARF IN THAT COLOR...
しゅん…
SNIF...
AH!
S-SORRY ...!
HER NAME'S A TABOO WITH RUKA-CHAN!
...IT'S ALL RIGHT.
I KNOW THAT YOU LOVE HER AND STUFF, KAZUYA-KUN...
DAH!
I MEAN, NOT LOVE, BUT...!
BUT I KNOW NOW!
IF YOU REALLY WANT SOMEONE TO LOVE YOU...
YOU CAN'T DO ANYTHING BUT PUSH YOUR OWN FEELINGS ON THEM!

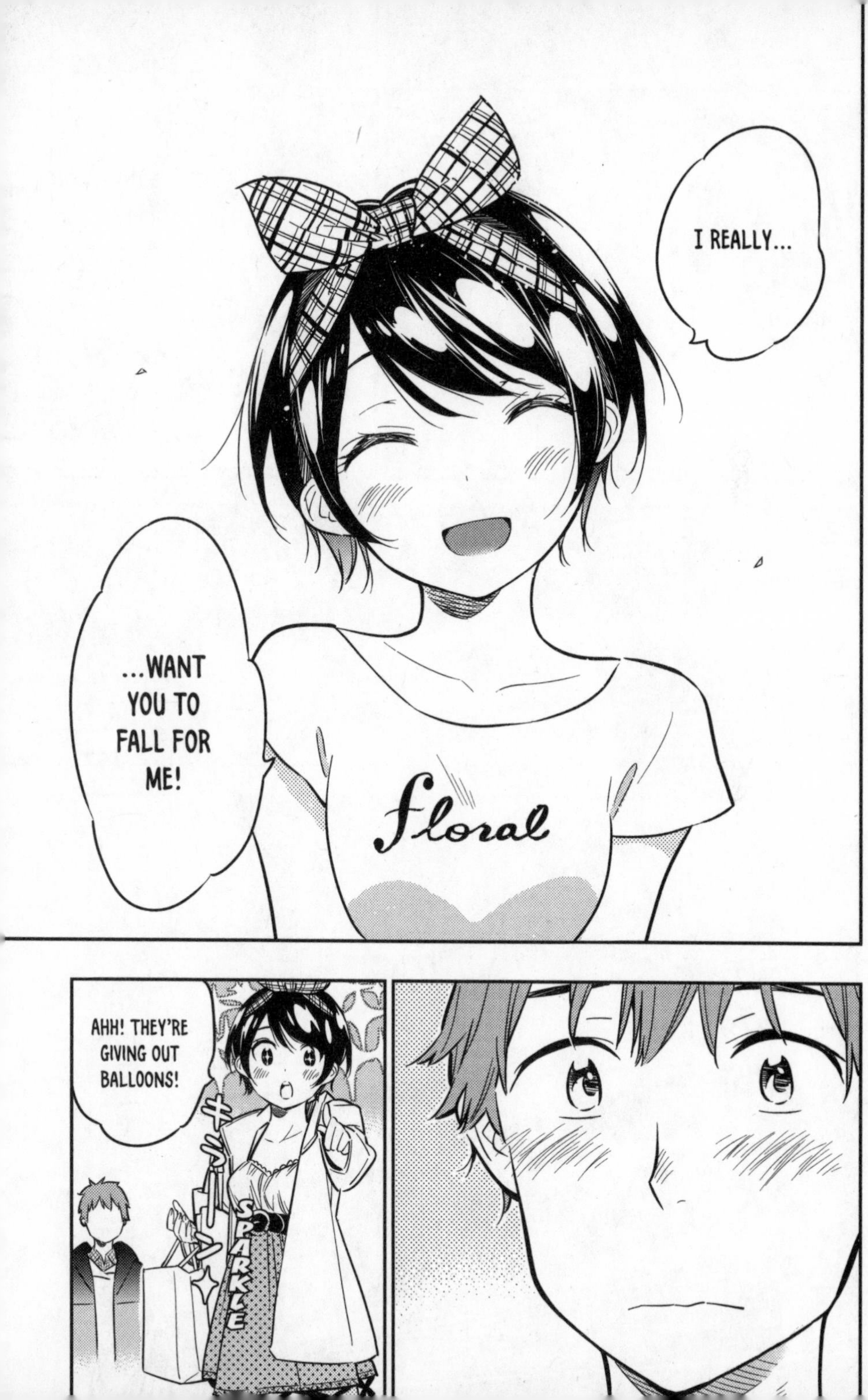
I REALLY...
...WANT YOU TO FALL FOR ME!
AHH! THEY'RE GIVING OUT BALLOONS!
キラ
SPARKLE

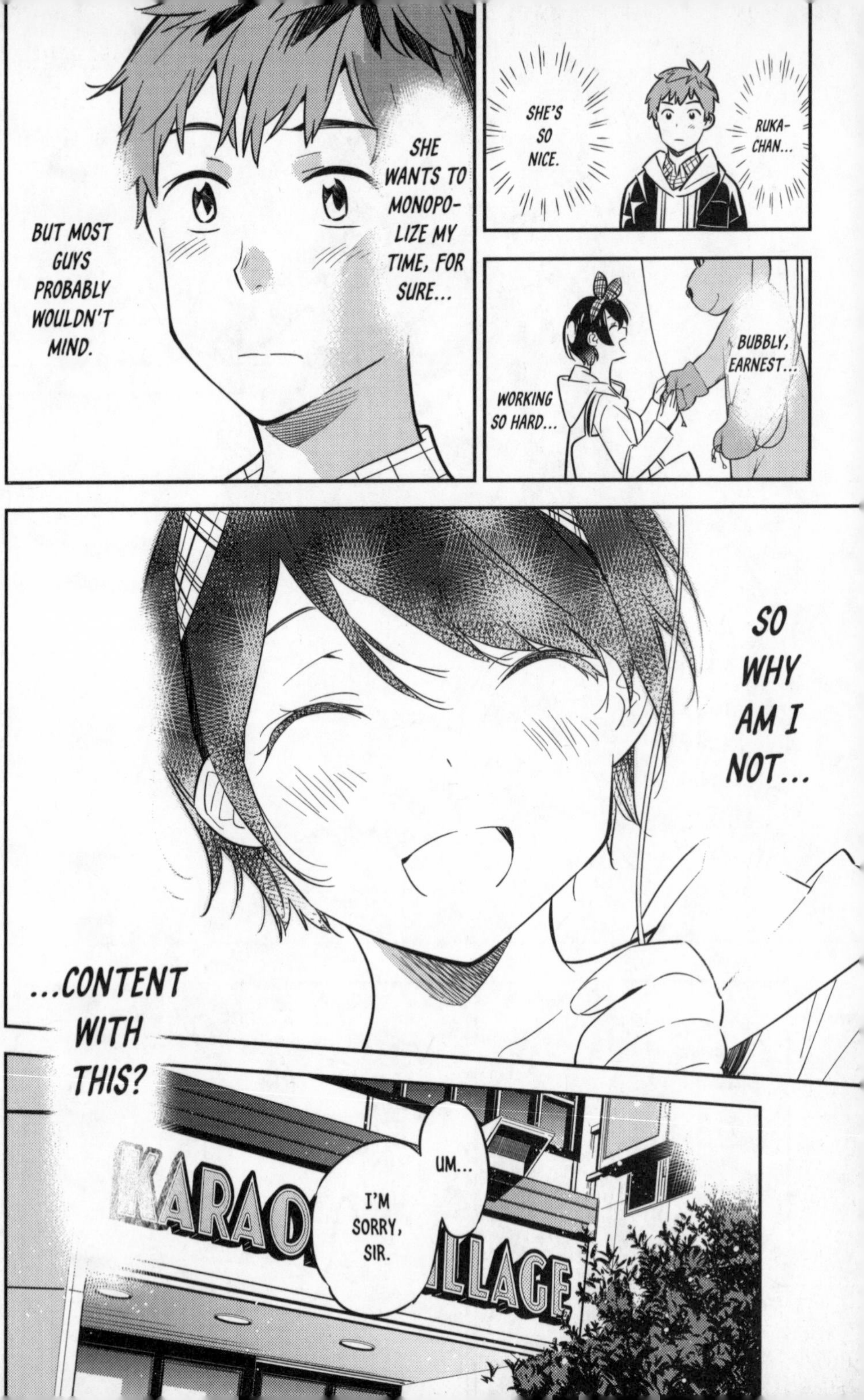
RUKA-CHAN...
SHE'S SO NICE.
BUBBLY, EARNEST...
WORKING SO HARD...
SHE WANTS TO MONOPOLIZE MY TIME, FOR SURE...
BUT MOST GUYS PROBABLY WOULDN'T MIND.
SO WHY AM I NOT...
...CONTENT WITH THIS?
UM...
I'M SORRY, SIR.

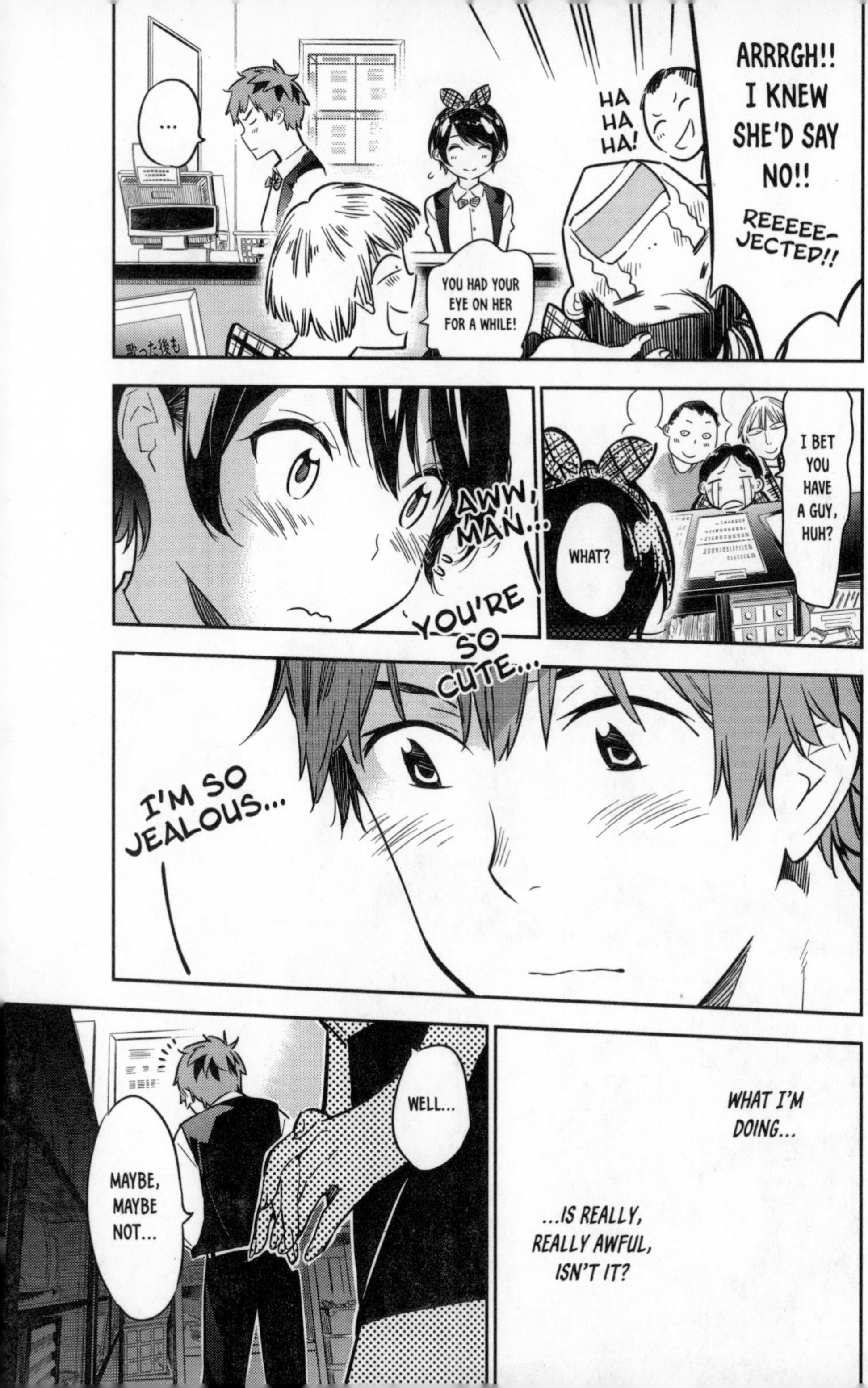
ARRRGH!! I KNEW SHE'D SAY NO!!
REEEEE-JECTED!!
HA HA HA!
YOU HAD YOUR EYE ON HER FOR A WHILE!
...
歌った後も
I BET YOU HAVE A GUY, HUH?
WHAT?
AWW, MAN...
YOU'RE SO CUTE...
I'M SO JEALOUS...
WHAT I'M DOING...
...IS REALLY, REALLY AWFUL, ISN'T IT?
WELL...
MAYBE, MAYBE NOT...

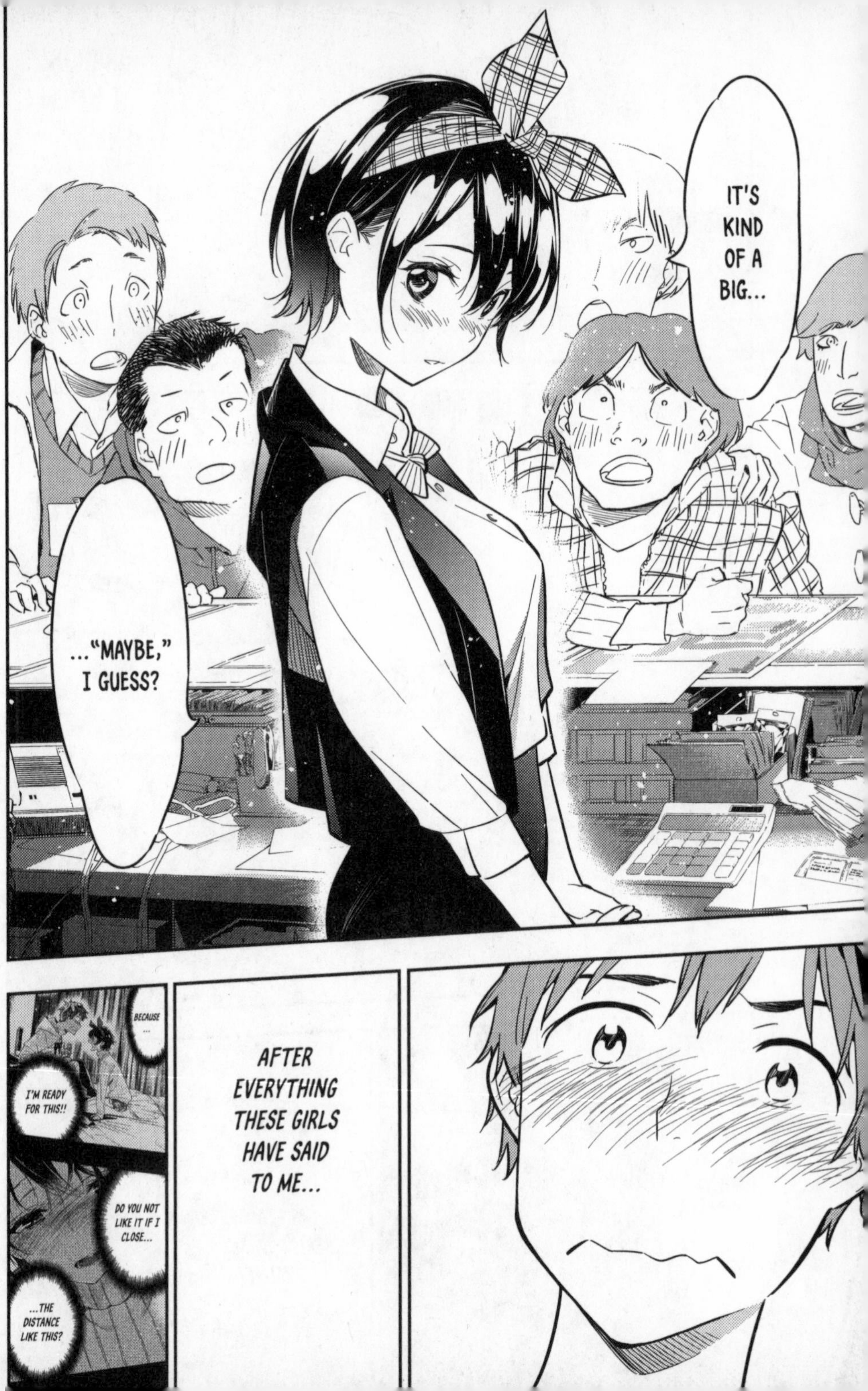
IT'S KIND OF A BIG...
..."MAYBE," I GUESS?
AFTER EVERYTHING THESE GIRLS HAVE SAID TO ME...
BECAUSE ...
I'M READY FOR THIS!!
DO YOU NOT LIKE IT IF I CLOSE...
...THE DISTANCE LIKE THIS?

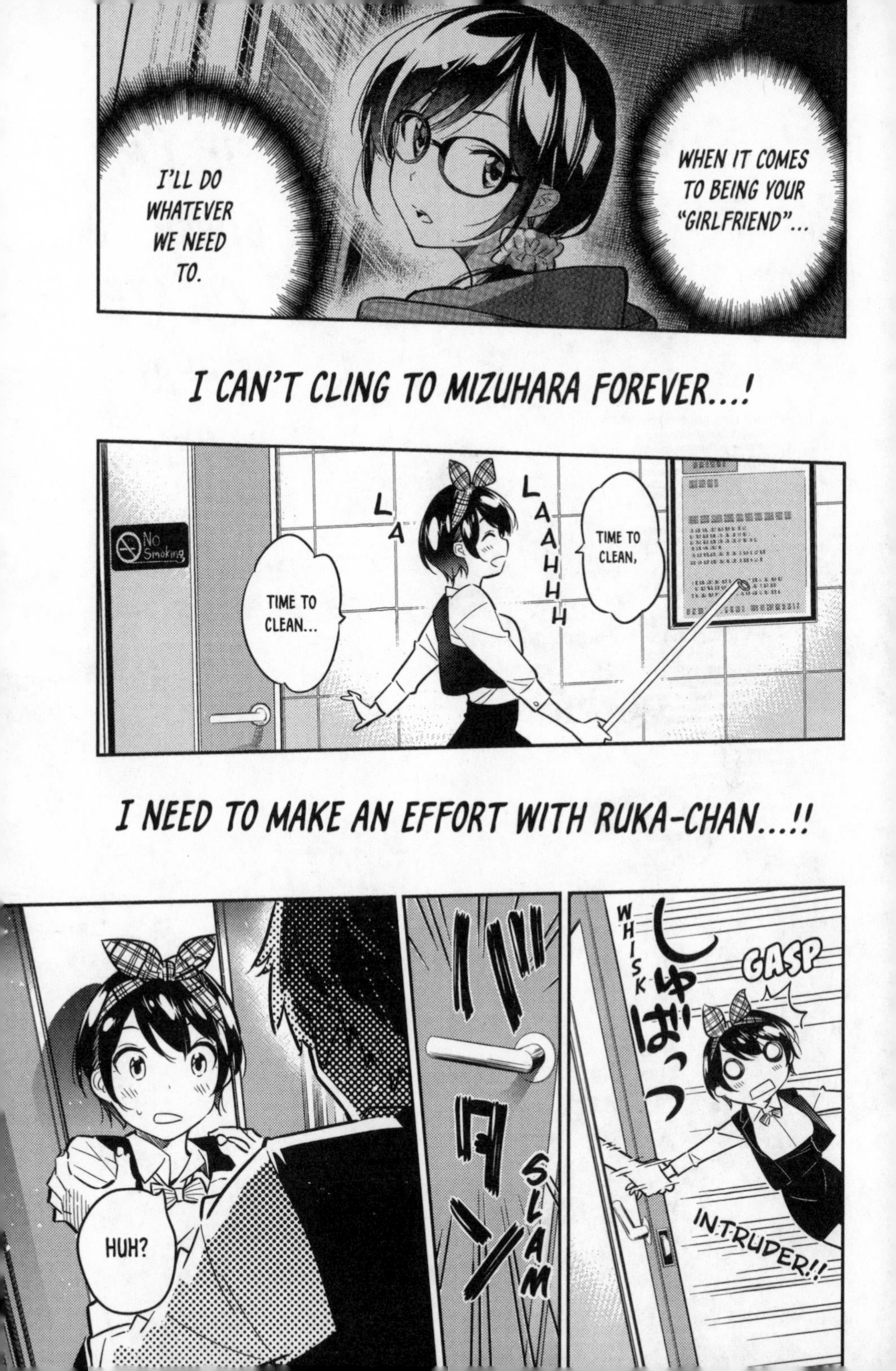
WHEN IT COMES TO BEING YOUR "GIRLFRIEND"...
I'LL DO WHATEVER WE NEED TO.
I CAN'T CLING TO MIZUHARA FOREVER...!
TIME TO CLEAN,
LAAHHHH
LA
TIME TO CLEAN...
No Smoking
I NEED TO MAKE AN EFFORT WITH RUKA-CHAN...!!
WHISK
しゅぱっっ
GASP
INTRUDER!!
バタン
SLAM
HUH?

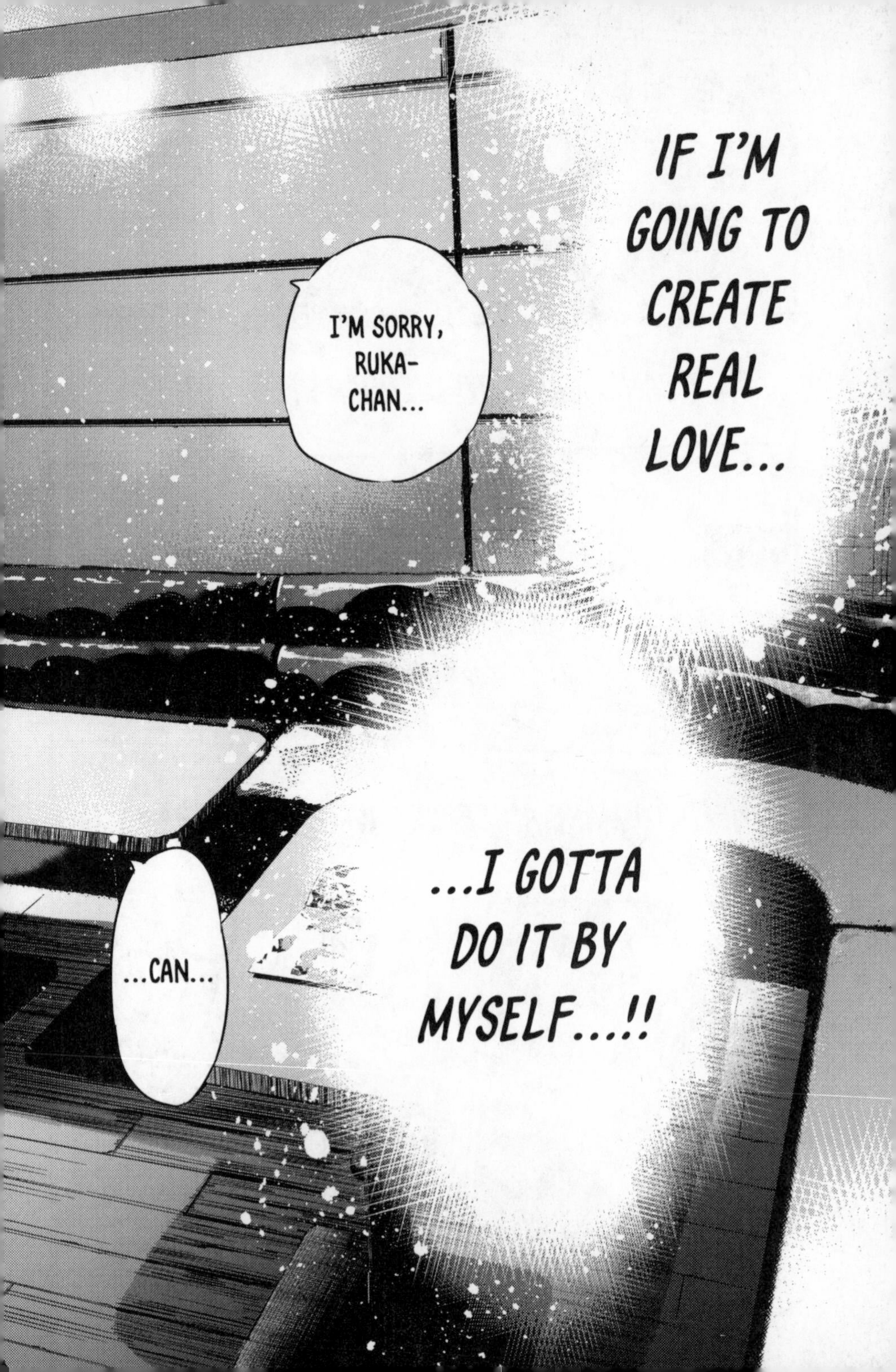
IF I'M GOING TO CREATE REAL LOVE...
I'M SORRY, RUKA-CHAN...
...I GOTTA DO IT BY MYSELF...!!
...CAN...

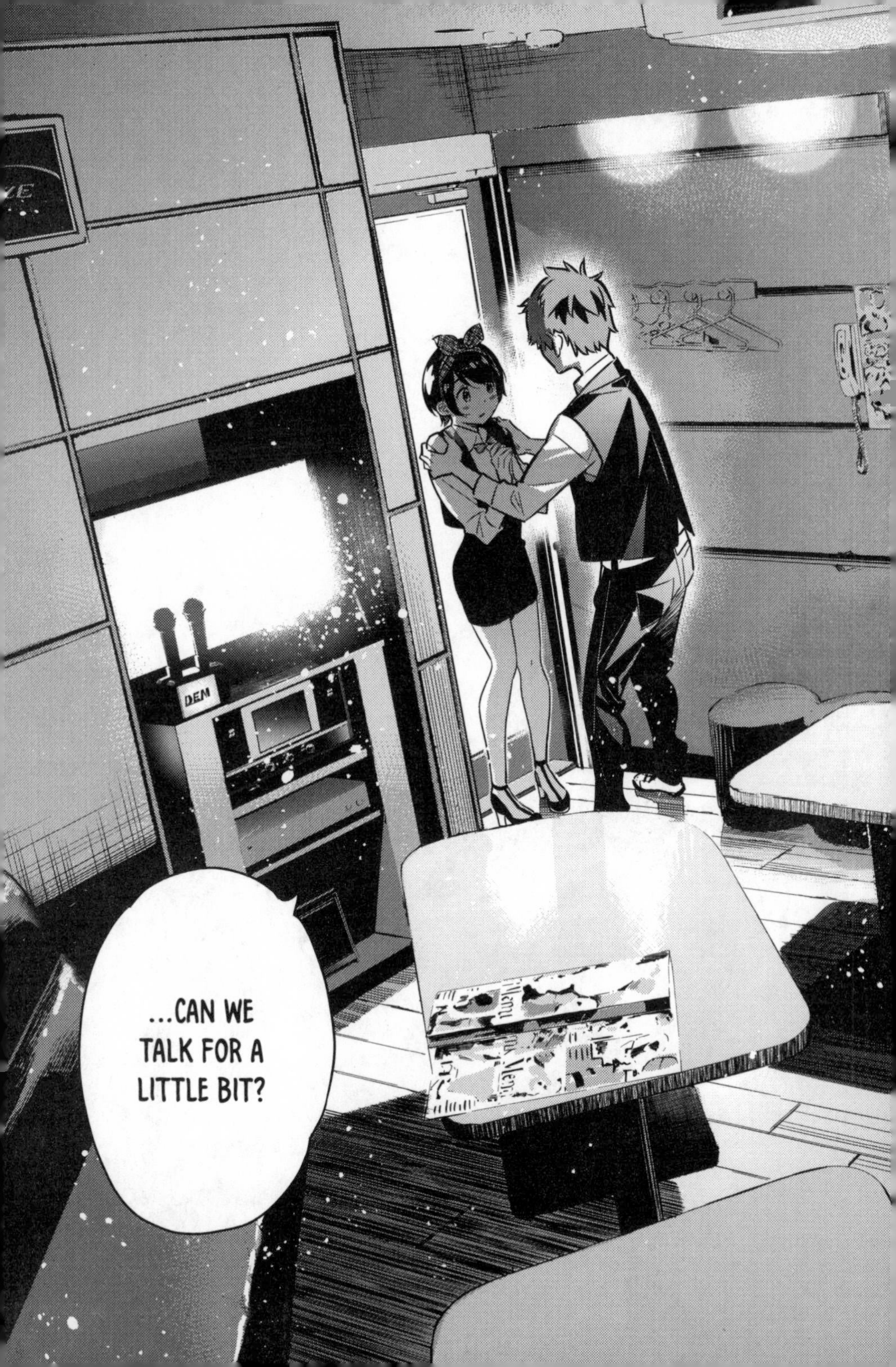
DEN
...CAN WE TALK FOR A LITTLE BIT?

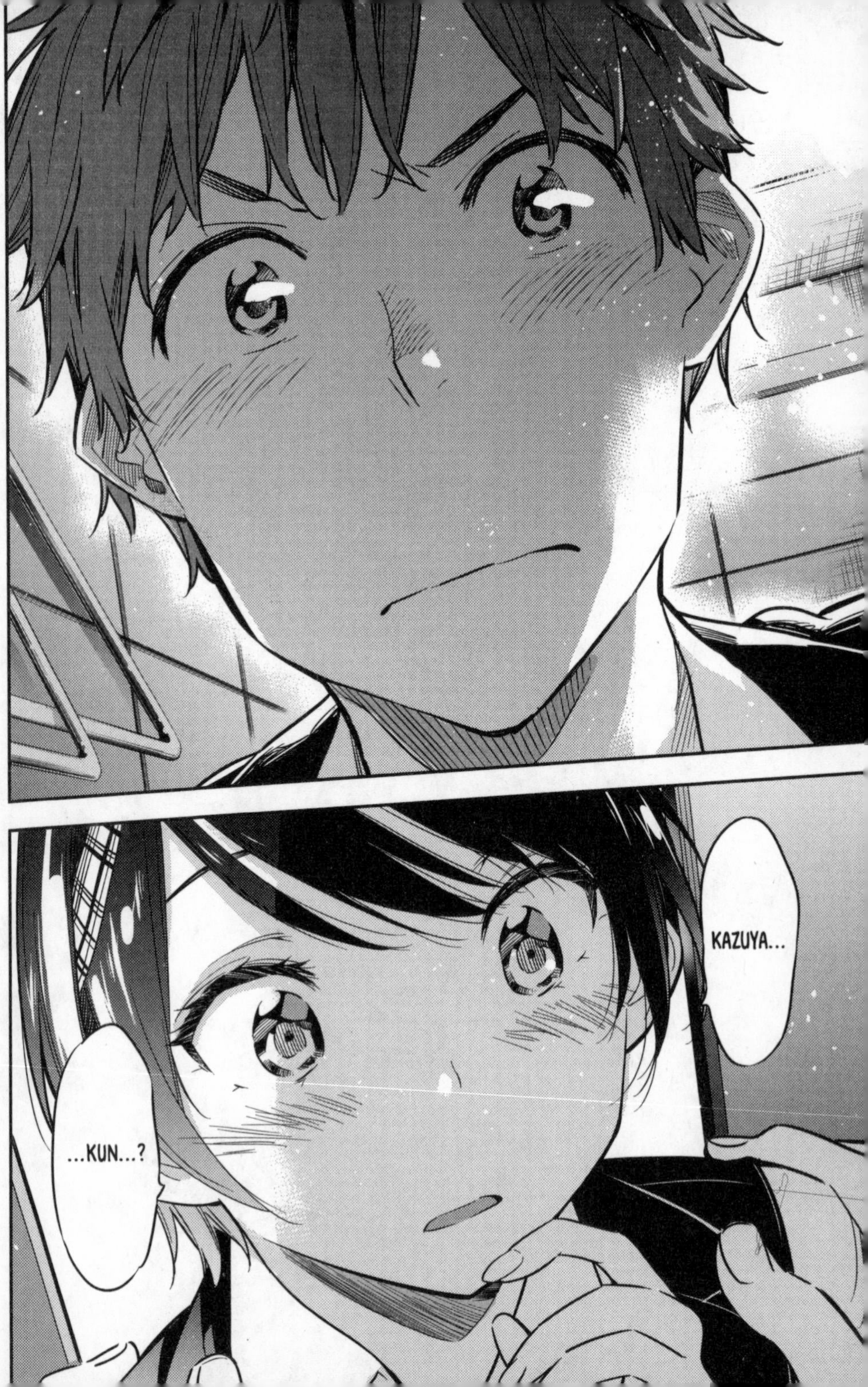
KAZUYA...
...KUN...?

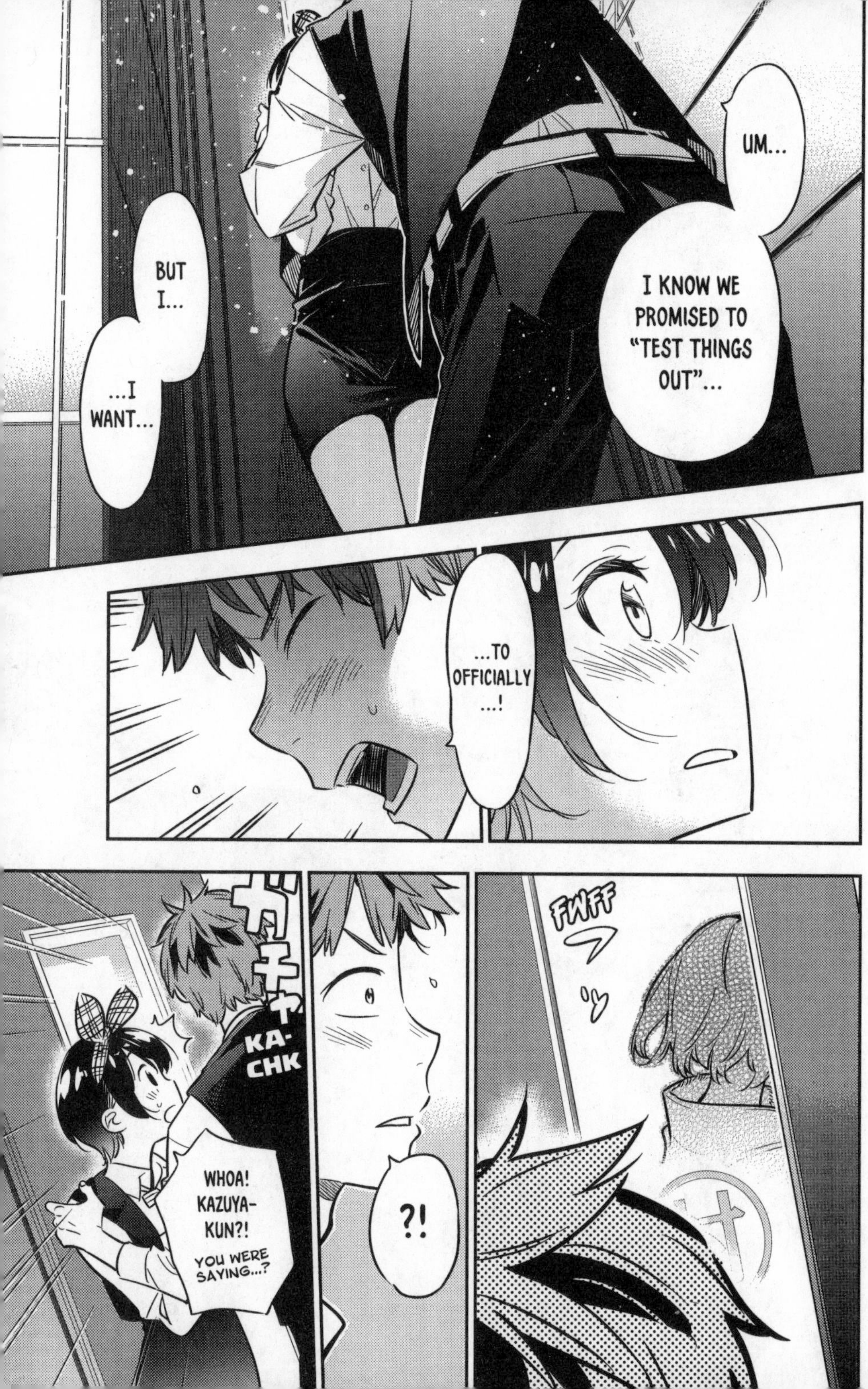
UM...
I KNOW WE PROMISED TO "TEST THINGS OUT"...
BUT I...
...I WANT...
...TO OFFICIALLY ...!
FWFF
?!
KA-CHK
WHOA! KAZUYA-KUN?!
YOU WERE SAYING...?

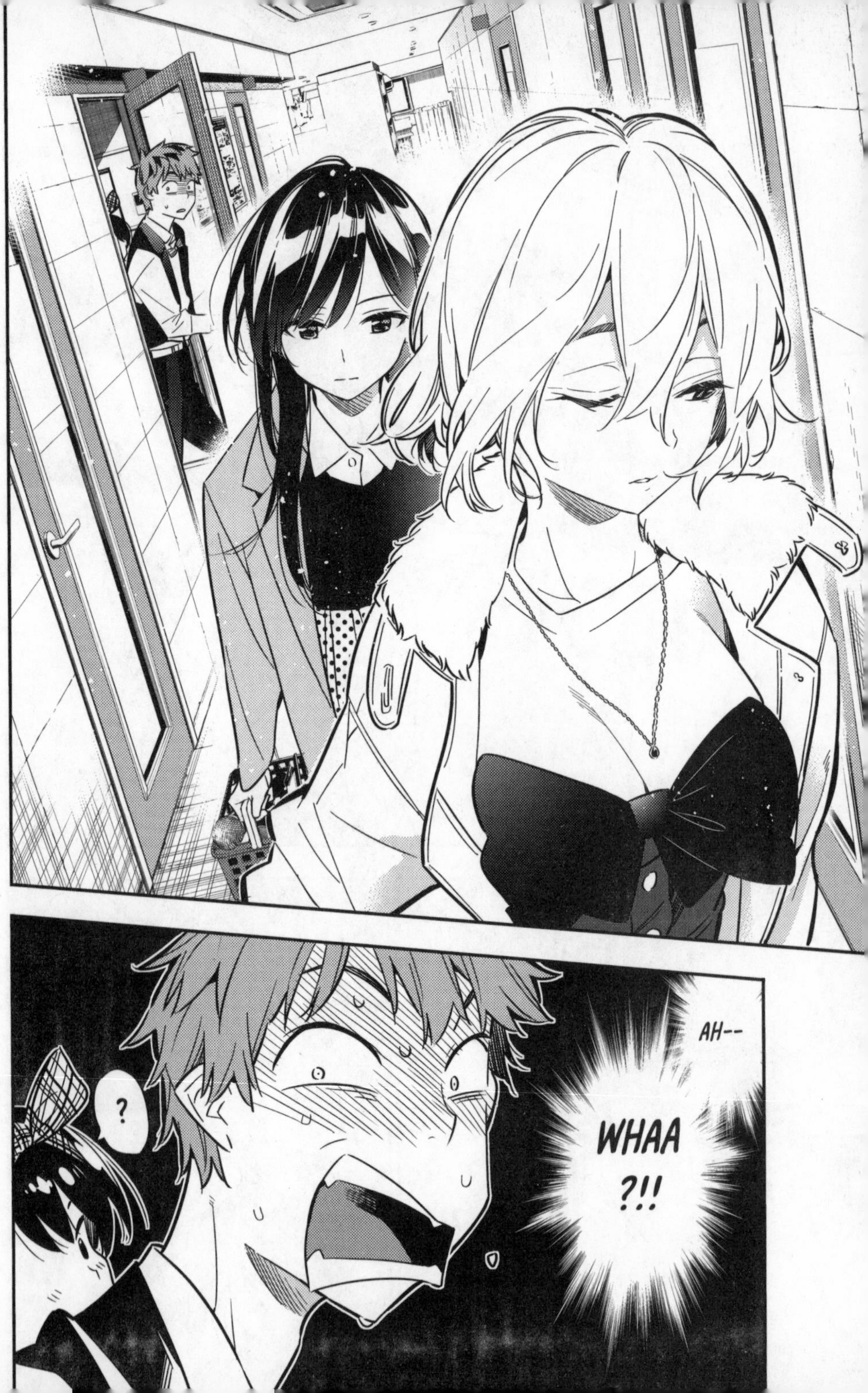
AH--
WHAA ?!!
?

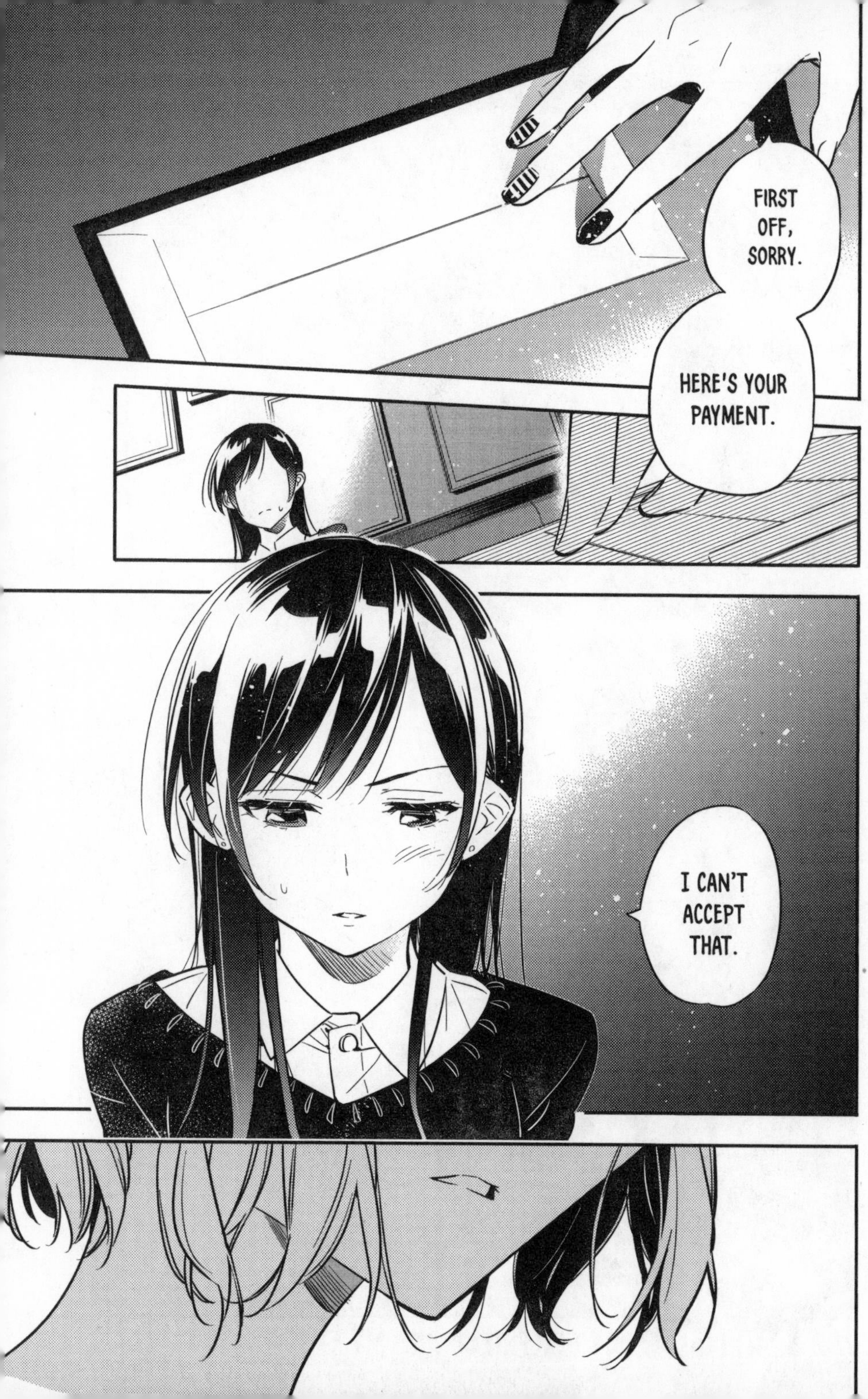
FIRST OFF, SORRY.
HERE'S YOUR PAYMENT.
I CAN'T ACCEPT THAT.

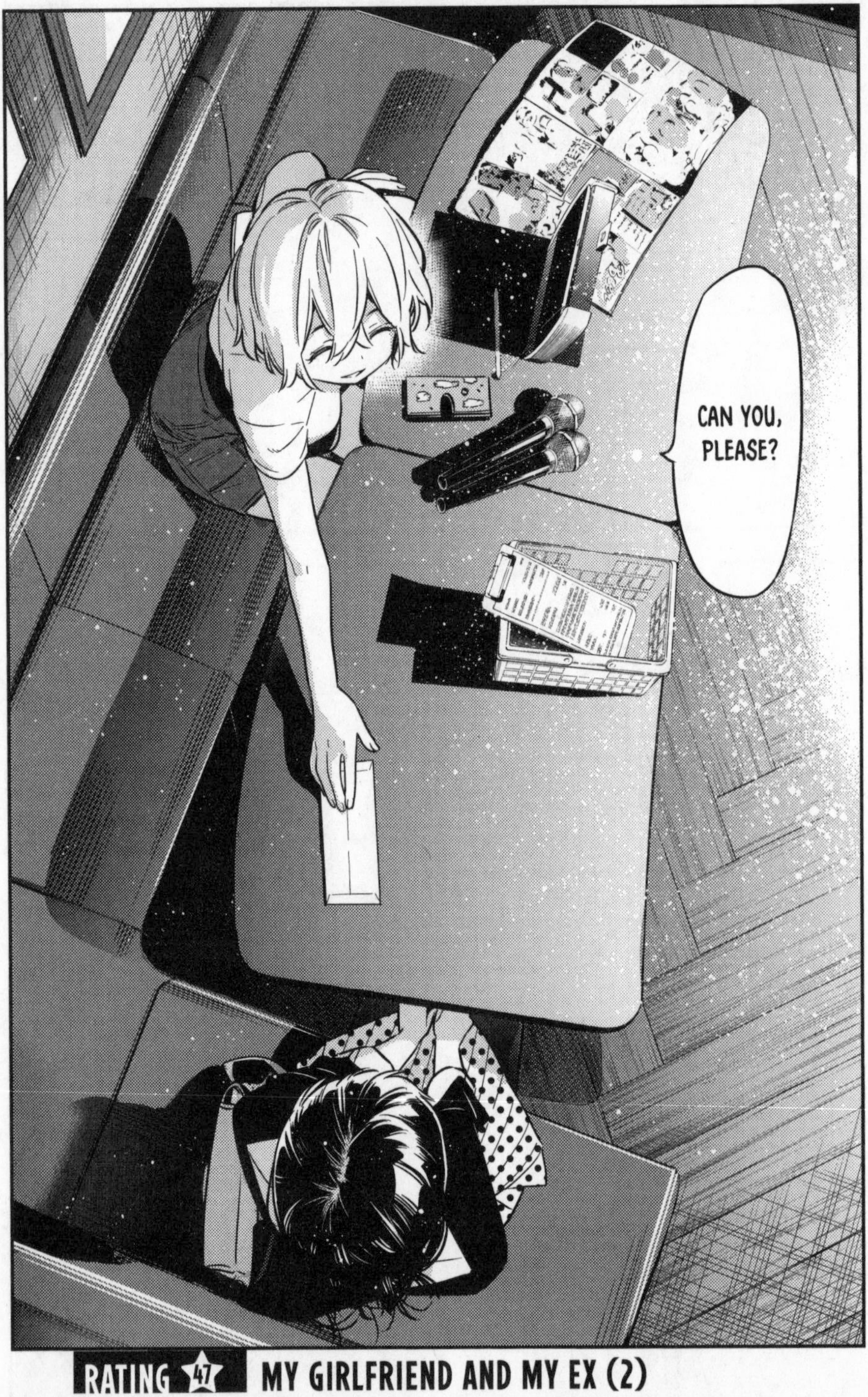
CAN YOU, PLEASE?

RATING 47 MY GIRLFRIEND AND MY EX (2)

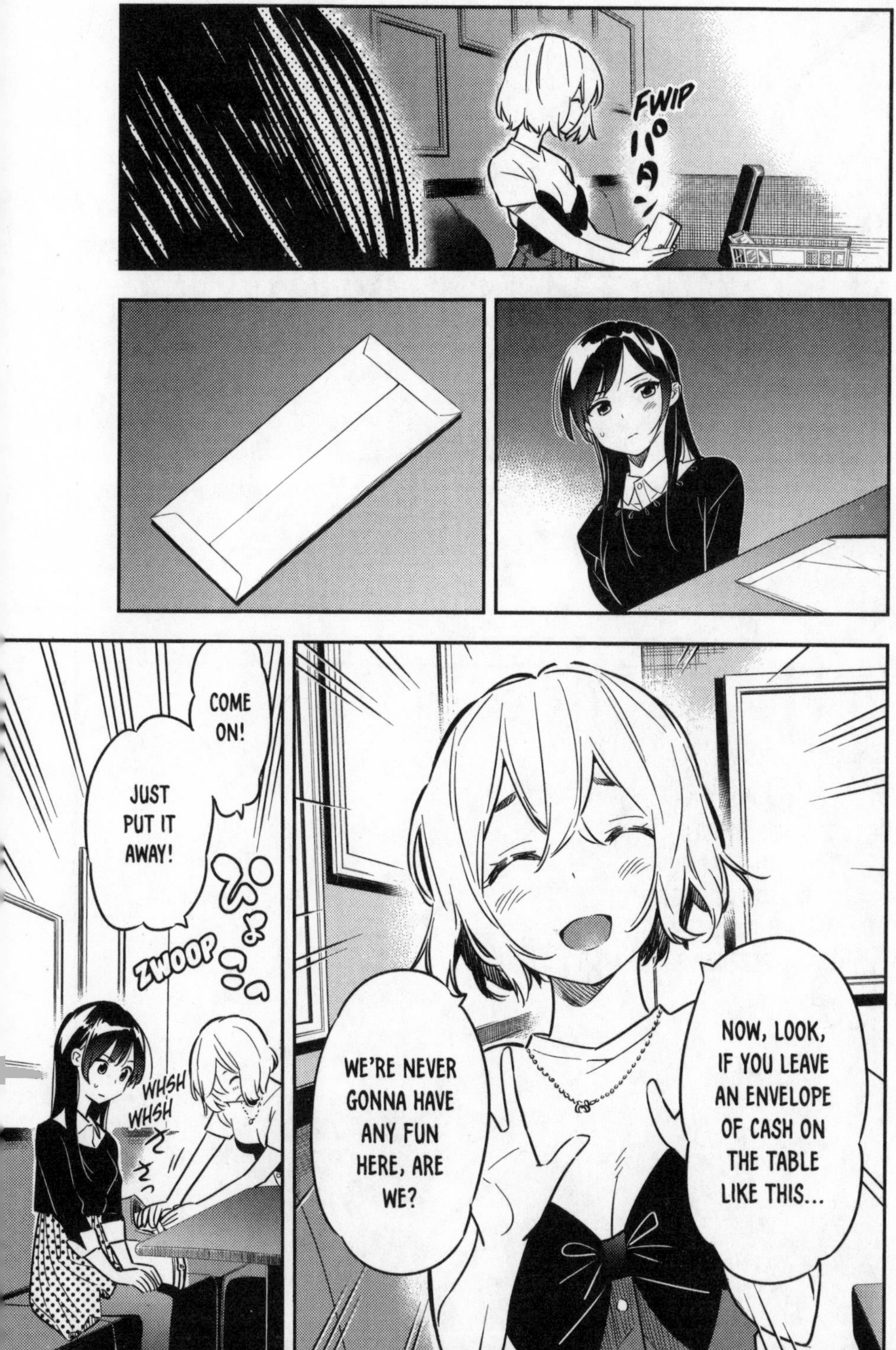
FWIP
パタン
NOW, LOOK, IF YOU LEAVE AN ENVELOPE OF CASH ON THE TABLE LIKE THIS...
WE'RE NEVER GONNA HAVE ANY FUN HERE, ARE WE?
COME ON!
JUST PUT IT AWAY!
ZWOOP
WHSH WHSH
さっ

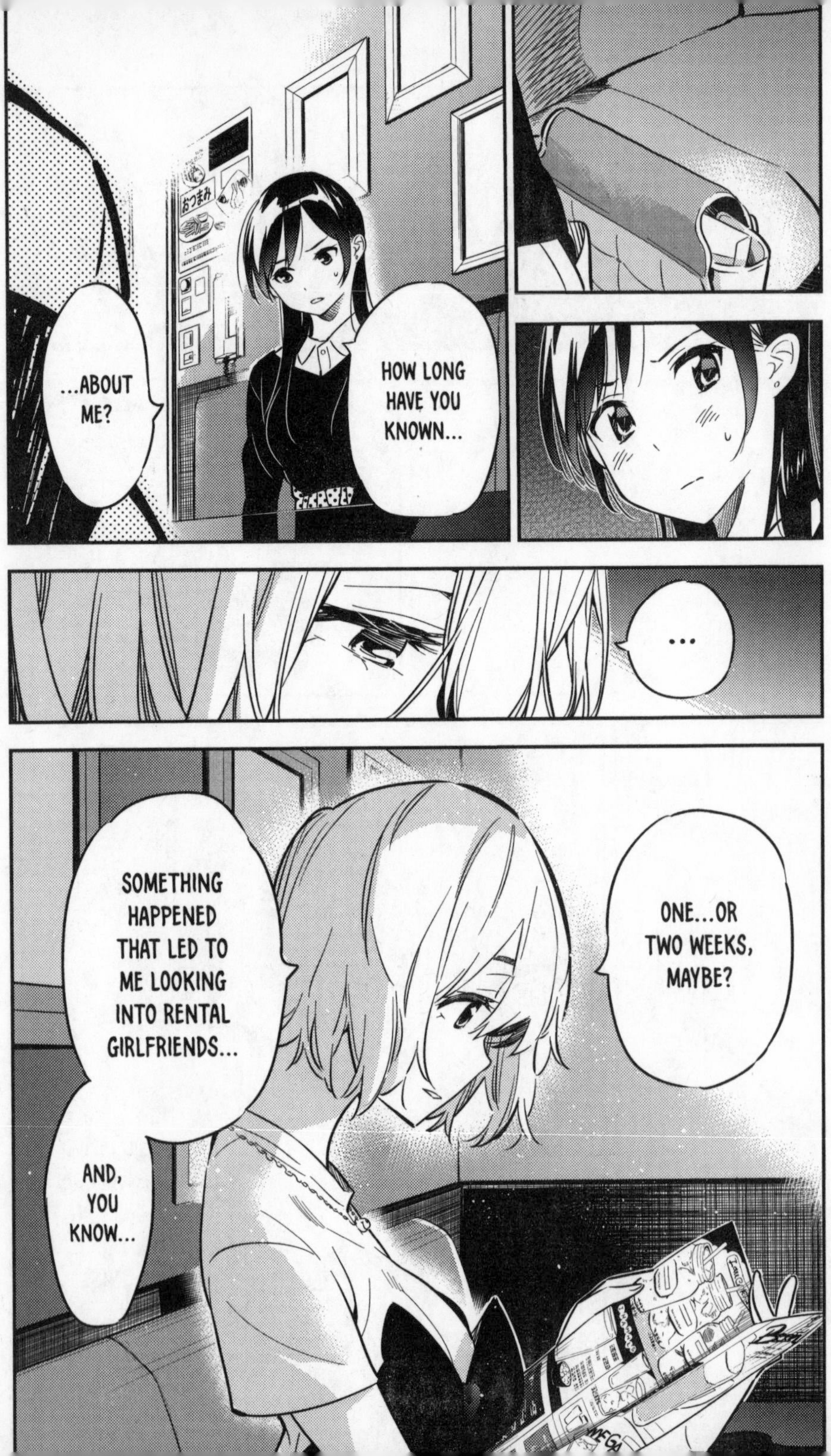
おつまみ
HOW LONG HAVE YOU KNOWN...
...ABOUT ME?
...
ONE...OR TWO WEEKS, MAYBE?
SOMETHING HAPPENED THAT LED TO ME LOOKING INTO RENTAL GIRLFRIENDS...
AND, YOU KNOW...

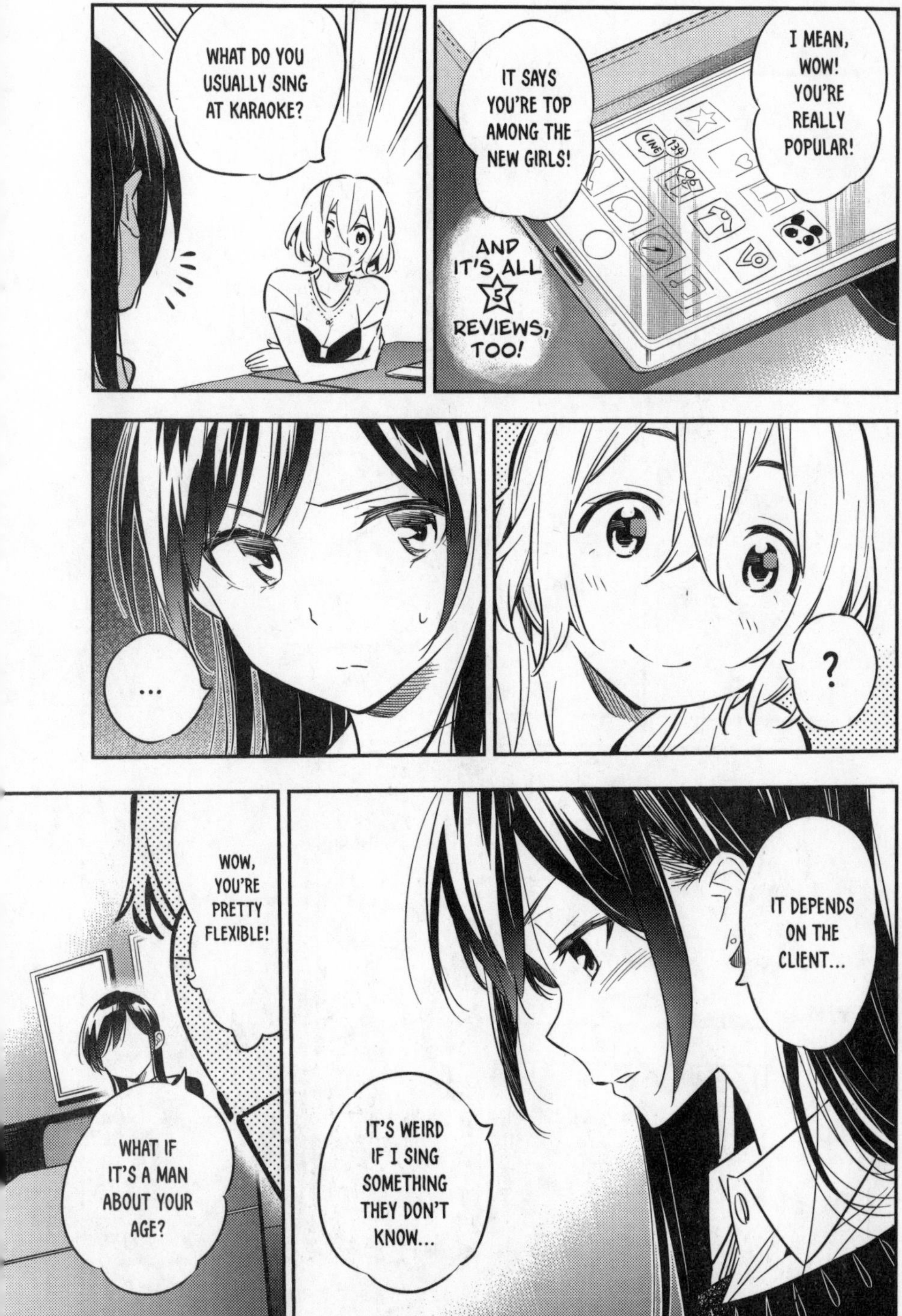
I MEAN, WOW! YOU'RE REALLY POPULAR!
IT SAYS YOU'RE TOP AMONG THE NEW GIRLS!
AND IT'S ALL 5 REVIEWS, TOO!
WHAT DO YOU USUALLY SING AT KARAOKE?
?
...
IT DEPENDS ON THE CLIENT...
IT'S WEIRD IF I SING SOMETHING THEY DON'T KNOW...
WOW, YOU'RE PRETTY FLEXIBLE!
WHAT IF IT'S A MAN ABOUT YOUR AGE?

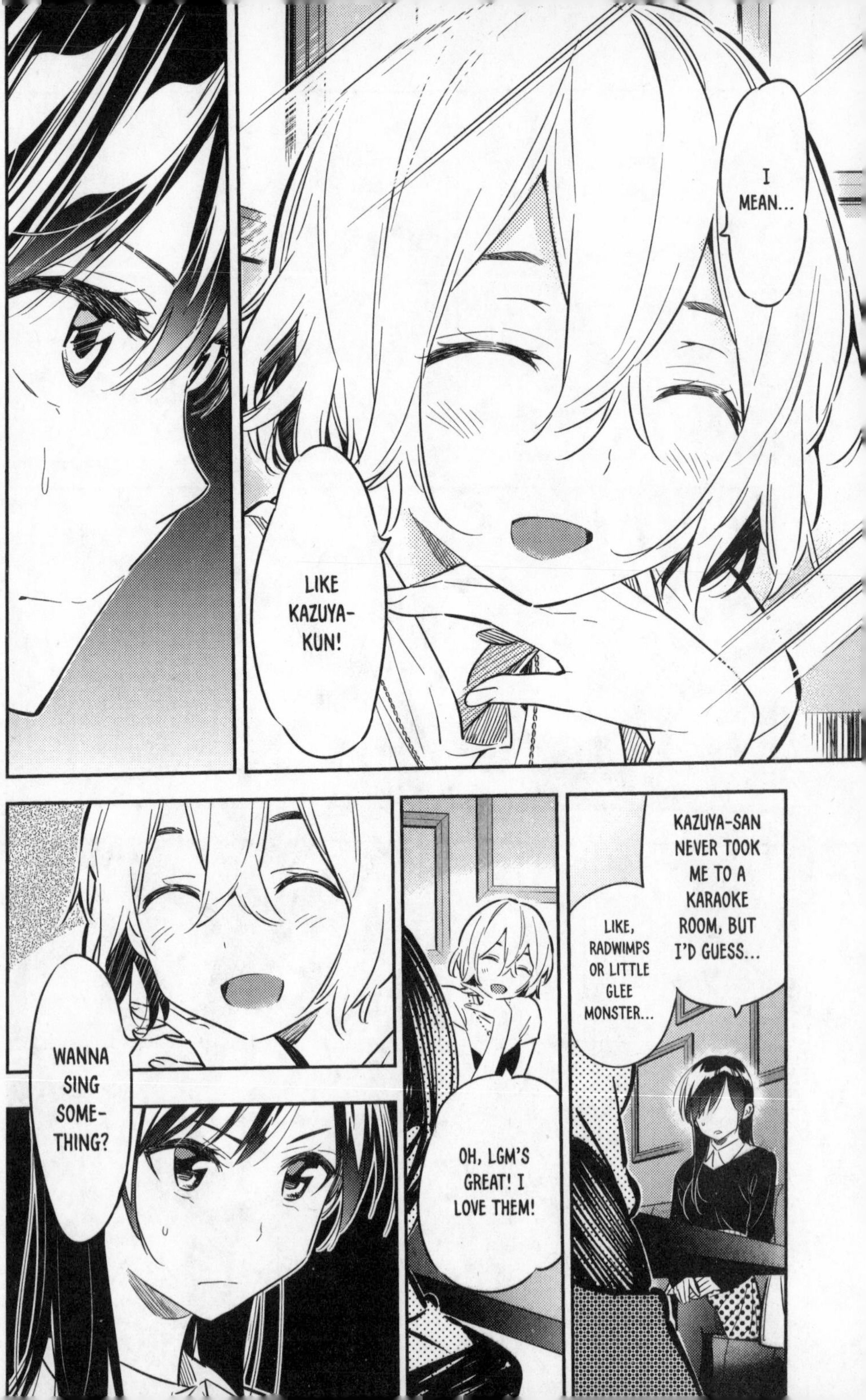
I MEAN...
LIKE KAZUYA-KUN!
KAZUYA-SAN NEVER TOOK ME TO A KARAOKE ROOM, BUT I'D GUESS...
LIKE, RADWIMPS OR LITTLE GLEE MONSTER...
OH, LGM'S GREAT! I LOVE THEM!
WANNA SING SOME-THING?

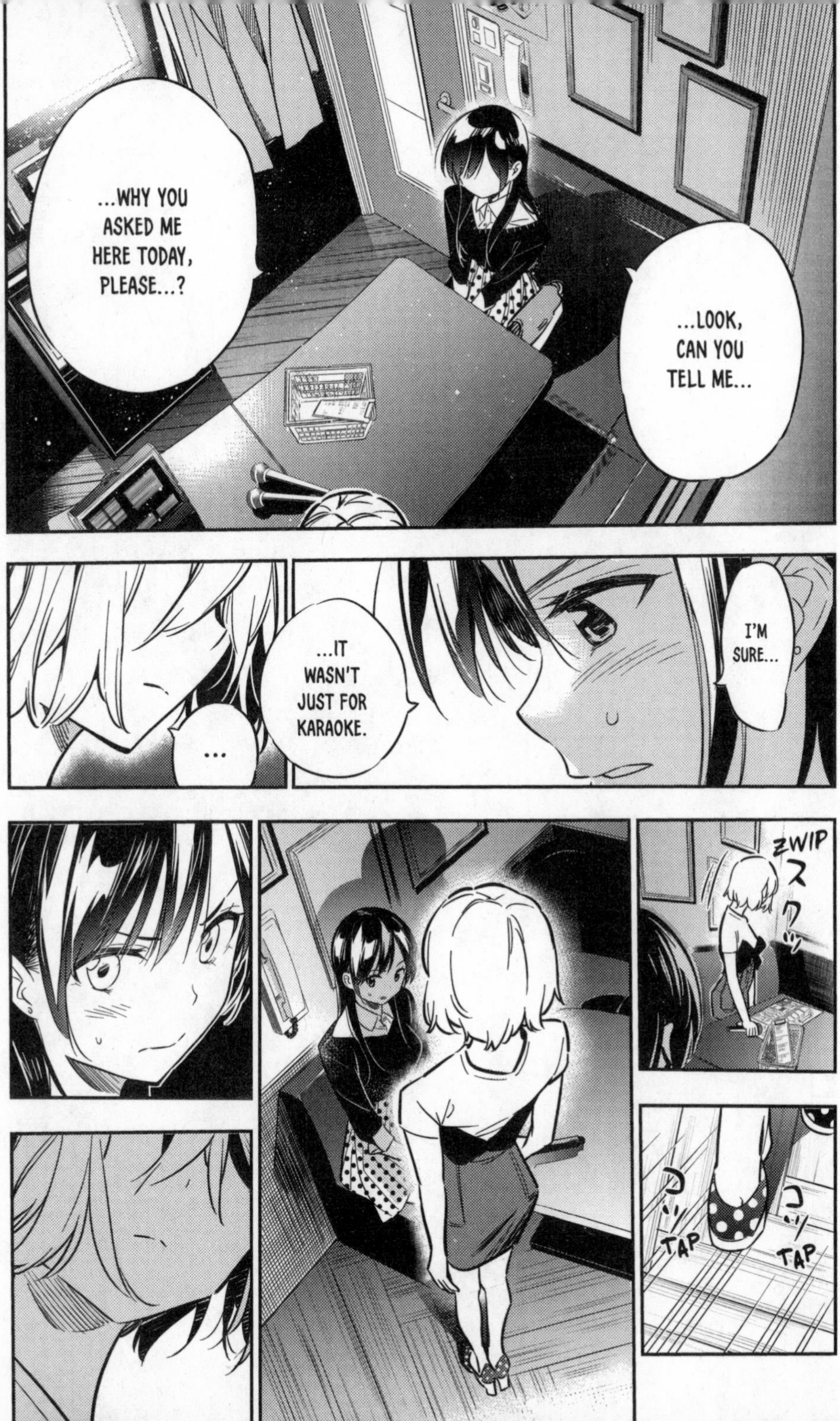
...LOOK, CAN YOU TELL ME...
...WHY YOU ASKED ME HERE TODAY, PLEASE...?
I'M SURE...
...IT WASN'T JUST FOR KARAOKE.
...
ZWIP
TAP
TAP

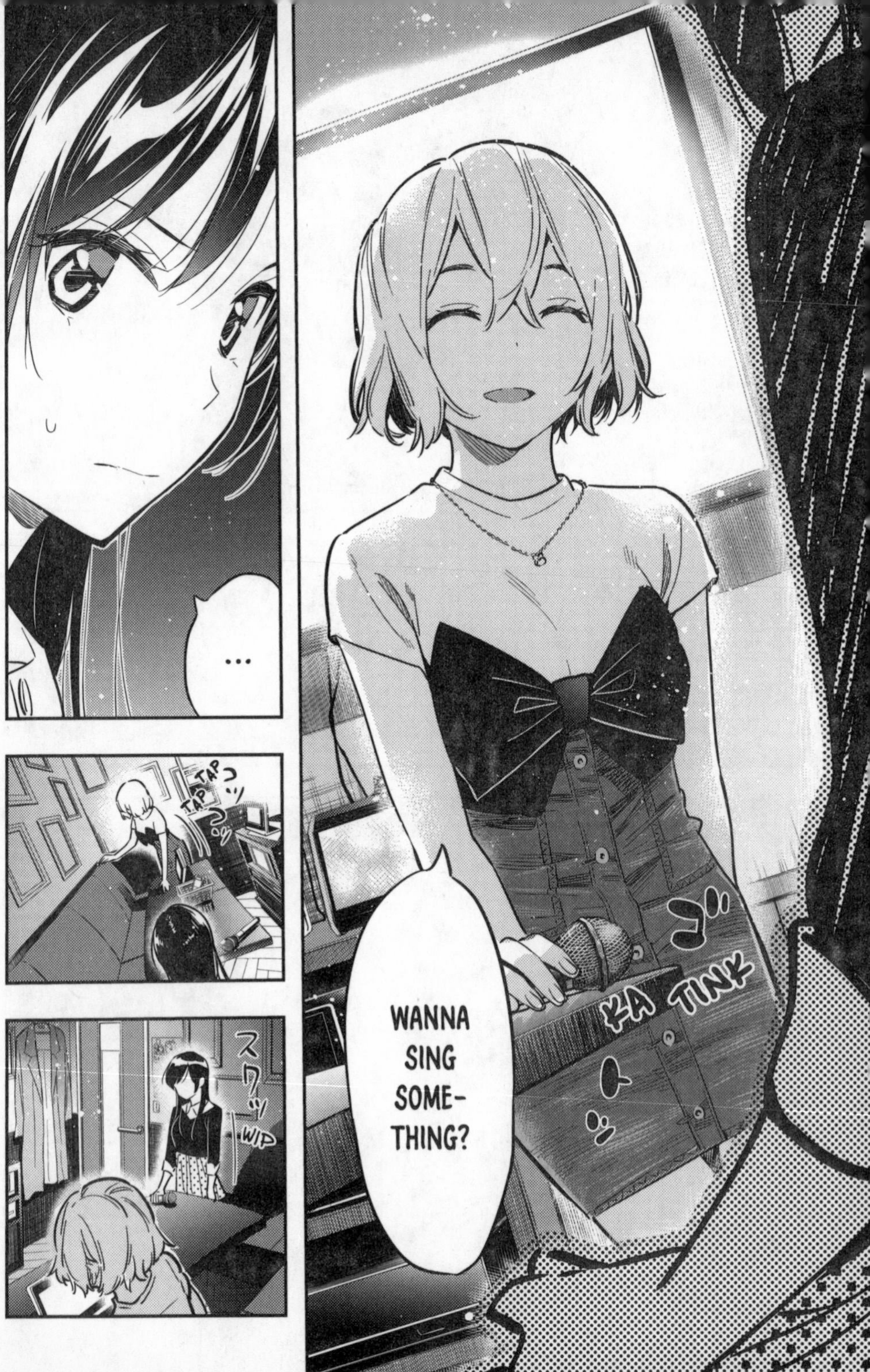
WANNA SING SOME-THING?
KA TINK
...
TAP TAP
WIP
スワッ

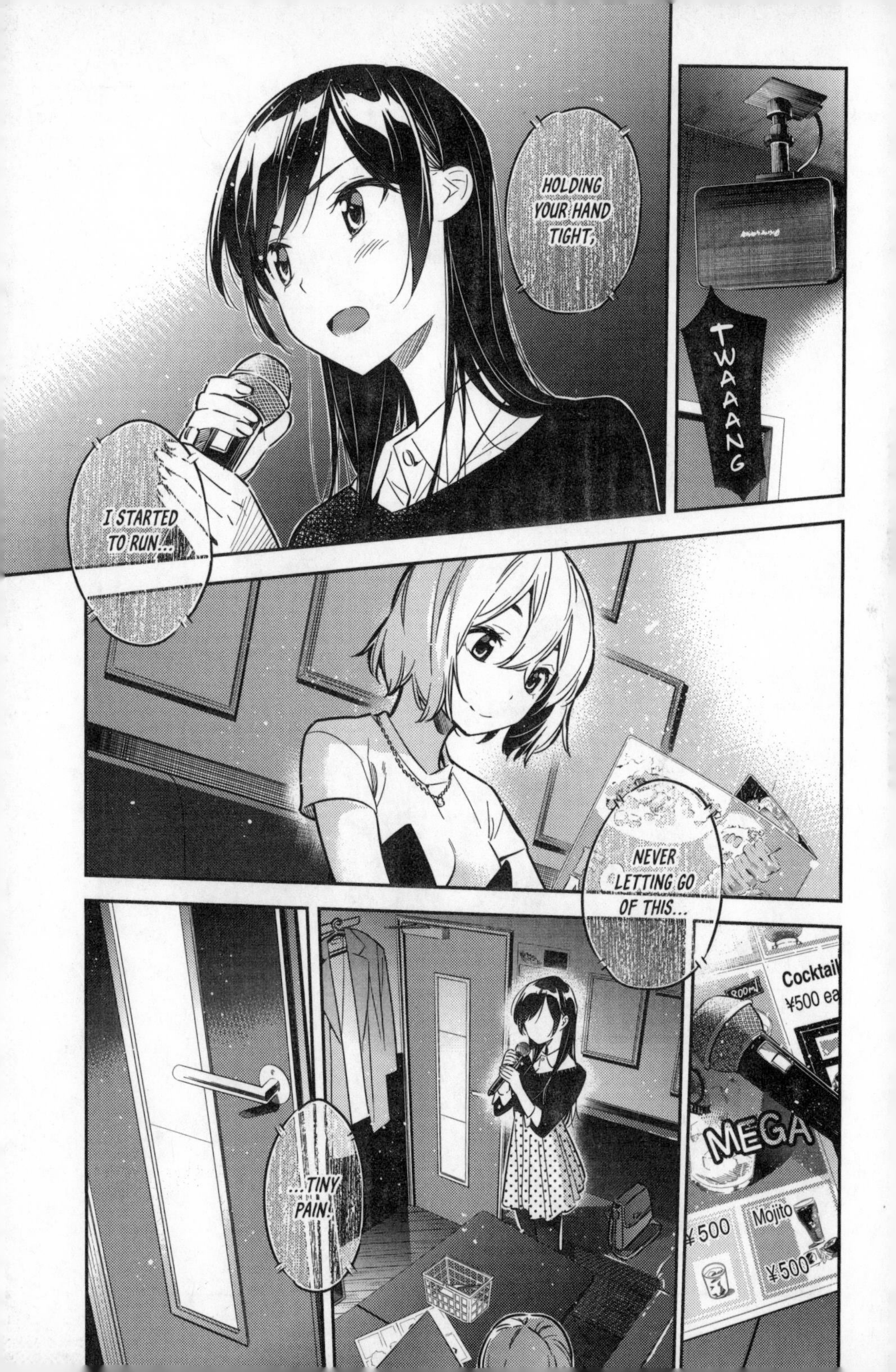
TWAAANG
HOLDING YOUR HAND TIGHT,
I STARTED TO RUN...
NEVER LETTING GO OF THIS...
Cocktail
¥500 ea
MEGA
¥500
Mojito
¥500
...TINY PAIN!

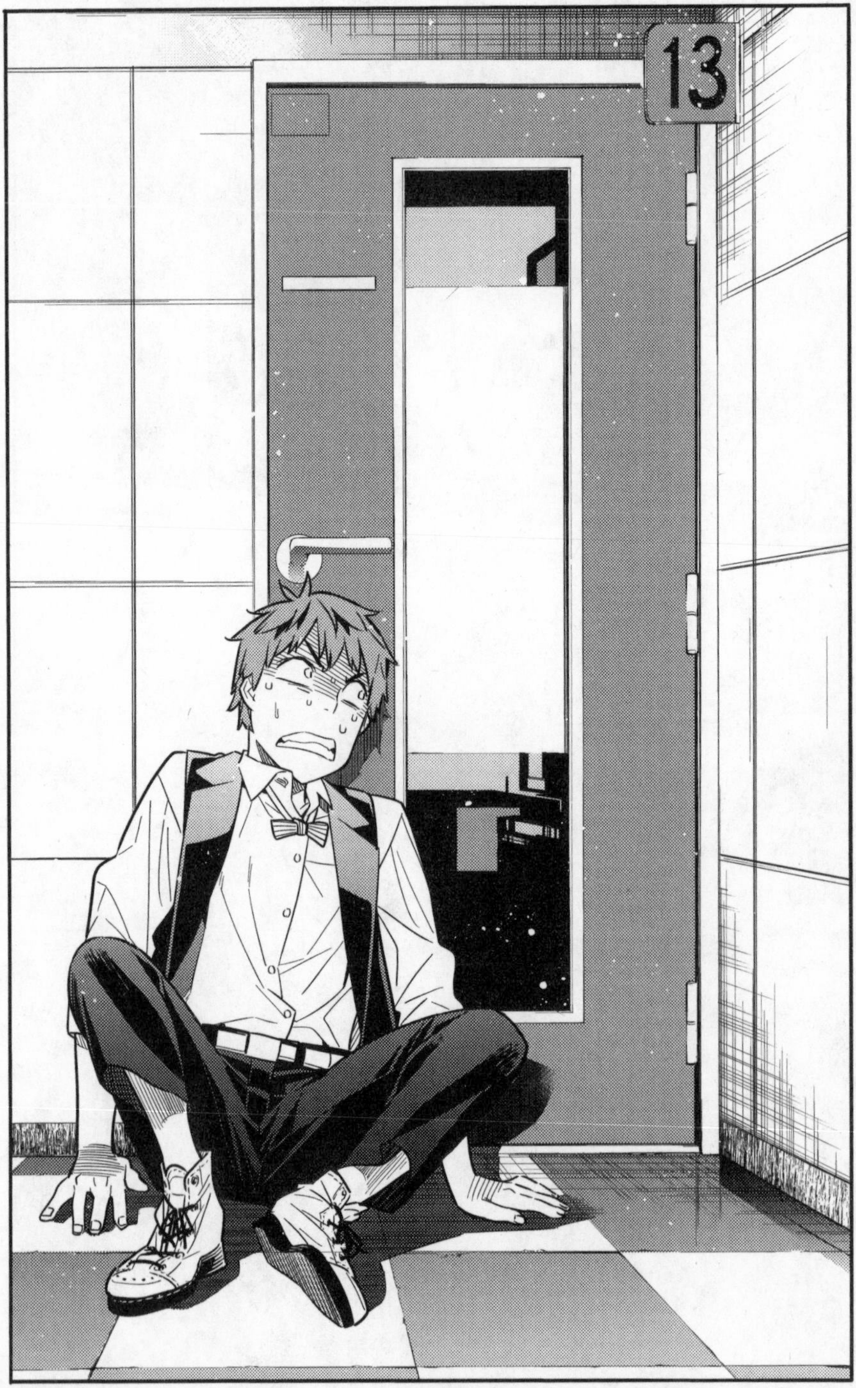
13

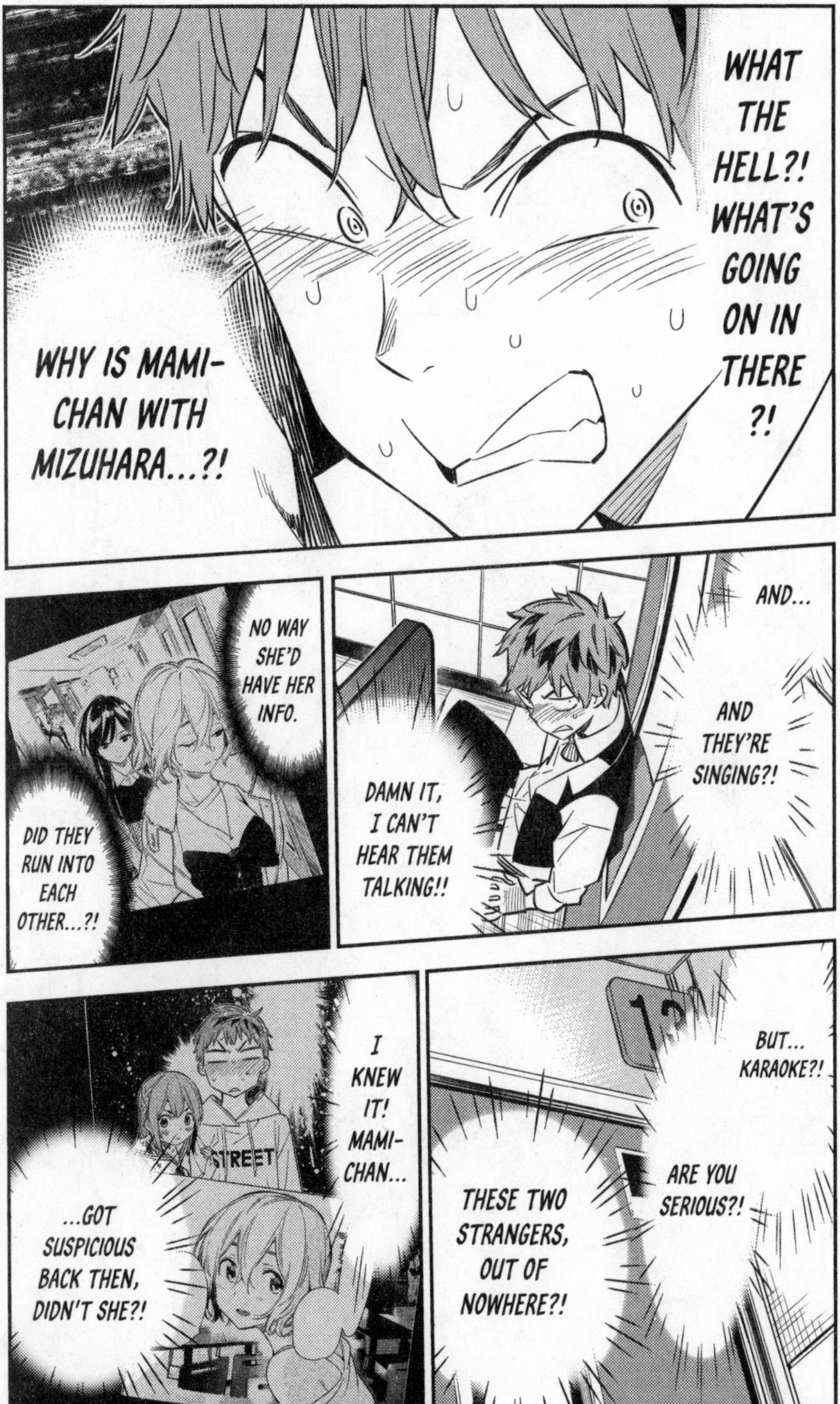
WHAT THE HELL?! WHAT'S GOING ON IN THERE?!
WHY IS MAMI-CHAN WITH MIZUHARA...?!
AND...
AND THEY'RE SINGING?!
DAMN IT, I CAN'T HEAR THEM TALKING!!
NO WAY SHE'D HAVE HER INFO.
DID THEY RUN INTO EACH OTHER...?!
BUT... KARAOKE?!
ARE YOU SERIOUS?!
THESE TWO STRANGERS, OUT OF NOWHERE?!
I KNEW IT! MAMI-CHAN...
STREET
...GOT SUSPICIOUS BACK THEN, DIDN'T SHE?!

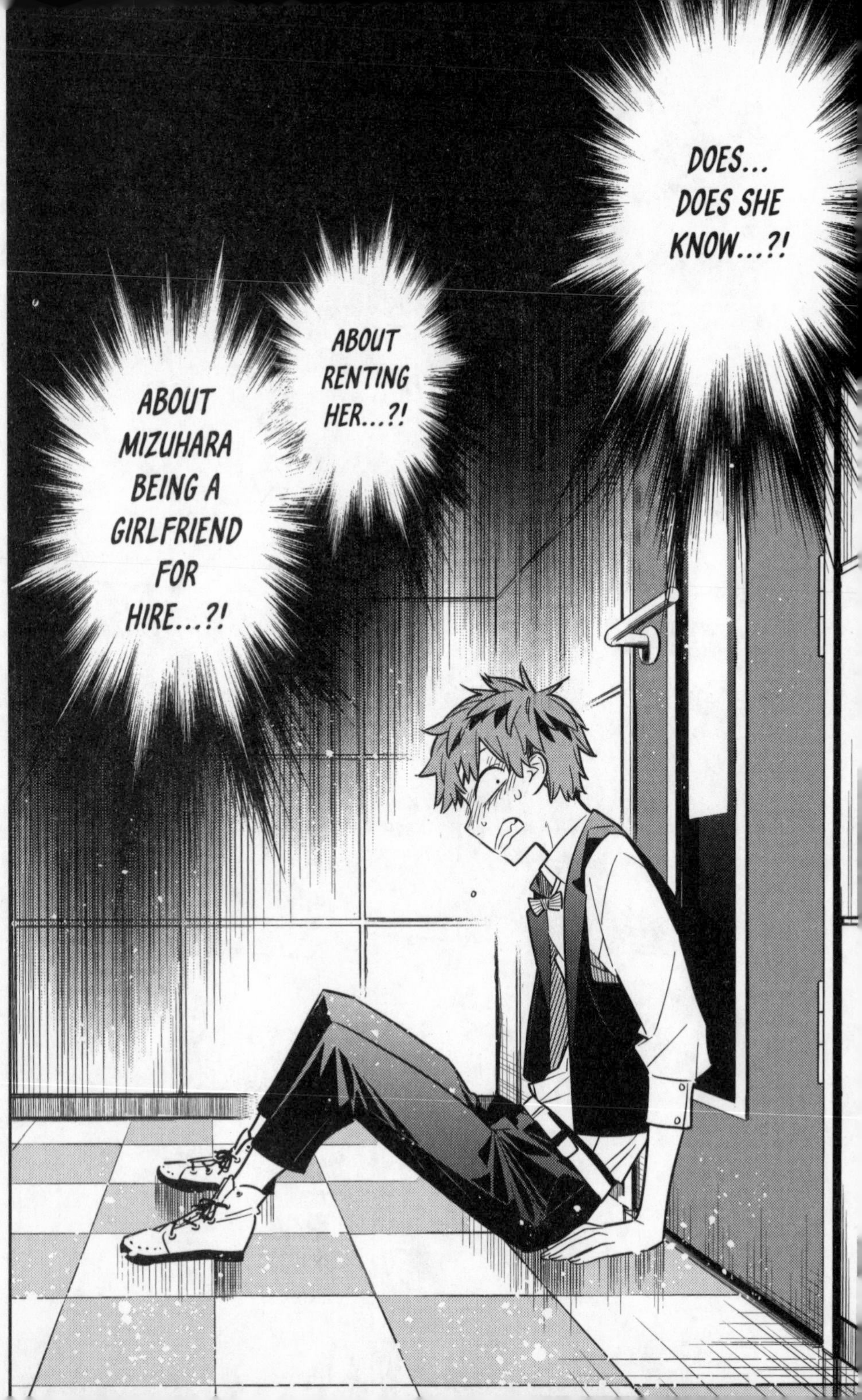
DOES... DOES SHE KNOW...?!
ABOUT RENTING HER...?!
ABOUT MIZUHARA BEING A GIRLFRIEND FOR HIRE...?!

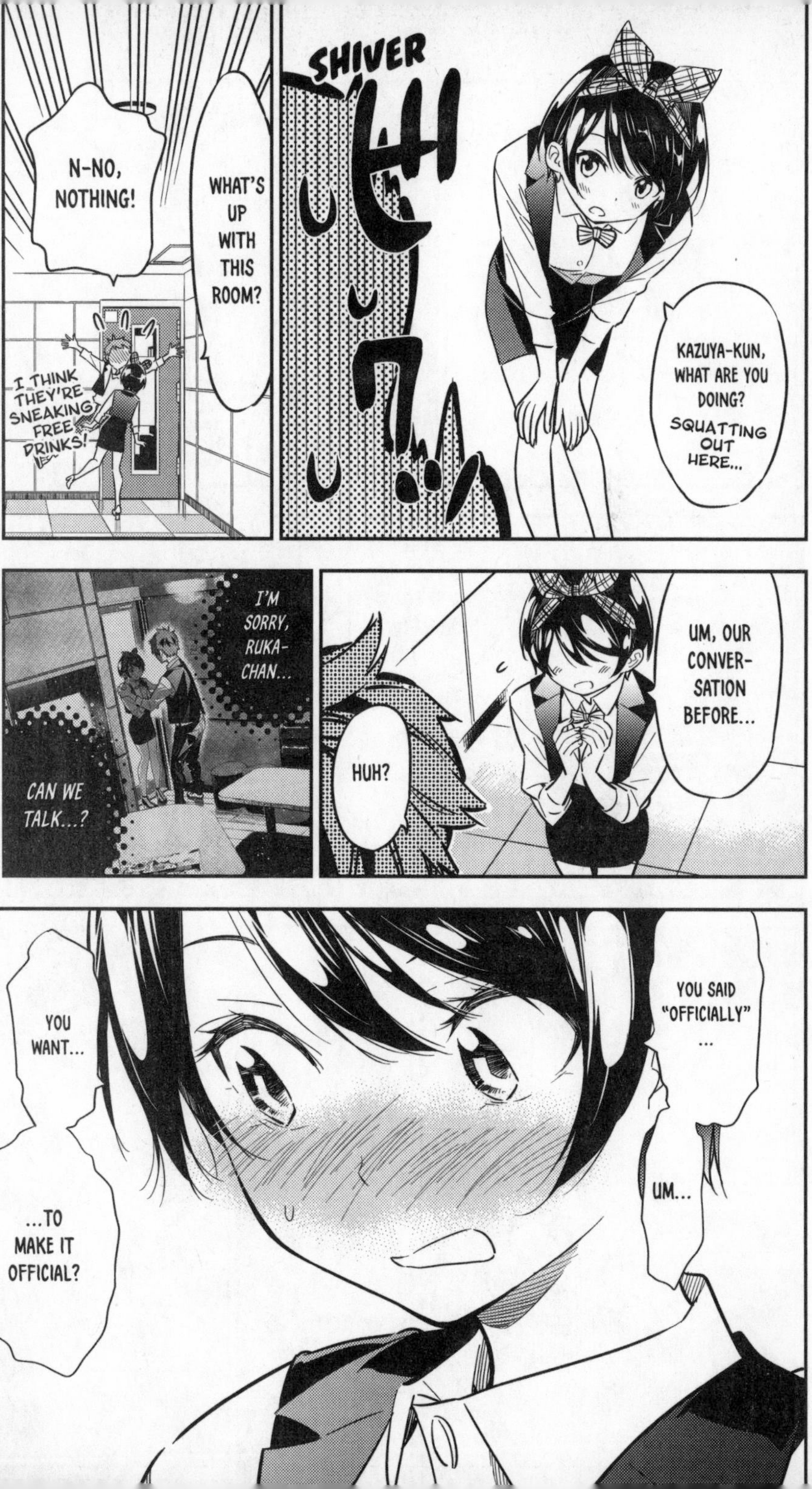
KAZUYA-KUN, WHAT ARE YOU DOING? SQUATTING OUT HERE...
SHIVER
WHAT'S UP WITH THIS ROOM?
N-NO, NOTHING!
I THINK THEY'RE SNEAKING FREE DRINKS!
UM, OUR CONVER-SATION BEFORE...
HUH?
I'M SORRY, RUKA-CHAN...
CAN WE TALK...?
YOU SAID "OFFICIALLY" ...
UM...
YOU WANT...
...TO MAKE IT OFFICIAL?

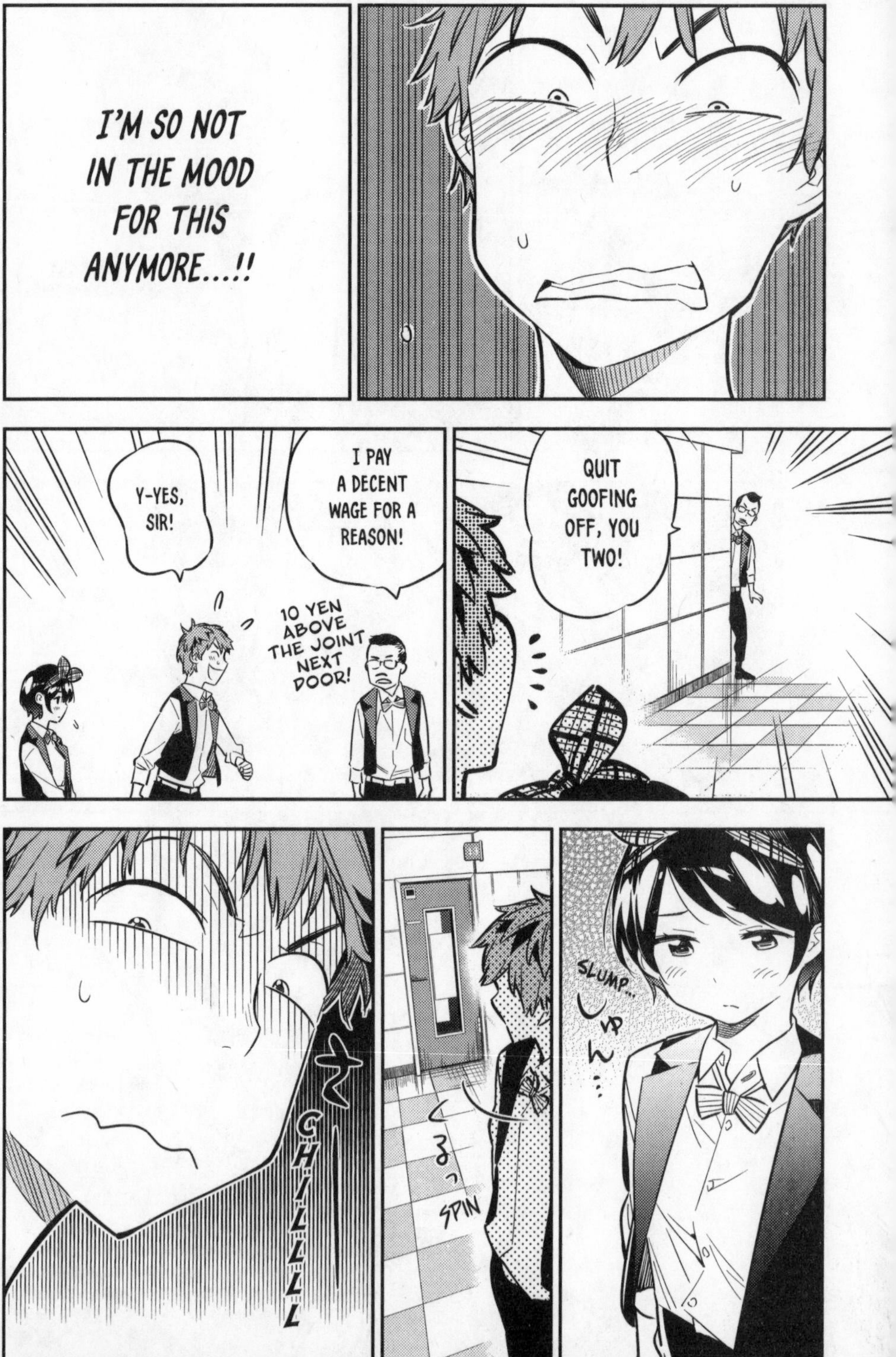
I'M SO NOT IN THE MOOD FOR THIS ANYMORE...!!
QUIT GOOFING OFF, YOU TWO!
I PAY A DECENT WAGE FOR A REASON!
10 YEN ABOVE THE JOINT NEXT DOOR!
Y-YES, SIR!
SLUMP...
しゅん…
くるっ
SPIN
CHILLLL

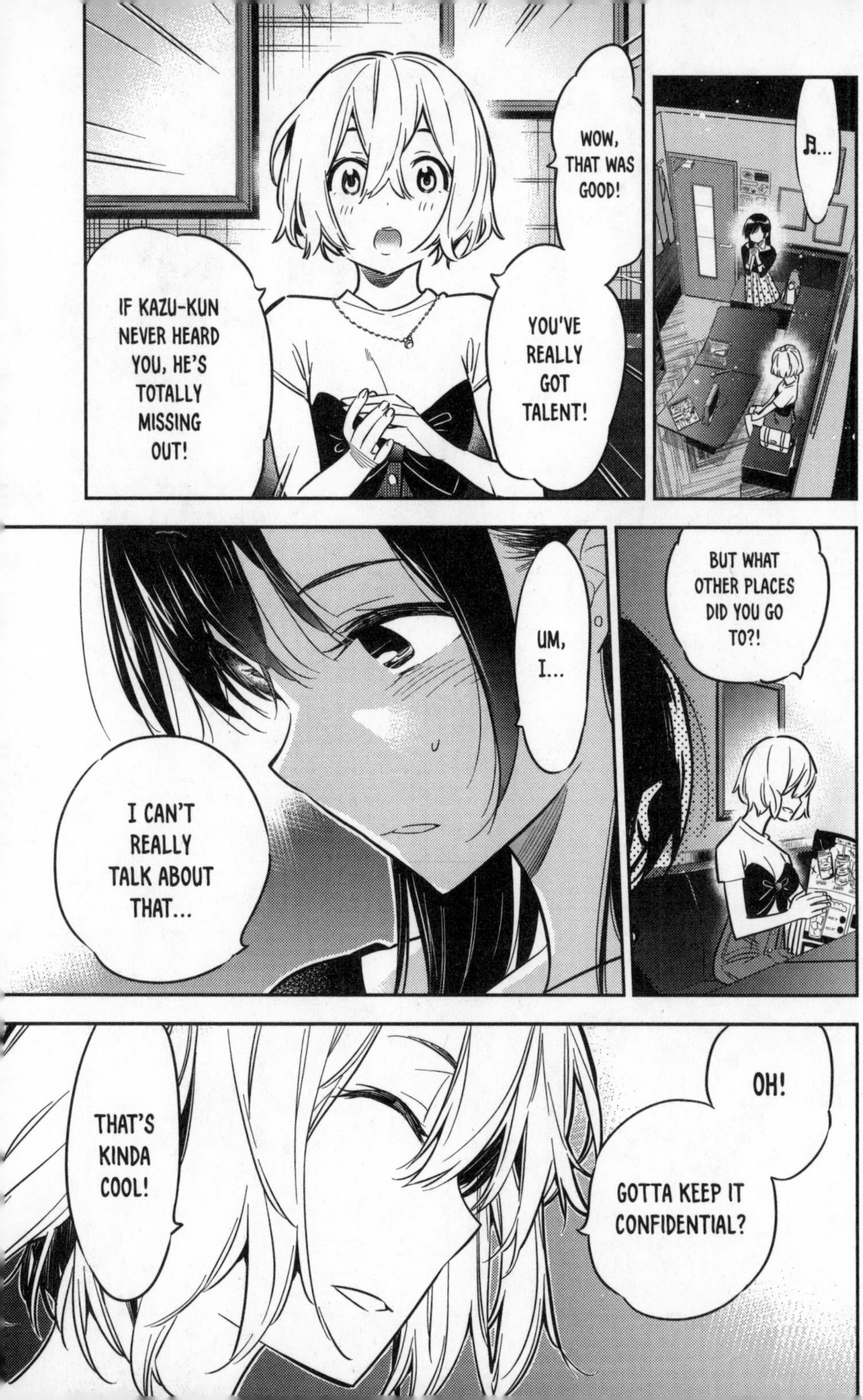
♫...
WOW, THAT WAS GOOD!
YOU'VE REALLY GOT TALENT!
IF KAZU-KUN NEVER HEARD YOU, HE'S TOTALLY MISSING OUT!
BUT WHAT OTHER PLACES DID YOU GO TO?!
UM, I...
I CAN'T REALLY TALK ABOUT THAT...
OH!
GOTTA KEEP IT CONFIDENTIAL?
THAT'S KINDA COOL!

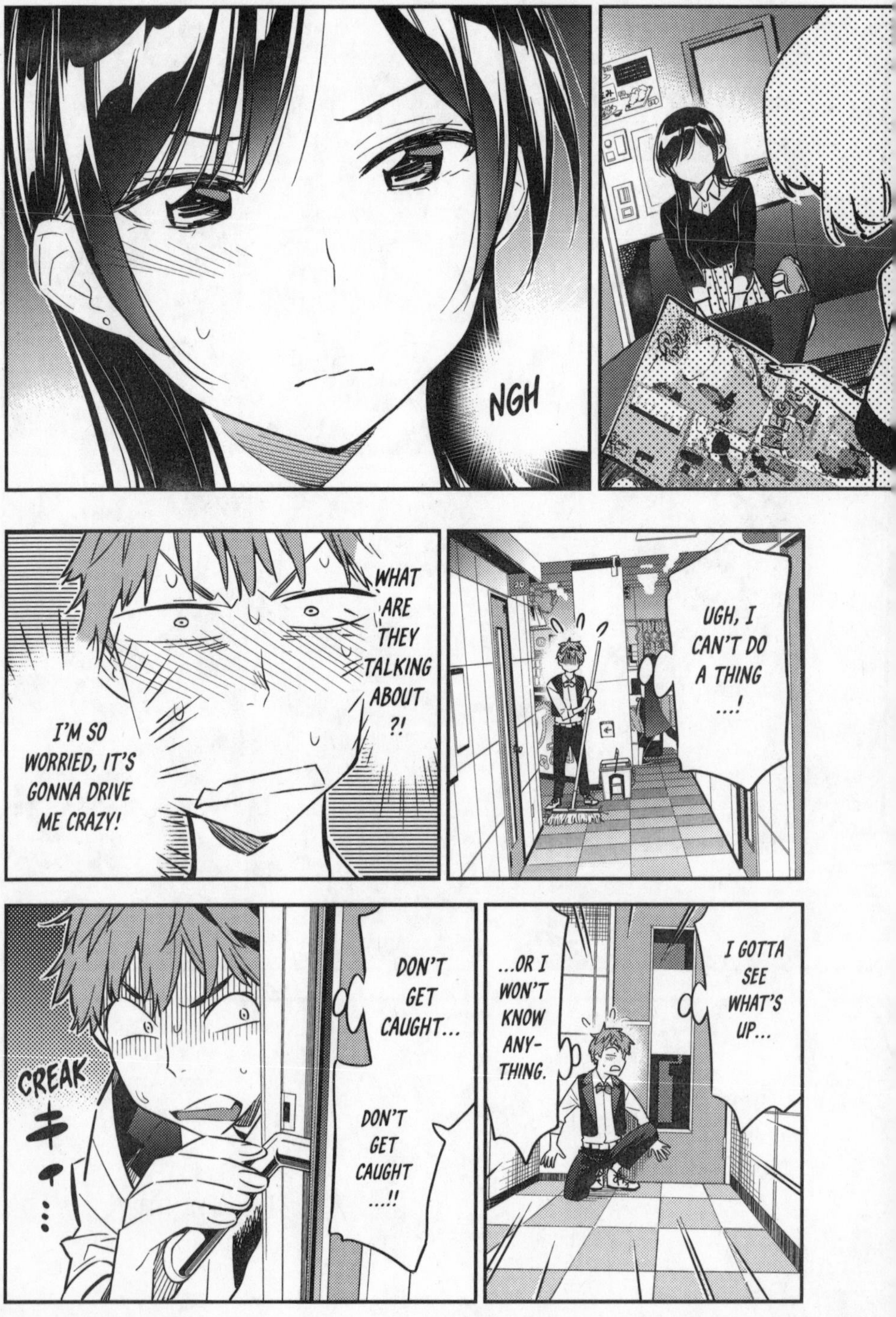
NGH
UGH, I CAN'T DO A THING ...!
WHAT ARE THEY TALKING ABOUT ?!
I'M SO WORRIED, IT'S GONNA DRIVE ME CRAZY!
I GOTTA SEE WHAT'S UP...
...OR I WON'T KNOW ANY-THING.
DON'T GET CAUGHT...
DON'T GET CAUGHT ...!!
CREAK
キィ…

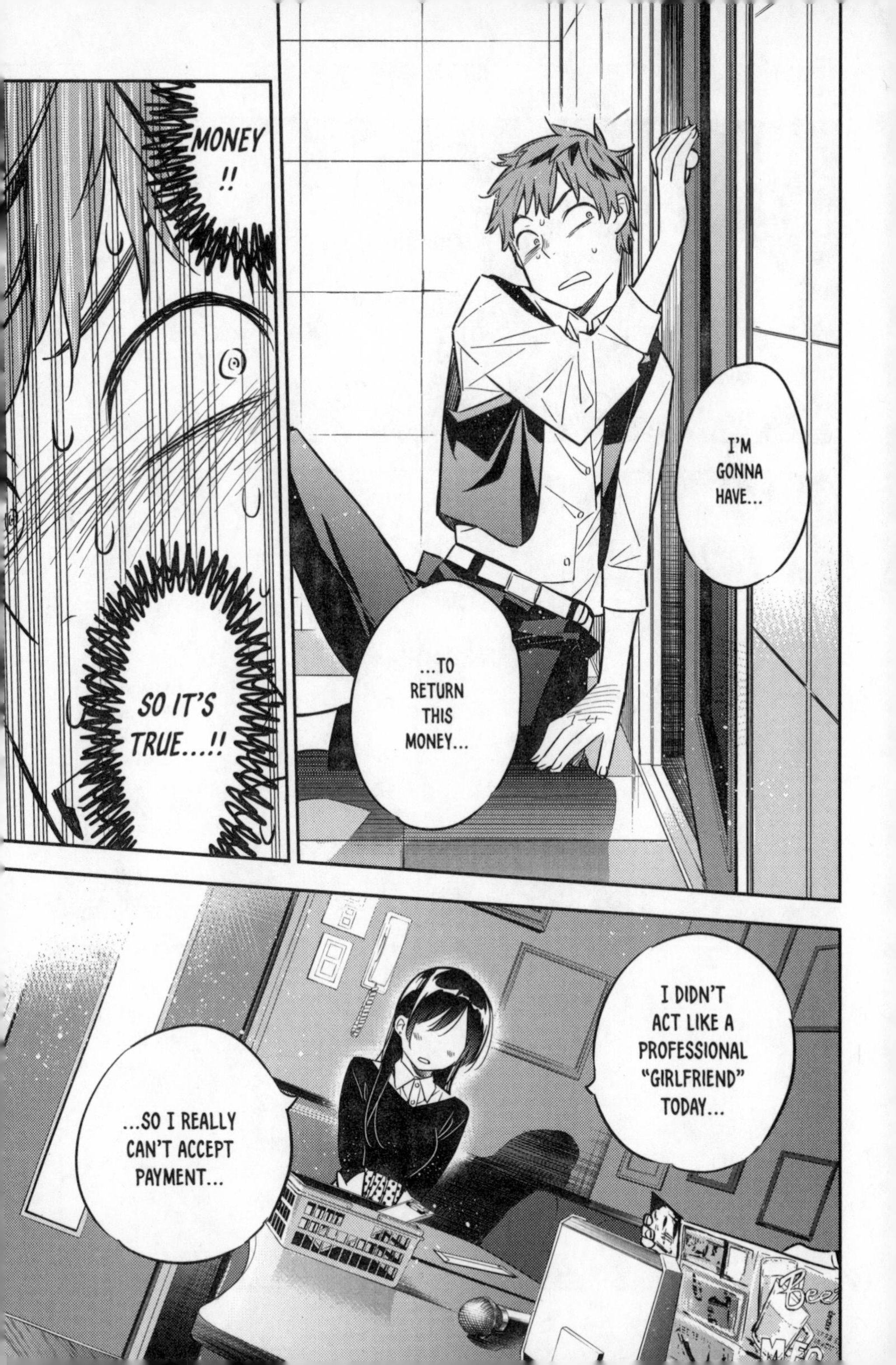
I'M GONNA HAVE...
...TO RETURN THIS MONEY...
MONEY !!
SO IT'S TRUE...!!
I DIDN'T ACT LIKE A PROFESSIONAL "GIRLFRIEND" TODAY...
...SO I REALLY CAN'T ACCEPT PAYMENT...

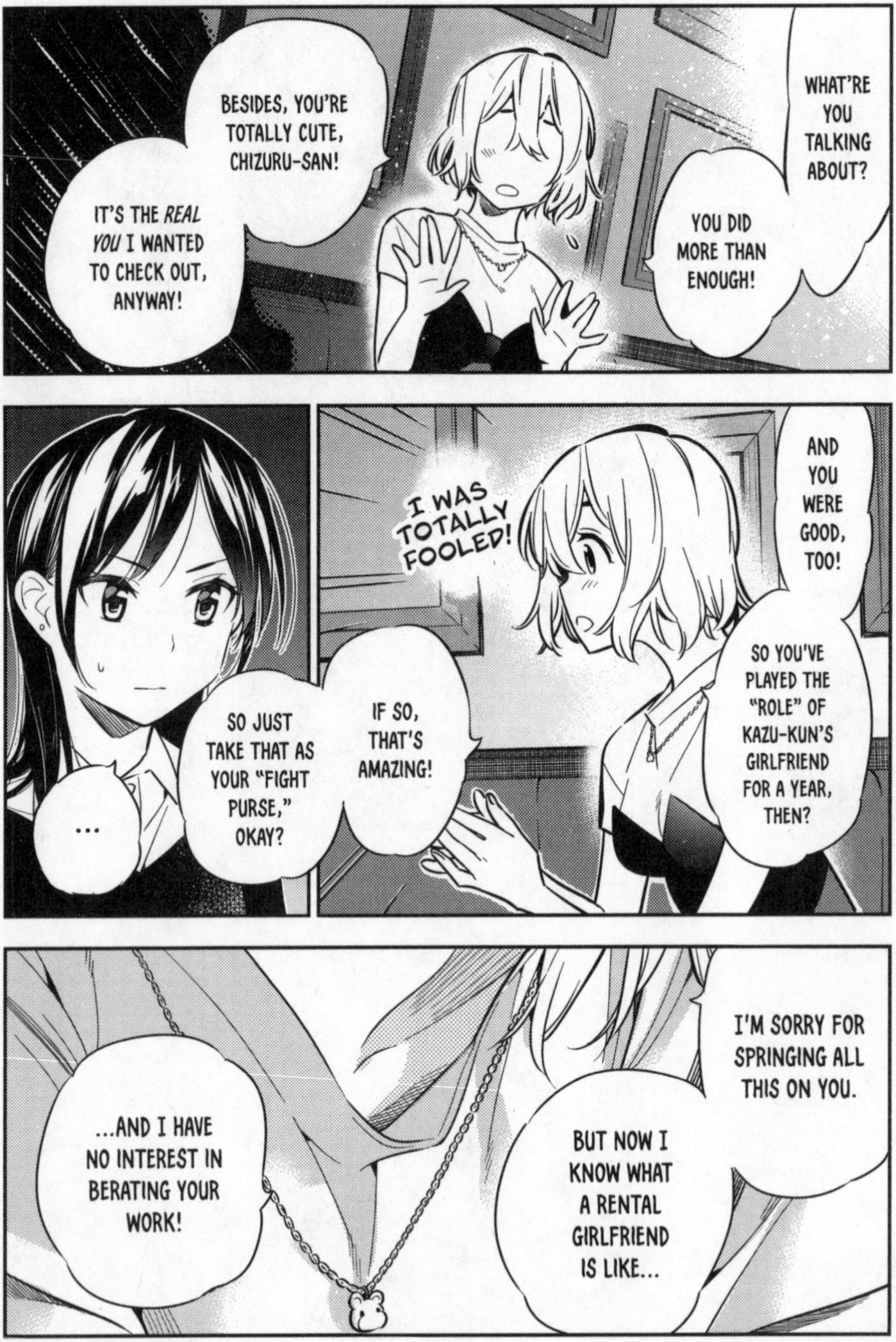
WHAT'RE YOU TALKING ABOUT?
YOU DID MORE THAN ENOUGH!
BESIDES, YOU'RE TOTALLY CUTE, CHIZURU-SAN!
IT'S THE *REAL YOU* I WANTED TO CHECK OUT, ANYWAY!
AND YOU WERE GOOD, TOO!
I WAS TOTALLY FOOLED!
SO YOU'VE PLAYED THE "ROLE" OF KAZU-KUN'S GIRLFRIEND FOR A YEAR, THEN?
IF SO, THAT'S AMAZING!
SO JUST TAKE THAT AS YOUR "FIGHT PURSE," OKAY?
...
I'M SORRY FOR SPRINGING ALL THIS ON YOU.
BUT NOW I KNOW WHAT A RENTAL GIRLFRIEND IS LIKE...
...AND I HAVE NO INTEREST IN BERATING YOUR WORK!

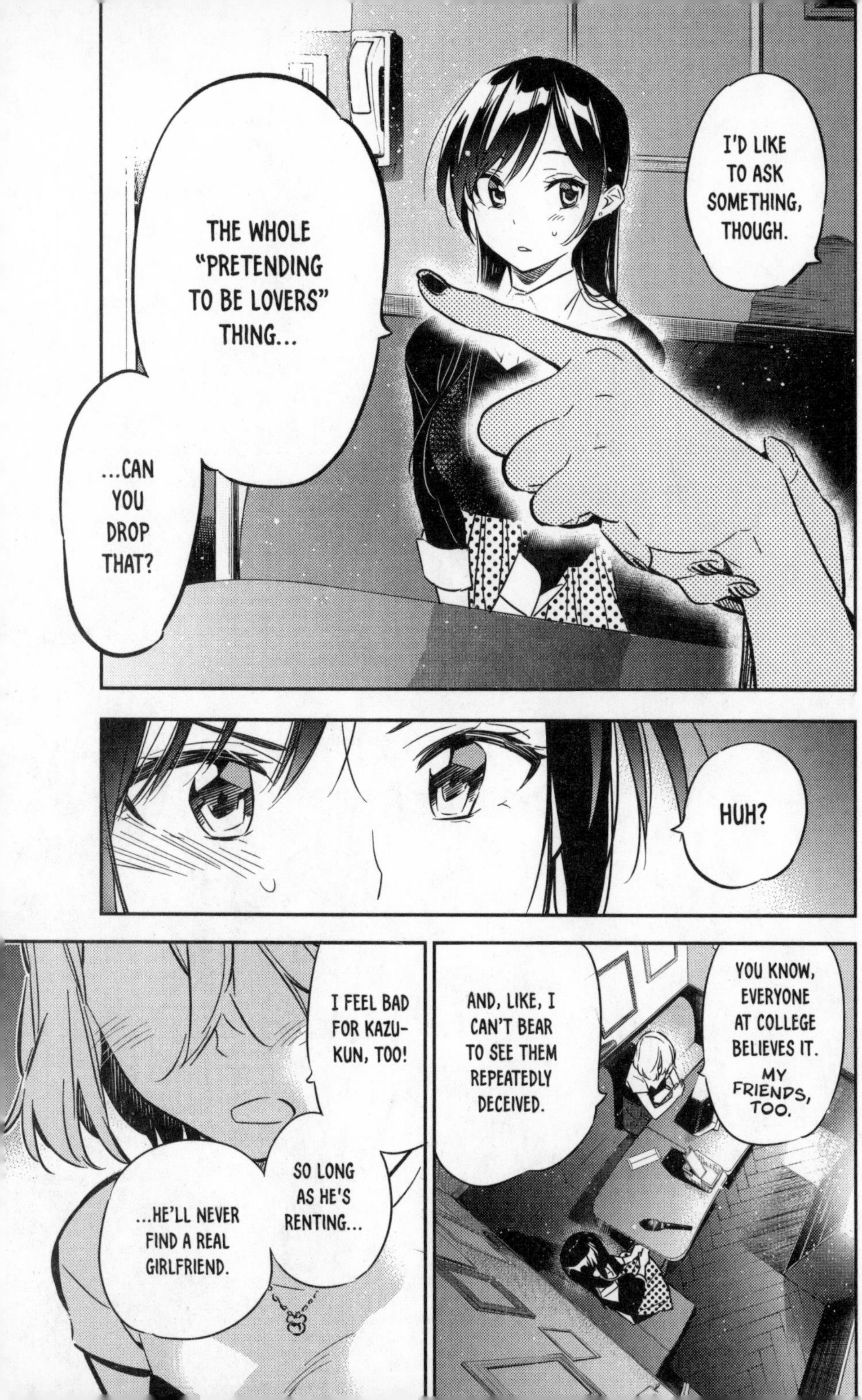
I'D LIKE TO ASK SOMETHING, THOUGH.
THE WHOLE "PRETENDING TO BE LOVERS" THING...
...CAN YOU DROP THAT?
HUH?
YOU KNOW, EVERYONE AT COLLEGE BELIEVES IT. MY FRIENDS, TOO.
AND, LIKE, I CAN'T BEAR TO SEE THEM REPEATEDLY DECEIVED.
I FEEL BAD FOR KAZU-KUN, TOO!
SO LONG AS HE'S RENTING...
...HE'LL NEVER FIND A REAL GIRLFRIEND.

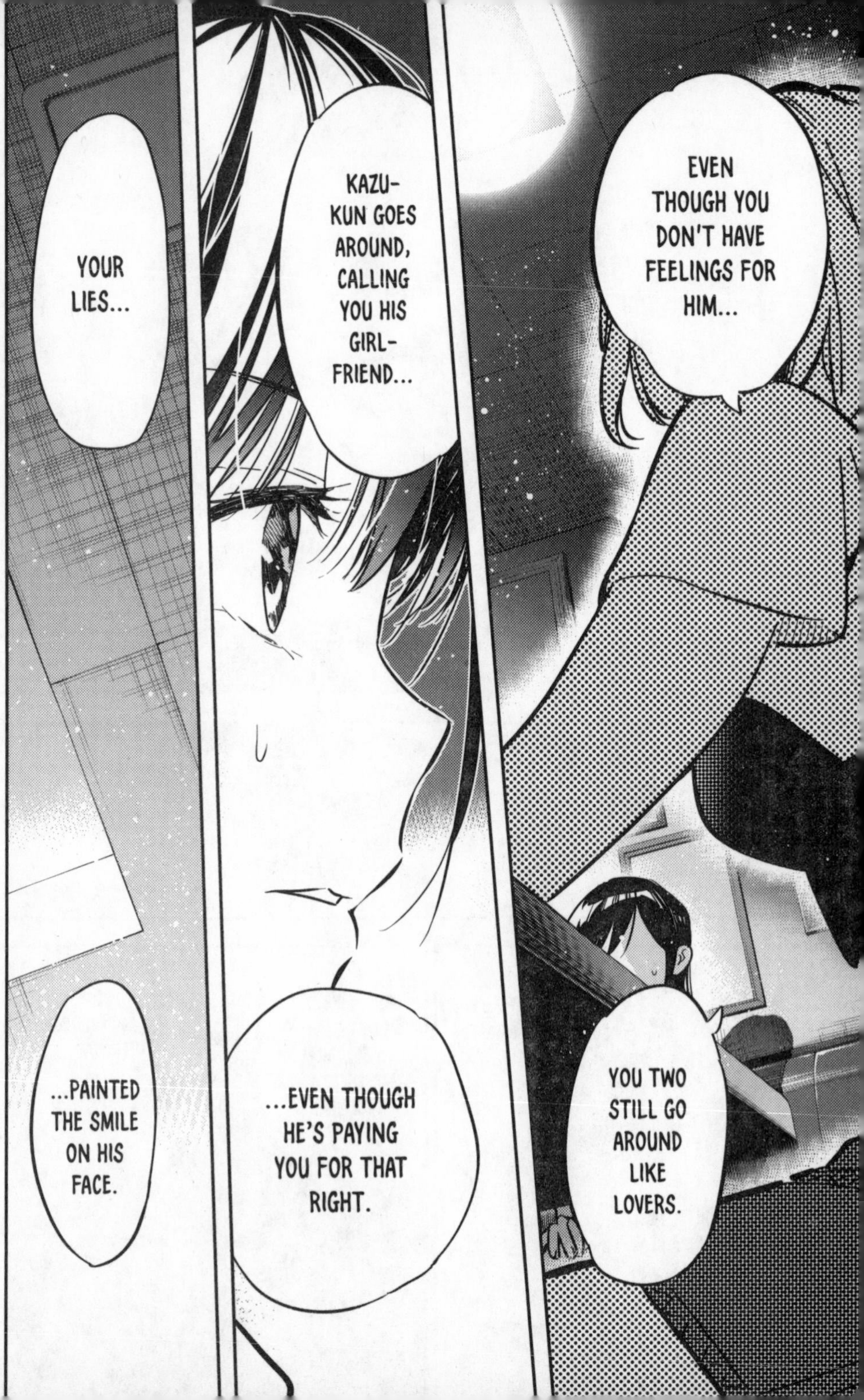
EVEN THOUGH YOU DON'T HAVE FEELINGS FOR HIM...
YOU TWO STILL GO AROUND LIKE LOVERS.
KAZU-KUN GOES AROUND, CALLING YOU HIS GIRL-FRIEND...
...EVEN THOUGH HE'S PAYING YOU FOR THAT RIGHT.
YOUR LIES...
...PAINTED THE SMILE ON HIS FACE.

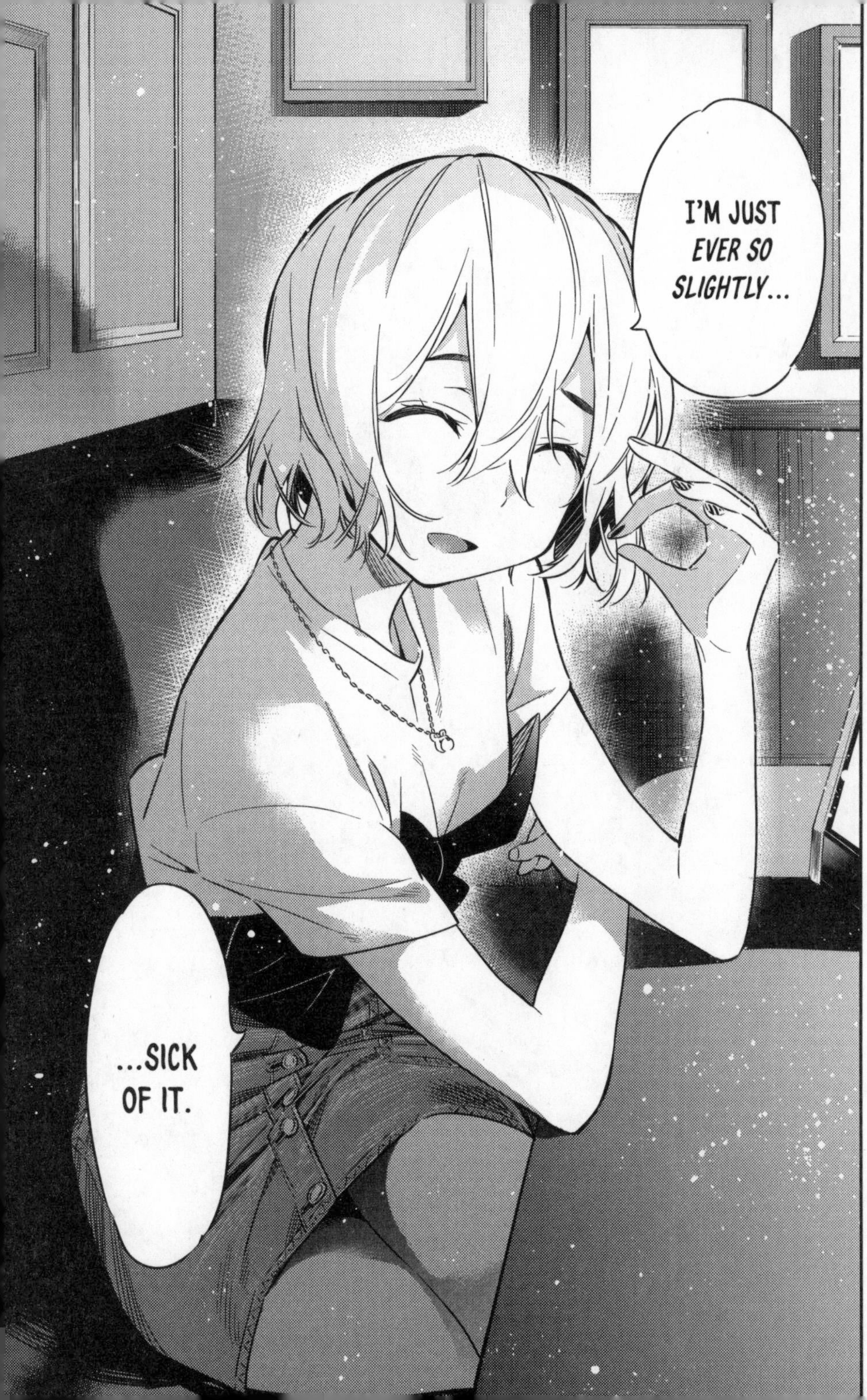
I'M JUST EVER SO SLIGHTLY...
...SICK OF IT.

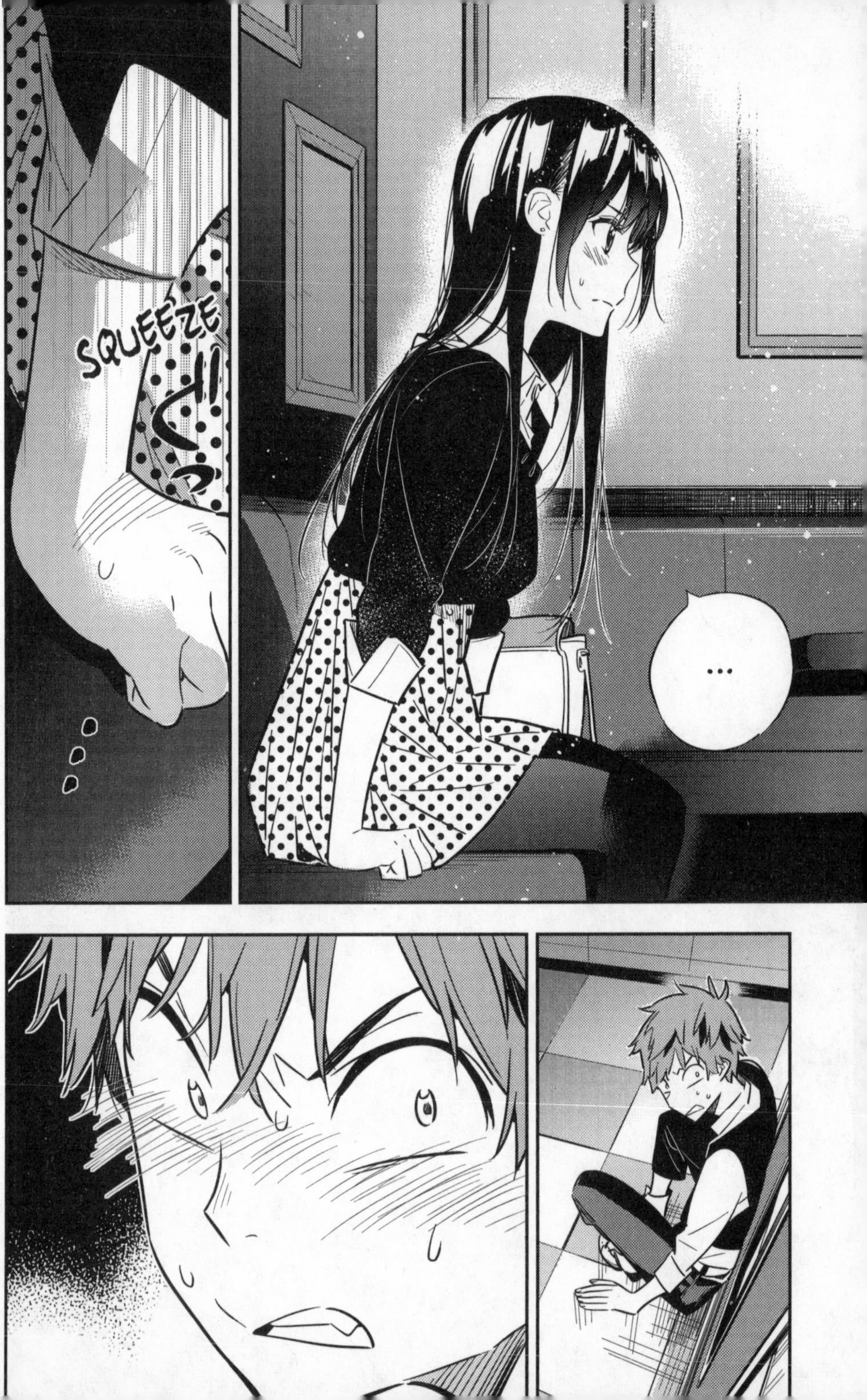
…
SQUEEZE

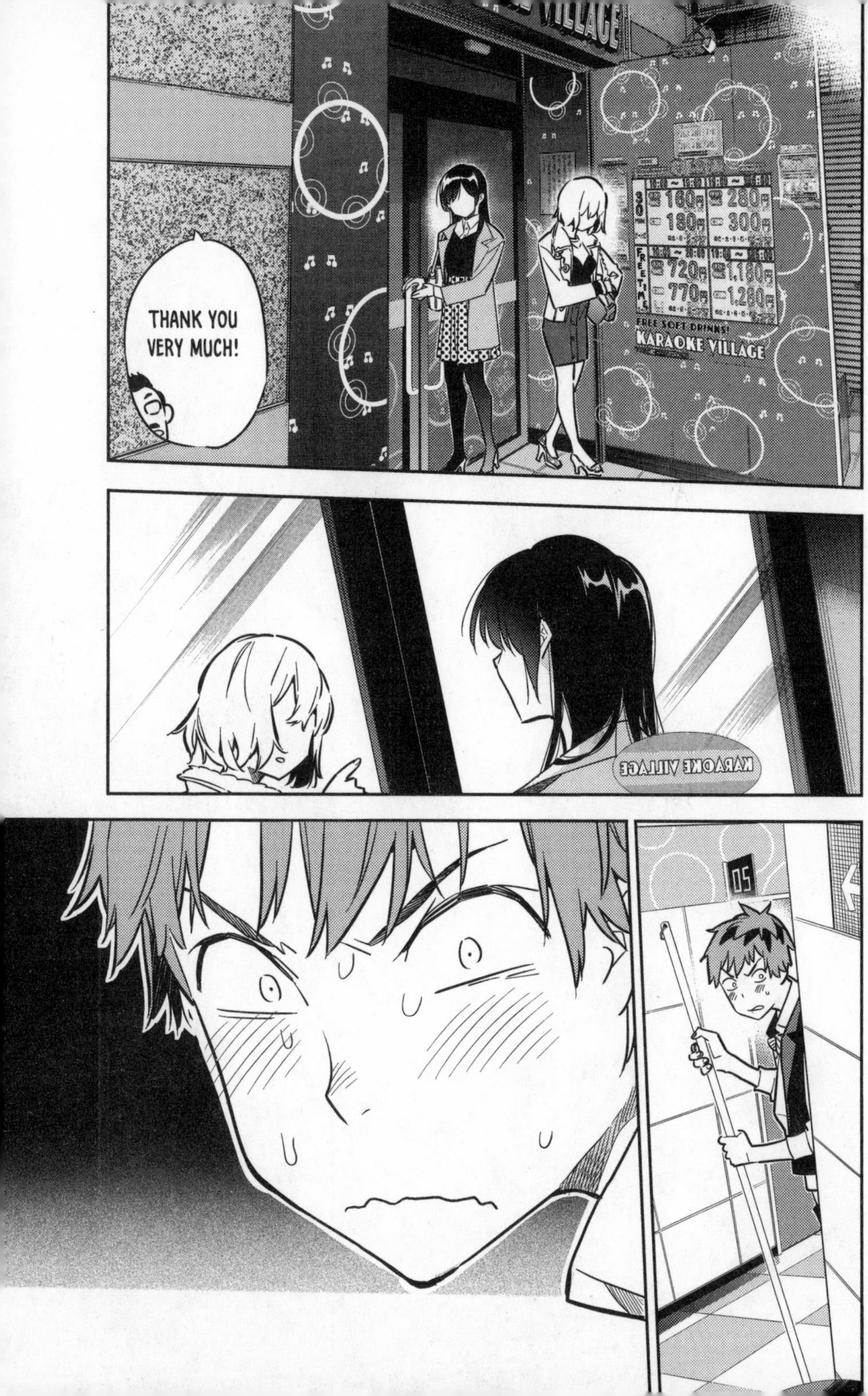
VILLAGE
THANK YOU VERY MUCH!
FREE SOFT DRINKS!
KARAOKE VILLAGE
05

RATING 48 MY GIRLFRIEND AND MY EX (3)

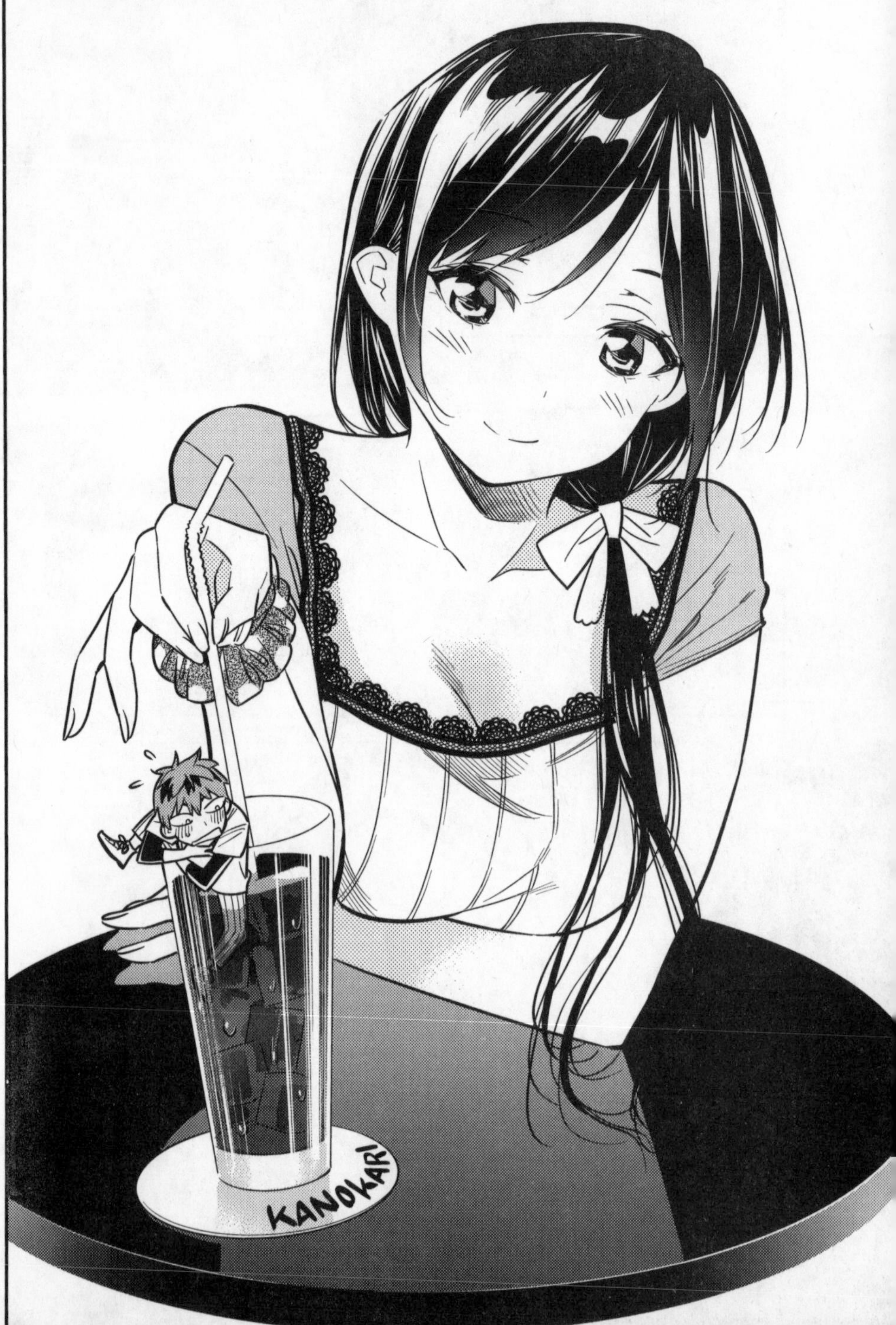
KANOKARI

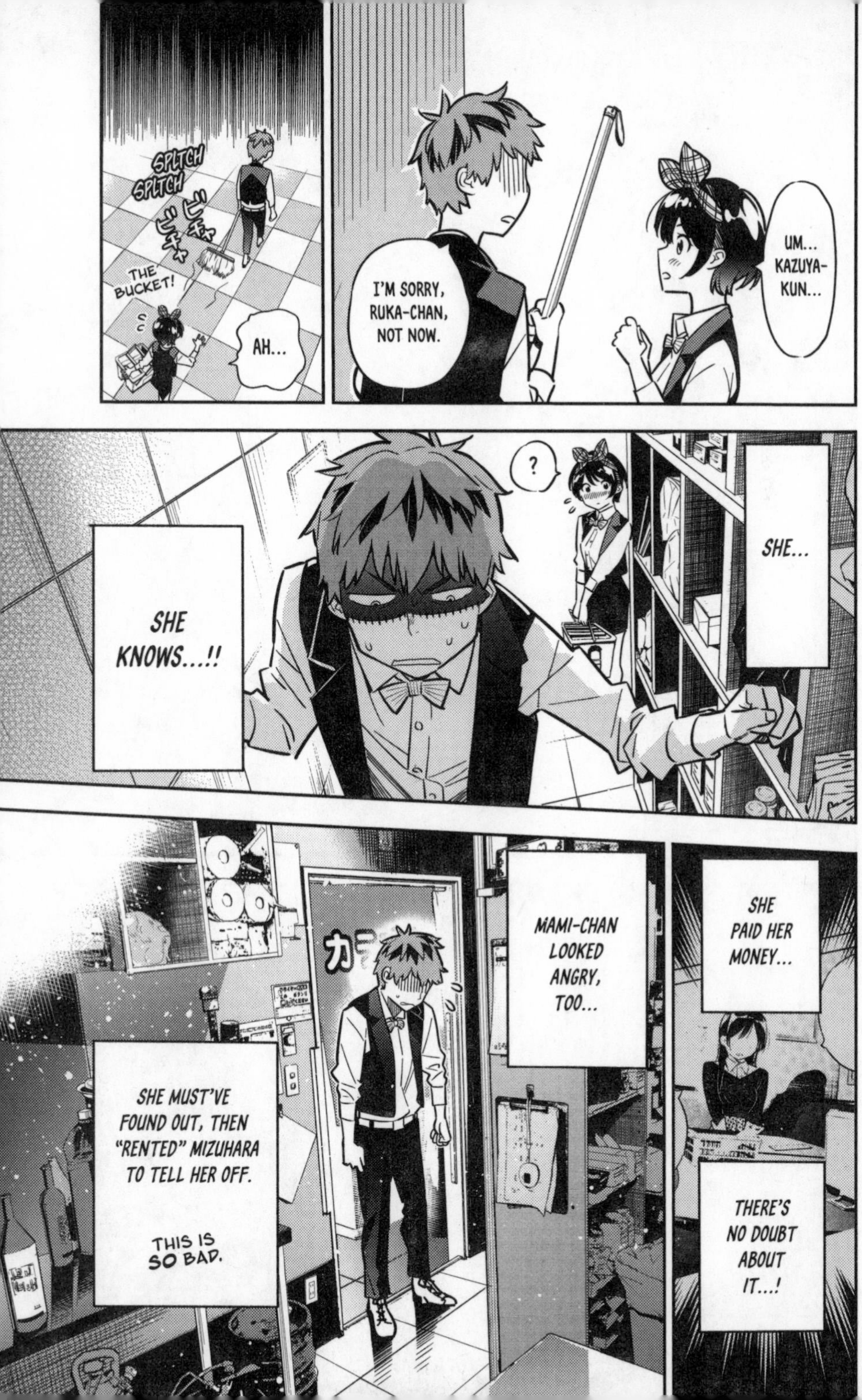
UM... KAZUYA-KUN...
I'M SORRY, RUKA-CHAN, NOT NOW.
SPLTCH SPLTCH
ビチャ ビチャ
THE BUCKET!
AH...
SHE...
?
SHE KNOWS...!!
SHE PAID HER MONEY...
THERE'S NO DOUBT ABOUT IT...!
MAMI-CHAN LOOKED ANGRY, TOO...
カ
SHE MUST'VE FOUND OUT, THEN "RENTED" MIZUHARA TO TELL HER OFF.
THIS IS SO BAD.

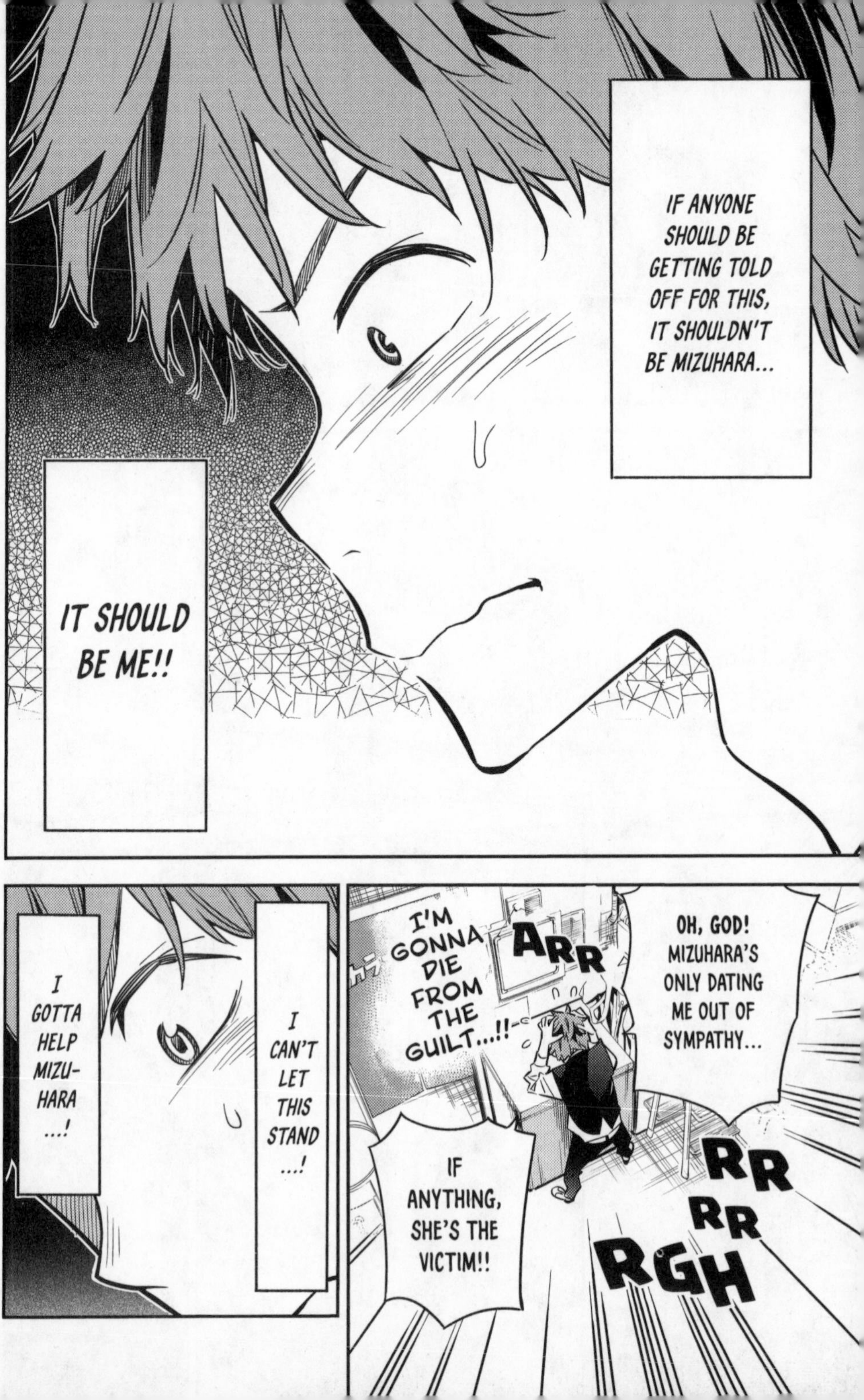
IF ANYONE SHOULD BE GETTING TOLD OFF FOR THIS, IT SHOULDN'T BE MIZUHARA...
IT SHOULD BE ME!!
OH, GOD! MIZUHARA'S ONLY DATING ME OUT OF SYMPATHY...
IF ANYTHING, SHE'S THE VICTIM!!
I'M GONNA DIE FROM THE GUILT...!!
ARRRRRRRGH
I CAN'T LET THIS STAND...!
I GOTTA HELP MIZU-HARA...!

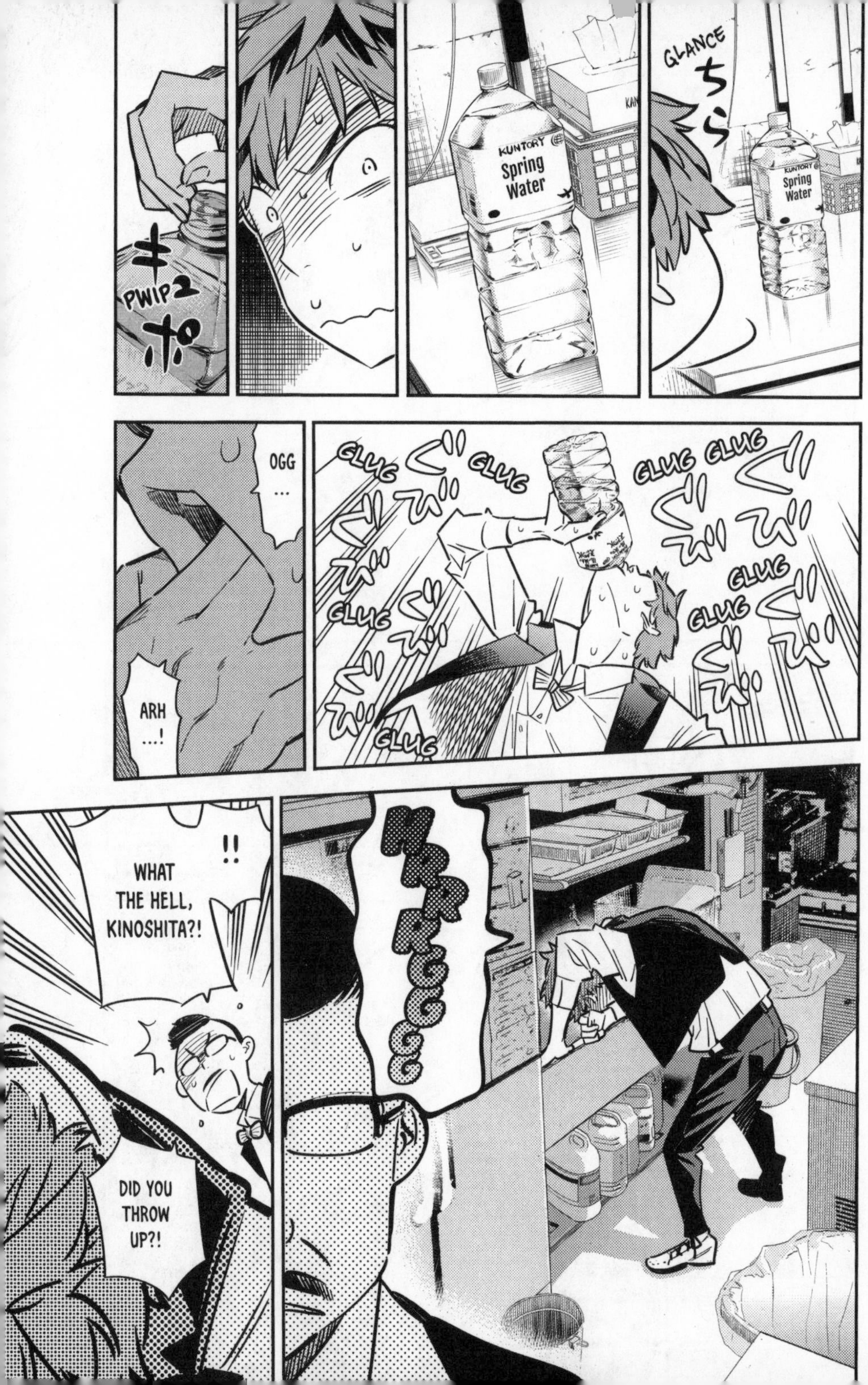
GLANCE
ちら
KUNTORY
Spring Water
KUNTORY
Spring Water
キ
PWIP
ポ
GLUG
ぐび
GLUG
ぐび
GLUG GLUG
ぐび
ぐび
GLUG
ぐび
GLUG
ぐび
GLUG
ぐび
GLUG
OGG...
ARH...!
HRRRGGG
!!
WHAT THE HELL, KINOSHITA?!
DID YOU THROW UP?!

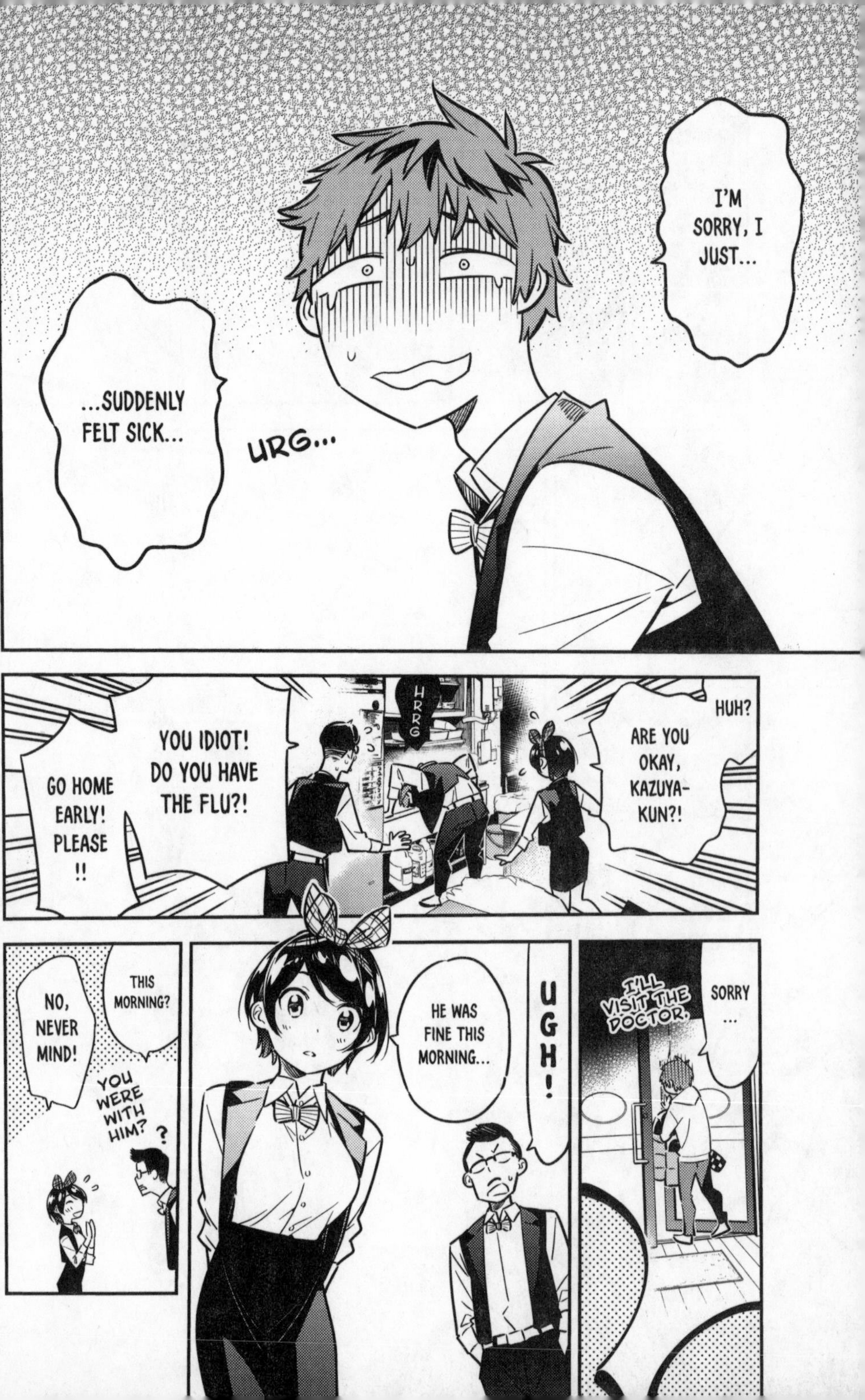
I'M SORRY, I JUST...
URG...
...SUDDENLY FELT SICK...
HUH?
ARE YOU OKAY, KAZUYA-KUN?!
HRRG
YOU IDIOT! DO YOU HAVE THE FLU?!
GO HOME EARLY! PLEASE !!
SORRY ...
I'LL VISIT THE DOCTOR.
UGH!
HE WAS FINE THIS MORNING...
THIS MORNING?
NO, NEVER MIND!
YOU WERE WITH HIM?
?

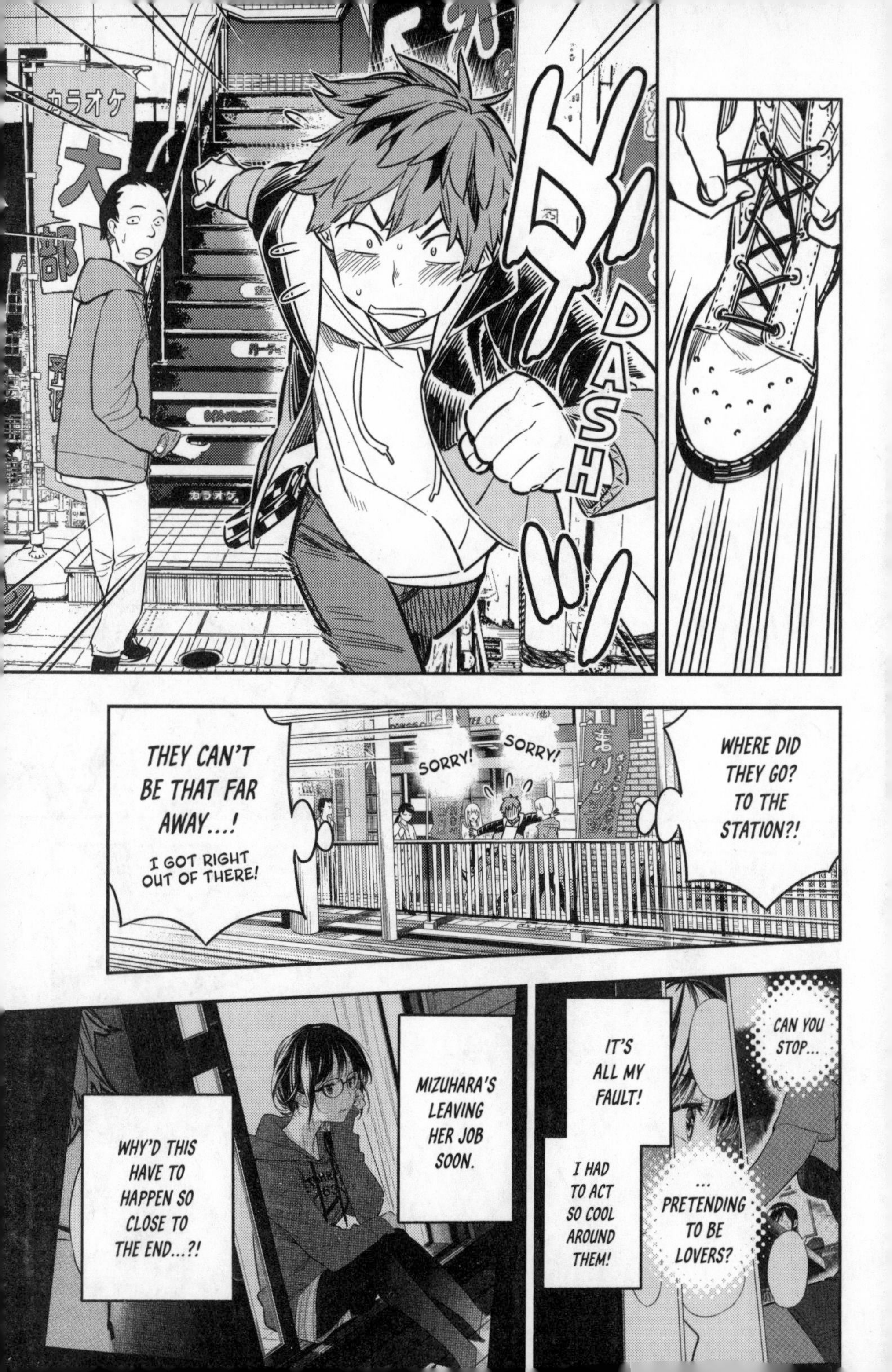

カラオケ
DASH
WHERE DID THEY GO? TO THE STATION?!
SORRY!
SORRY!
THEY CAN'T BE THAT FAR AWAY...!
I GOT RIGHT OUT OF THERE!
CAN YOU STOP...
... PRETENDING TO BE LOVERS?
IT'S ALL MY FAULT!
I HAD TO ACT SO COOL AROUND THEM!
MIZUHARA'S LEAVING HER JOB SOON.
WHY'D THIS HAVE TO HAPPEN SO CLOSE TO THE END...?!

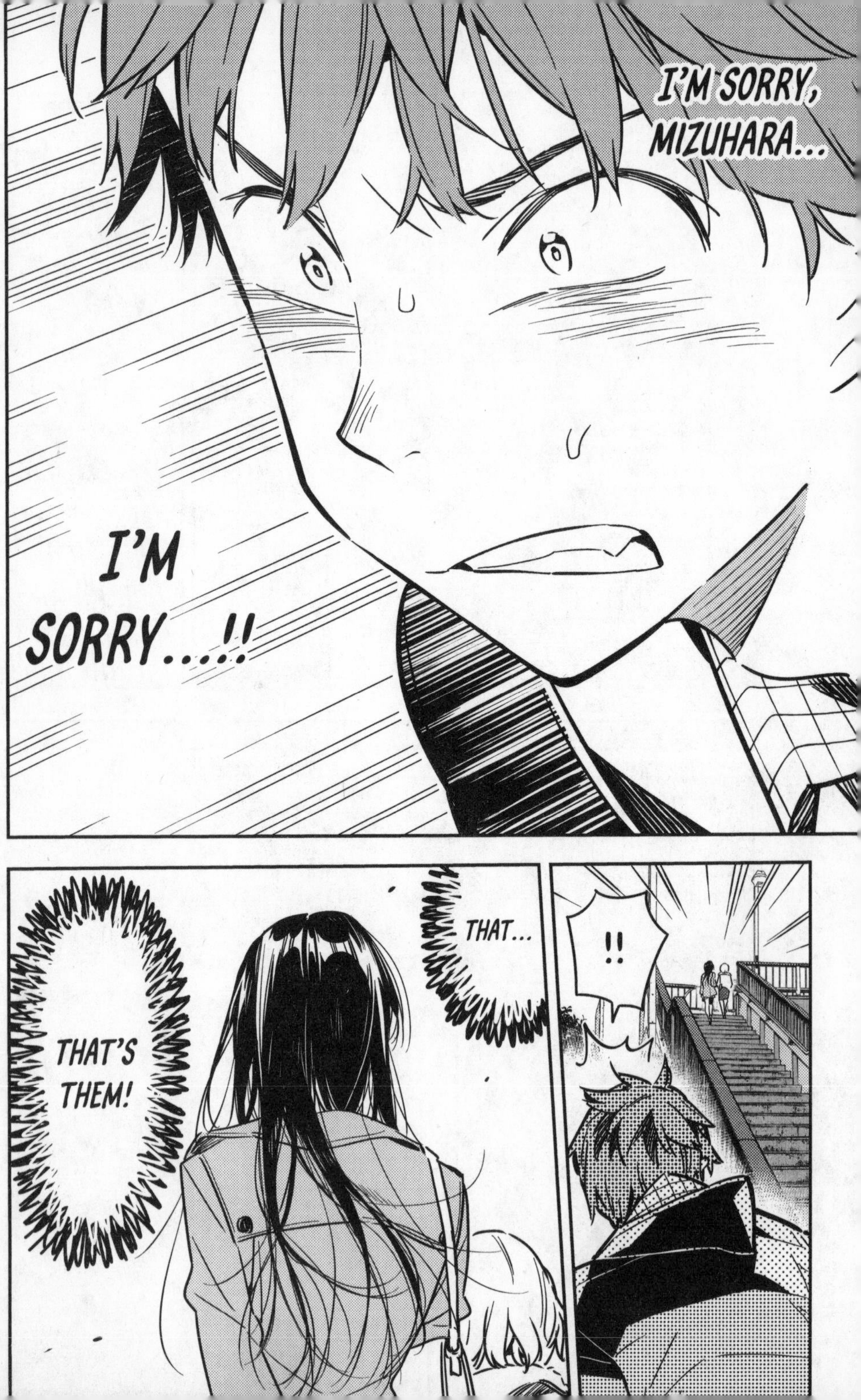
I'M SORRY, MIZUHARA...
I'M SORRY...!!
!!
THAT...
THAT'S THEM!

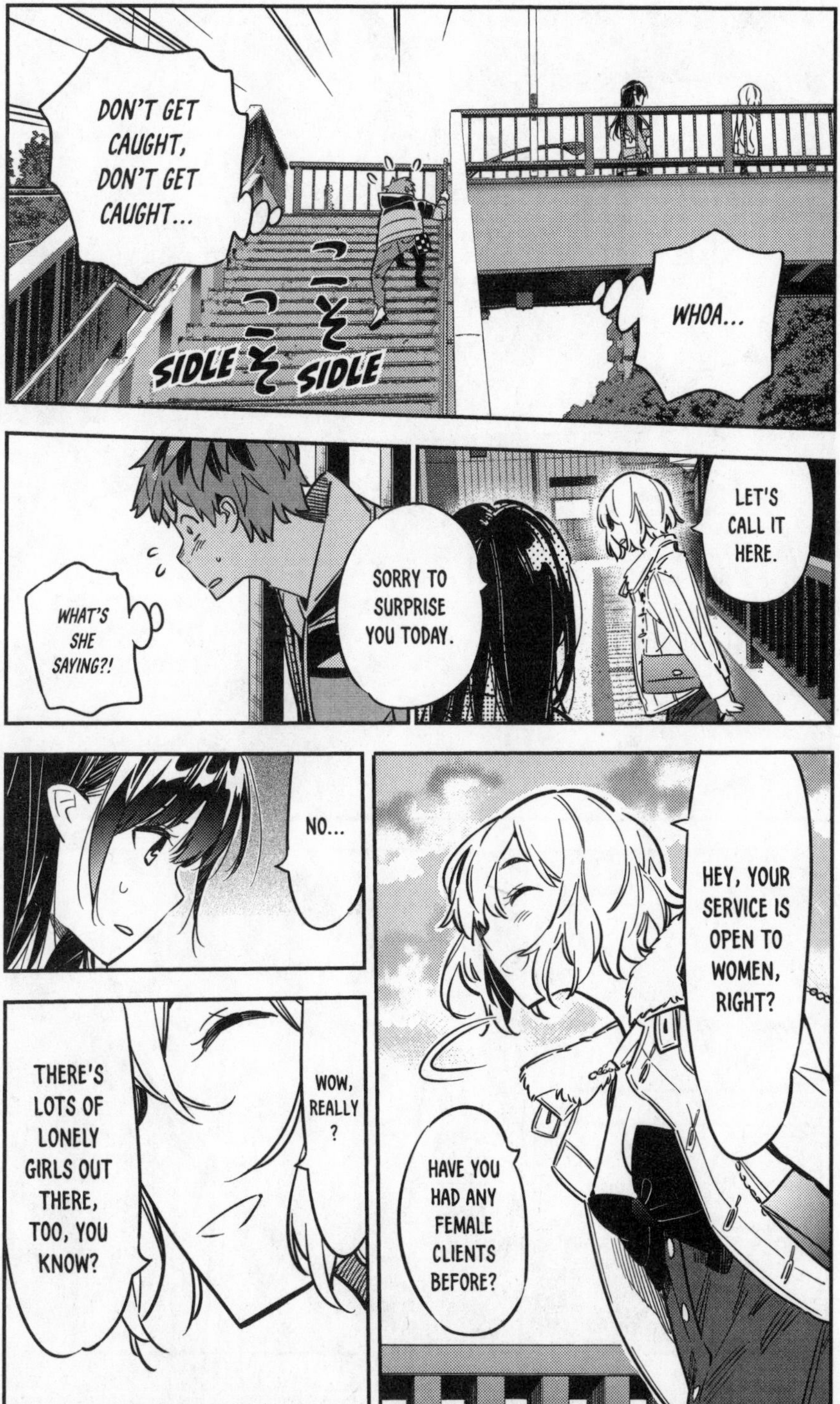
DON'T GET CAUGHT, DON'T GET CAUGHT...
SIDLE SIDLE
WHOA...
LET'S CALL IT HERE.
SORRY TO SURPRISE YOU TODAY.
WHAT'S SHE SAYING?!
HEY, YOUR SERVICE IS OPEN TO WOMEN, RIGHT?
HAVE YOU HAD ANY FEMALE CLIENTS BEFORE?
NO...
WOW, REALLY?
THERE'S LOTS OF LONELY GIRLS OUT THERE, TOO, YOU KNOW?

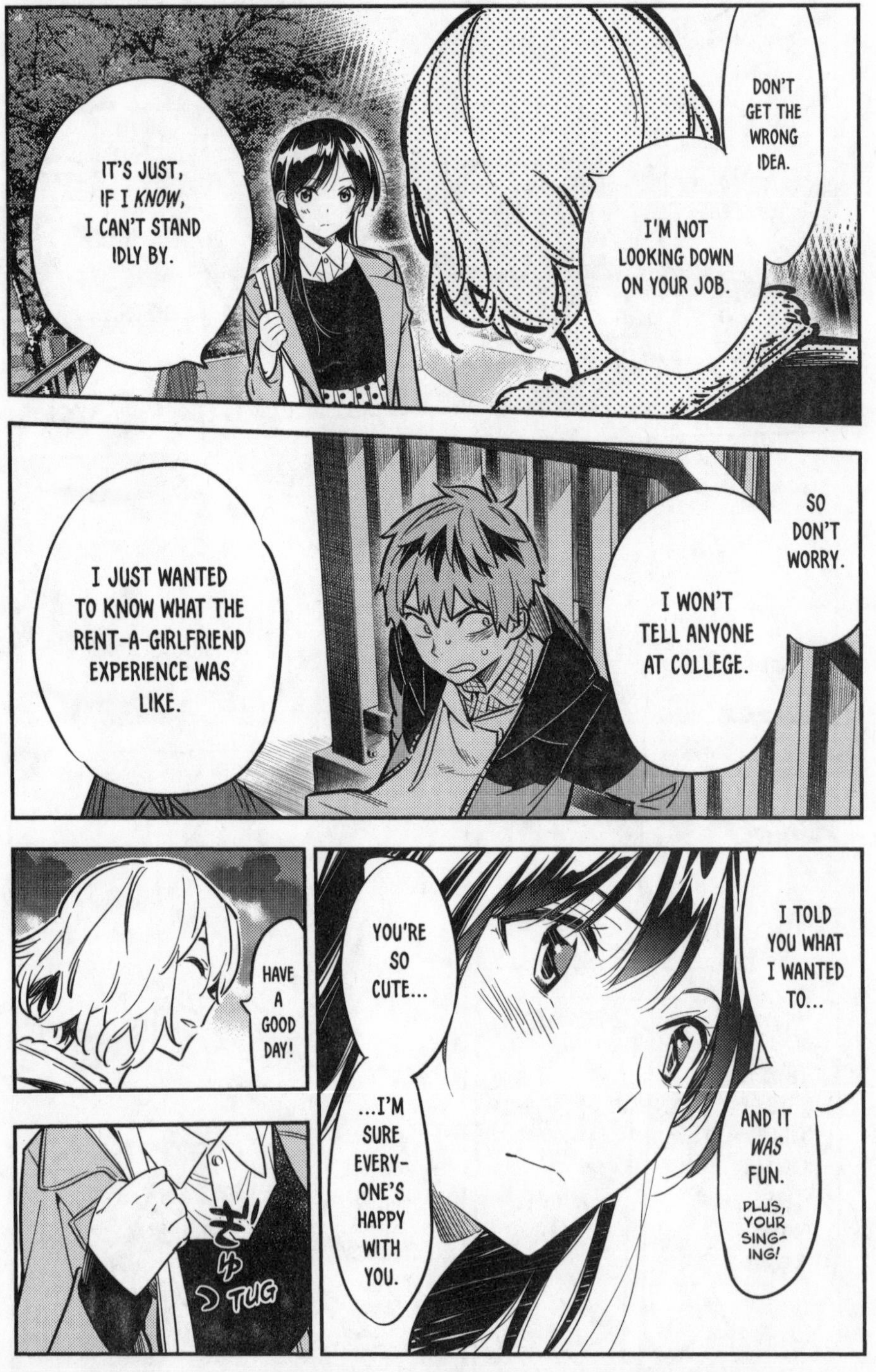
DON'T GET THE WRONG IDEA.
I'M NOT LOOKING DOWN ON YOUR JOB.
IT'S JUST, IF I *KNOW*, I CAN'T STAND IDLY BY.
SO DON'T WORRY.
I WON'T TELL ANYONE AT COLLEGE.
I JUST WANTED TO KNOW WHAT THE RENT-A-GIRLFRIEND EXPERIENCE WAS LIKE.
I TOLD YOU WHAT I WANTED TO...
AND IT *WAS* FUN.
PLUS, YOUR SINGING!
YOU'RE SO CUTE...
...I'M SURE EVERYONE'S HAPPY WITH YOU.
HAVE A GOOD DAY!
ぎゅっ
TUG

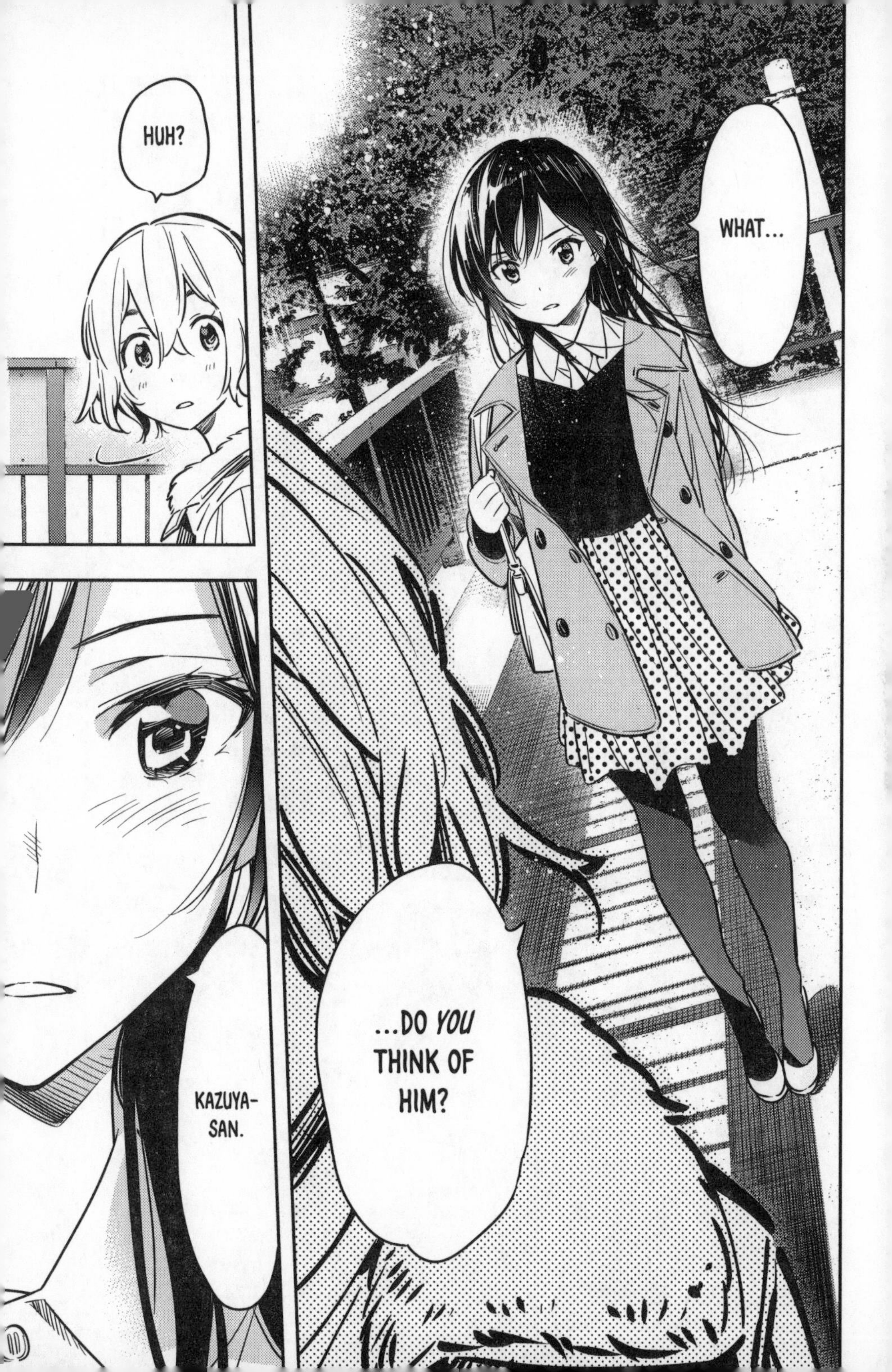
WHAT...
...DO YOU THINK OF HIM?
HUH?
KAZUYA-SAN.

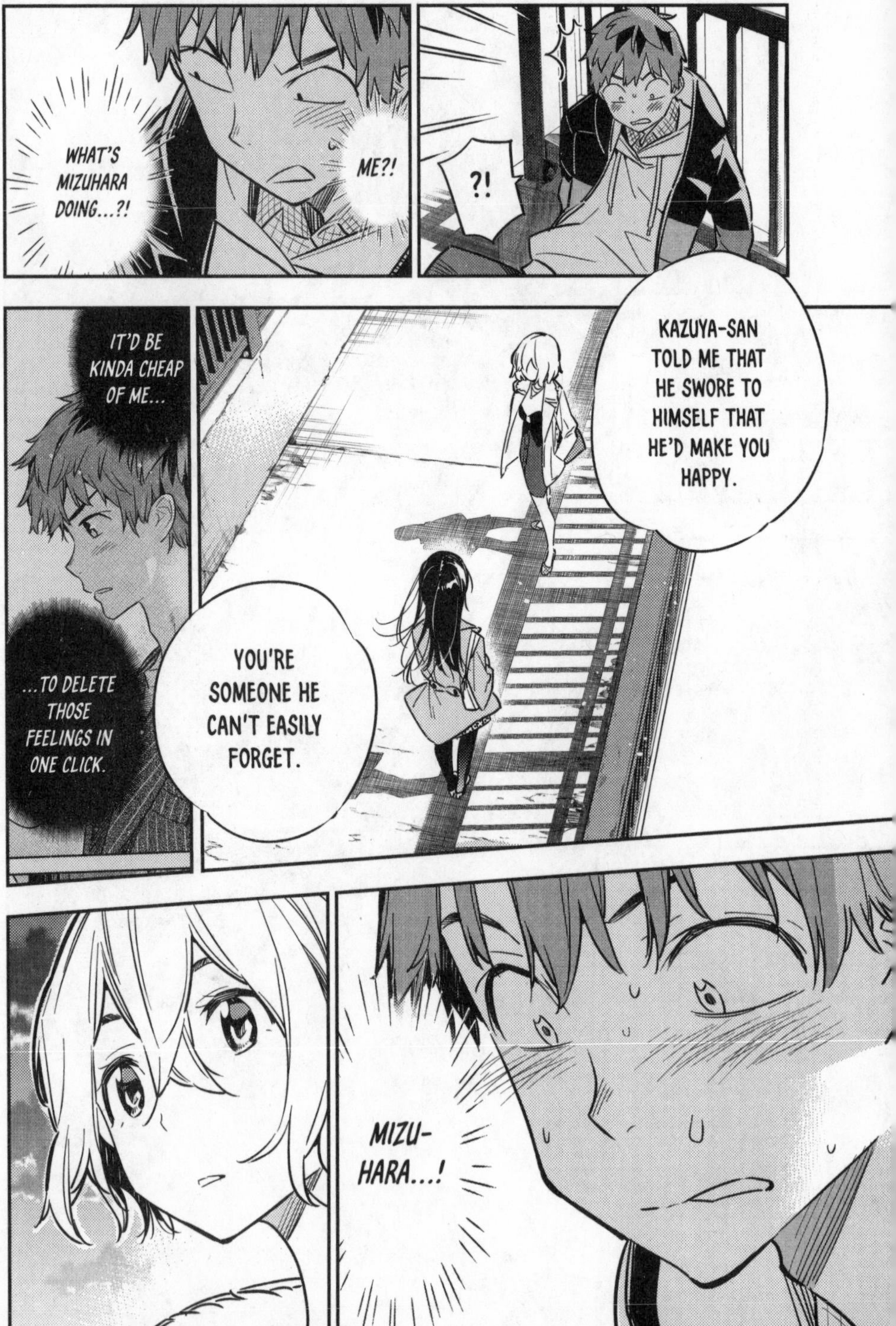
?!
ME?!
WHAT'S MIZUHARA DOING...?!
KAZUYA-SAN TOLD ME THAT HE SWORE TO HIMSELF THAT HE'D MAKE YOU HAPPY.
YOU'RE SOMEONE HE CAN'T EASILY FORGET.
IT'D BE KINDA CHEAP OF ME...
...TO DELETE THOSE FEELINGS IN ONE CLICK.
MIZU-HARA...!

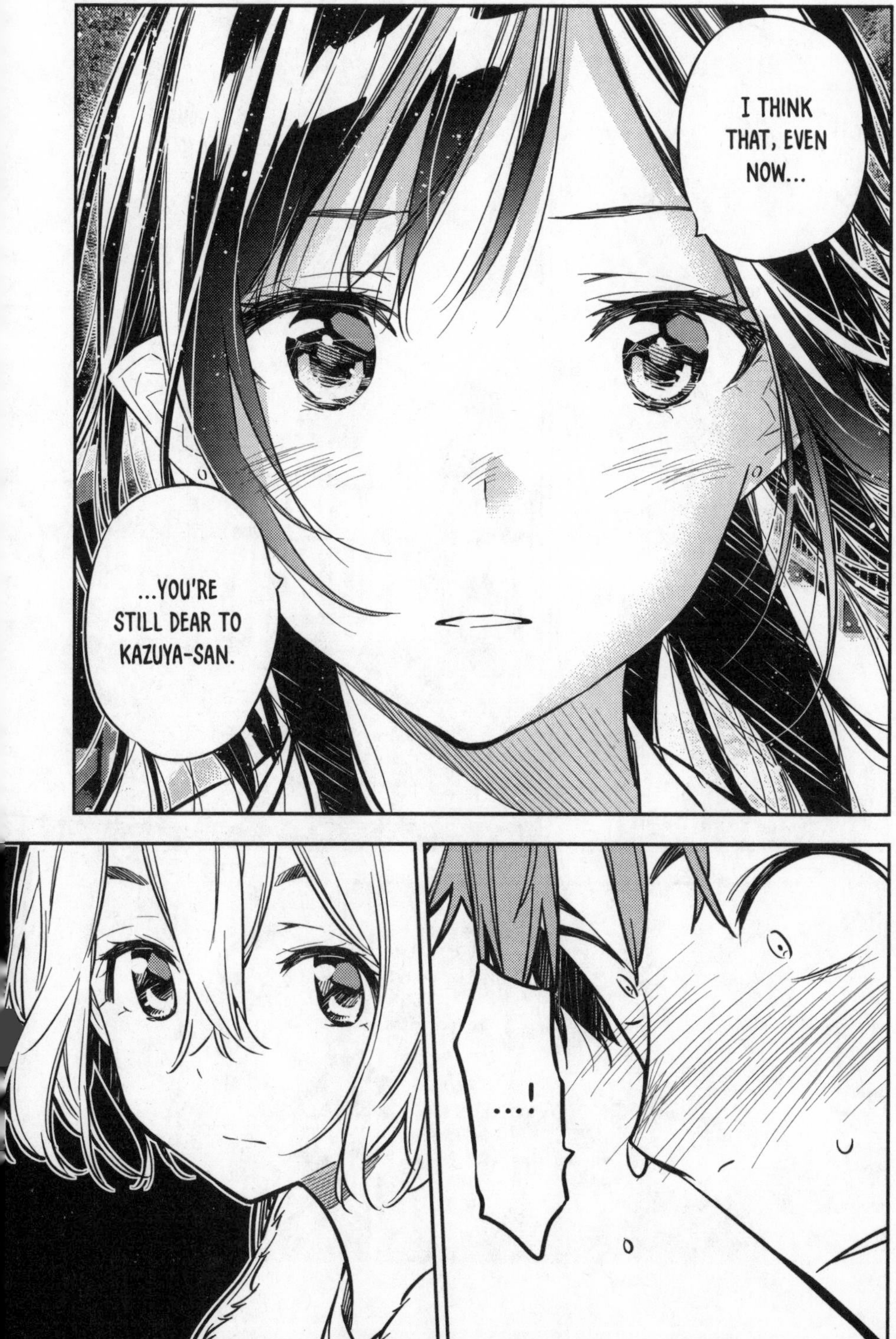
I THINK THAT, EVEN NOW...
...YOU'RE STILL DEAR TO KAZUYA-SAN.
...!

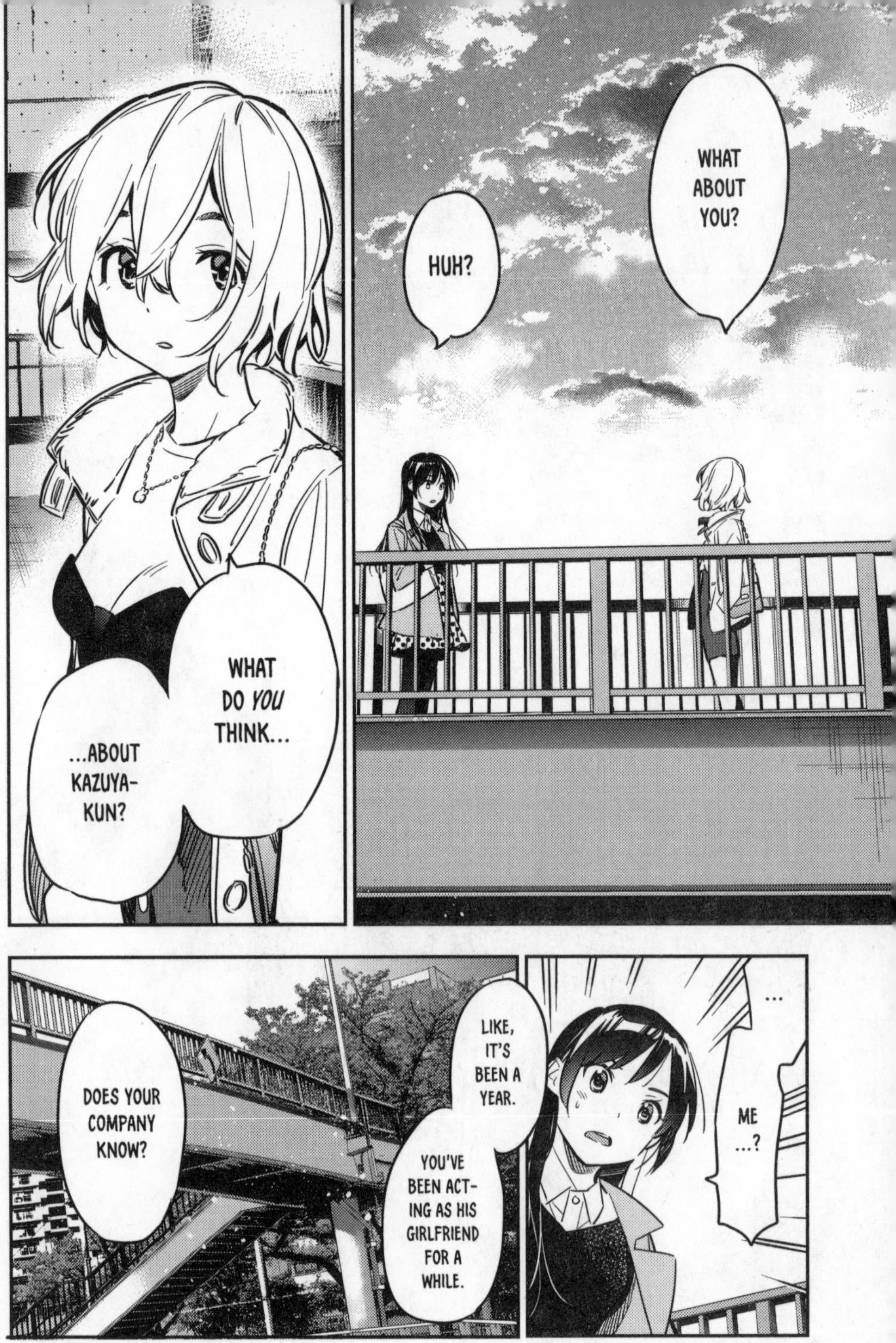
WHAT ABOUT YOU?
HUH?
WHAT DO *YOU* THINK...
...ABOUT KAZUYA-KUN?
...
ME ...?
LIKE, IT'S BEEN A YEAR.
YOU'VE BEEN ACT-ING AS HIS GIRLFRIEND FOR A WHILE.
DOES YOUR COMPANY KNOW?

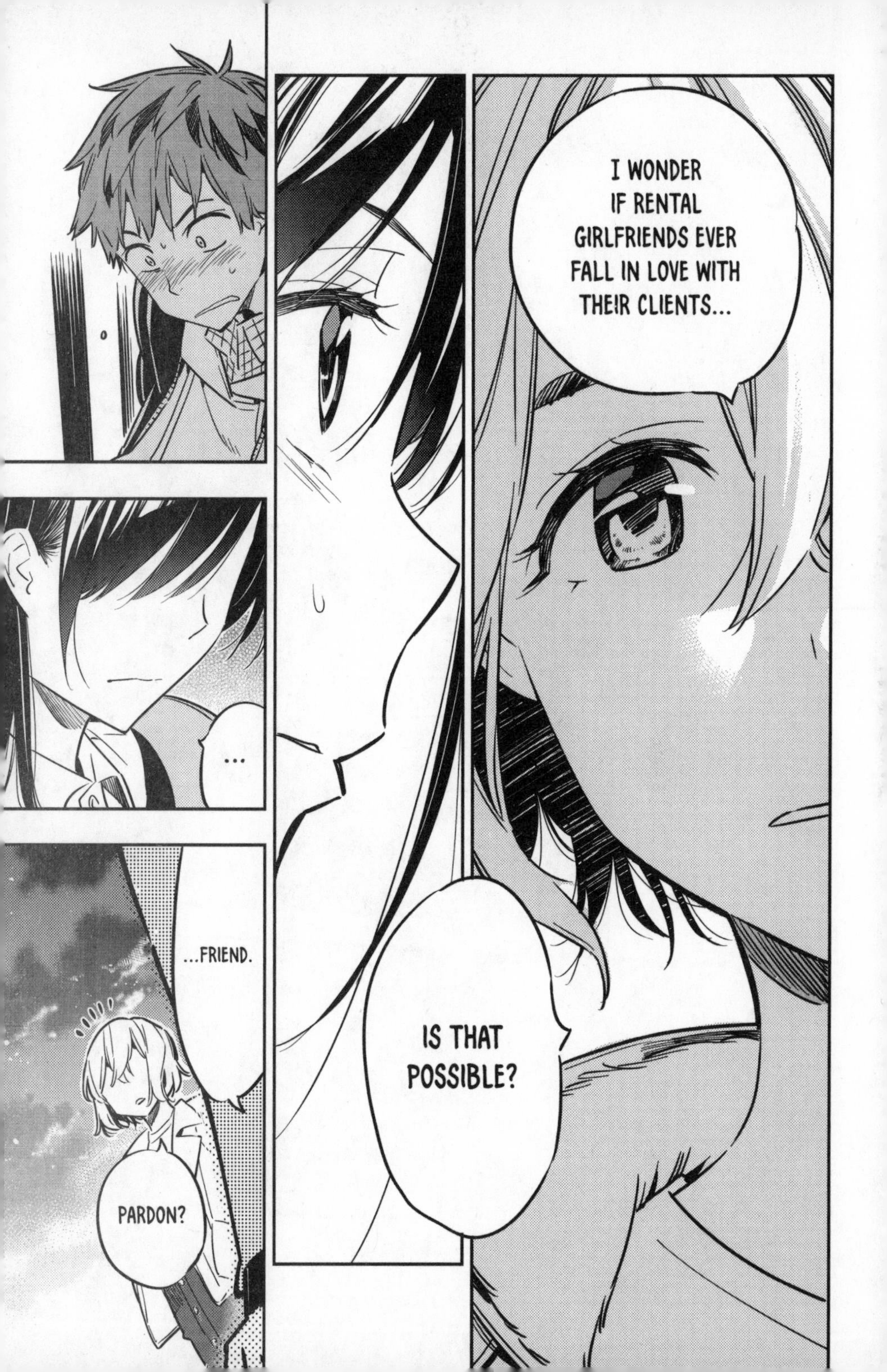
I WONDER IF RENTAL GIRLFRIENDS EVER FALL IN LOVE WITH THEIR CLIENTS...
IS THAT POSSIBLE?
...
...FRIEND.
PARDON?

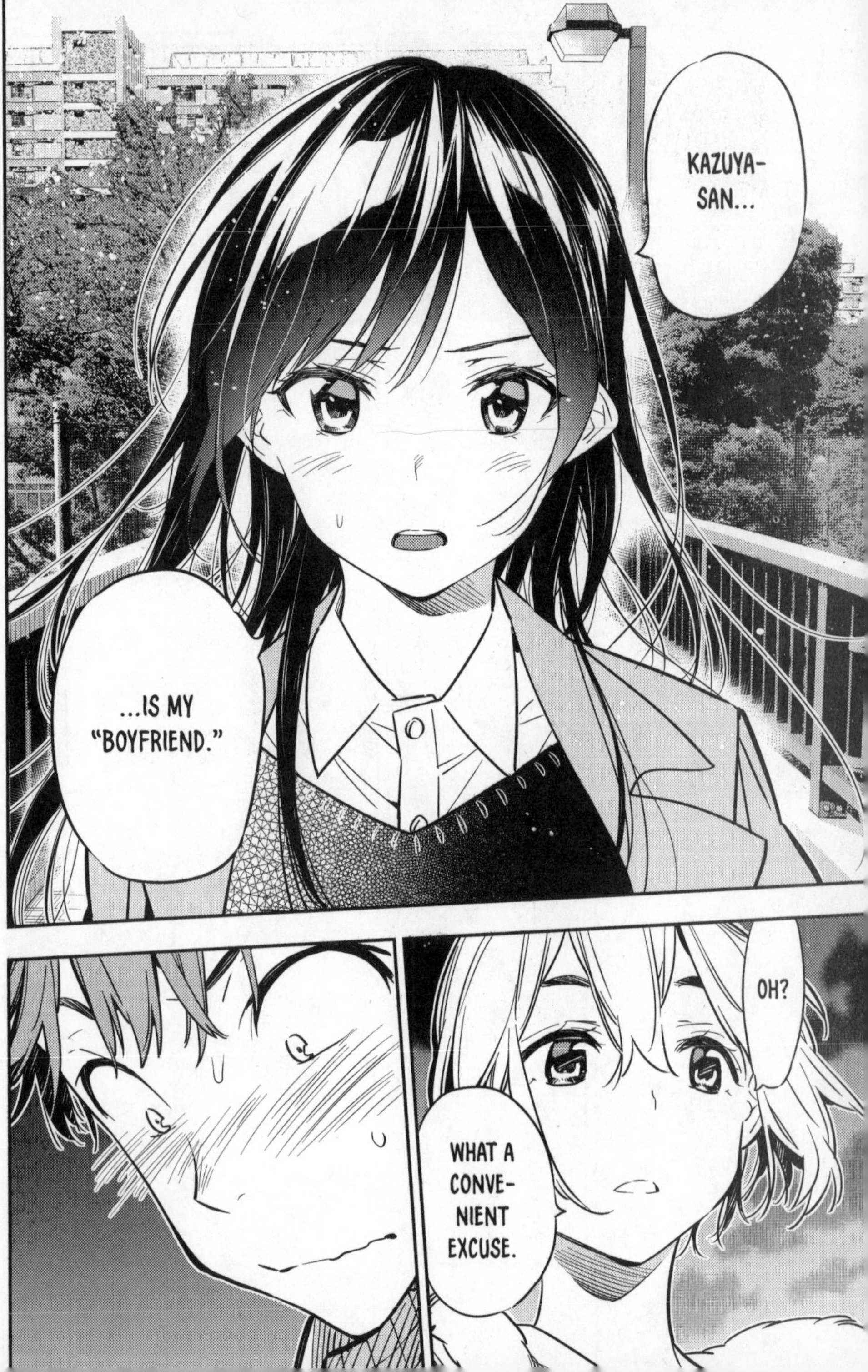
KAZUYA-SAN...
...IS MY "BOYFRIEND."
OH?
WHAT A CONVE-NIENT EXCUSE.

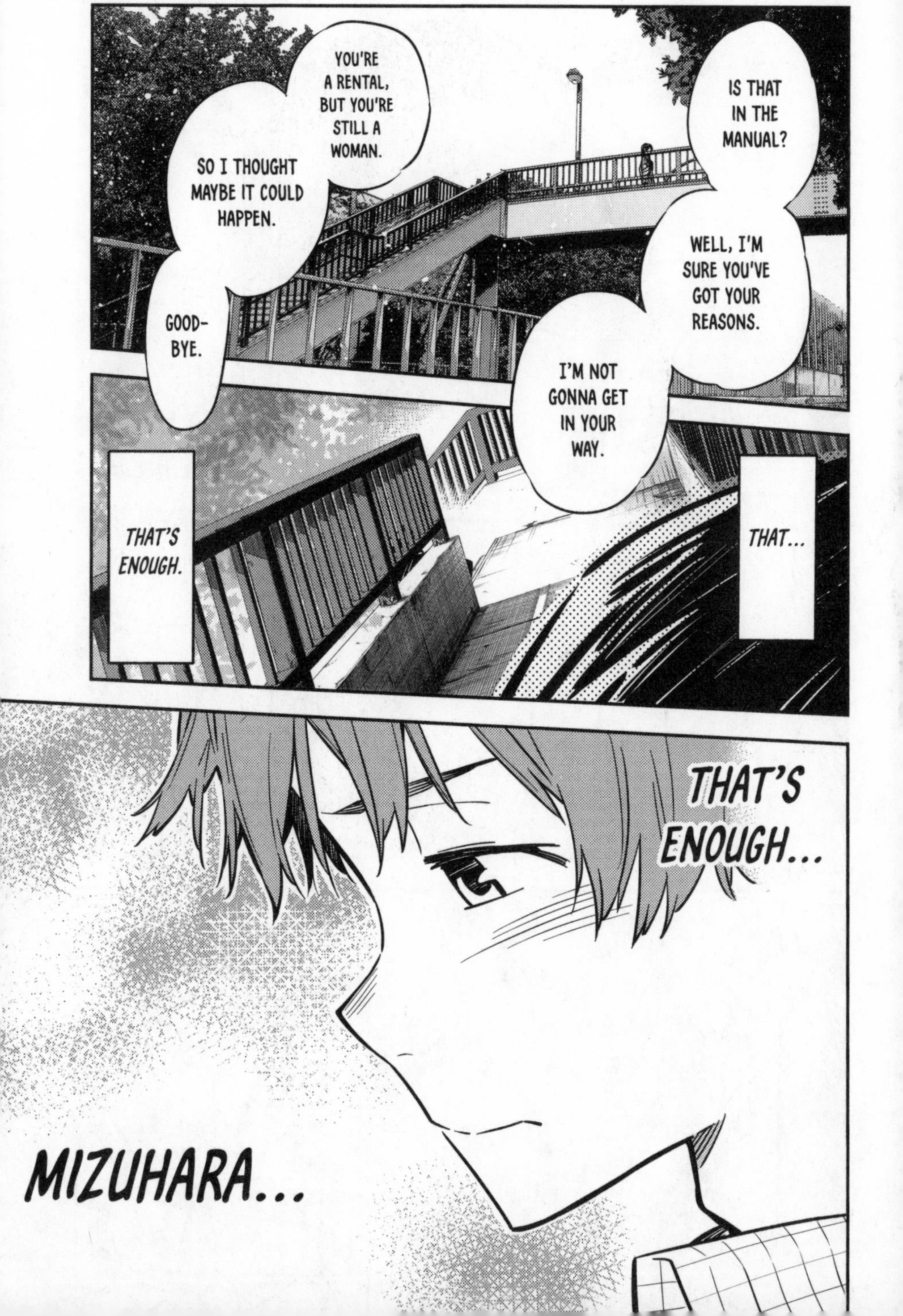
IS THAT IN THE MANUAL?
WELL, I'M SURE YOU'VE GOT YOUR REASONS.
I'M NOT GONNA GET IN YOUR WAY.
YOU'RE A RENTAL, BUT YOU'RE STILL A WOMAN.
SO I THOUGHT MAYBE IT COULD HAPPEN.
GOOD-BYE.
THAT...
THAT'S ENOUGH.
THAT'S ENOUGH...
MIZUHARA...

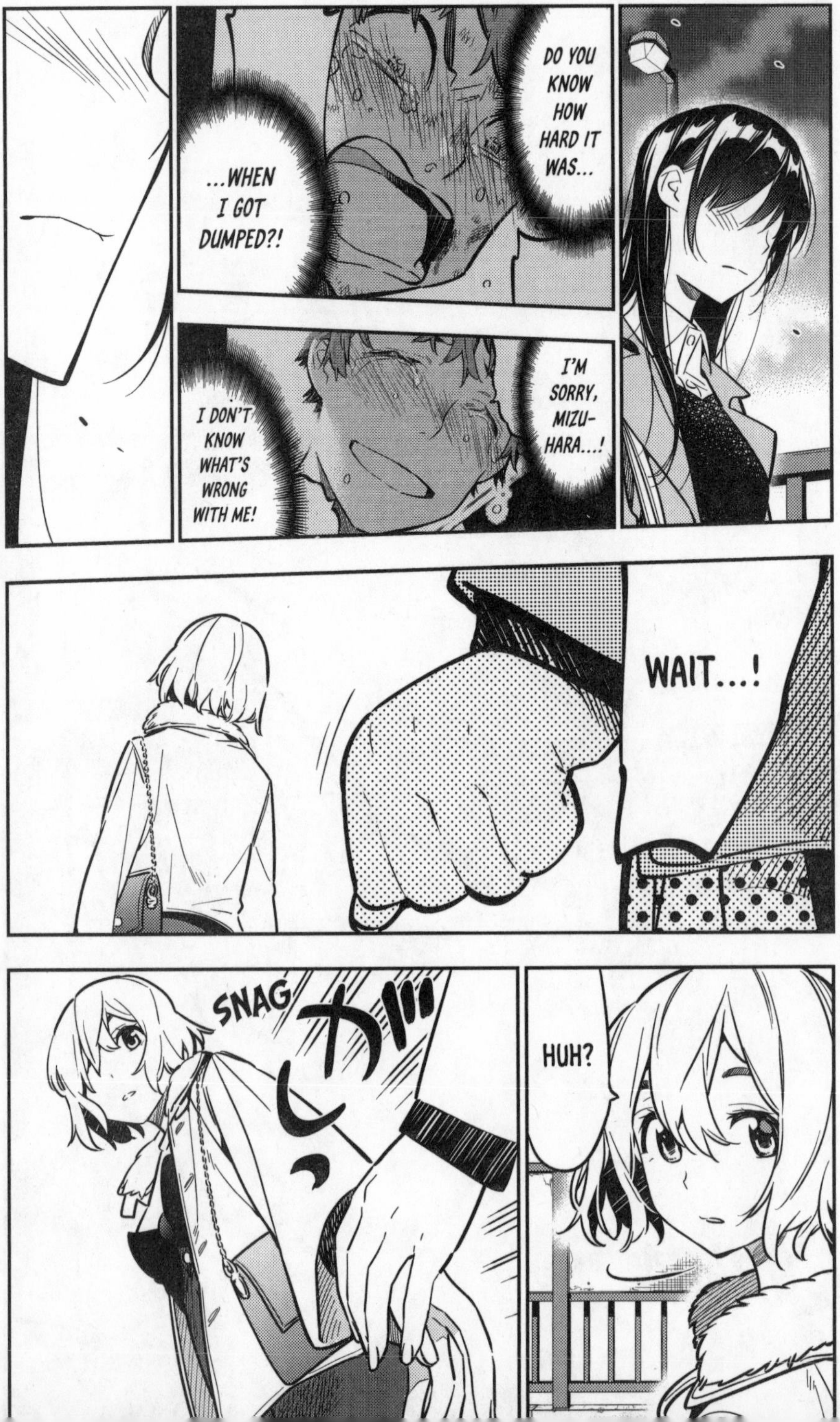
DO YOU KNOW HOW HARD IT WAS...
...WHEN I GOT DUMPED?!
I'M SORRY, MIZUHARA...!
I DON'T KNOW WHAT'S WRONG WITH ME!
WAIT...!
HUH?
SNAG

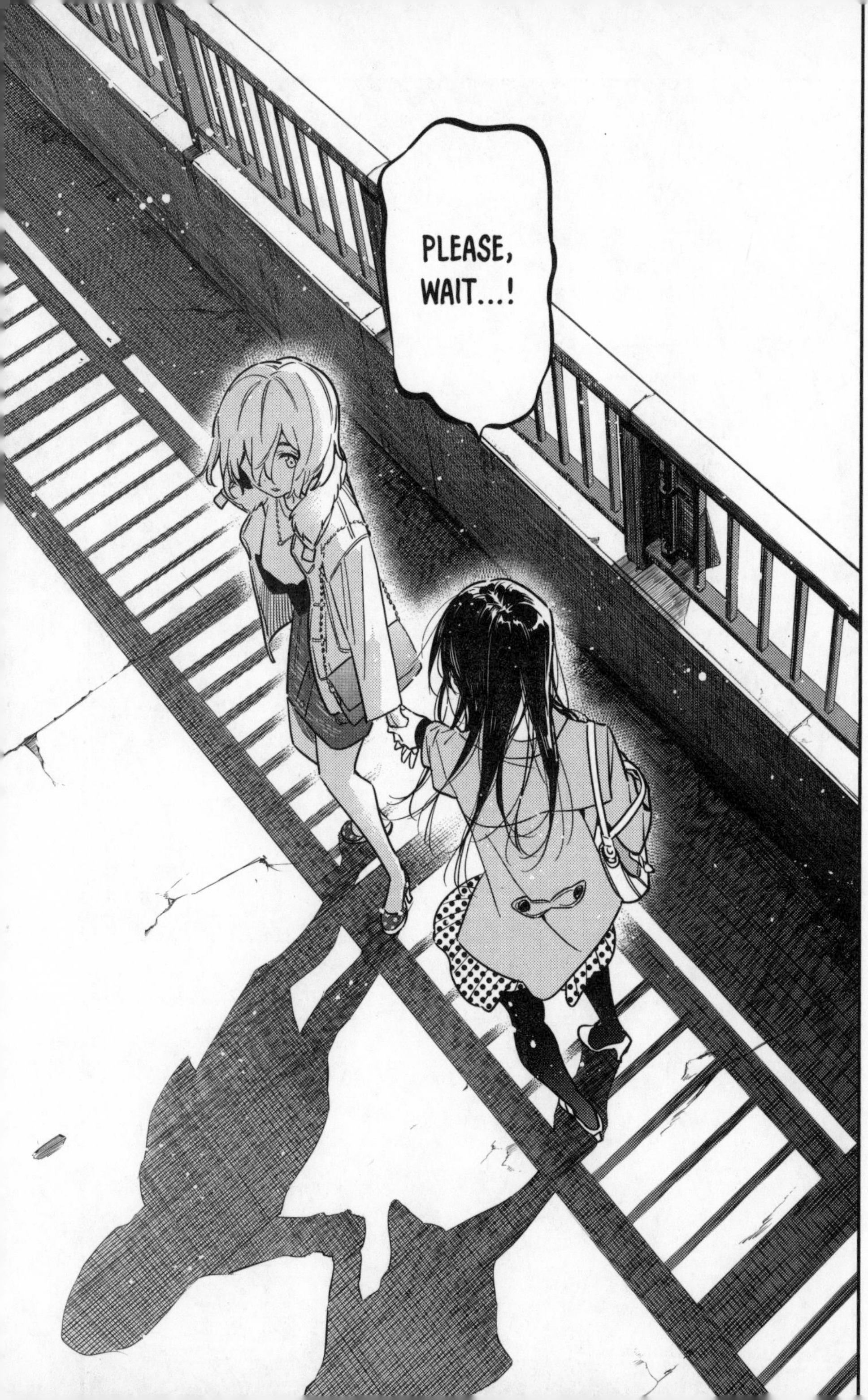
PLEASE, WAIT...!

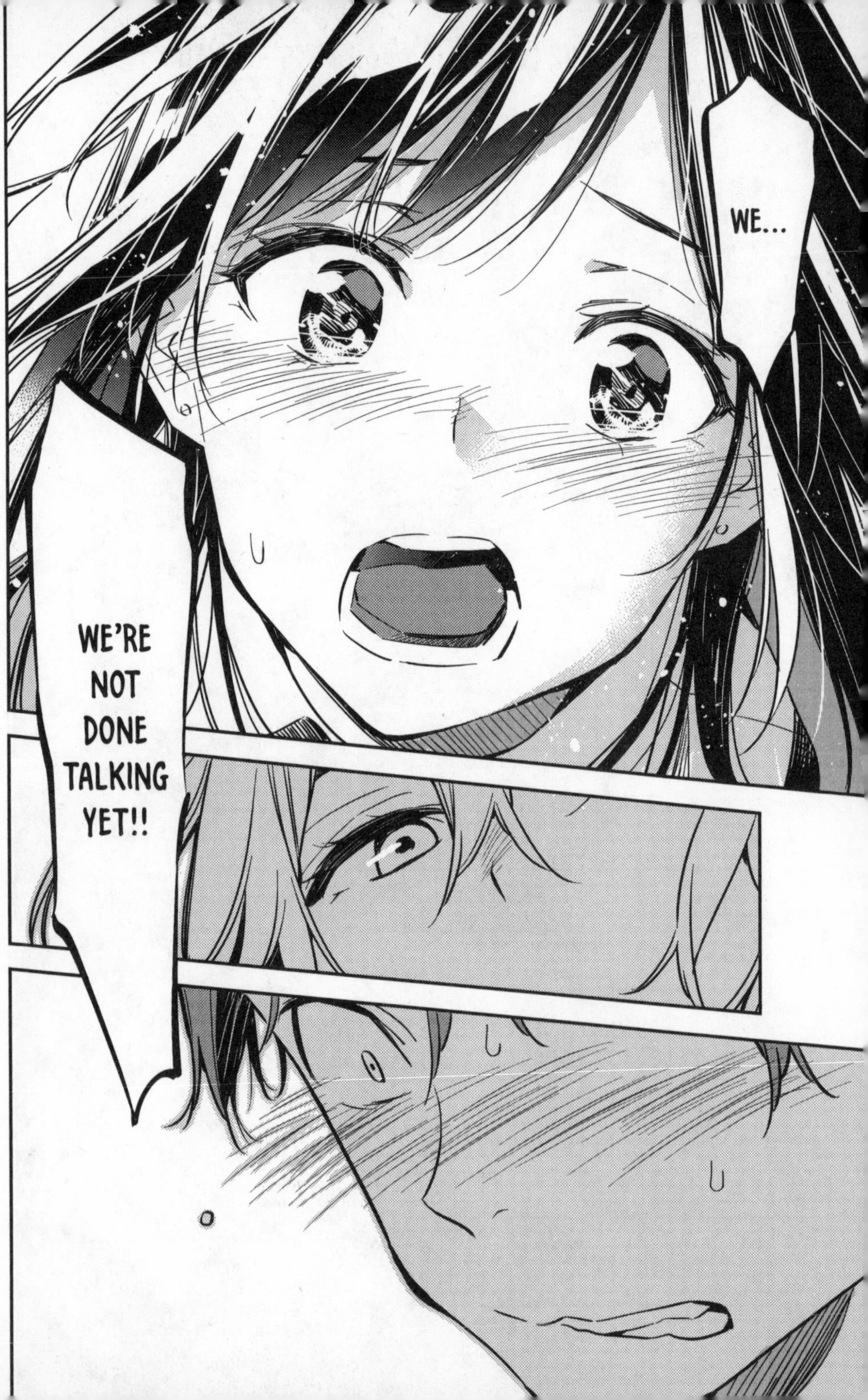
WE...
WE'RE NOT DONE TALKING YET!!

RATING 49 THE CONFESSION AND MY GIRLFRIEND

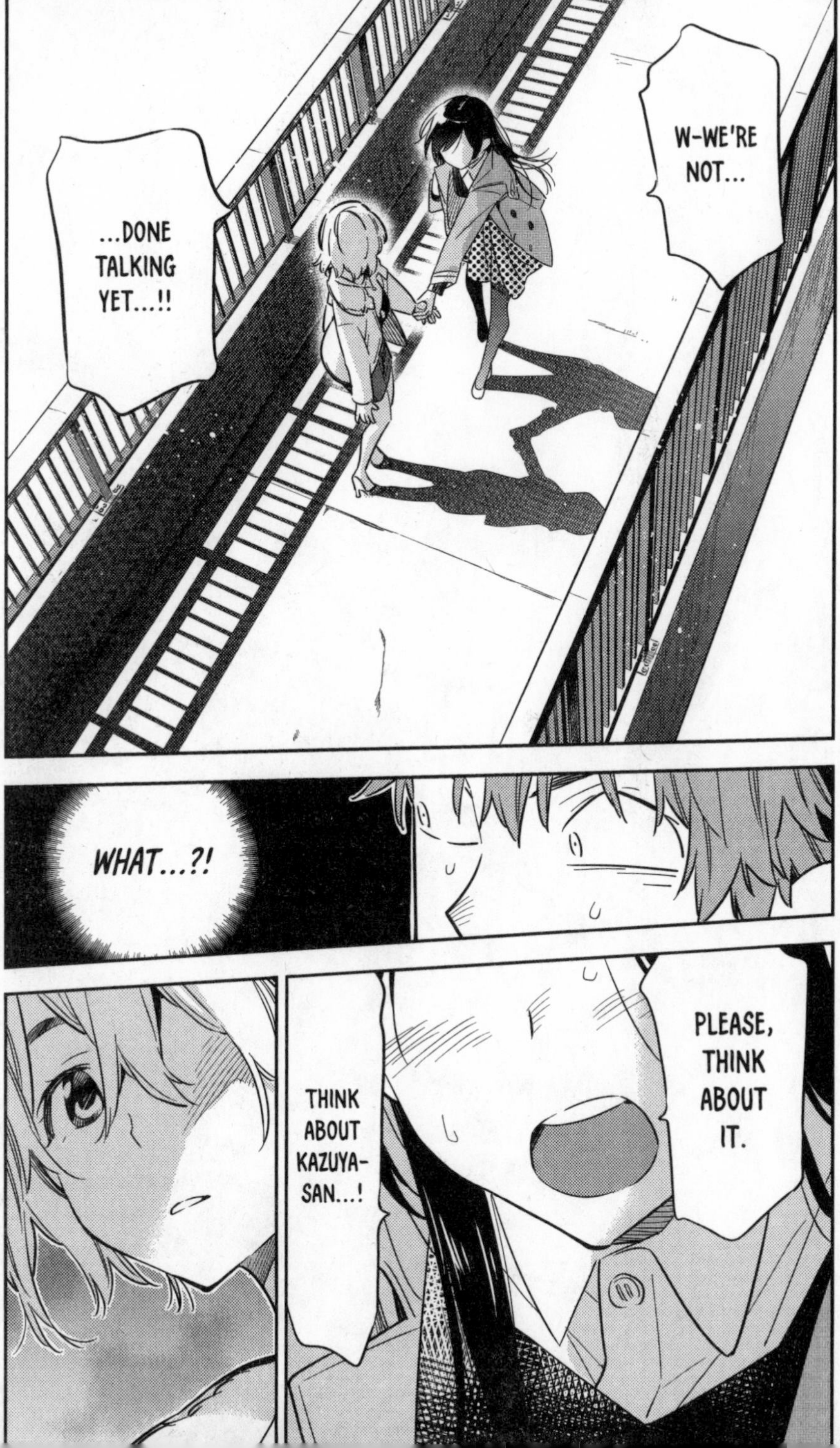
W-WE'RE NOT...
...DONE TALKING YET...!!
WHAT...?!
PLEASE, THINK ABOUT IT.
THINK ABOUT KAZUYA-SAN...!

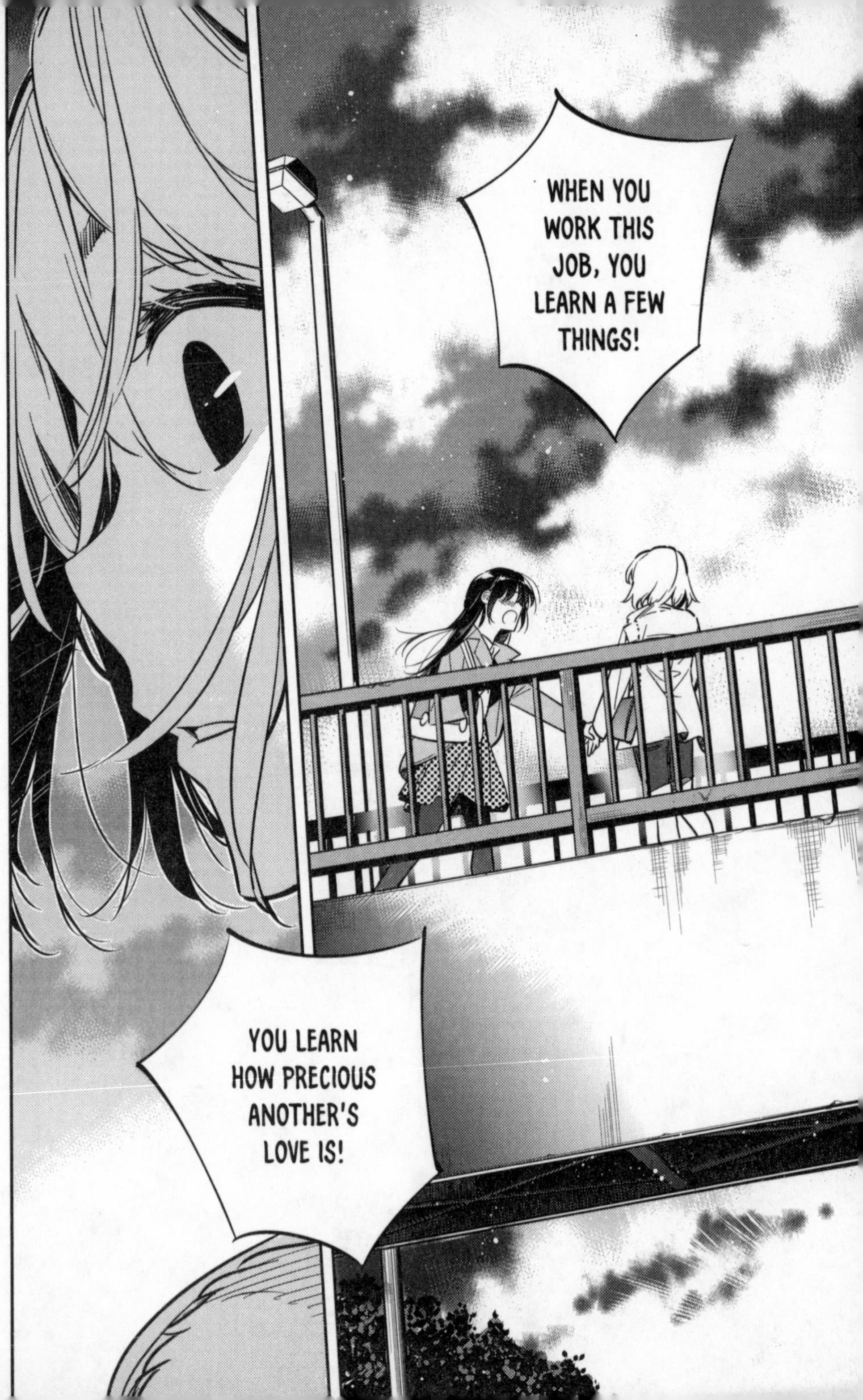
WHEN YOU WORK THIS JOB, YOU LEARN A FEW THINGS!
YOU LEARN HOW PRECIOUS ANOTHER'S LOVE IS!

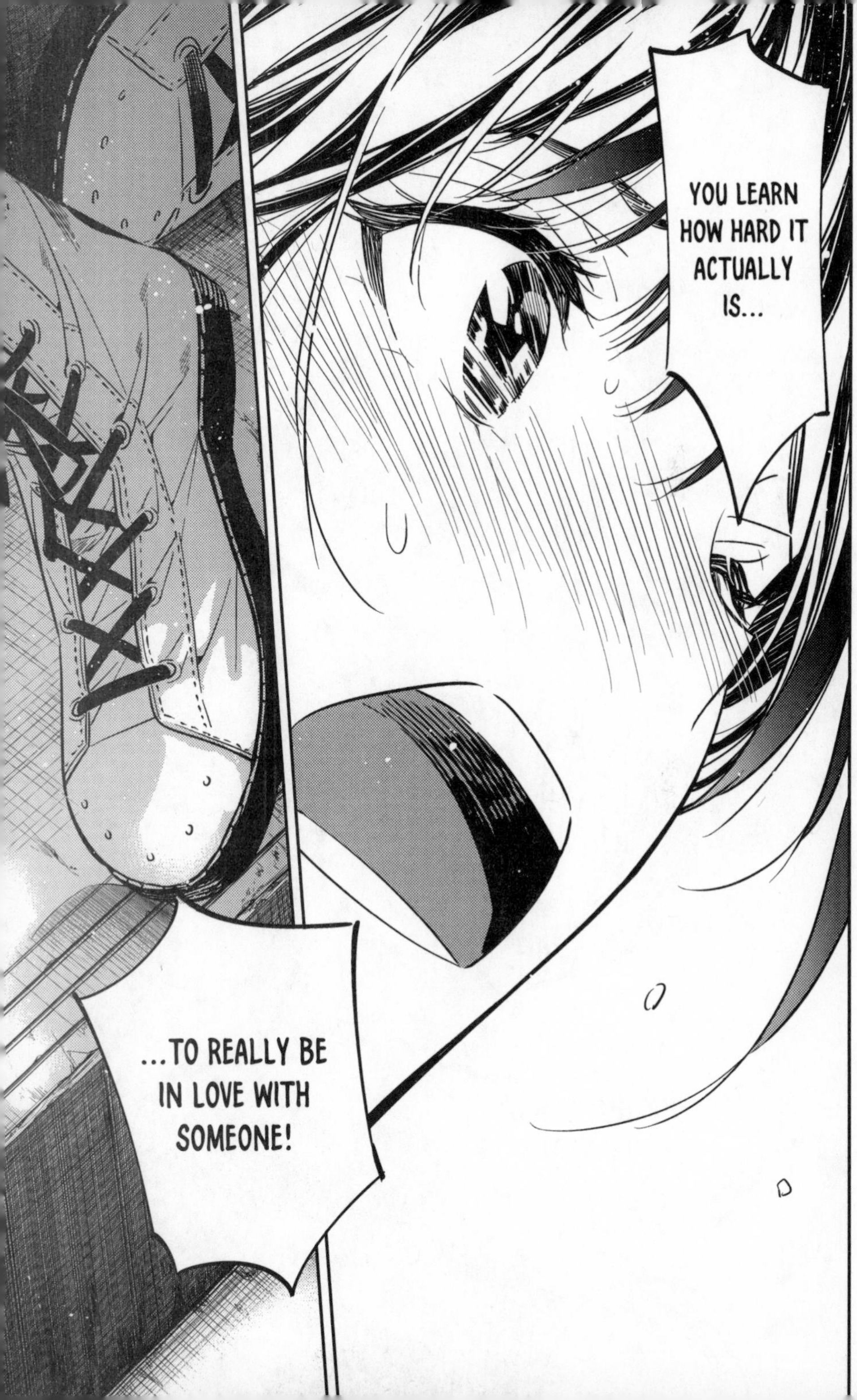
YOU LEARN HOW HARD IT ACTUALLY IS...
...TO REALLY BE IN LOVE WITH SOMEONE!

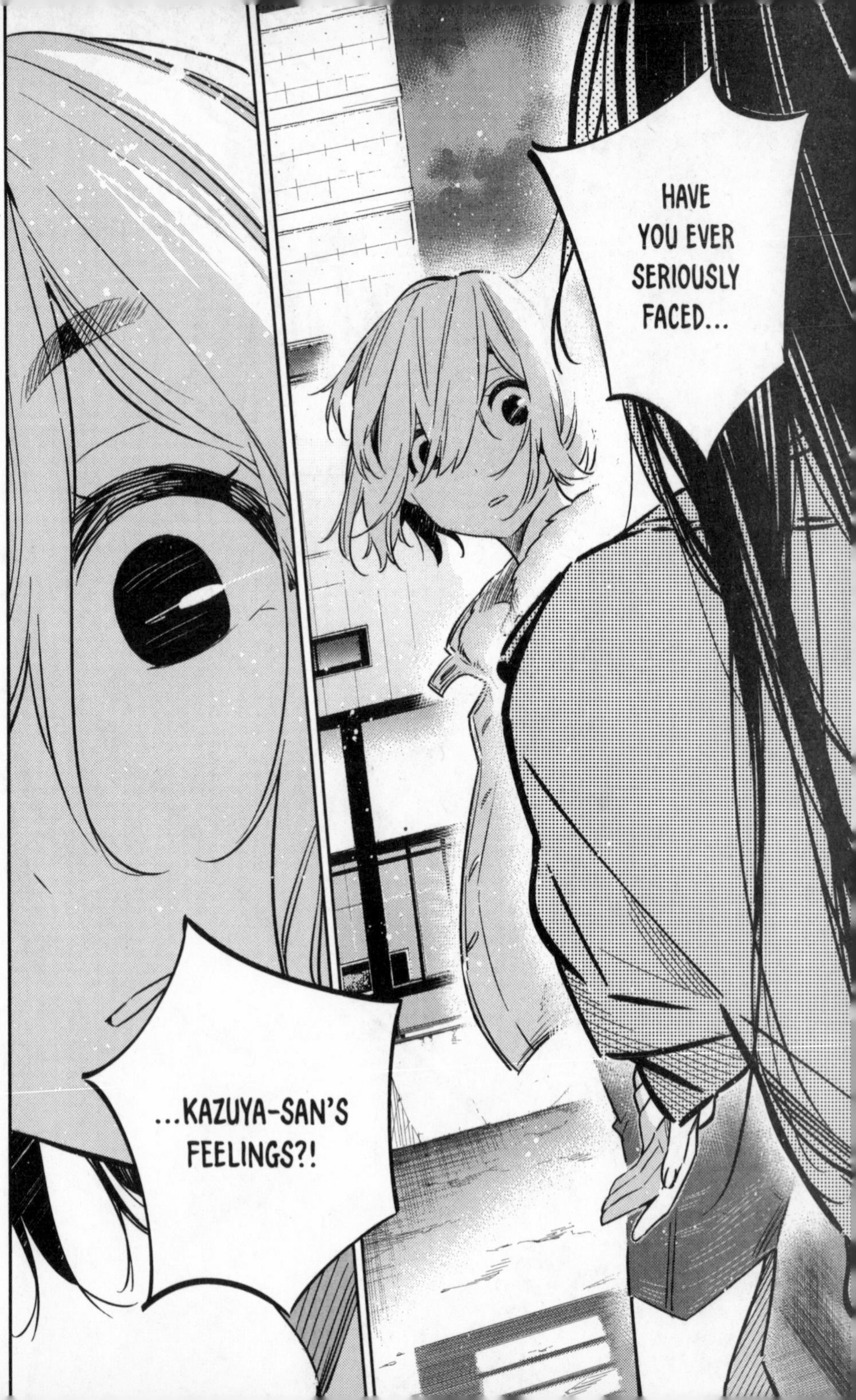
HAVE YOU EVER SERIOUSLY FACED...
...KAZUYA-SAN'S FEELINGS?!

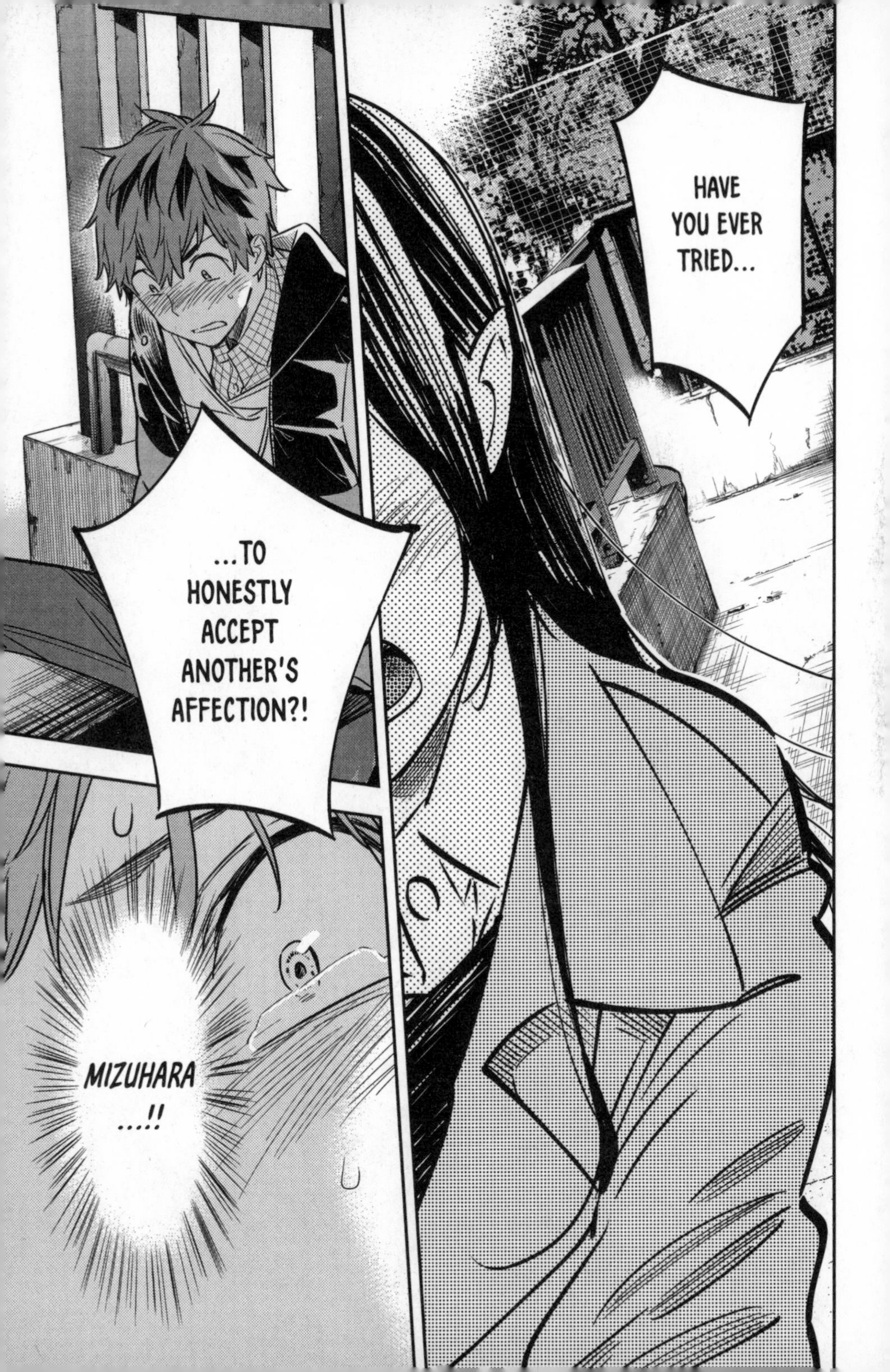
HAVE YOU EVER TRIED...
...TO HONESTLY ACCEPT ANOTHER'S AFFECTION?!
MIZUHARA ...!!

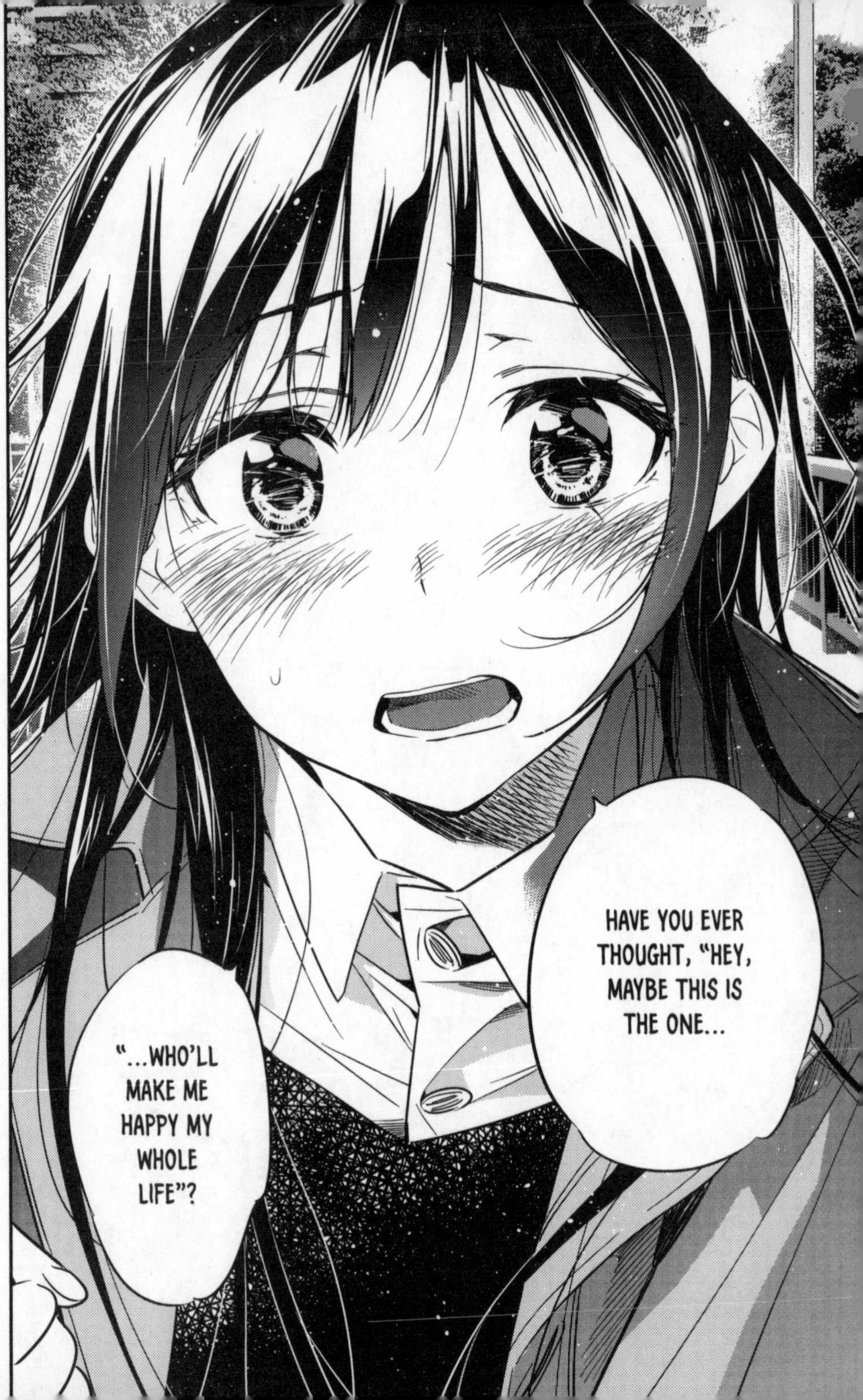
HAVE YOU EVER THOUGHT, "HEY, MAYBE THIS IS THE ONE...
"...WHO'LL MAKE ME HAPPY MY WHOLE LIFE"?

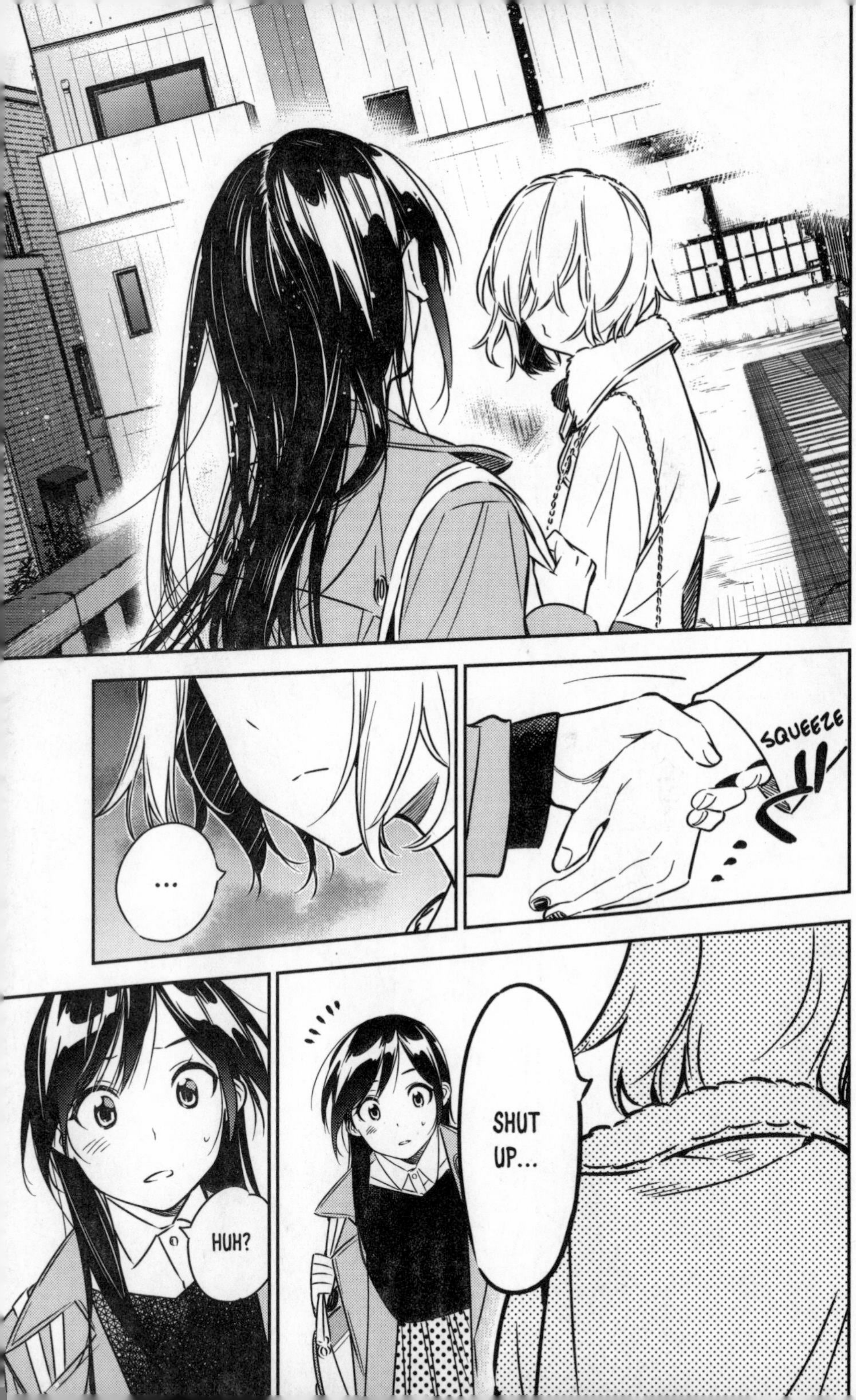
SQUEEZE
...
SHUT UP...
HUH?

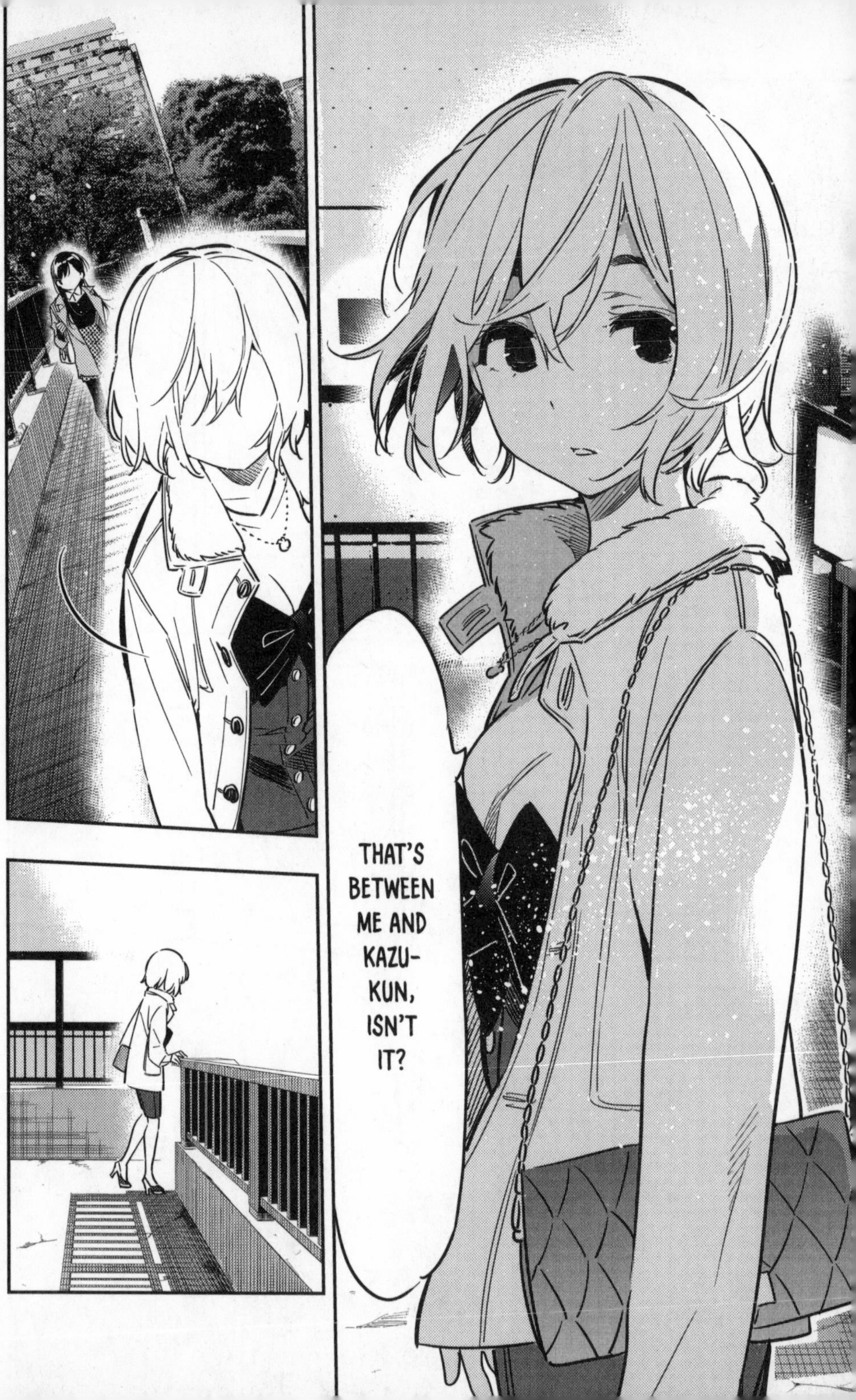
THAT'S BETWEEN ME AND KAZU-KUN, ISN'T IT?

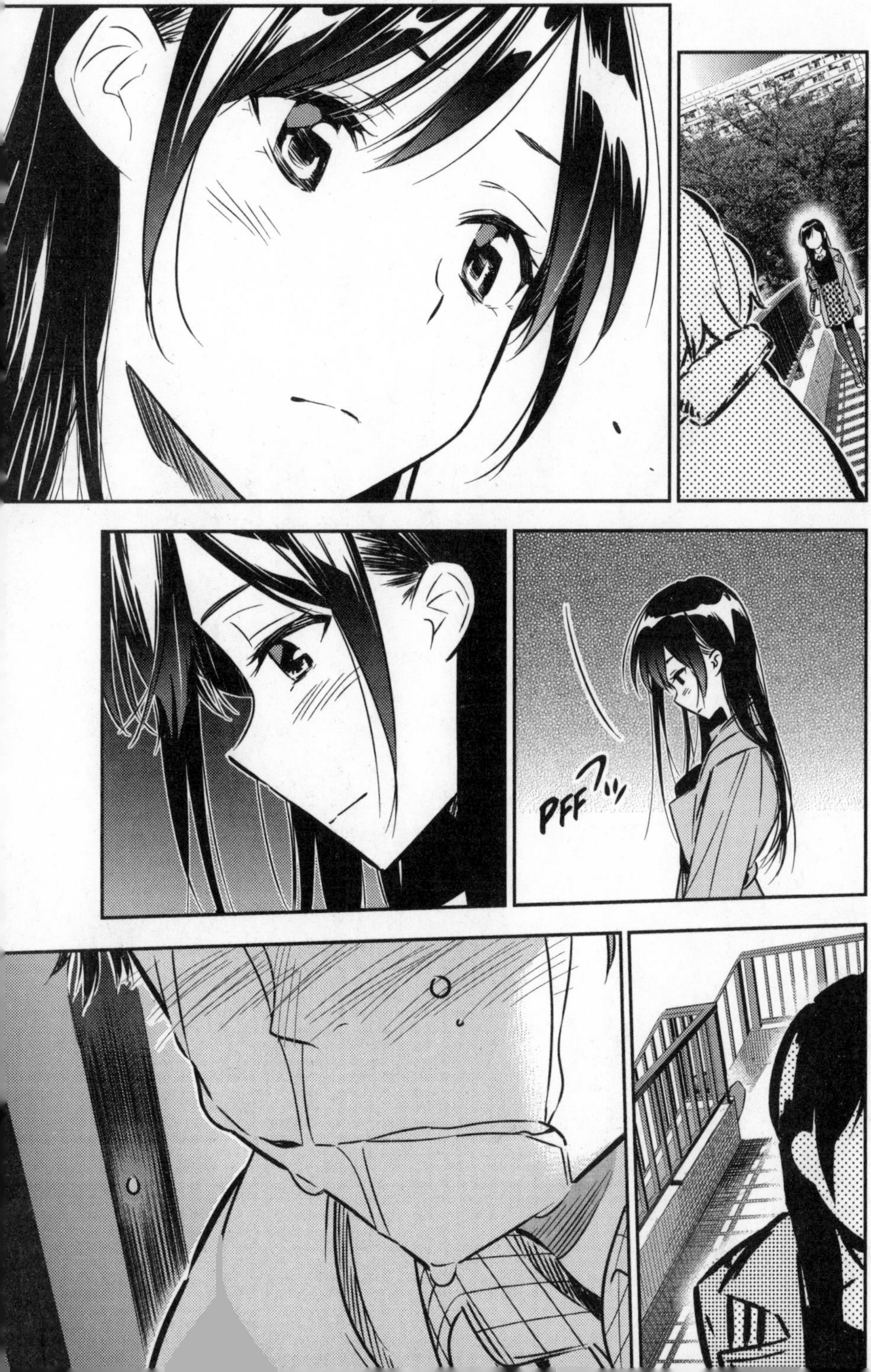
PFF

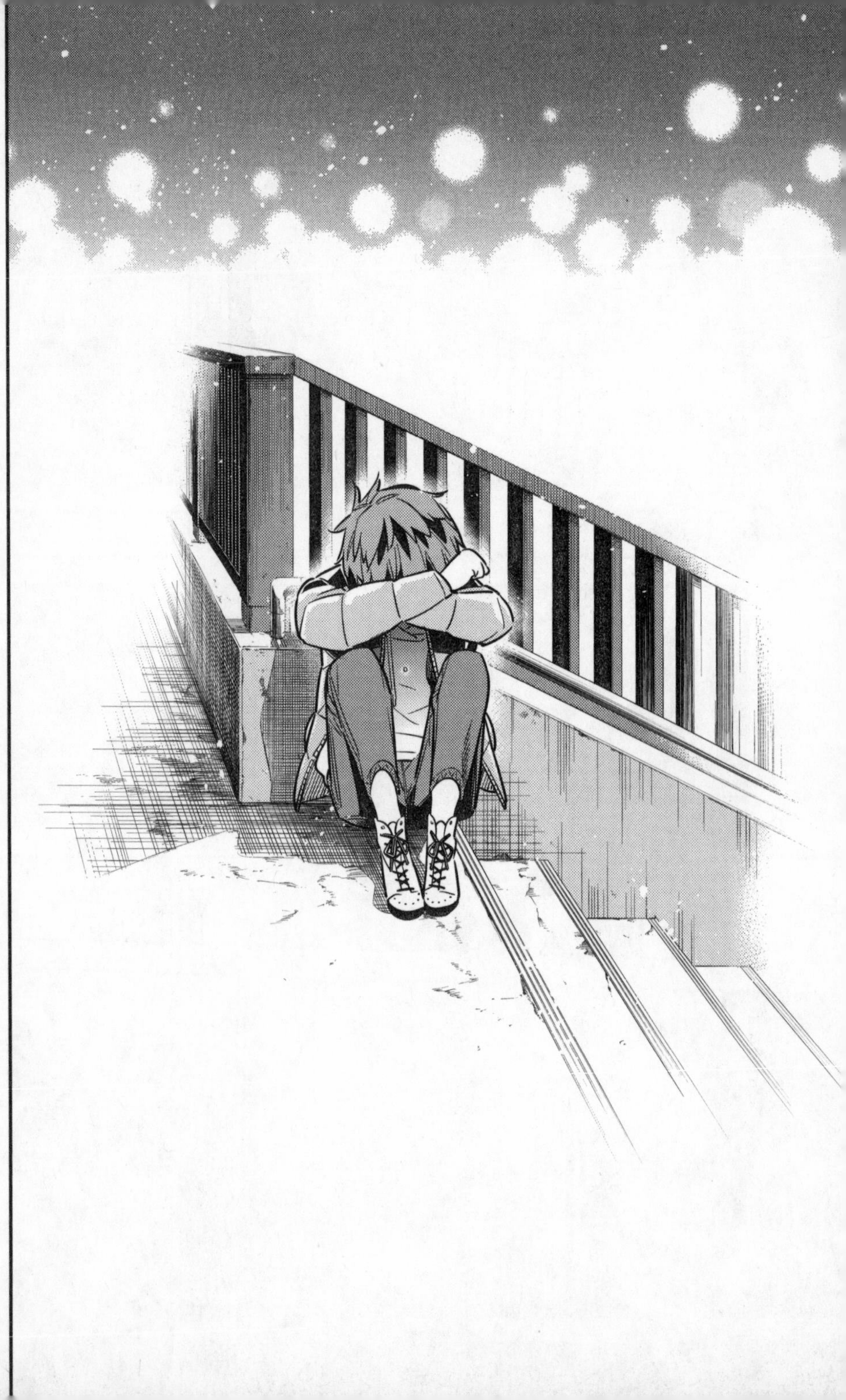

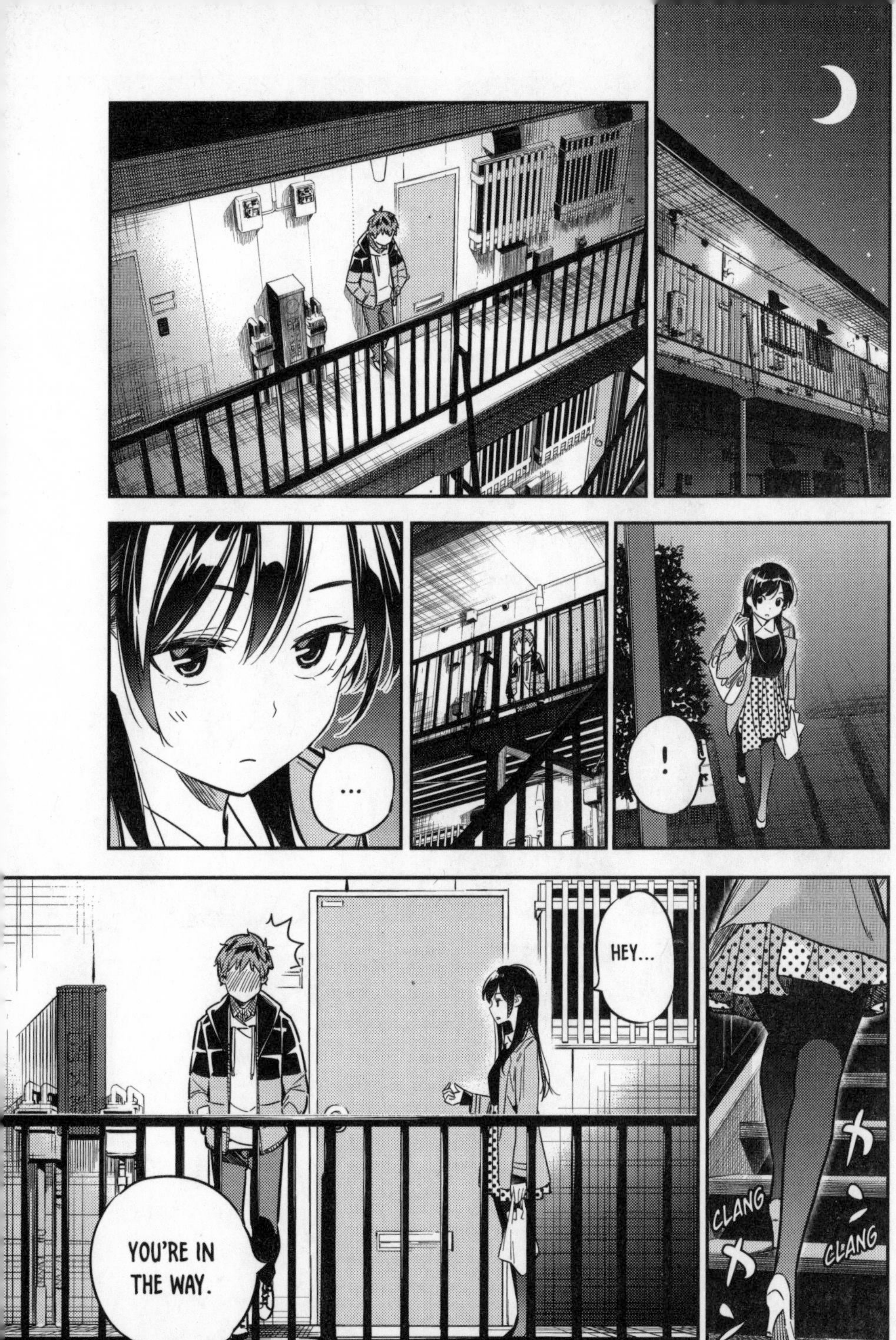
!
...
CLANG
CLANG
HEY...
YOU'RE IN THE WAY.

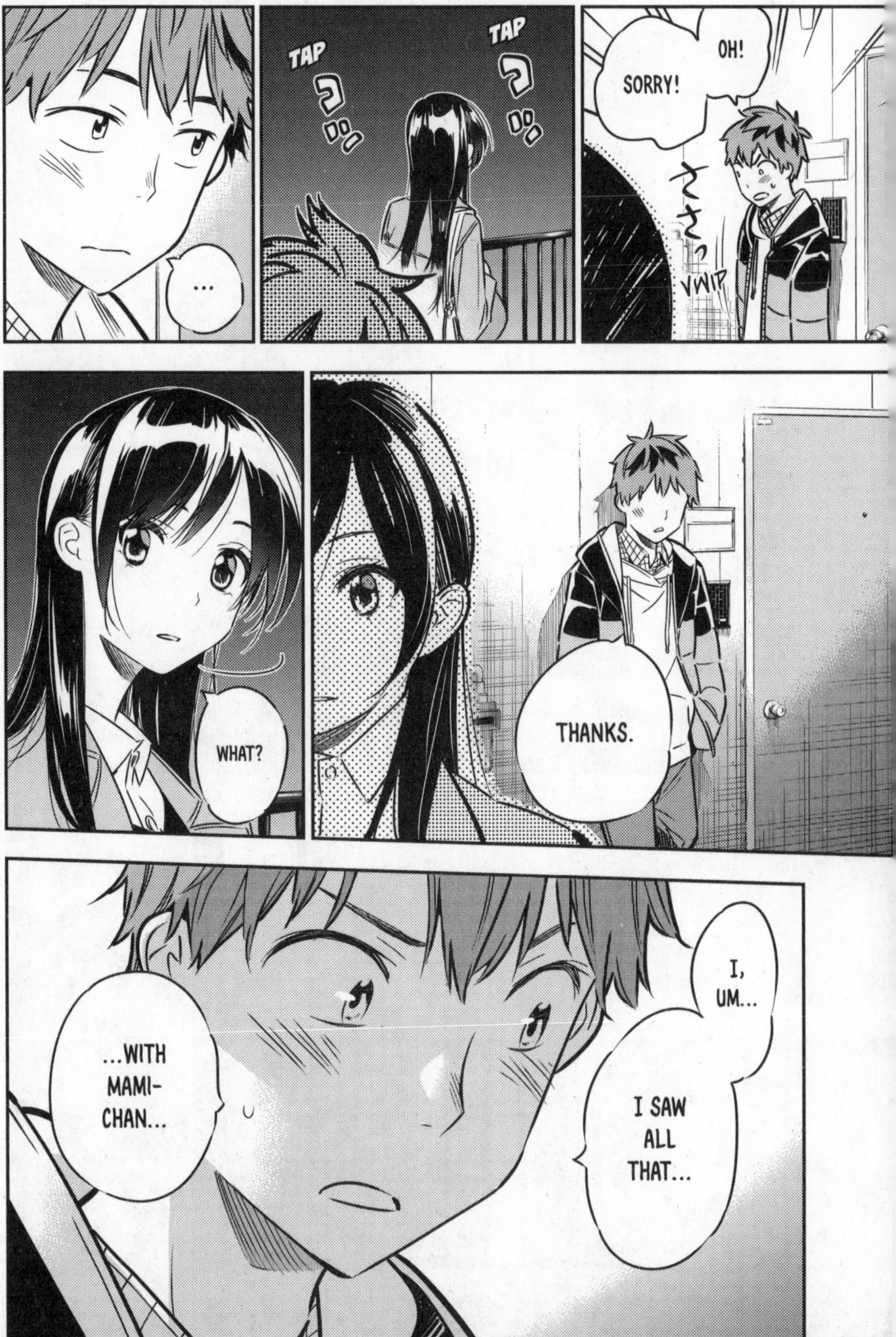
OH!
SORRY!
ささっ
VWIP
TAP
TAP
...
THANKS.
WHAT?
I, UM...
I SAW ALL THAT...
...WITH MAMI-CHAN...

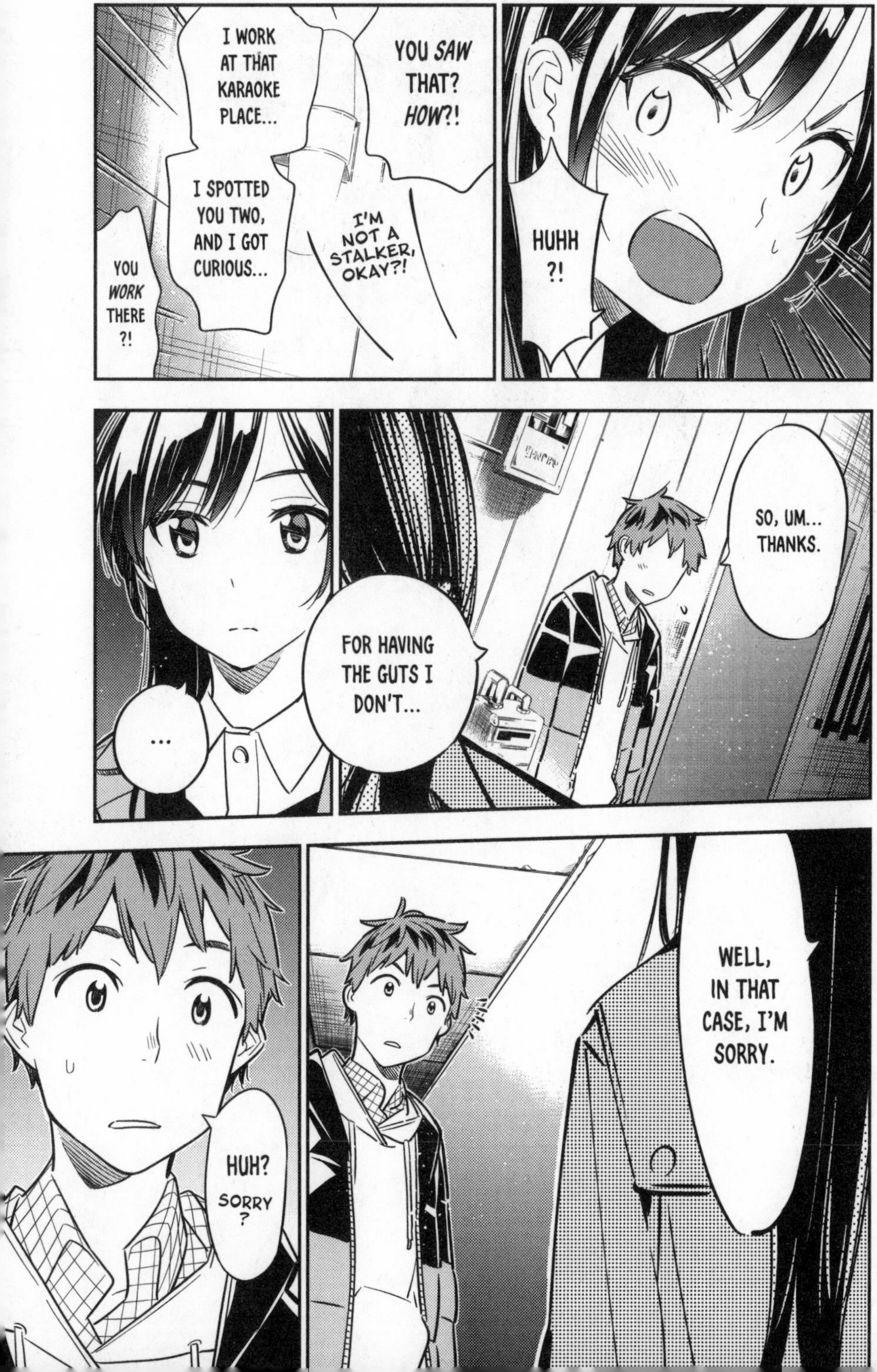
HUHH?!
YOU SAW THAT? HOW?!
I WORK AT THAT KARAOKE PLACE...
I'M NOT A STALKER, OKAY?!
I SPOTTED YOU TWO, AND I GOT CURIOUS...
YOU WORK THERE?!
SO, UM... THANKS.
FOR HAVING THE GUTS I DON'T...
...
WELL, IN THAT CASE, I'M SORRY.
HUH?
SORRY?

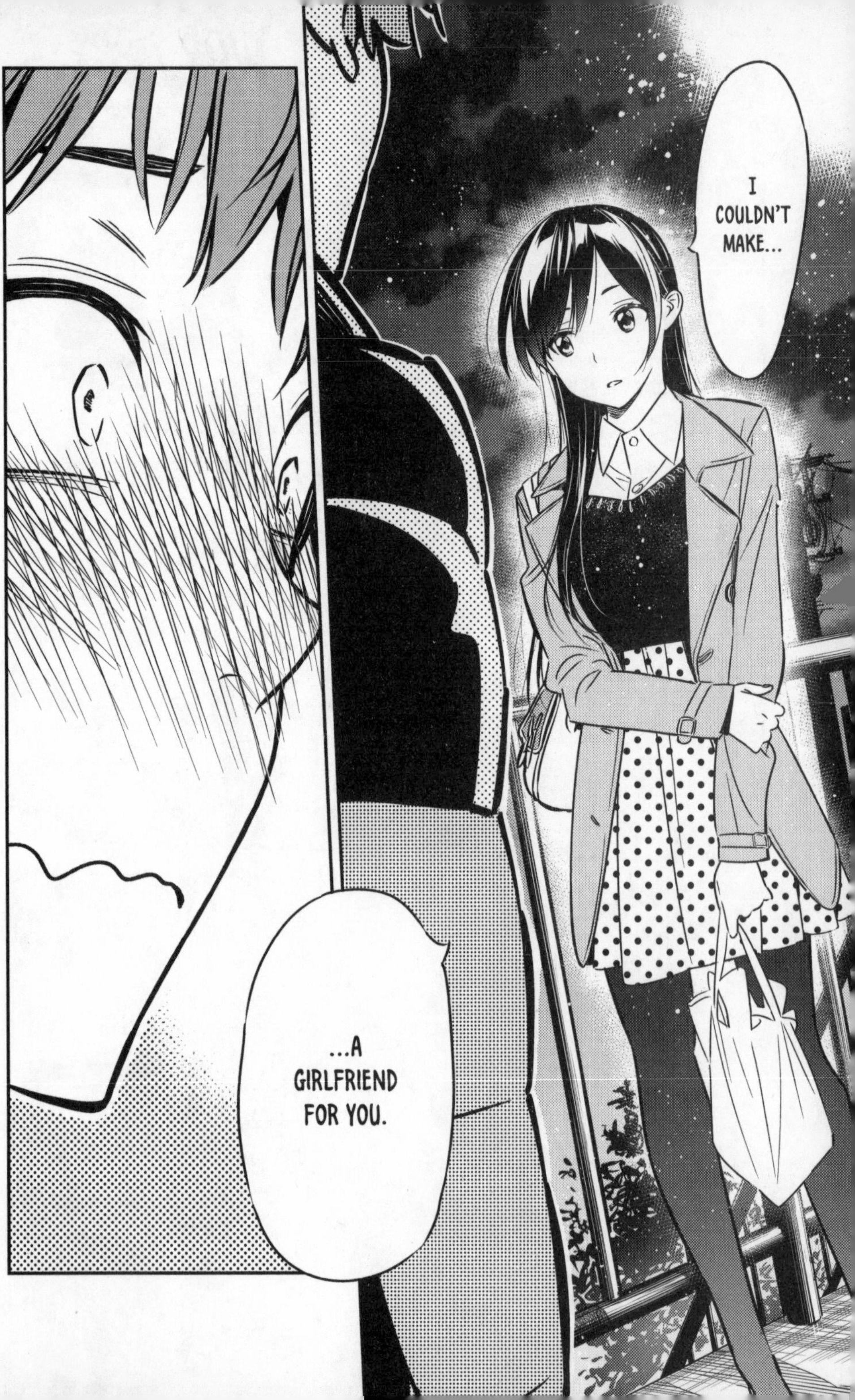
I COULDN'T MAKE...
...A GIRLFRIEND FOR YOU.

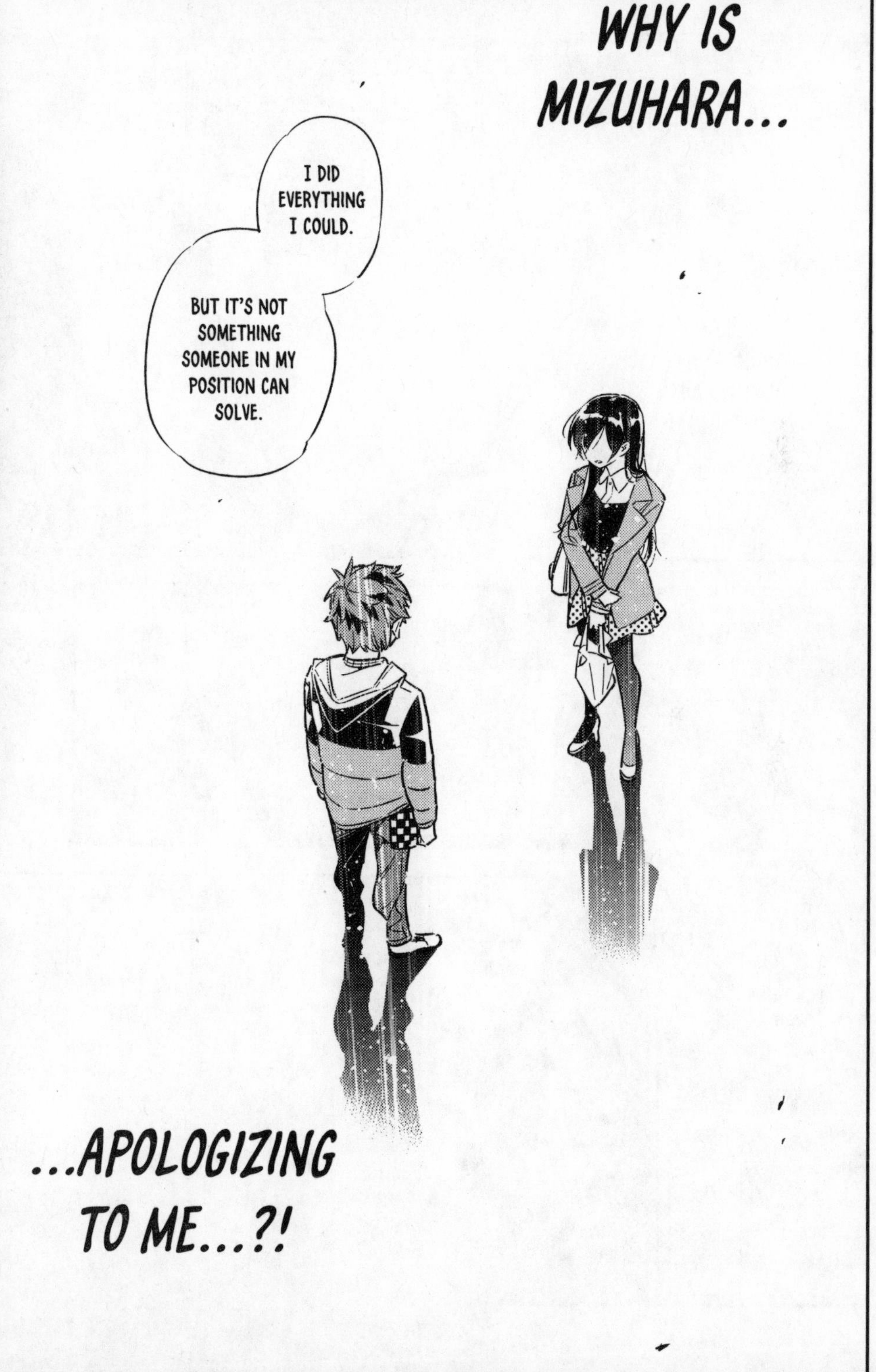
WHY IS MIZUHARA...
I DID EVERYTHING I COULD.
BUT IT'S NOT SOMETHING SOMEONE IN MY POSITION CAN SOLVE.
...APOLOGIZING TO ME...?!

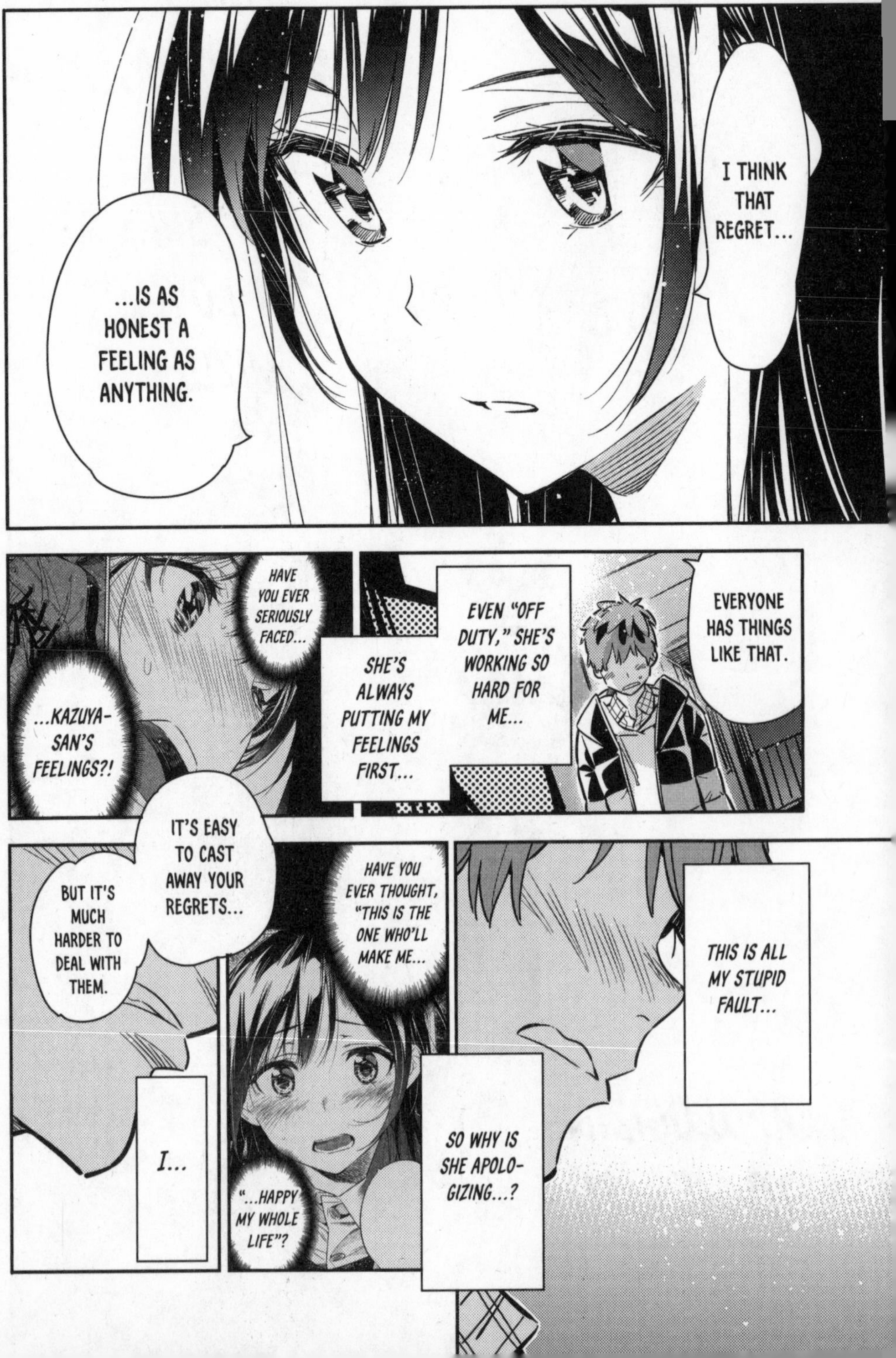
I THINK THAT REGRET...
...IS AS HONEST A FEELING AS ANYTHING.
EVERYONE HAS THINGS LIKE THAT.
EVEN "OFF DUTY," SHE'S WORKING SO HARD FOR ME...
SHE'S ALWAYS PUTTING MY FEELINGS FIRST...
HAVE YOU EVER SERIOUSLY FACED...
...KAZUYA-SAN'S FEELINGS?!
THIS IS ALL MY STUPID FAULT...
SO WHY IS SHE APOLO-GIZING...?
HAVE YOU EVER THOUGHT, "THIS IS THE ONE WHO'LL MAKE ME...
"...HAPPY MY WHOLE LIFE"?
IT'S EASY TO CAST AWAY YOUR REGRETS...
BUT IT'S MUCH HARDER TO DEAL WITH THEM.
I...

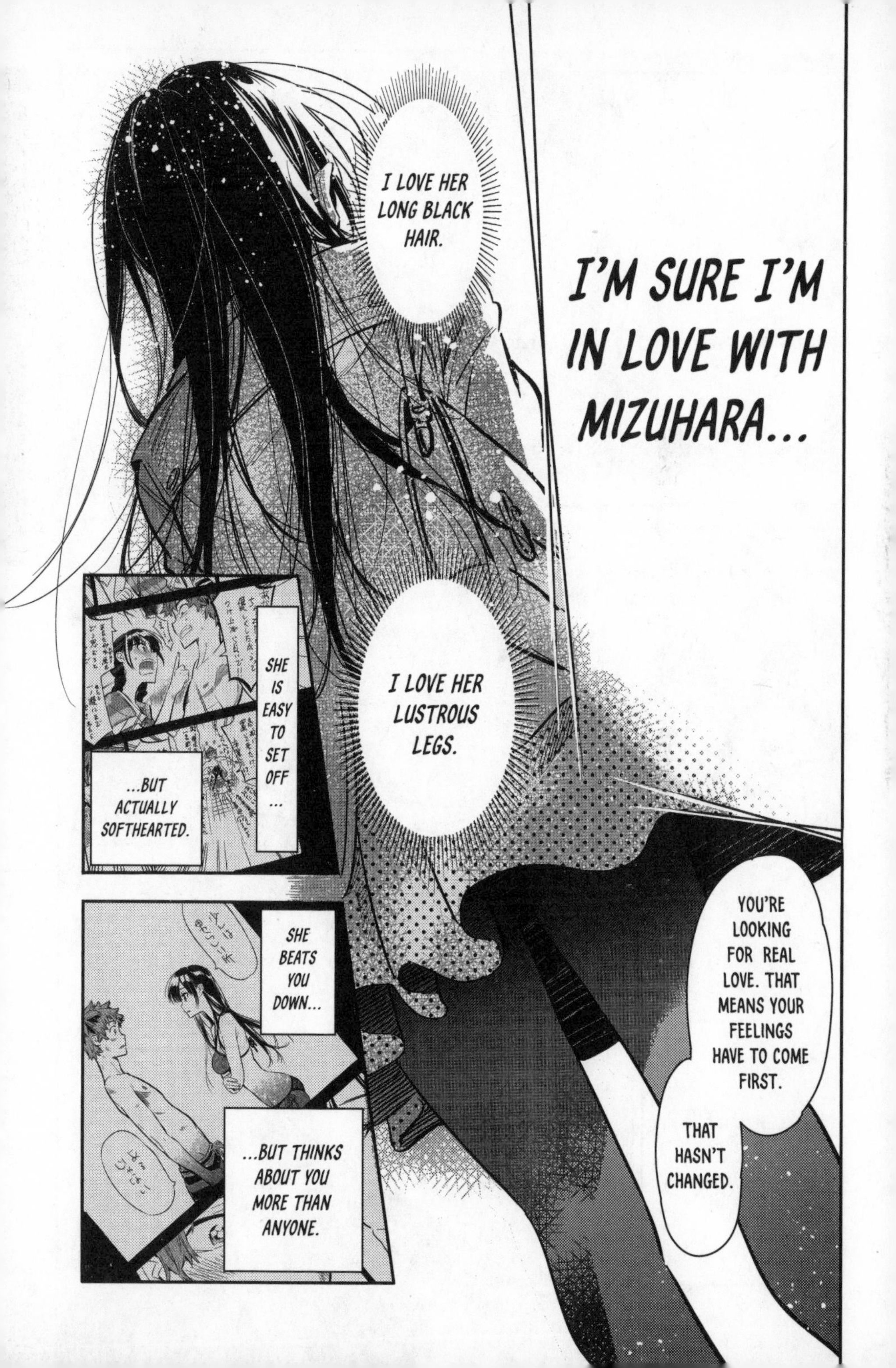
I LOVE HER LONG BLACK HAIR.
I'M SURE I'M IN LOVE WITH MIZUHARA...
I LOVE HER LUSTROUS LEGS.
YOU'RE LOOKING FOR REAL LOVE. THAT MEANS YOUR FEELINGS HAVE TO COME FIRST.
THAT HASN'T CHANGED.
SHE IS EASY TO SET OFF ...
...BUT ACTUALLY SOFTHEARTED.
SHE BEATS YOU DOWN...
...BUT THINKS ABOUT YOU MORE THAN ANYONE.

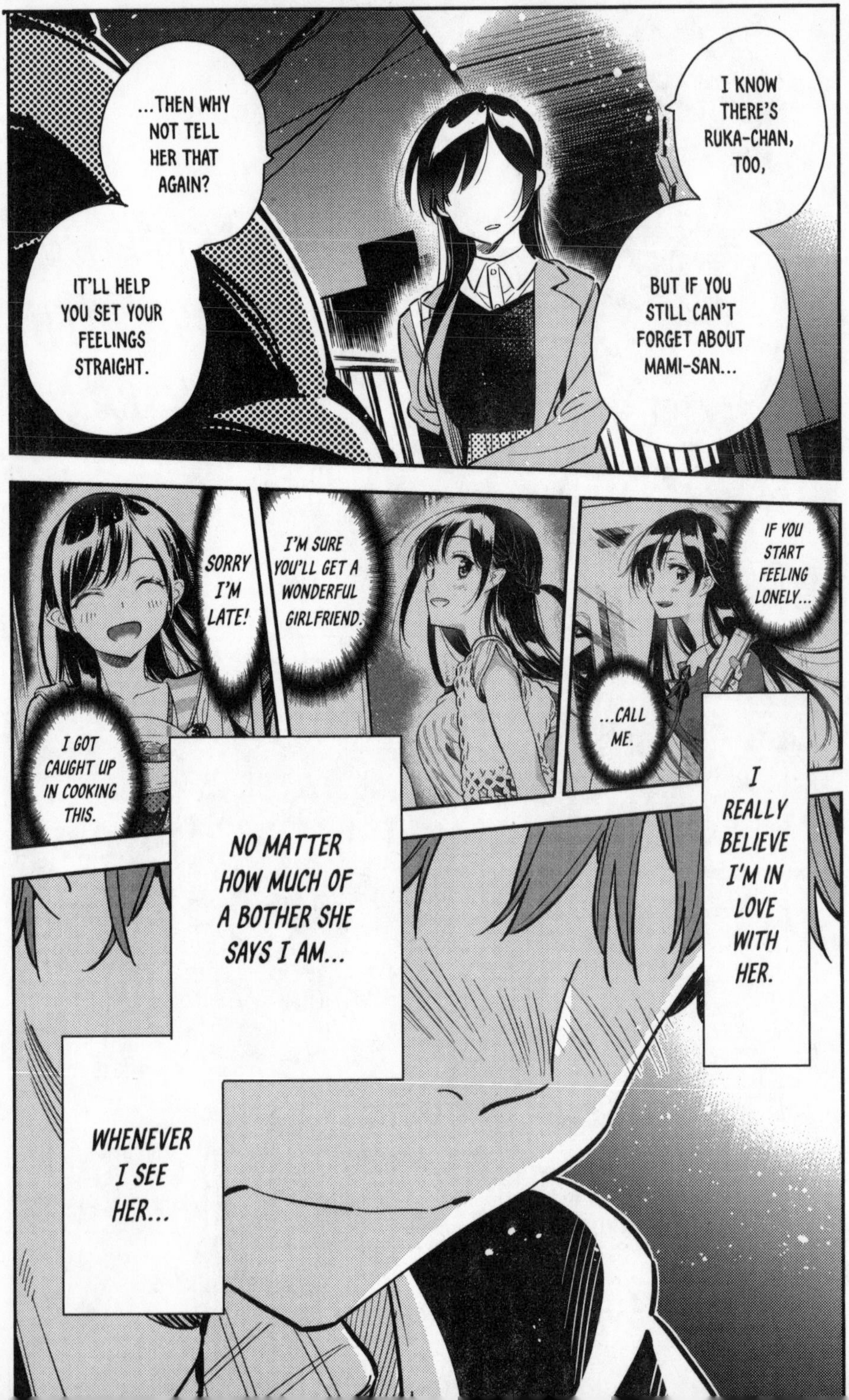
I KNOW THERE'S RUKA-CHAN, TOO,
BUT IF YOU STILL CAN'T FORGET ABOUT MAMI-SAN...
...THEN WHY NOT TELL HER THAT AGAIN?
IT'LL HELP YOU SET YOUR FEELINGS STRAIGHT.
IF YOU START FEELING LONELY...
...CALL ME.
I'M SURE YOU'LL GET A WONDERFUL GIRLFRIEND.
SORRY I'M LATE!
I GOT CAUGHT UP IN COOKING THIS.
I REALLY BELIEVE I'M IN LOVE WITH HER.
NO MATTER HOW MUCH OF A BOTHER SHE SAYS I AM...
WHENEVER I SEE HER...

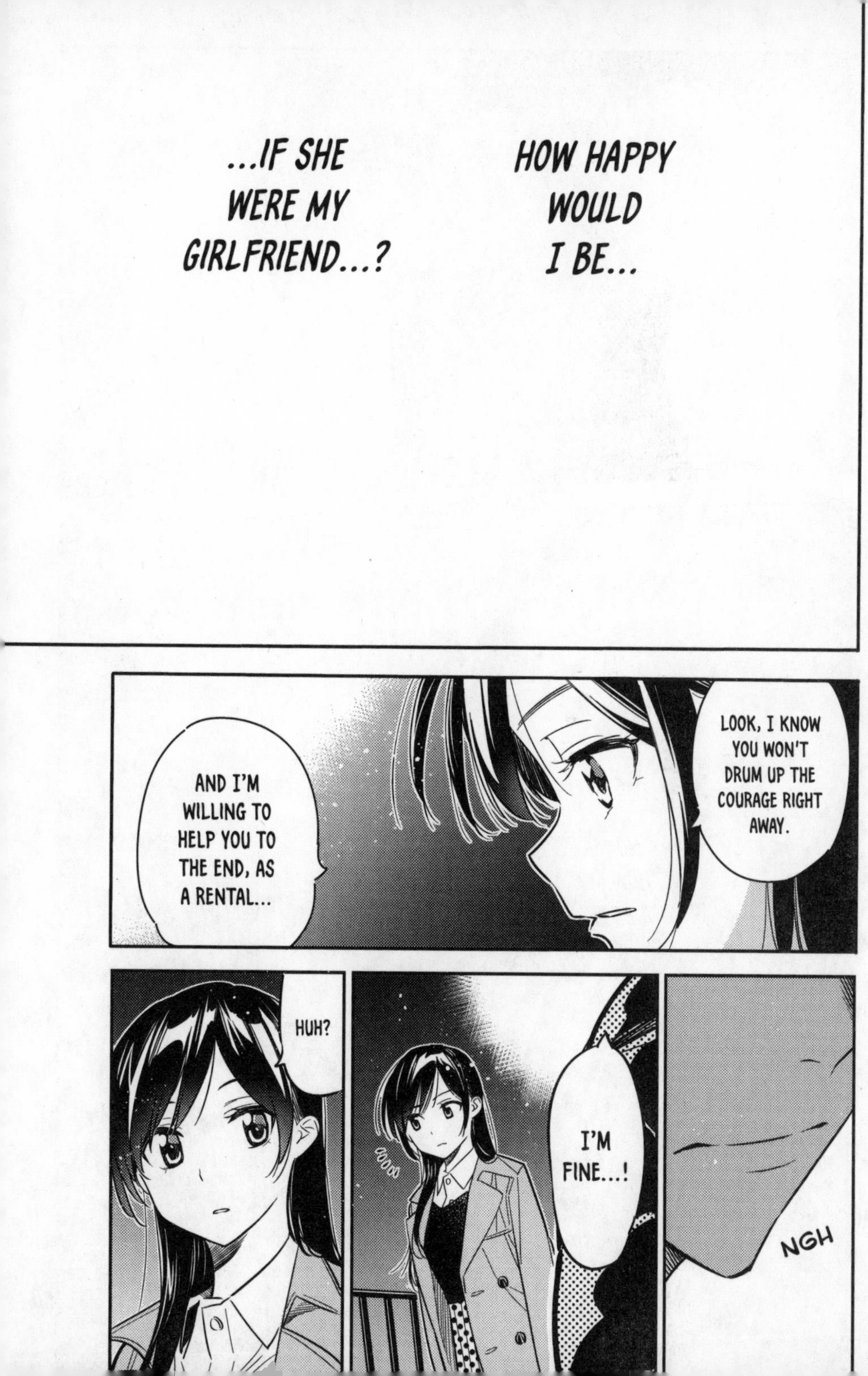
HOW HAPPY WOULD I BE...
...IF SHE WERE MY GIRLFRIEND...?
LOOK, I KNOW YOU WON'T DRUM UP THE COURAGE RIGHT AWAY.
AND I'M WILLING TO HELP YOU TO THE END, AS A RENTAL...
NGH
I'M FINE...!
HUH?

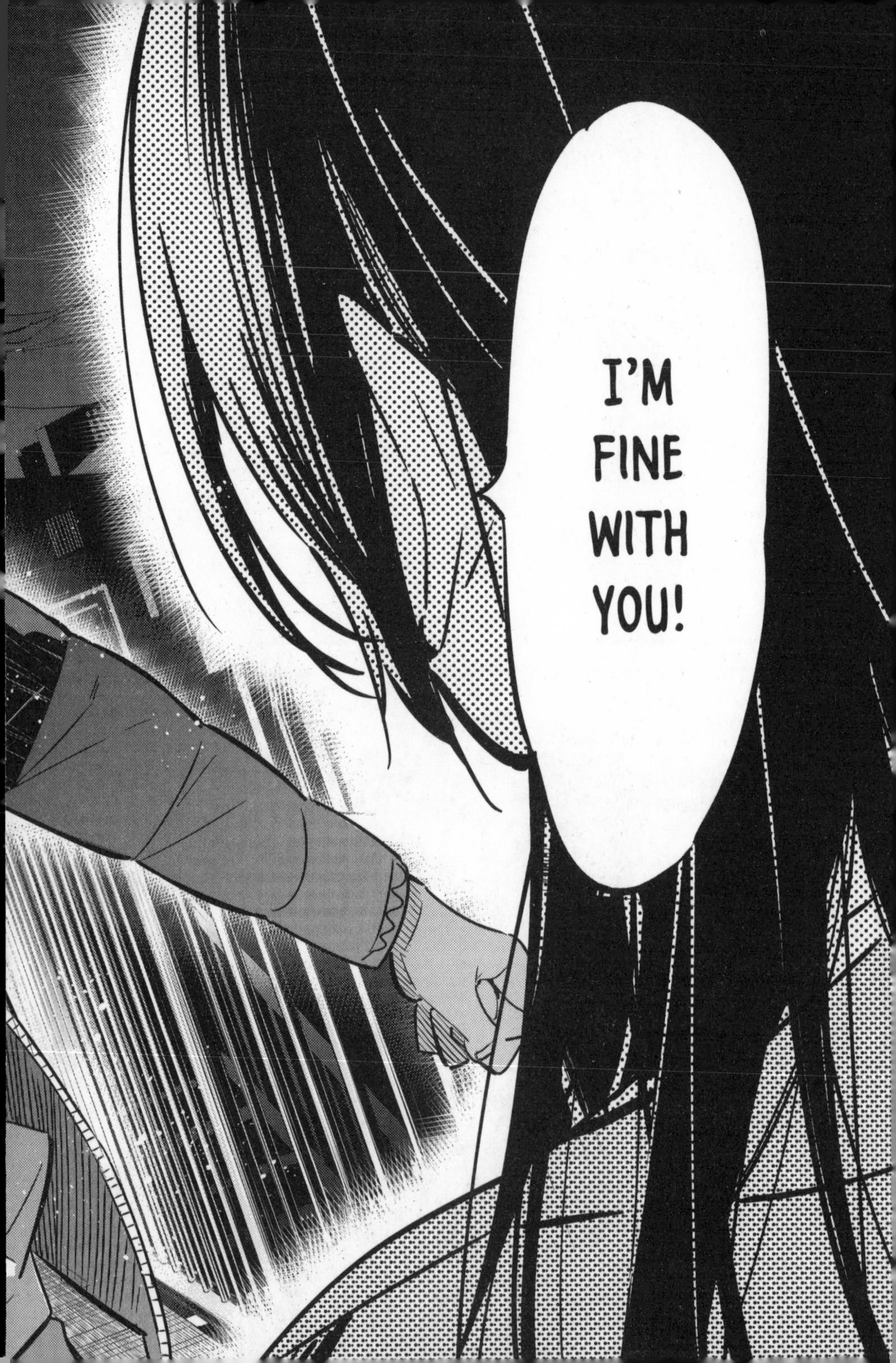
I'M FINE WITH YOU!

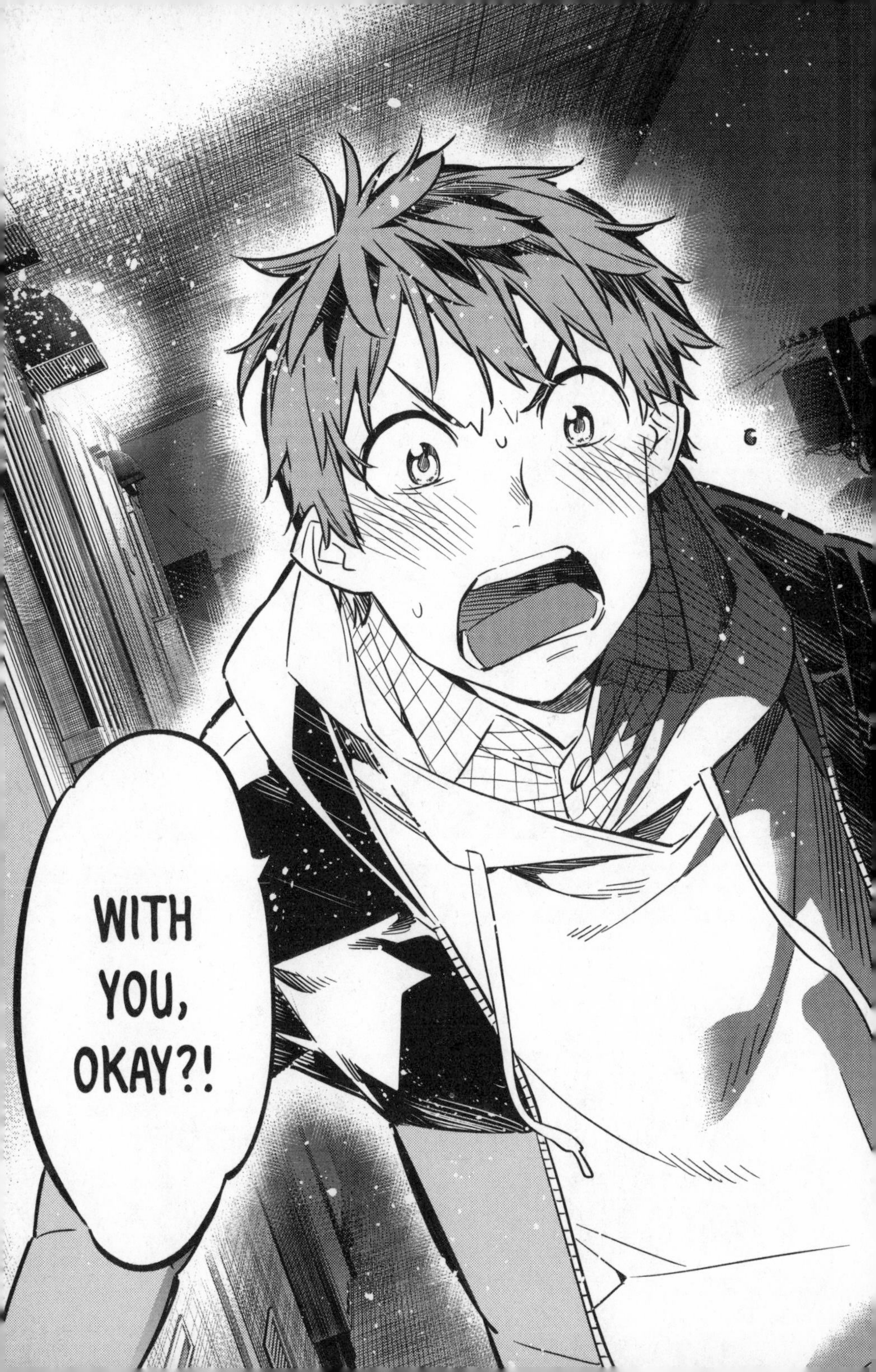
WITH YOU, OKAY?!

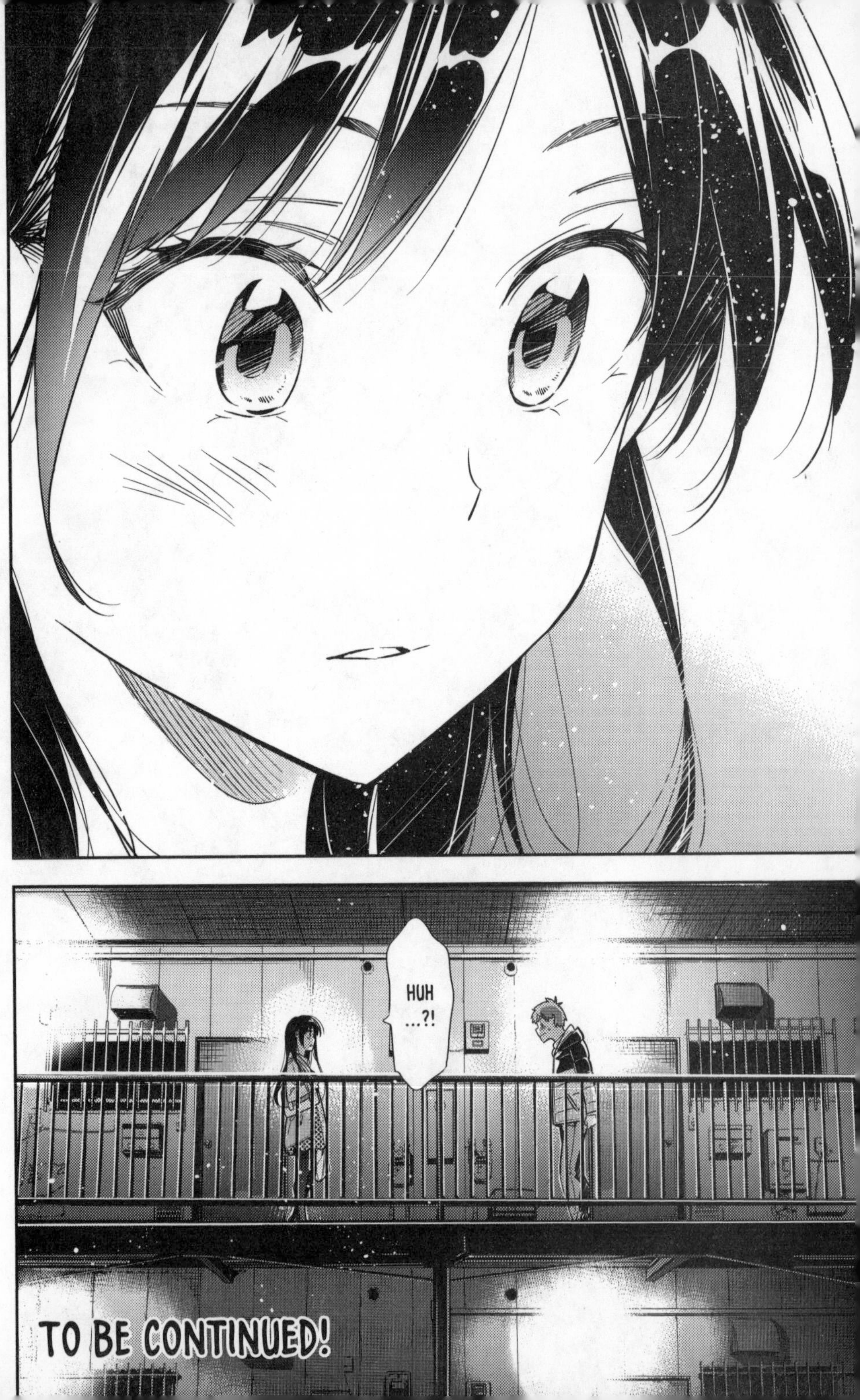
HUH ...?!
TO BE CONTINUED!

RENT-A-GIRLFRIEND

Bonus: Rent-A-Girlfriend × Senryu Girl

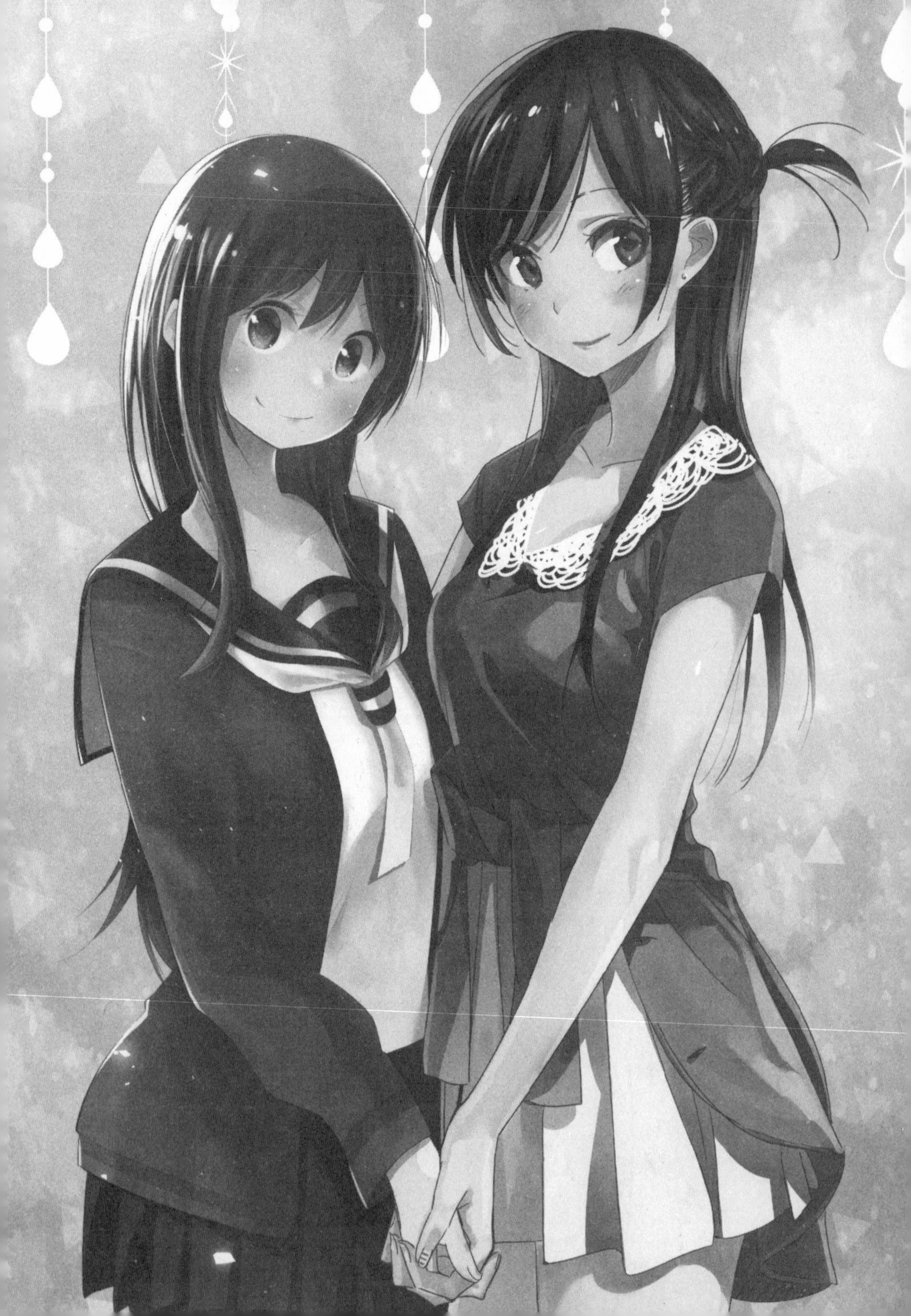

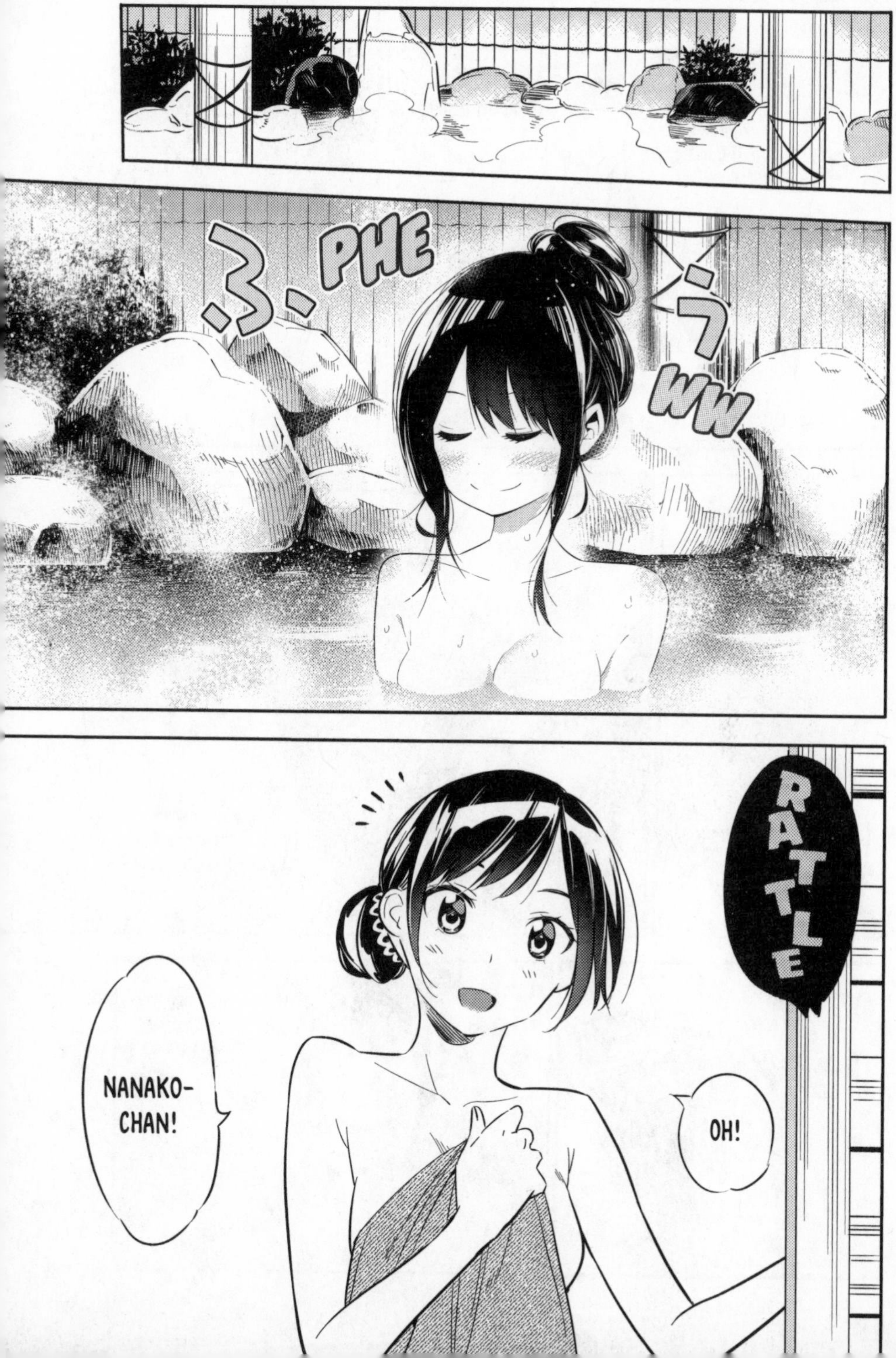

ふ PHE
う WW
RATTLE
OH!
NANAKO-CHAN!

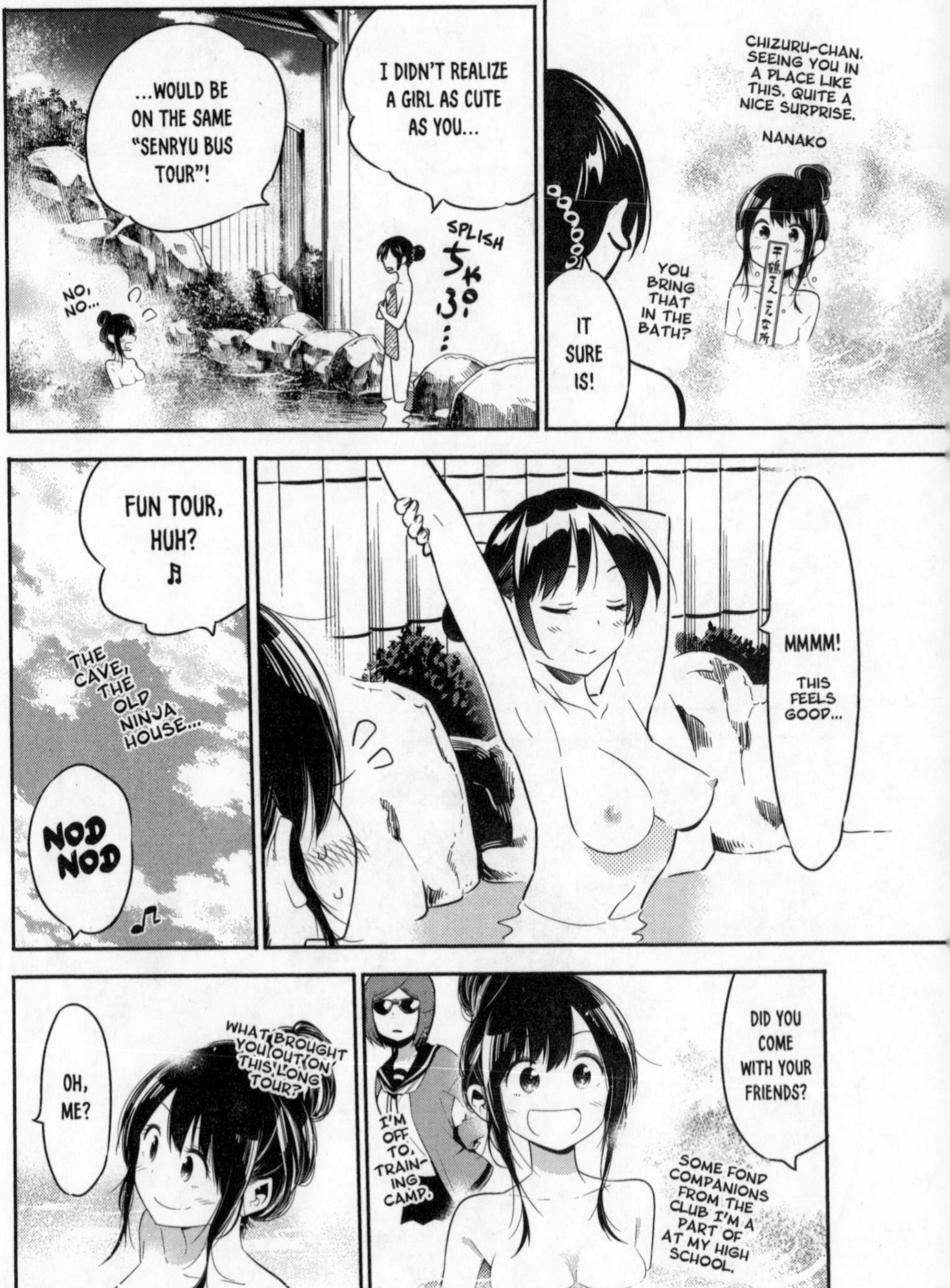
CHIZURU-CHAN. SEEING YOU IN A PLACE LIKE THIS. QUITE A NICE SURPRISE.
NANAKO
千鶴さん こんな所
YOU BRING THAT IN THE BATH?
IT SURE IS!
I DIDN'T REALIZE A GIRL AS CUTE AS YOU...
...WOULD BE ON THE SAME "SENRYU BUS TOUR"!
SPLISH
ちゃぷ…
NO, NO...
MMMM!
THIS FEELS GOOD...
FUN TOUR, HUH? ♫
THE CAVE, THE OLD NINJA HOUSE...
NOD NOD ♫
DID YOU COME WITH YOUR FRIENDS?
SOME FOND COMPANIONS FROM THE CLUB I'M A PART OF AT MY HIGH SCHOOL.
I'M OFF TO TRAINING CAMP.
WHAT BROUGHT YOU OUT ON THIS LONG TOUR?
OH, ME?

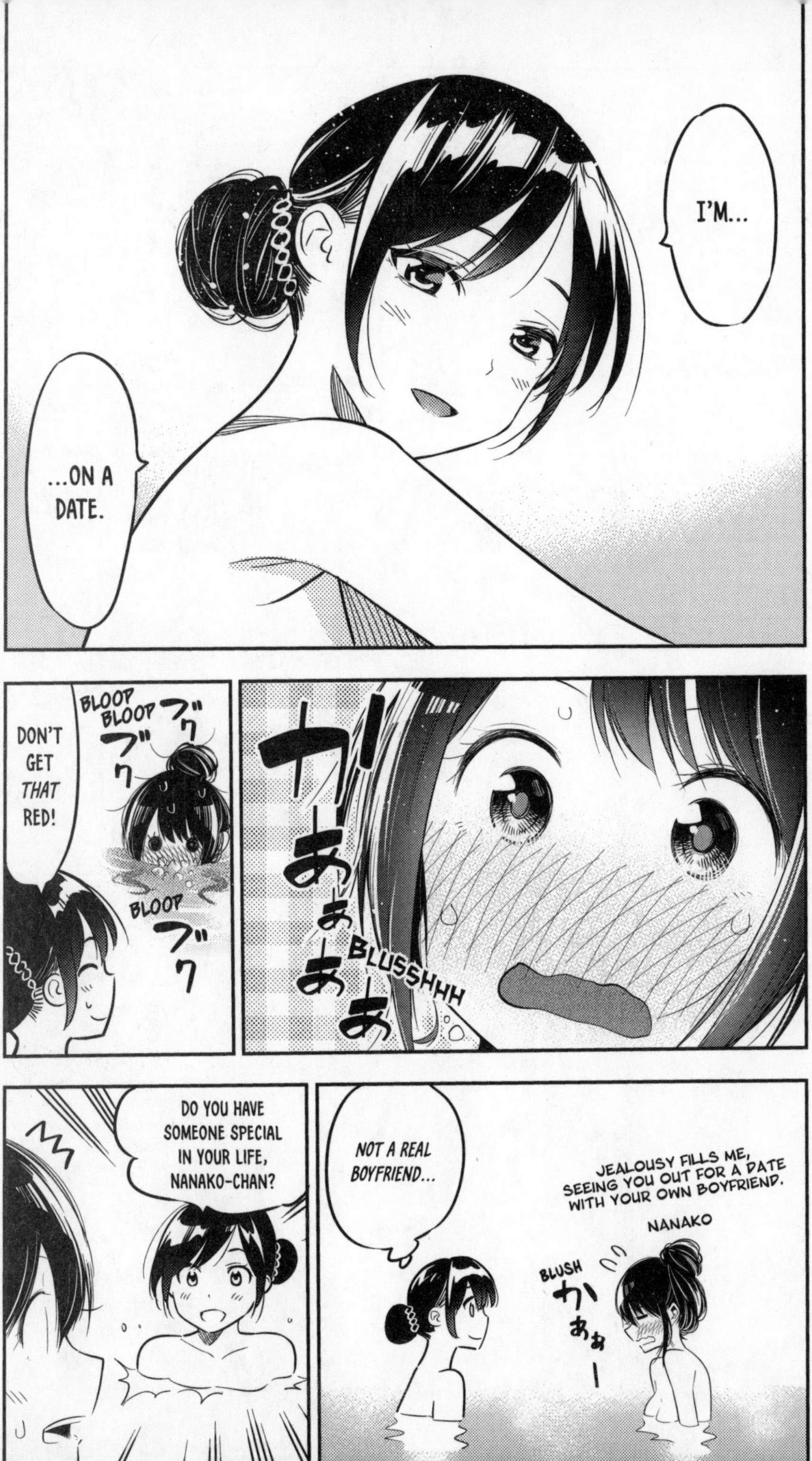
I'M...
...ON A DATE.
BLUSSHHH
BLOOP BLOOP ブク ブク
DON'T GET *THAT* RED!
BLOOP ブク
JEALOUSY FILLS ME, SEEING YOU OUT FOR A DATE WITH YOUR OWN BOYFRIEND.
NANAKO
NOT A REAL BOYFRIEND...
BLUSH かぁぁー
DO YOU HAVE SOMEONE SPECIAL IN YOUR LIFE, NANAKO-CHAN?

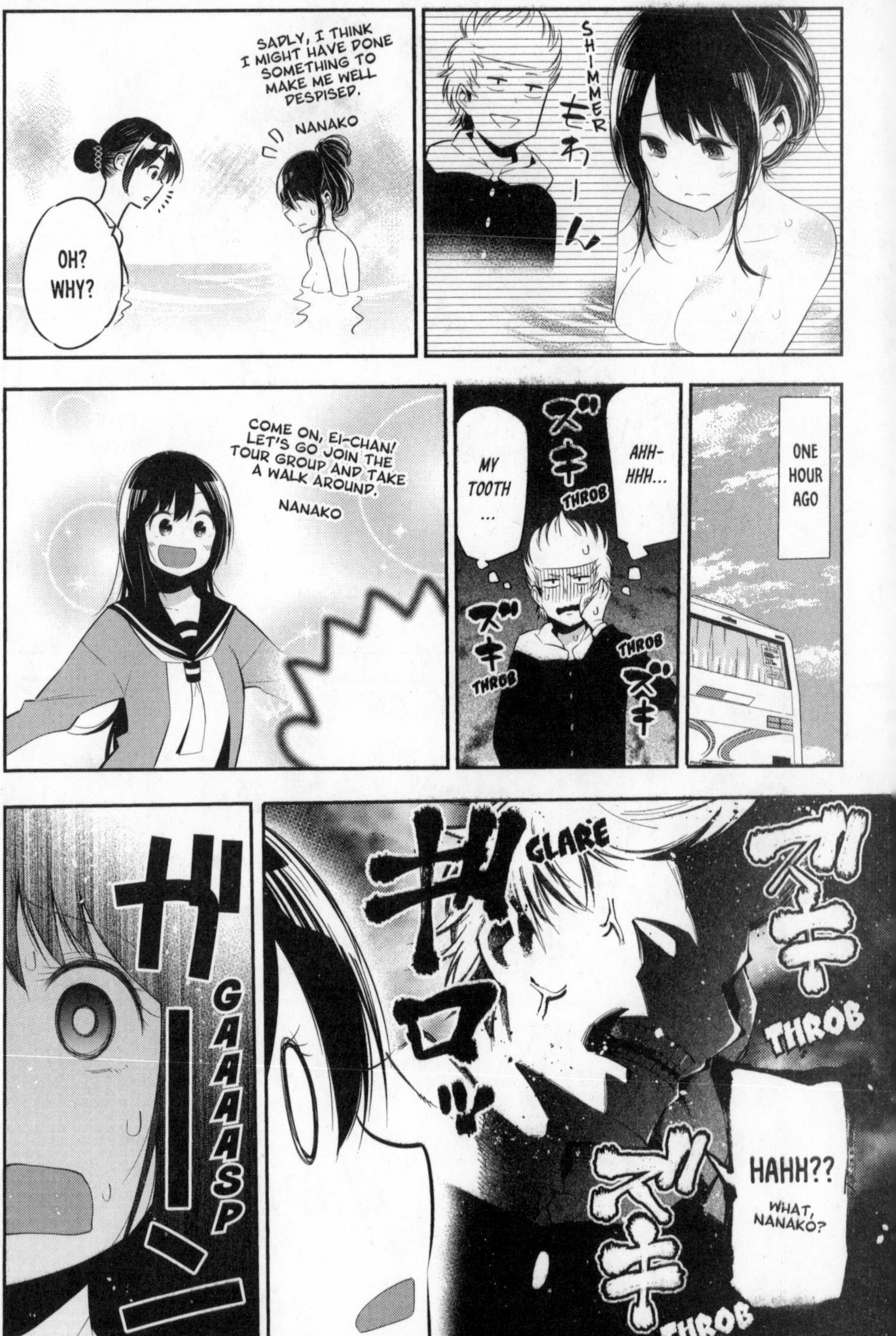
SHIMMER
SADLY, I THINK I MIGHT HAVE DONE SOMETHING TO MAKE ME WELL DESPISED.
NANAKO
OH? WHY?
ONE HOUR AGO
AHH-HHH...
MY TOOTH ...
THROB
THROB
THROB
COME ON, EI-CHAN! LET'S GO JOIN THE TOUR GROUP AND TAKE A WALK AROUND.
NANAKO
THROB
GLARE
HAHH??
WHAT, NANAKO?
THROB
GAAAAASP

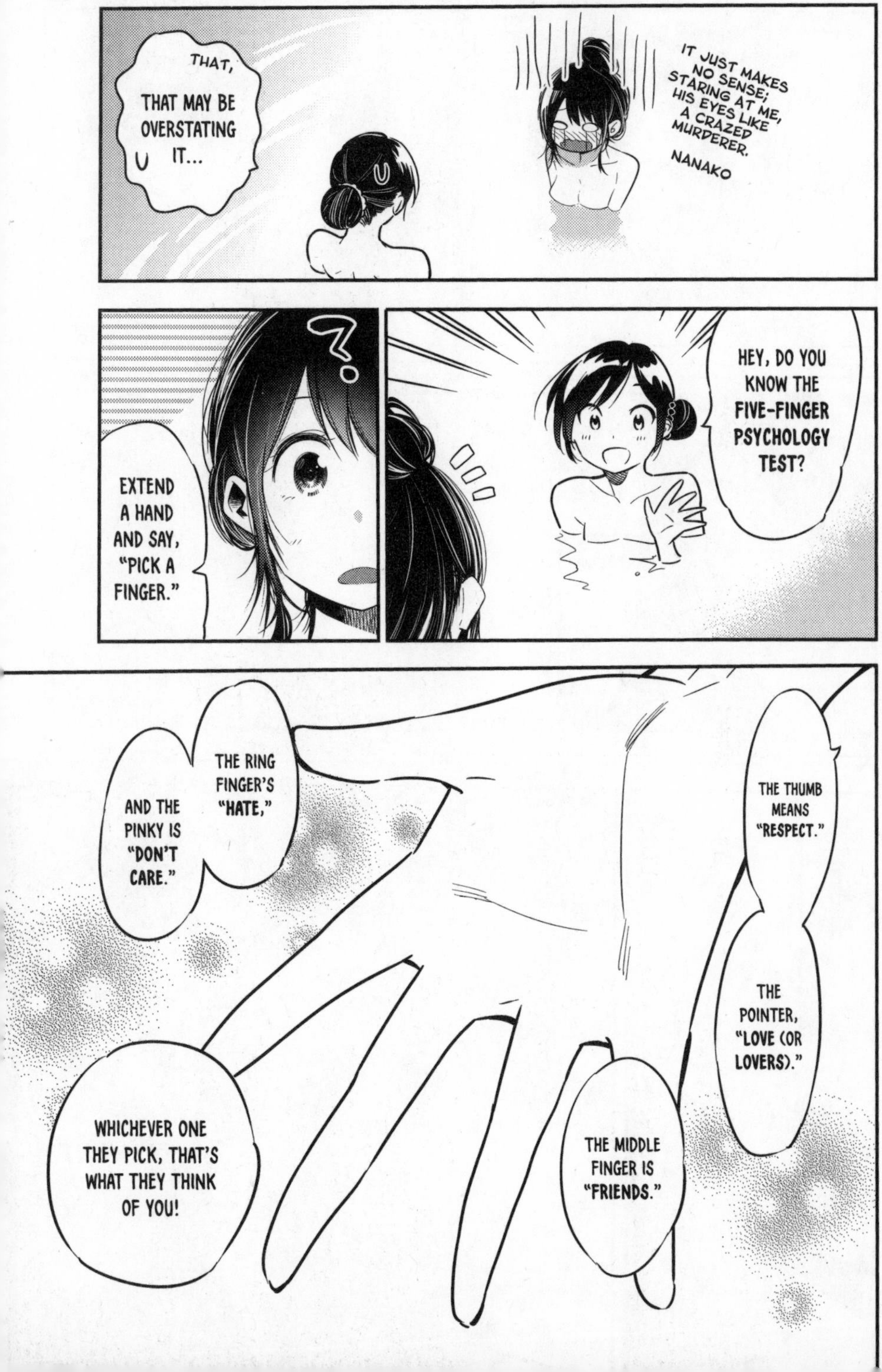
IT JUST MAKES NO SENSE; STARING AT ME, HIS EYES LIKE A CRAZED MURDERER.
NANAKO
THAT, THAT MAY BE OVERSTATING IT...
HEY, DO YOU KNOW THE FIVE-FINGER PSYCHOLOGY TEST?
EXTEND A HAND AND SAY, "PICK A FINGER."
THE THUMB MEANS "RESPECT."
THE POINTER, "LOVE (OR LOVERS)."
THE MIDDLE FINGER IS "FRIENDS."
THE RING FINGER'S "HATE,"
AND THE PINKY IS "DON'T CARE."
WHICHEVER ONE THEY PICK, THAT'S WHAT THEY THINK OF YOU!

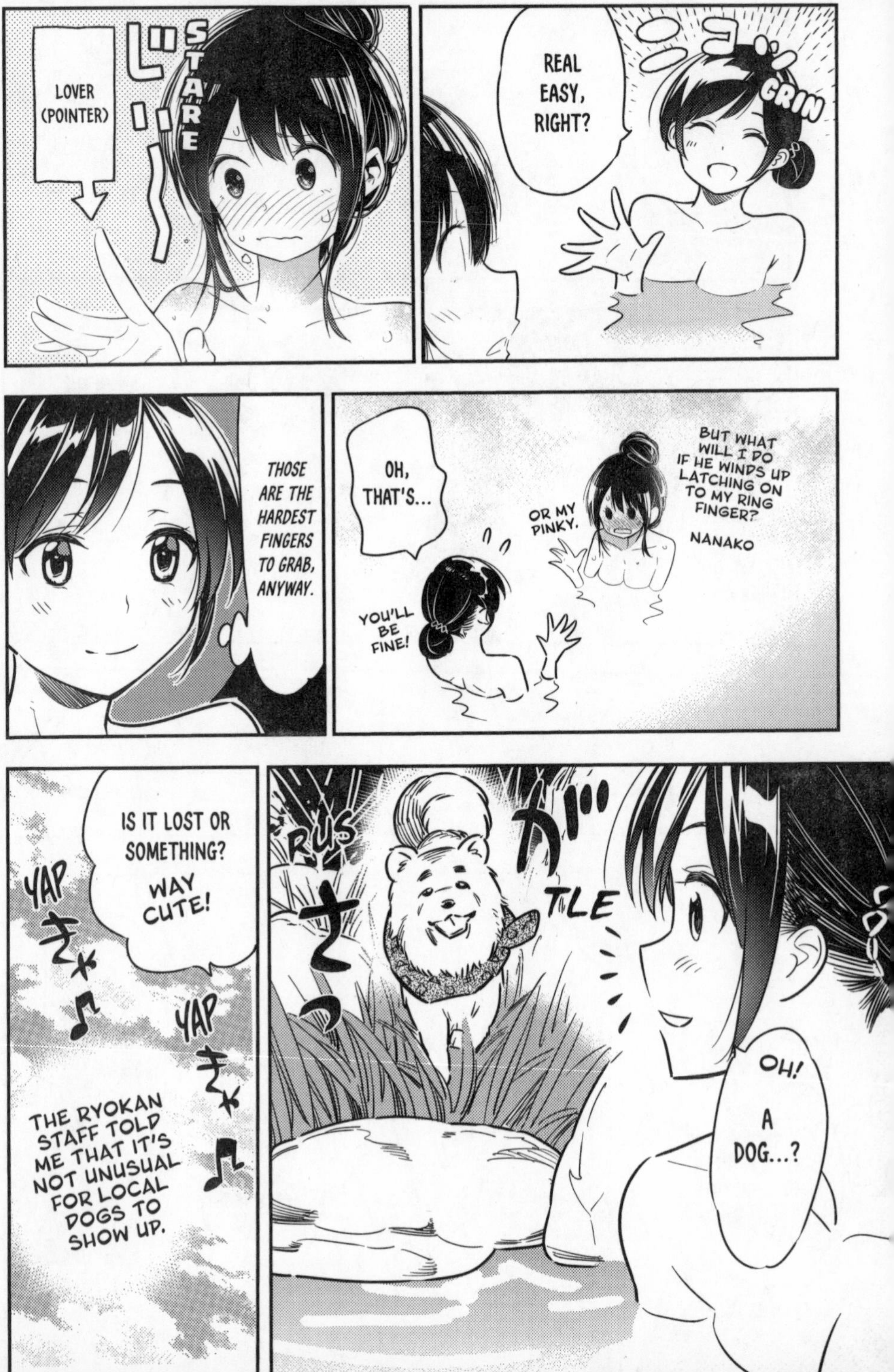
REAL EASY, RIGHT?
GRIN
STARE
LOVER (POINTER)
OH, THAT'S...
YOU'LL BE FINE!
OR MY PINKY.
BUT WHAT WILL I DO IF HE WINDS UP LATCHING ON TO MY RING FINGER?
NANAKO
THOSE ARE THE HARDEST FINGERS TO GRAB, ANYWAY.
RUS
TLE
OH!
A DOG...?
IS IT LOST OR SOMETHING?
WAY CUTE!
YAP
YAP
THE RYOKAN STAFF TOLD ME THAT IT'S NOT UNUSUAL FOR LOCAL DOGS TO SHOW UP.

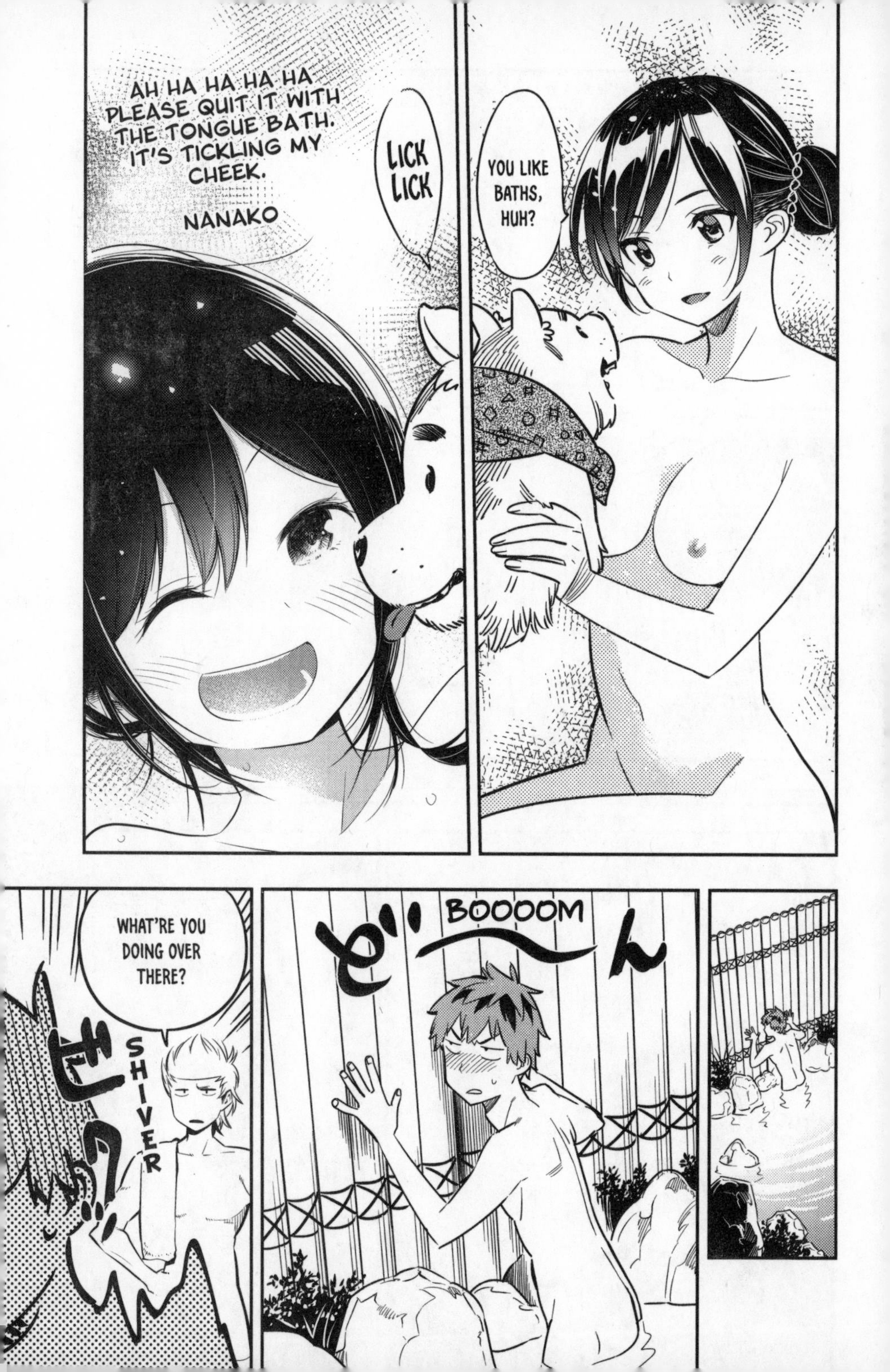
YOU LIKE BATHS, HUH?
LICK LICK
AH HA HA HA HA PLEASE QUIT IT WITH THE TONGUE BATH. IT'S TICKLING MY CHEEK.
NANAKO
BOOOM
ど〜ん
WHAT'RE YOU DOING OVER THERE?
SHIVER

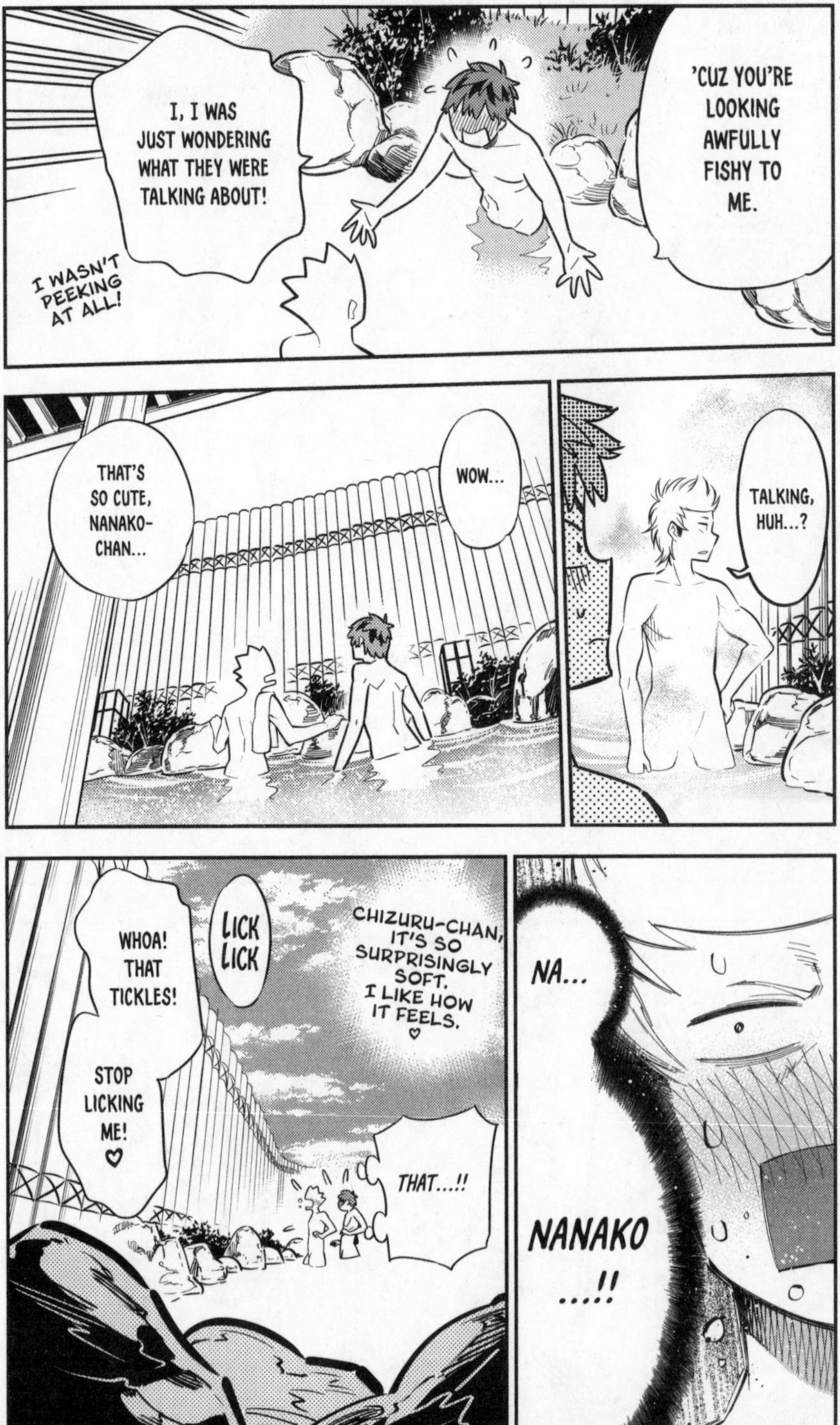
'CUZ YOU'RE LOOKING AWFULLY FISHY TO ME.
I, I WAS JUST WONDERING WHAT THEY WERE TALKING ABOUT!
I WASN'T PEEKING AT ALL!
TALKING, HUH...?
WOW...
THAT'S SO CUTE, NANAKO-CHAN...
NA...
NANAKO ....!!
CHIZURU-CHAN, IT'S SO SURPRISINGLY SOFT. I LIKE HOW IT FEELS. ♡
LICK LICK
WHOA! THAT TICKLES!
STOP LICKING ME! ♡
THAT...!!

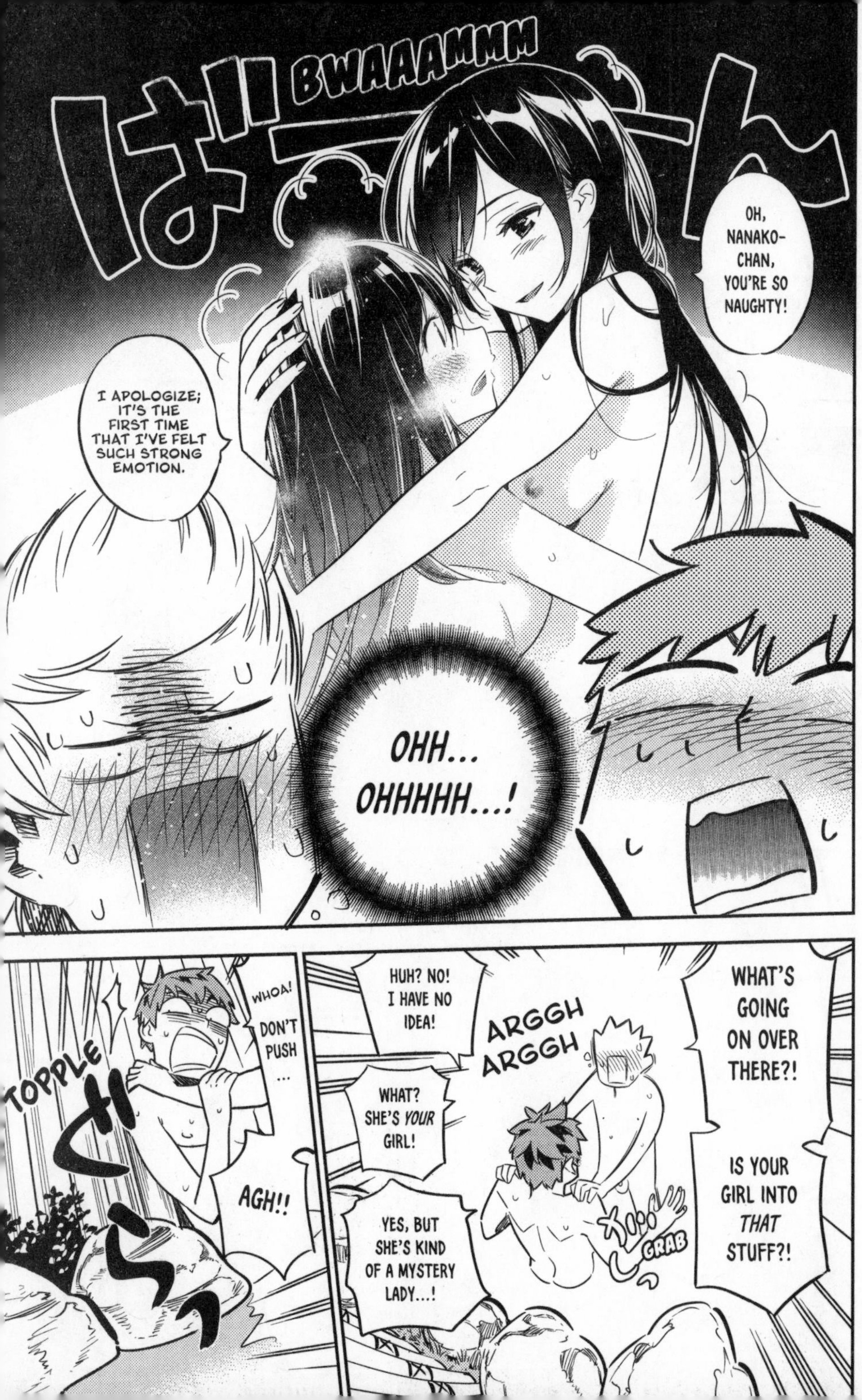
BWAAAMMM
OH, NANAKO-CHAN, YOU'RE SO NAUGHTY!
I APOLOGIZE; IT'S THE FIRST TIME THAT I'VE FELT SUCH STRONG EMOTION.
OHH... OHHHHH...!
WHAT'S GOING ON OVER THERE?!
IS YOUR GIRL INTO THAT STUFF?!
HUH? NO! I HAVE NO IDEA!
ARGGH ARGGH
WHAT? SHE'S YOUR GIRL!
GRAB
YES, BUT SHE'S KIND OF A MYSTERY LADY...!
WHOA! DON'T PUSH ...
TOPPLE
AGH!!

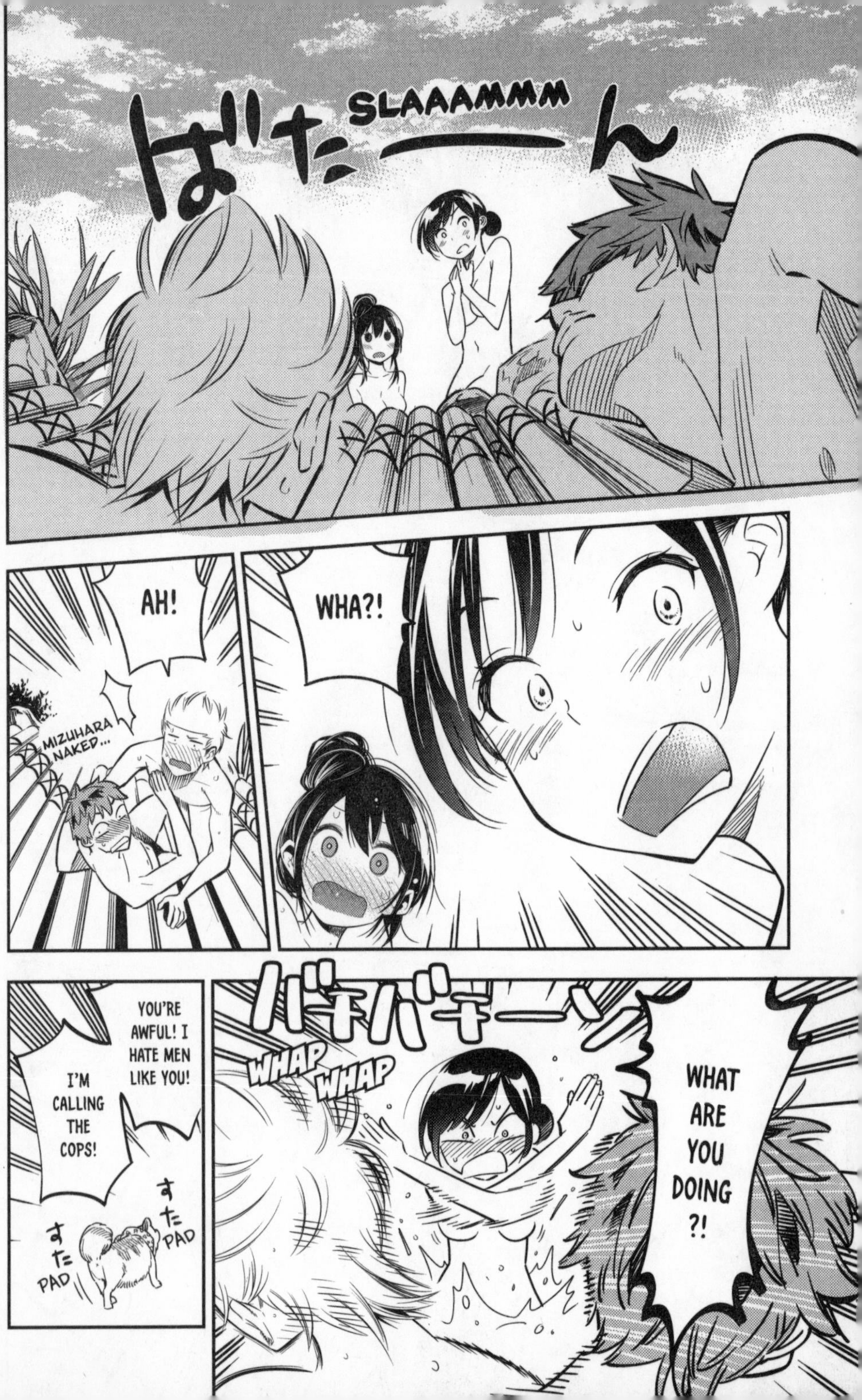

ばたーーん
SLAAAMMMM
WHA?!
AH!
MIZUHARA NAKED...
バチバチーン
WHAP WHAP
WHAT ARE YOU DOING?!
YOU'RE AWFUL! I HATE MEN LIKE YOU!
I'M CALLING THE COPS!
すた
PAD
すた
PAD

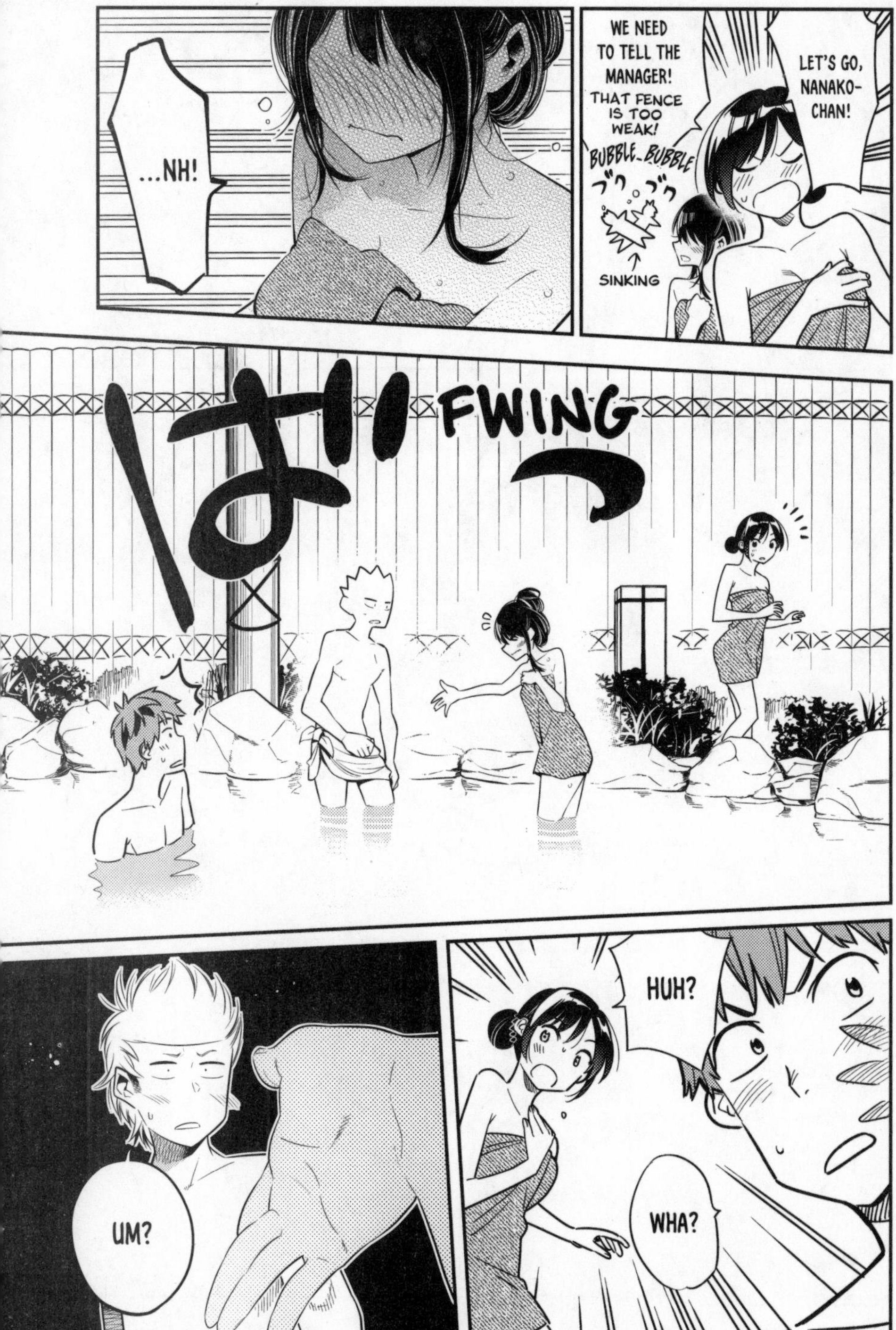
LET'S GO, NANAKO-CHAN!
WE NEED TO TELL THE MANAGER!
THAT FENCE IS TOO WEAK!
BUBBLE BUBBLE
ブクブク
SINKING
...NH!
はっ
FWING
HUH?
WHA?
UM?

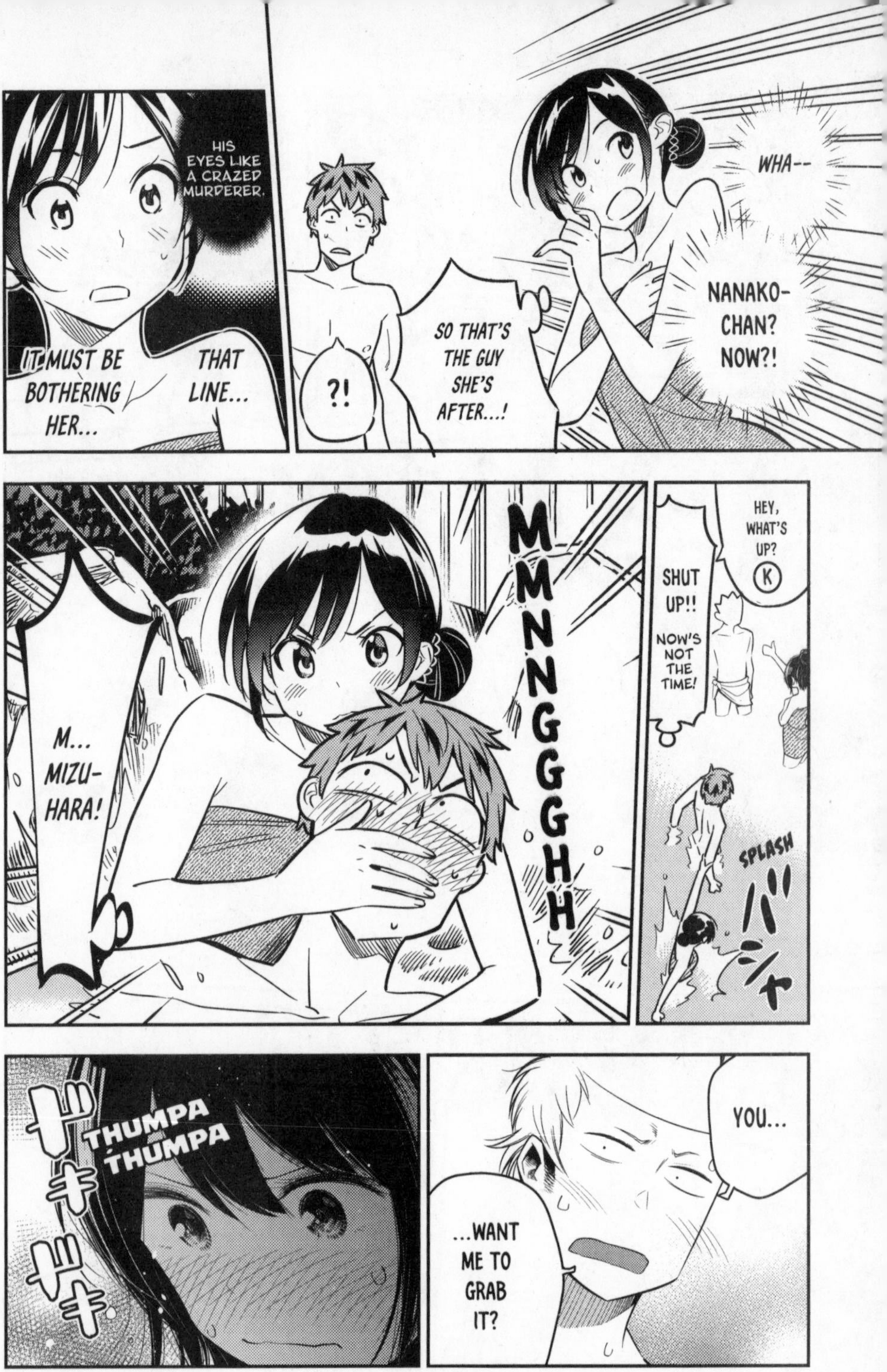
WHA--
NANAKO-CHAN? NOW?!
SO THAT'S THE GUY SHE'S AFTER...!
?!
HIS EYES LIKE A CRAZED MURDERER.
THAT LINE...
IT MUST BE BOTHERING HER...
HEY, WHAT'S UP? (K)
SHUT UP!! NOW'S NOT THE TIME!
SPLASH
バシャ
MMNNGGGH
M... MIZUHARA!
YOU...
...WANT ME TO GRAB IT?
THUMPA THUMPA
ドキドキ

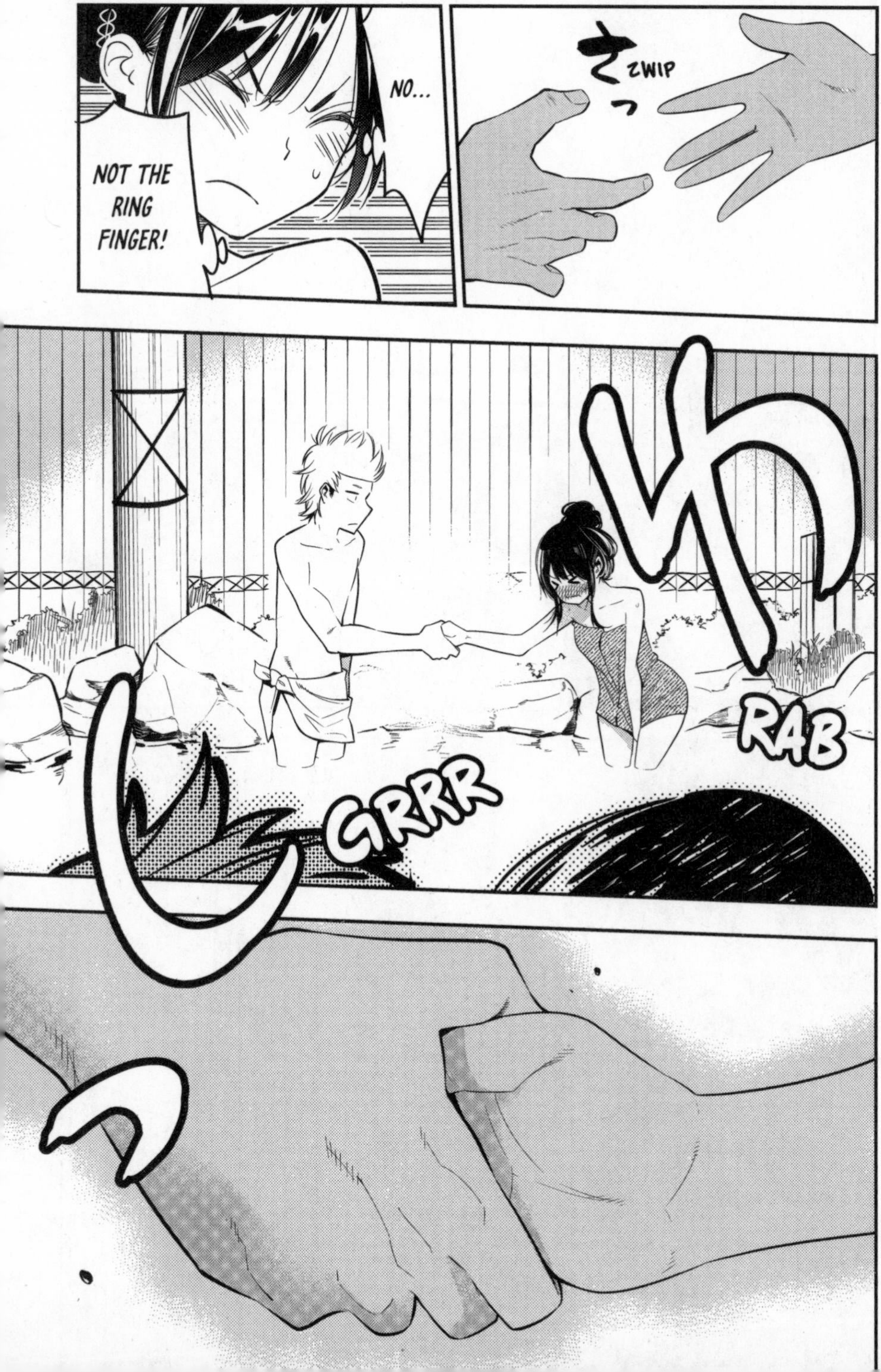
さっ
ZWIP
NO...
NOT THE RING FINGER!
RAB
GRRR

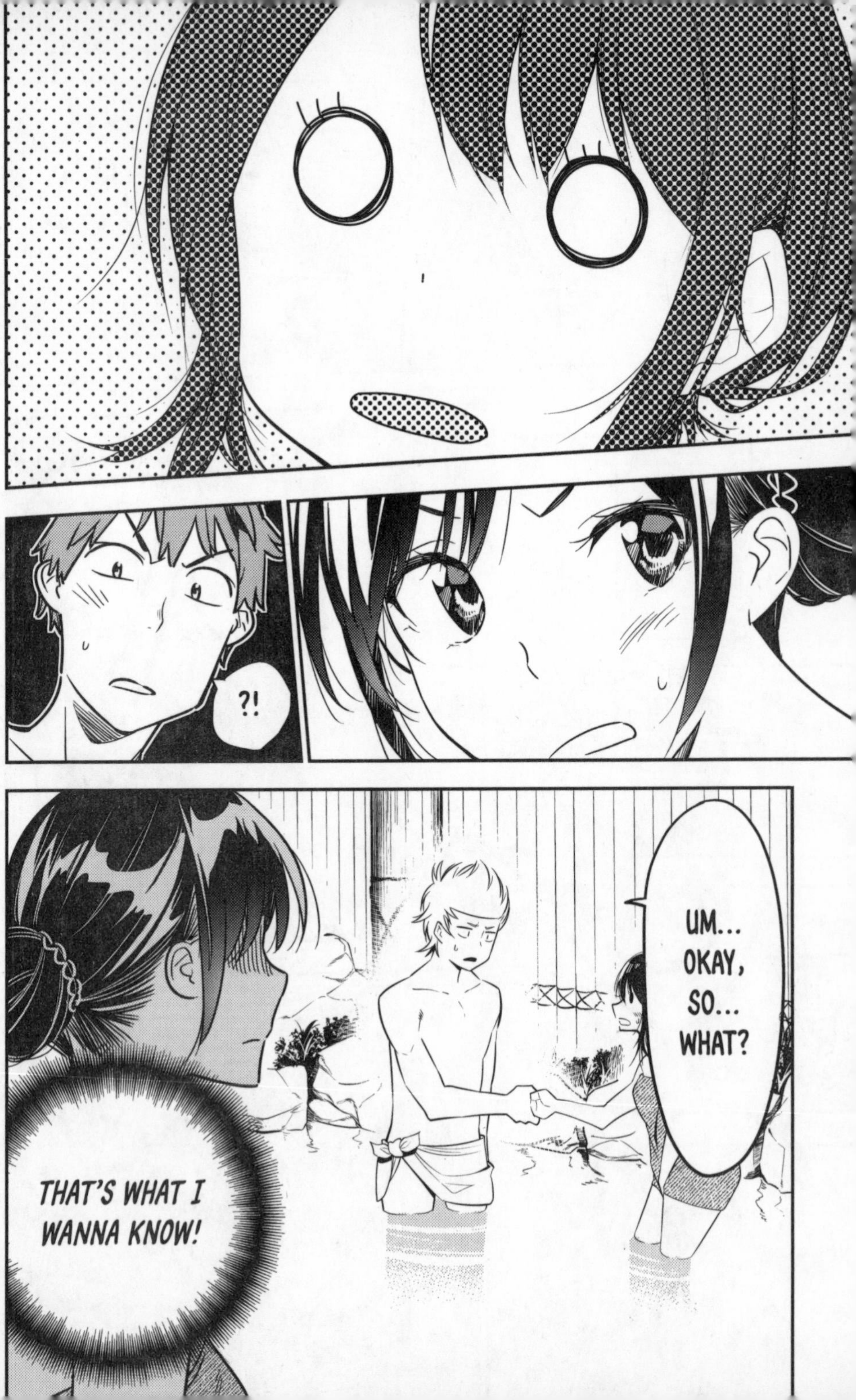
?!
UM... OKAY, SO... WHAT?
THAT'S WHAT I WANNA KNOW!

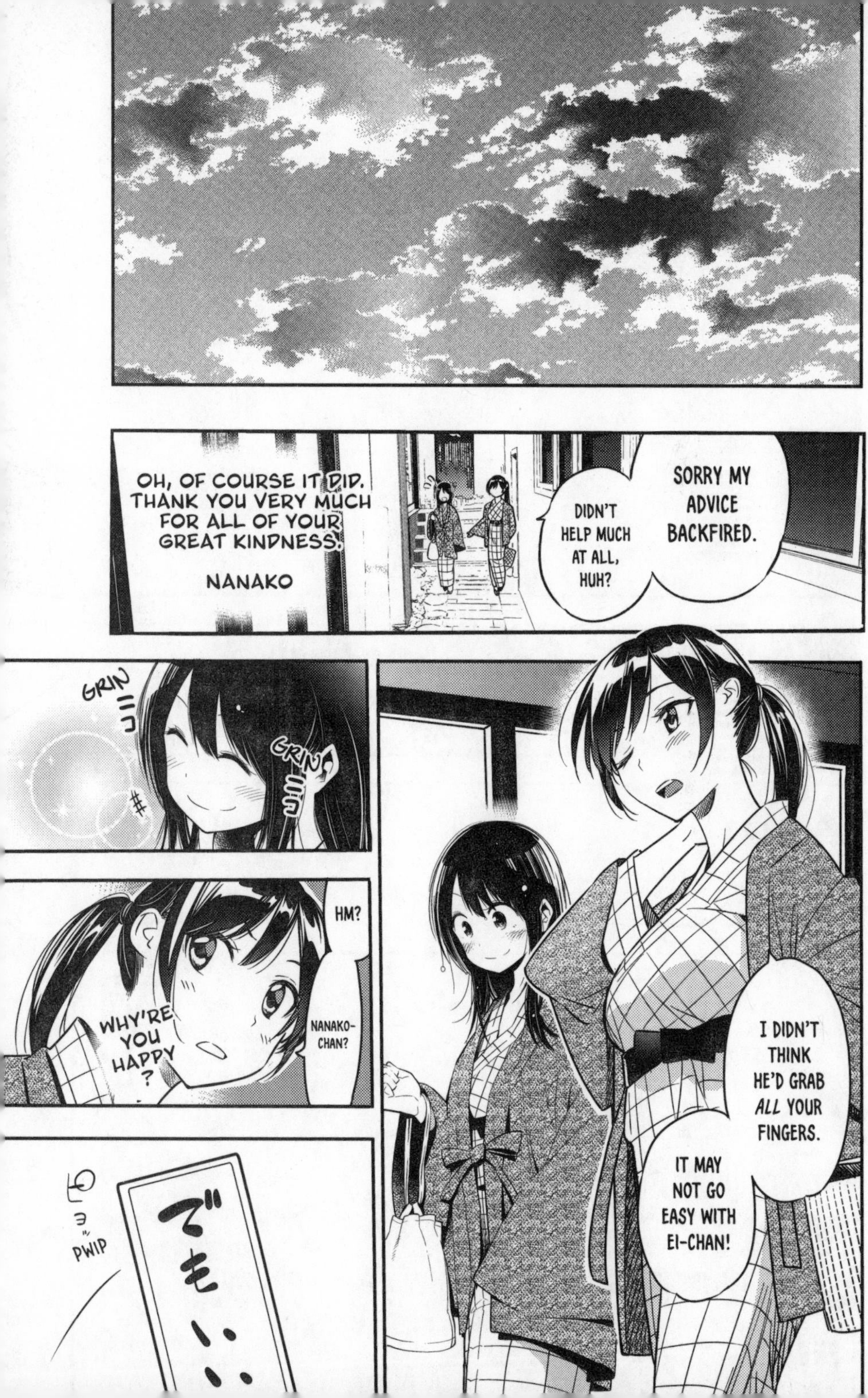
SORRY MY ADVICE BACKFIRED.
DIDN'T HELP MUCH AT ALL, HUH?
OH, OF COURSE IT DID. THANK YOU VERY MUCH FOR ALL OF YOUR GREAT KINDNESS.
NANAKO
I DIDN'T THINK HE'D GRAB *ALL* YOUR FINGERS.
IT MAY NOT GO EASY WITH EI-CHAN!
GRIN
ニコ
GRIN
ニコ
HM?
NANAKO-CHAN?
WHY'RE YOU HAPPY?
でも…
ピョ
PWIP

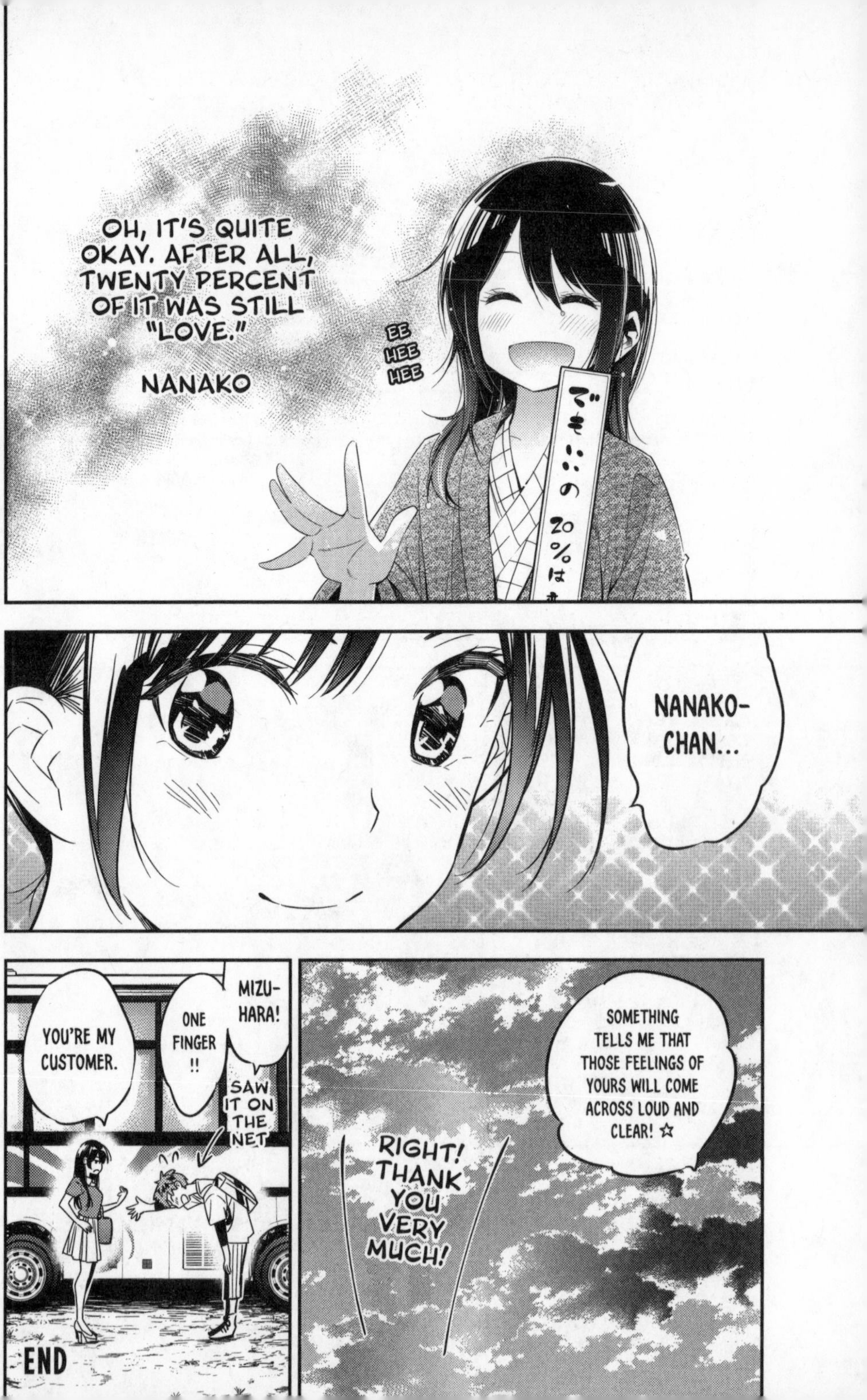
OH, IT'S QUITE OKAY. AFTER ALL, TWENTY PERCENT OF IT WAS STILL "LOVE."
NANAKO
EE HEE HEE
NANAKO-CHAN...
SOMETHING TELLS ME THAT THOSE FEELINGS OF YOURS WILL COME ACROSS LOUD AND CLEAR! ☆
RIGHT! THANK YOU VERY MUCH!
MIZU-HARA!
ONE FINGER !!
YOU'RE MY CUSTOMER.
SAW IT ON THE NET
END

A BONUS WRITTEN IN ADVANCE OF THE OBON HOLIDAY, WITH MY HEART ALREADY IN FULL OBON MODE.

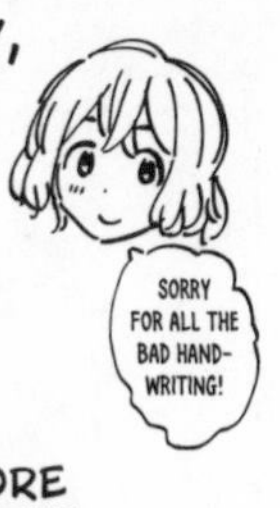
SORRY FOR ALL THE BAD HAND-WRITING!

THANK YOU FOR PURCHASING VOLUME 6 OF RENT-A-GIRLFRIEND!

YOU KNOW, I'VE GOT JUST ONE MORE PAGE TO WRITE BEFORE MY TIME OFF. BUT THAT'S MY PROBLEM, NOT YOURS. THE BONUS PAGE FROM THE LAST VOLUME WAS PRETTY WELL RECEIVED, SO I'M TRYING IT OUT AGAIN (FOR THE LAST TIME).

THIS TIME I THINK I'LL WRITE ABOUT WHY I DECIDED TO GET INTO MANGA (IN CLASSIC AFTERWORD STYLE). I'M THE THIRD SON FROM A FAMILY IN A RURAL PART OF THE NAGANO PREFECTURE. MY INTEREST IN MANGA WAS ENTIRELY BECAUSE OF MY OLDEST BROTHER. BACK WHEN I WAS IN KINDERGARTEN, HE WOULD PURCHASE SHONEN JUMP EVERY WEEK, READ IT, AND THEN PASS IT ON TO ME. AS A VERY SENSITIVE YOUNG CHILD, IT ALL STABBED INTO MY HEART LIKE A DAGGER.

I WAS ON THE BASEBALL TEAM AS A KID, SO I PROBABLY WROTE IN MY GRADE-SCHOOL GRADUATION ESSAY THAT I WANTED TO BE A PRO ATHLETE LIKE EVERYONE ELSE (THOUGH I'M NOT COMPLETELY SURE ANYMORE). HOWEVER, DURING MY LAST GAME IN MIDDLE SCHOOL, MY TENDENCY TO GET EXTREMELY EXCITED AROUND OTHER PEOPLE GOT THE BETTER OF ME, AND I MADE THREE OR FOUR ERRORS IN A ROW. AS CAPTAIN, I THUS LED OUR TEAM TO ONE IMPRESSIVE LOSS. (APOLOGIES TO MY OLD TEAMMATES, I STILL FEEL TERRIBLE ABOUT IT... IT'S SERIOUSLY ONE OF THE WORST TRAUMAS OF MY LIFE...)

AS A RESULT, I DROPPED OUT OF BASEBALL IN HIGH SCHOOL. (SERIOUSLY, I COULD NEVER CAUSE THAT MUCH TROUBLE FOR A TEAM AGAIN... I'M SURE I'M NEVER GOING TO HEAVEN...) AFTER THAT, I'D JUST GO HOME AND KICK A SOCCER BALL AROUND ALL DAY (⟵ MAKES NO SENSE).

OF COURSE, ONCE YOU REACH YOUR LATE TEENS, YOU START TO SERIOUSLY THINK ABOUT THE FUTURE. AS SOMEONE THAT WAS MAJORLY, AND CONTINUALLY, INFLUENCED BY ALL THE FAMOUS MANGA OF THE ERA, I NATURALLY STARTED TO THINK, "I GUESS I LIKE MANGA MOST OF ALL." ⟵ ONE-TRACK MIND

SO, AFTER GRADUATION, I WENT TO AN ART SCHOOL AND BEGAN MAKING SUBMISSIONS. I CHOSE SHONEN MAGAZINE (IGNORING THE FACT THAT I THOUGHT I WAS ENOUGH OF A GENIUS TO ROCKET TO THE TOP NO MATTER WHICH MAGAZINE I WENT WITH) ON A RECOMMENDATION FROM MY EDITOR. NATURALLY, I HAD MY UPS AND DOWNS. SOMETIMES I'D BE OVERJOYED AND SOMETIMES I'D FEEL LIKE I WAS ABOUT TO DIE...BUT LOOKING BACK, I'M ABLE TO DO WHAT I LIKE FOR A LIVING, DRAWING MANGA IS FUN, AND IF I SCREW UP, I CAN TAKE RESPONSIBILITY FOR IT MYSELF. (AGAIN, SERIOUSLY, I'M SORRY, TEAMMATES...THE BALL JUST KEPT VANISHING ON ME... IT WAS A REGULAR POP-UP, BUT I COMPLETELY FORGOT HOW TO MOVE MY BODY LIKE BEFORE...AND THEN THE BALL HIT MY LEG, AND I KICKED IT AWAY... I CAN STILL HEAR THE OPPOSING TEAM'S BENCH SHOUT "GO FOR THIRD! GO FOR THIRD!" IN MY EARS...ARGH...)

REGARDLESS, MANGA'S A RAUCOUS BLAST, SO IT'S ALL GOOD. IT KEEPS ME CONNECTED TO ALL OF YOU, TOO. ALSO, YOU KNOW, I GOT JUST ONE MORE PAGE TO WRITE BEFORE MY TIME OFF. BUT THAT'S MY PROBLEM, NOT YOURS.

COPY/PASTE

VOLUME 7 IS ON SALE NOW! REIJI MIYAJIMA

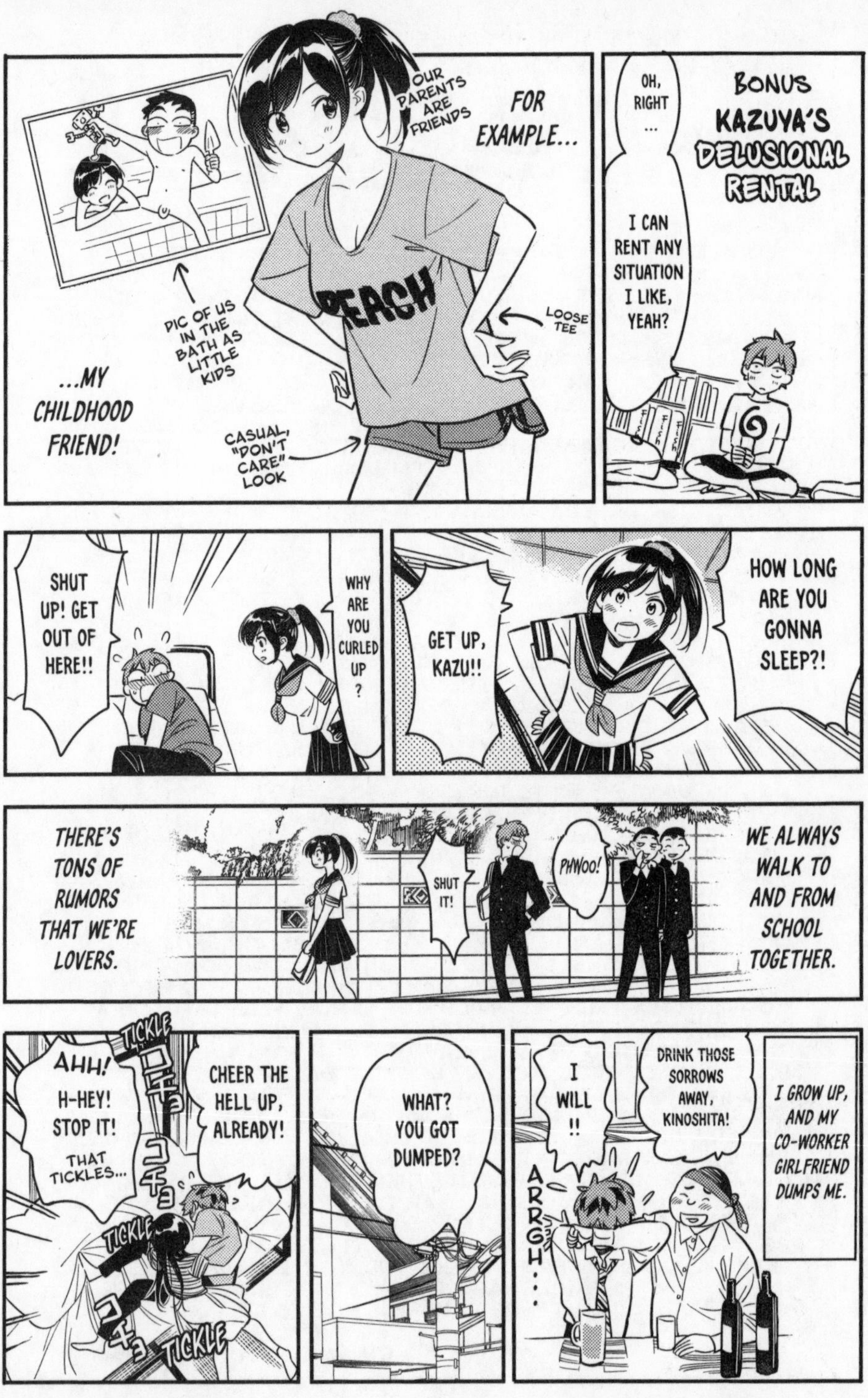
BONUS KAZUYA'S DELUSIONAL RENTAL
OH, RIGHT ...
I CAN RENT ANY SITUATION I LIKE, YEAH?
FOR EXAMPLE...
OUR PARENTS ARE FRIENDS
PIC OF US IN THE BATH AS LITTLE KIDS
PEACH
LOOSE TEE
...MY CHILDHOOD FRIEND!
CASUAL, "DON'T CARE" LOOK
HOW LONG ARE YOU GONNA SLEEP?!
GET UP, KAZU!!
WHY ARE YOU CURLED UP ?
SHUT UP! GET OUT OF HERE!!
WE ALWAYS WALK TO AND FROM SCHOOL TOGETHER.
PHWOO!
SHUT IT!
THERE'S TONS OF RUMORS THAT WE'RE LOVERS.
I GROW UP, AND MY CO-WORKER GIRLFRIEND DUMPS ME.
DRINK THOSE SORROWS AWAY, KINOSHITA!
I WILL !!
ARRGH...
WHAT? YOU GOT DUMPED?
CHEER THE HELL UP, ALREADY!
TICKLE
AHH! H-HEY! STOP IT! THAT TICKLES...
TICKLE
TICKLE

RENT-A-GIRLFRIEND STAFF: A, IROHKI, TEMAENO, KUSUMI, MITSUKI

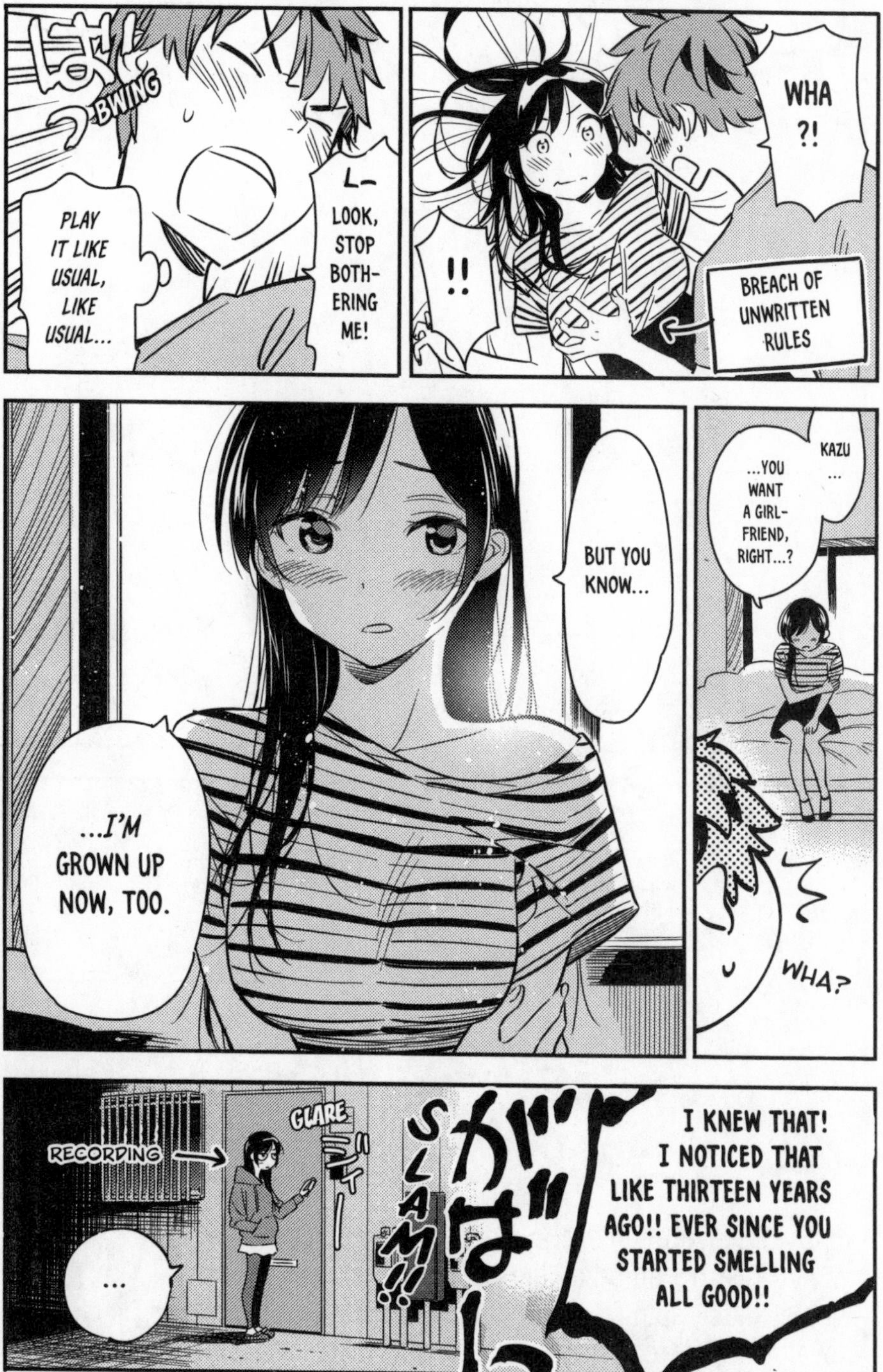
WHA ?!
!!
BREACH OF UNWRITTEN RULES
BWING
L— LOOK, STOP BOTH-ERING ME!
PLAY IT LIKE USUAL, LIKE USUAL...
KAZU ...
...YOU WANT A GIRL-FRIEND, RIGHT...?
WHA?
BUT YOU KNOW...
...I'M GROWN UP NOW, TOO.
I KNEW THAT! I NOTICED THAT LIKE THIRTEEN YEARS AGO!! EVER SINCE YOU STARTED SMELLING ALL GOOD!!
SLAM!!
GLARE
RECORDING
...

EDITORS: HIRAOKA-SAN, HIRATSUKA-SAN, HARA-SAN, CHOKAI-SAN. ALSO THANKS TO EVERYBODY WHO PICKED UP THIS BOOK!! SEE YOU SOON! ♡

THE SWEET SCENT OF LOVE IS IN THE AIR! FOR FANS OF OFFBEAT ROMANCES LIKE *WOTAKOI*

Sweat and Soap © Kintetsu Yamada / Kodansha Ltd.

In an office romance, there's a fine line between sexy and awkward... and that line is where Asako — a woman who sweats copiously — meets Koutarou — a perfume developer who can't get enough of Asako's, er, scent. Don't miss a romcom manga like no other!

KC KODANSHA COMICS

Young characters and steampunk setting, like *Howl's Moving Castle* and *Battle Angel Alita*

Beyond the Clouds © 2018 Nicke / Ki-oon

A boy with a talent for machines and a mysterious girl whose wings he's fixed will take you beyond the clouds! In the tradition of the high-flying, resonant adventure stories of Studio Ghibli comes a gorgeous tale about the longing of young hearts for adventure and friendship!

THE WORLD OF CLAMP!

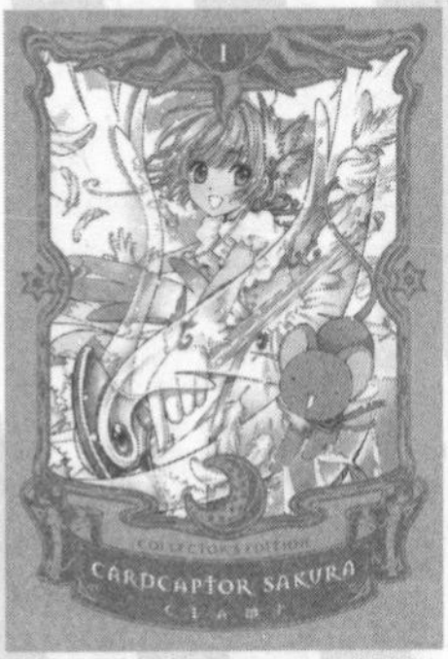
CARDCAPTOR SAKURA

Cardcaptor Sakura
Collector's Edition

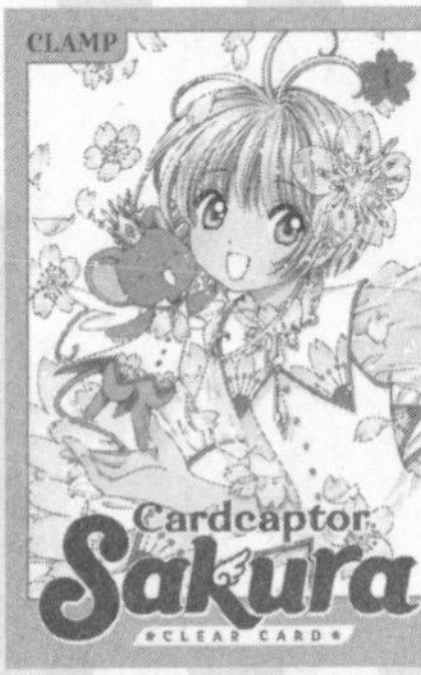
CLAMP
Cardcaptor
Sakura
CLEAR CARD

Cardcaptor Sakura:
Clear Card

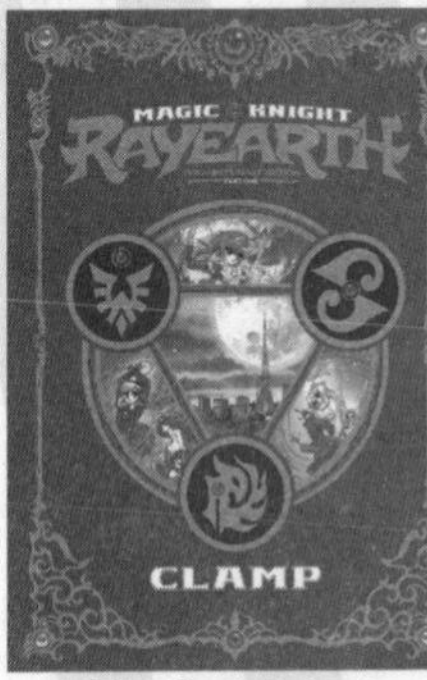
MAGIC KNIGHT
RAYEARTH
CLAMP

Magic Knight Rayearth
25th Anniversary Box Set

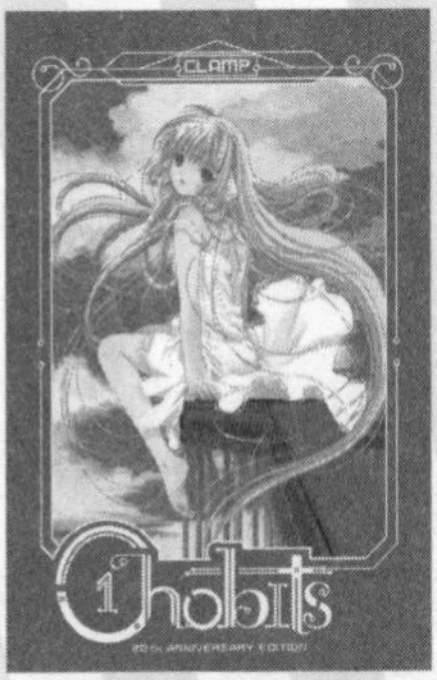
CLAMP
1
Chobits

Chobits

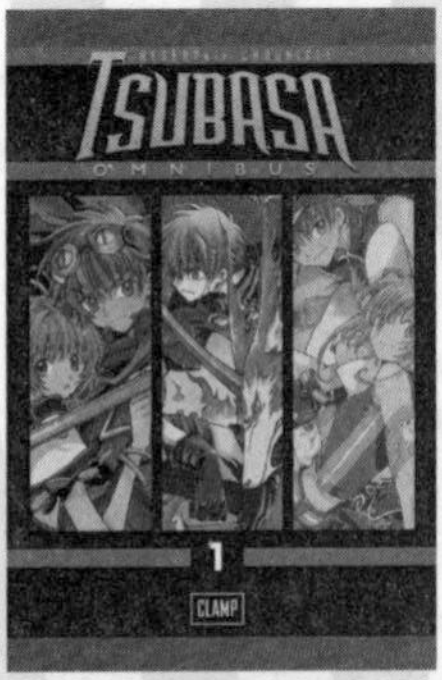
TSUBASA
OMNIBUS
1
CLAMP

TSUBASA Omnibus

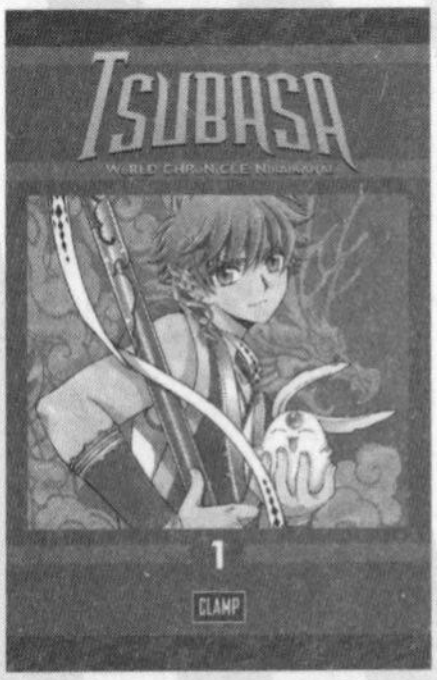
TSUBASA
1
CLAMP

TSUBASA WoRLD CHRoNiCLE

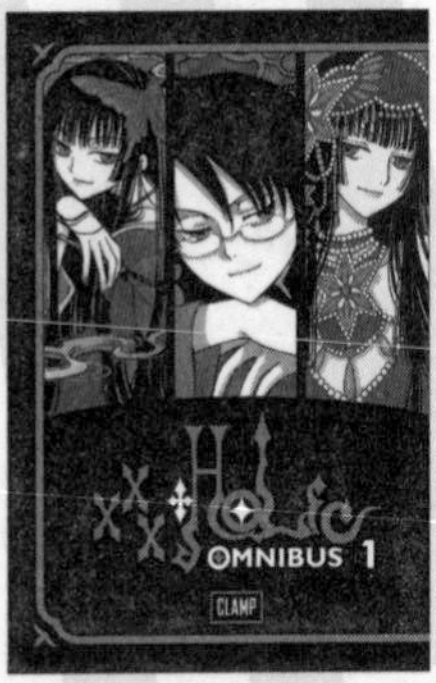
xxxHOLiC
OMNIBUS 1
CLAMP

xxxHOLiC Omnibus

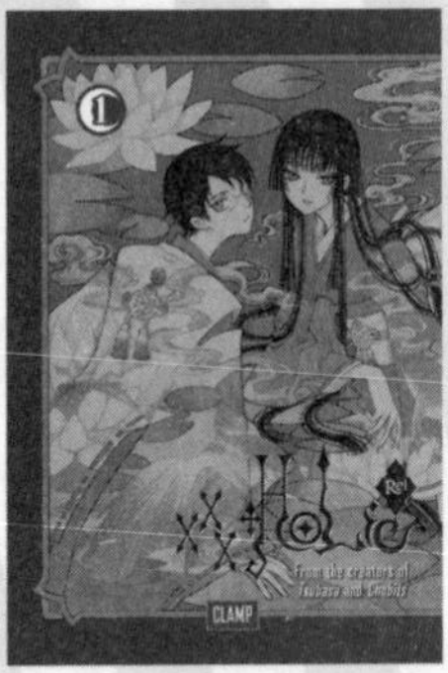
1
xxxHOLiC
Rei
CLAMP

xxxHOLiC Rei

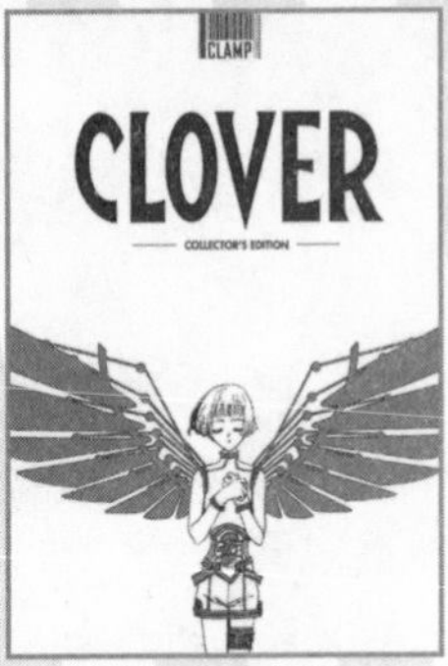
CLAMP
CLOVER
COLLECTOR'S EDITION

CLOVER Collector's Edition

KC KODANSHA COMICS

Kodansha Comics welcomes you to explore the expansive world of CLAMP, the all-female artist collective that has produced some of the most acclaimed manga of the century. Our growing catalog includes icons like *Cardcaptor Sakura* and *Magic Knight Rayearth*, each crafted with CLAMP's one-of-a-kind style and characters!

The art-deco cyberpunk classic from the creators of *xxxHOLiC* and *Cardcaptor Sakura*!

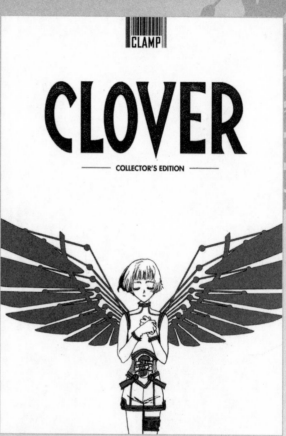

"Starred Review. This experimental sci-fi work from CLAMP reads like a romantic version of *AKIRA*."
—Publishers Weekly

CLAMP
CLOVER
COLLECTOR'S EDITION

Su was born into a bleak future, where the government keeps tight control over children with magical powers—codenamed "Clovers." With Su being the only "four-leaf" Clover in the world, she has been kept isolated nearly her whole life. Can ex-military agent Kazuhiko deliver her to the happiness she seeks? Experience the complete series in this hardcover edition, which also includes over twenty pages of ravishing color art!

KC
KODANSHA COMICS

Knight of the Ice ©Yayoi Ogawa/Kodansha Ltd.

SKATING THRILLS AND ICY CHILLS WITH THIS NEW TINGLY ROMANCE SERIES!

A rom-com on ice, perfect for fans of *Princess Jellyfish* and *Wotakoi*. Kokoro is the talk of the figure-skating world, winning trophies and hearts. But little do they know... he's actually a huge nerd! From the beloved creator of *You're My Pet* (*Tramps Like Us*).

Chitose is a serious young woman, working for the health magazine *SASSO*. Or at least, she would be, if she wasn't constantly getting distracted by her childhood friend, international figure skating star Kokoro Kijinami! In the public eye and on the ice, Kokoro is a gallant, flawless knight, but behind his glittery costumes and breathtaking spins lies a secret: He's actually a hopelessly romantic otaku, who can only land his quad jumps when Chitose is on hand to recite a spell from his favorite magical girl anime!

KC
KODANSHA
COMICS

A SMART, NEW ROMANTIC COMEDY FOR FANS OF *SHORTCAKE CAKE* AND *TERRACE HOUSE*!

A romance manga starring high school girl Meeko, who learns to live on her own in a boarding house whose living room is home to the odd (but handsome) Matsunaga-san. She begins to adjust to her new life away from her parents, but Meeko soon learns that no matter how far away from home she is, she's still a young girl at heart — especially when she finds herself falling for Matsunaga-san.

PERFECT WORLD

Rie Aruga

A TOUCHING NEW SERIES ABOUT LOVE AND COPING WITH DISABILITY

An office party reunites Tsugumi with her high school crush Itsuki. He's realized his dream of becoming an architect, but along the way, he experienced a spinal injury that put him in a wheelchair. Now Tsugumi's rekindled feelings will butt up against prejudices she never considered — and Itsuki will have to decide if he's ready to let someone into his heart...

"Depicts with great delicacy and courage the difficulties some with disabilities experience getting involved in romantic relationships... Rie Aruga refuses to romanticize, pushing her heroine to face the reality of disability. She invites her readers to the same tasks of empathy, knowledge and recognition."
—Slate.fr

"An important entry [in manga romance]... The emotional core of both plot and characters indicates thoughtfulness... [Aruga's] research is readily apparent in the text and artwork, making this feel like a real story."
—Anime News Network

SAINT ☆ YOUNG MEN

A LONG AWAITED ARRIVAL IN PREMIUM 2-IN-1 HARDCOVER

After centuries of hard work, Jesus and Buddha take a break from their heavenly duties to relax among the people of Japan, and their adventures in this lighthearted buddy comedy are sure to bring mirth and merriment to all!

"Brilliant...the physical comedy and facial expressions will make you literally LOL."
—Sam Humphries
(host of *DC Daily*;
writer, *Green Lanterns*,
Legendary Star-Lord)

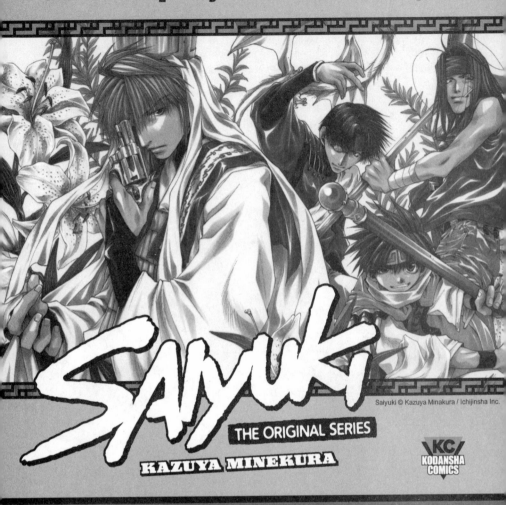

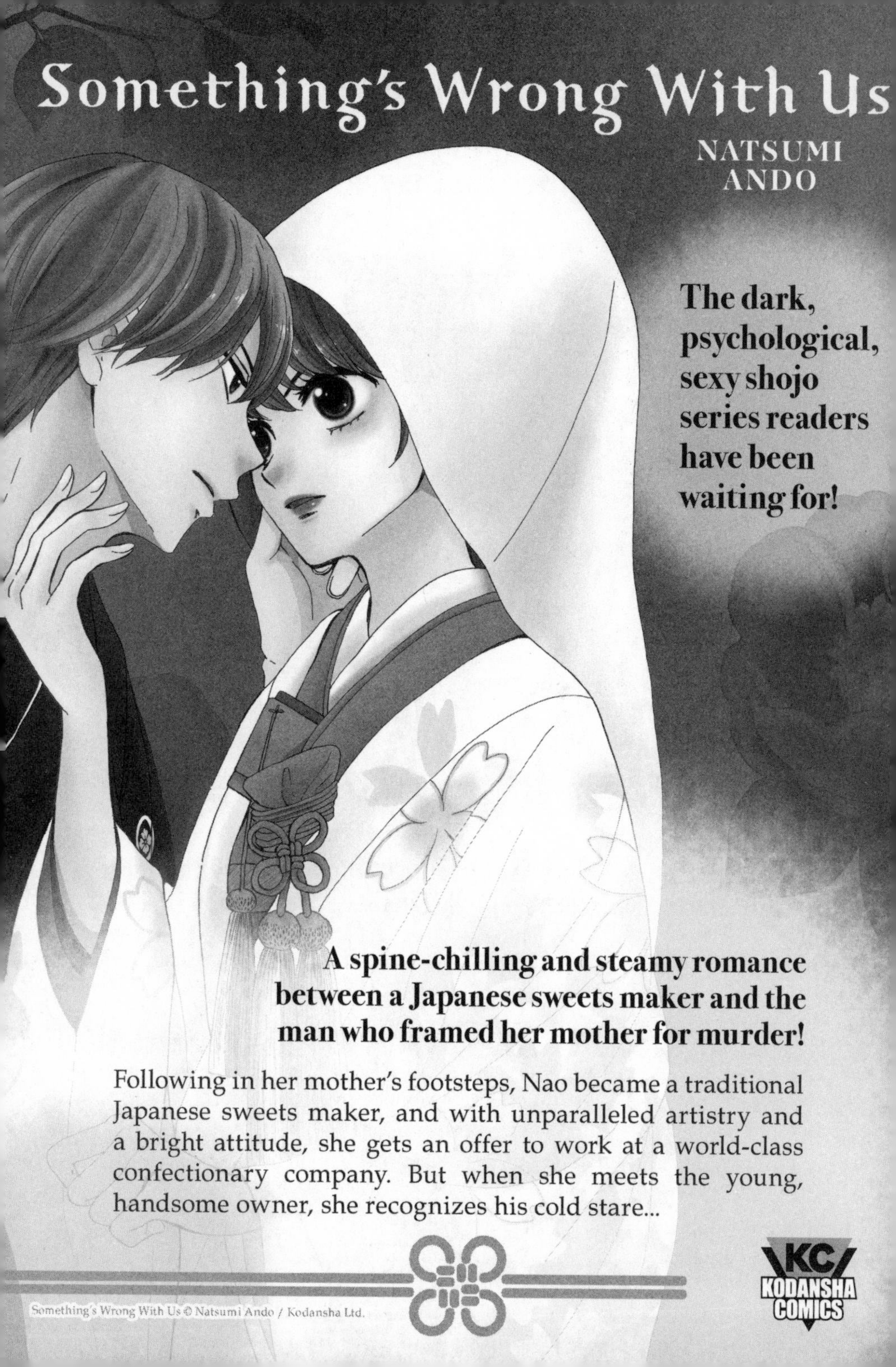
Something's Wrong With Us
NATSUMI ANDO
The dark, psychological, sexy shojo series readers have been waiting for!
A spine-chilling and steamy romance between a Japanese sweets maker and the man who framed her mother for murder!
Following in her mother's footsteps, Nao became a traditional Japanese sweets maker, and with unparalleled artistry and a bright attitude, she gets an offer to work at a world-class confectionary company. But when she meets the young, handsome owner, she recognizes his cold stare...
KC KODANSHA COMICS
Something's Wrong With Us © Natsumi Ando / Kodansha Ltd.

The beloved characters from *Cardcaptor Sakura* return in a brand new, reimagined fantasy adventure!

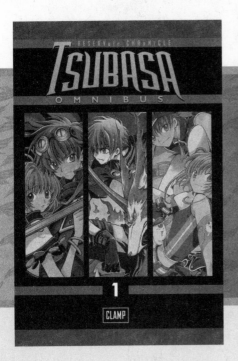

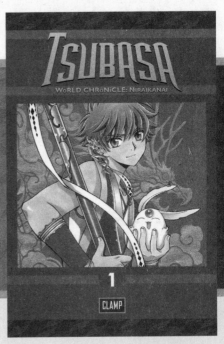

"[*Tsubasa*] takes readers on a fantastic ride that only gets more exhilarating with each successive chapter." —Anime News Network

In the Kingdom of Clow, an archaeological dig unleashes an incredible power, causing Princess Sakura to lose her memories. To save her, her childhood friend Syaoran must follow the orders of the Dimension Witch and travel alongside Kurogane, an unrivaled warrior; Fai, a powerful magician; and Mokona, a curiously strange creature, to retrieve Sakura's dispersed memories!

The adorable new odd-couple cat comedy manga from the creator of the beloved *Chi's Sweet Home*, in full color!

Sue & Tai-chan
Konami Kanata

Sue is an aging housecat who's looking forward to living out her life in peace... but her plans change when the mischievous black tomcat Tai-chan enters the picture! Hey! Sue never signed up to be a catsitter! *Sue & Tai-chan* is the latest from the reigning meow-narch of cute kitty comics, Konami Kanata.

KC KODANSHA COMICS

A Kodansha Comics Trade Paperback Original
Rent-A-Girlfriend 5 copyright © 2018 Reiji Miyajima
English translation copyright © 2021 Reiji Miyajima

Published in the United States by Kodansha Comics, an imprint of Kodansha USA Publishing, LLC, New York.

Publication rights for this English edition arranged through Kodansha Ltd., Tokyo.

First published in Japan in 2018 by Kodansha Ltd., Tokyo as Kanojo, okarishimasu, volume 6.

ISBN 978-1-64651-090-0

Original cover design by Kohei Nawata Design Office

Printed in the United States of America.

www.kodanshacomics.com

9 8 7 6 5 4 3 2 1
Translation: Kevin Gifford
Lettering: Paige Pumphrey
Editing: Jordan Blanco
Kodansha Comics edition cover design by Phil Balsman

Publisher: Kiichiro Sugawara

Director of publishing services: Ben Applegate
Associate director of operations: Stephen Pakula
Publishing services associate managing editor: Madison Salters
Assistant production manager: Emi Lotto, Angela Zurlo
Logo and character art ©Kodansha USA Publishing, LLC